IL OSE AUSSI DOUTER

Quinton

The History Primer

THE History Primer

Primer

J. H. HEXTER

BASIC BOOKS, INC., Publishers

NEW YORK   LONDON

© 1971 by Basic Books, Inc.
Library of Congress Catalog Card Number: 74–135551
SBN 465–03027–0
Manufactured in the United States of America
DESIGNED BY VINCENT TORRE

To

WILLIAM O. AYDELOTTE

CARL HEMPEL

SHEILA RYAN JOHANNSEN

LOUIS MINK

QUENTIN SKINNER

PAUL WARD

who helped me by not quite agreeing with me,
or by not agreeing at all.

PREFACE

I<small>T</small> is not possible to thank all the people who have helped me with this book. Sporadically, for more than a quarter century, I have given thought to the matters it concerns itself with. In that time I have argued one point or another that is made in it with dozens and before hundreds of people. From the many to whom I am obliged I have chosen to dedicate *The History Primer* to a half-dozen who have pressed me hardest at considerable cost to themselves in time and patience.

It really started, I suppose, at Queens College in 1941, when I heard my then colleague Carl Hempel read his paper, "The Function of General Laws in History." Somehow I disagreed with his argument, but it took a long time for me to find out why and how much I disagreed, and to get it down in writing. In the interval both my disagreement with and my fond respect for Carl Hempel have steadily increased.

Adverse criticism sharpens the wits, but praise helps in another way. It props a writer's crumbling ego and enables him to carry through, for better or worse, to the completion of his work. For kind encouragement I owe a large debt to Bea and Irving Kristol, and for time to think and write to the Center for Advanced Study in the Behavioral Sciences and to Yale University.

New Haven
1971

Acknowledgments and Explanations

I wish to thank the *International Encyclopedia of the Social Sciences* and Crowell Collier Macmillan, Inc. for permission to reproduce part of Bernard Berelson's article, "BEHAVIORAL SCIENCES."

For reasons suggested on pp. 19–20, a bibliography seemed an inappropriate appendage to *The History Primer*. So did an index. A detailed table of contents has been provided instead.

CONTENTS

CHAPTER I

CHAPTER VI

CHAPTER VII

CHAPTER VIII

CHAPTER IX

CHAPTER X

The History Primer

NONCHAPTER: *or*
Why Did You Do It
That Way?

Iᴛ may not be a very good idea to start a book with a section that nobody actually needs to read. Nevertheless, nobody needs to read the Nonchapter that follows. None of the main notions in *The History Primer* will depend on what is said here, so that a reader who skips it and starts right in with Chapter 1 will not miss much, if anything.

Using the Nonchapter

I am starting with a nonchapter because between deciding on the title and putting the final touches on the book, I made a number of decisions as to how I would go about the job, and while some of these decisions can readily be inferred from the chapters themselves, others may be hard to figure out, and a few may seem odd to the point where they become annoying to some readers. Such readers may be put off by ways of proceeding that strike them as irritating, unduly eccentric, or perplexing. The purpose of this Nonchapter is, as far as possible, to foresee where friction points will occur and deal with them in advance. This seems preferable to waiting to deal with them as they arise, because within the structure of discourse of a given chapter an explanatory detour may interrupt a line of argument that otherwise is moving directly to its appointed conclusion.

Readers therefore have three options with respect to this Nonchapter: (1) They can skip it at the outset, and if thereafter they find smooth passage through the book, they can skip it altogether. (2) By reading the whole Nonchapter through at once they probably can spare themselves a bit of nuisance later. (3) Or they may wait till they come to a part of the exposition that bothers them and then turn back to the Nonchapter to see if the problem is taken care of there. To make this search easier, the Contents lists for ready reference the main points taken up in the Nonchapter. Since written discourse is a linear operation, however, and since some statements have implications that are, so to speak, logically simultaneous, rather than sequential, it has occasionally been necessary for me to decide the sequence of argument on non-logical grounds. So some of the matters that are perhaps left irritatingly unstated at the point where comment first seems appropriate are handled later, and these will not appear in the Nonchapter. Finally, a considerable number of topics of major importance for understanding history will not concern us at all in this Primer for reasons to be made explicit shortly.

First about the title of the book, *The History Primer*. A good many of the characteristics of the book may become more intelligible by means of an explanation of my choice of a title. As a matter of tactical convenience I shall start with "History," go on to "Primer," and then return to "The."

The Use of "History"

Some years ago an eminent historian, E. H. Carr, wrote a book called *What Is History?* A couple of millennia back another man of considerable eminence asked a question similar in form and stayed not for an answer. Mr. Carr did not stay very long either; but unlike Pilate he promptly produced what he believed to be the answer. What follows here has a somewhat more restricted purpose: not to legislate about what history "really" is, but simply to indicate how I shall use the term "history" in this primer. It is a term of many uses, one whole range of which I intend to exclude consistently and entirely, not at all on grounds that such uses are illegitimate, but as matter of convenience in discourse. "History" is often used to mean "the past" as such, or any part of it, or even more broadly "the past and the future," or any part of them. I do not intend to use the term in any of these senses in this primer. This book, in short, is not an elementary account of what happened in the past. In referring to the past as such, I shall use the term "the past" or some unequivocal synonym,[1] in referring to the future, "the future" or some unequivocal synonym.

---

[1] E.g., "what was," "what has been," "what happened."

In its broadest sense in this book, "history" means any patterned, coherent account, intended to be true, of any past happenings involving human intention or doing or suffering. This jettisoning of the other meanings of the term "history" has no invidious intent whatever. It is just unfortunate that we often use the same word to designate "the human past" and "coherent statements about the human past." At best this leads to readily avoidable confusion and ambiguity, especially in a book like this, where the context may not always make clear which meaning is intended. At worst, in the hands of philosophical idealists it leads to mere mystagogy. Murky-minded men cite the above-mentioned dual designation, implying that a defect in nomenclature somehow creates between the subject of inquiry, "history," and what it is inquiry about, the past, a relation different from the one that subsists between any other subject, say zoology, and what it is about, animal life, or that it is a symptom of such a different relation. Of course, to be actually unable to distinguish between the account, the history, of the St. Bartholomew's Day massacre and the actual events, the massacre of Huguenots that began in Paris on August 24, 1572, would be a pretty clear indication of insanity. Therefore, to attach much significance to the linguistic oddity described above makes little sense, which of course has not prevented people, groping after an idea where there is none, from attaching it. If the relation between history and the past is different from the relation between zoology and animal life (and that is at least possible), it has nothing to do with the homonymy in question.

As defined for the purpose at hand, the sentence, "On August 19, 1967, my wife, my son Christopher, and I went to dinner at Ondine's in Sausalito" is history. So is the sentence, "By November 1648, Henry Ireton had decided that it was necessary to bring about the execution of Charles I." So is the collocation of sentences, "On August 19, 1967, my wife, my son Christopher, and I went to the ball game. Then to celebrate Chris's twenty-third birthday we went to dinner at Ondine's in Sausalito, where on our departure Chris accidentally left his camera." But the collocation of the sentences, "On August 19, 1967, my wife, my son Christopher, and I went to dinner at Ondine's in Sausalito. By November 1648, Henry Ireton had decided that it was necessary to bring about the execution of Charles I" is not history as defined, because it is not patterned or coherent. It might be possible to specify exhaustively the conditions of patterning and coherence as historians now conceive them; but it is not necessary here, since except possibly for a few marginal cases, neither historians nor anyone else has difficulty in recognizing historical pattern and coherence or their opposites.

We shall use the term "history" frequently in this generic sense of any patterned, coherent account of the human past intended to be true. We shall also use it frequently in another, highly specified sense. There it will signify the sort of patterned, coherent accounts of the past that professional historians nowadays write when they systematically study the record of the past with the aim of extending the current limits of historical knowledge. Clearly this is a very, very special case of the generic type. The requirement of writing, the systematic use of the record of the past, and the objective, the advancement (not just the dissemination) of historical knowledge, all reduce the initial large set to a much smaller subset. The omissions especially to keep in mind are the compendia, the compilations, the handbooks, the textbooks, the source books, and the edited sets of documents and of correspondence. All these are history; they are also written history, but in one way or another they do not qualify under the restrictive special definition of history offered above.[2] The things to remember are that the term "history" will be used either in the very broad sense indicated first or in the very narrow sense indicated second, and almost never in any other way. Usually it should be clear from the context which of the two senses is meant, or whether both are perhaps intended. Occasionally, when the context does not provide enough clues, there may be a reference to "written history." In that case the very narrow sense of the term is intended, not the intermediate sense which would include textbooks and so on. So much for "history."

What a Primer Is

A primer is a first book on a subject, a book that contains the rudiments of what one needs to know in order to think effectively and coherently about the activity it describes. It is, of course, possible to take part in an activity quite effectively without knowing the rudiments in a way that enables one to think coherently about it as a whole. From time immemorial, in a very wide range of activities from farming and fighting to baseball, such effective participation has been achieved through imitation, habituation, practice, and drill. This primer is concerned with thinking coherently about history as a whole, not with effective participation in history as a professional activity, per se. It will try, for example, to discern *whether* there are rules about written history, and if so, what some of the rules are like and why; it will not try to collect and codify the rules, or to offer practical exercises in history writing.

Primers are usually by intention simple and rather easy books, al-

[2] A very few textbooks sometimes display a skill and originality of synthesis that move them into the class of written history that will concern us further.

though they cannot always be so. Primers of nuclear physics, theory of numbers, and Indo-European philology could not, one supposes, be excessively simple or easy despite the best will of their authors to make them so. Other things being equal, however, for reasons that will be considered later,[3] a history primer, although its subject is a very complex activity, should theoretically be easy, presenting very few obstacles to the understanding of any reasonably intelligent reader. This primer would indeed be easy (probably too easy, too short, and intellectually too unchallenging to warrant publication), if other things were equal. But they are not at all equal; they are so unequal that for one practicing historian, writing a history primer has become at once the most arduous and the most perplexing intellectual exercise he has ever undertaken.

Obstacles to Understanding History

Behind the house where I lived some years ago was a low, readily traversable mountain range. In the autumn a great bank of fog rolled in from the sea and towered high above the mountains, which it completely covered and concealed. From distances not very great, those fog banks themselves looked much like mountains, immense and forbidding. If an old inhabitant phoned a newcomer and said, "Hiking in the mountains here is a pleasant mild exercise. Shall we do it this afternoon?" the newcomer might have been amazed at the inappropriateness of the old inhabitant's proposal and of the language in which he couched it. Mild exercise, indeed, among those stark cliffs, snow-covered folds, and hideous ravines! If the newcomer expressed some of his amazement at the proposal, the old inhabitant, who did not need to look at the mountains from a distance because he intimately knew them with his feet, might reply that of course there were rough patches of climbing best left to trained experts who sought them out, but that on the whole it was easy going for men of reasonable vigor.

If we extend this absurd misunderstanding indefinitely, we get an image of one of the things that are not equal, and that prevents a history primer from being as easy as it otherwise might be. For a long while many relatively straightforward facts about history have been hidden under towering cloud banks of illusion blown in from the sea of words. These illusions are the creation of all sorts of Deep Thinkers, but mainly of philosophers stretching all the way back to Plato and Aristotle. They are so much more picturesque and interesting, so much more intricate and involute, than the easy truths about history which they

[3] See Chapters 1 and 2.

conceal, that it is nearly impossible to persuade anyone who has not wandered about in history on his feet that those truths are what they are. He can scarcely believe that there is not a lot more to it.

Here, however, our analogy breaks down in two different ways. For first, as we shall see, in history in the general sense all men perforce wander about on their feet,[4] but this does not at all dispel their confusion about history's contours. And second, when they have talked about history in general instead of writing it in particular, next to the philosophers, professional historians themselves have made the most considerable contribution to the present confusion about it. As to the first anomaly, it exists primarily because most men fail to recognize as history what they have so comfortably managed their way around for so many years. The anomalous case of the professional historians is even more peculiar, and their contributions to the confusion about history at once larger and more ambivalent; they are also intelligible. Many historians have simply accepted notions about explanations, causes, knowing, truth, and understanding that philosophers and scientists developed to cope with other sorts of activity and have assumed that such notions were totally applicable to history because in fact some of them were partially applicable. Other historians, correctly observing that this assumption was false, made the opposite presumptions: either that history had nothing of consequence in common with other disciplines, or (with terrifying imperialism) that it superseded and subsumed them all.

To this confusion professional historians added a further dimension. Whatever their deficiencies in the matter of the mountains of mirage, many of them were in and by practice adroit scramblers over the actual terrain of history, and the actualities they had learned with their feet often obtruded into their consciousness and destroyed the orderliness of their illusions without dispelling the illusions themselves. Instead of the tightly constructed, precise delusional systems characteristic of some of the philosophies of history produced by logicians, the meditations of historians on the fundamentals of their craft have been with rare exception turbid and rather messy. In some respects this has been a great streak of good fortune for the practice of history writing. Historians have rarely been tempted to adjust their actual practice in writing history to their loftier view of the nature of history. Their speculations have been something for them to play with, their discipline something for them to work with, and the recreation and business have gone on in separate compartments not much interfering with or affecting each other.

While the rudiments of history are easy to understand, the masses of

[4] See Chapters 1 and 2.

illusion that overlay them are hard to get rid of. The mere statement of the rudimentary truths is not enough. To get rid of the illusions, it is necessary to show not only that the truths are true, but that the illusions are incompatible with them, and therefore must be swept away. This is not easy to do and the procedures may not be very easy to follow. My purpose is to make them no harder to follow than they need to be, to make the work of the reader as unburdensome as I can.

This purpose will help explain a trait of this primer which some readers may find annoying. A few points will be made with what may appear to be excessive emphasis and reiteration. This is, however, something that one might reasonably expect in a primer. Crucial points need not only to be made emphatically at the point where they first emerge from the matrix of discourse, they also need to be repeated and reviewed at points where they reemerge, and where to have them immediately in mind makes what follows easier to understand. The author has therefore intentionally sacrificed possibilities for elegance, subtlety, and economy of statement to the more uncomely and blunt requirements for writing a readily intelligible primer.

A Claim to Uniqueness

The definite article in the title of *The History Primer* indicates the conviction of its author that in one respect the book is unique: there is no other primer that deals directly and adequately with the rudiments of history in the two senses in which the term "history" is used in this book. W. B. Walsh's *Introduction to the Philosophy of History* is a partial exception. It does not, however, fully come to grips with the rudiments of history in the restrictive sense. Most manuals or primers about history are concerned with the techniques of historical research and investigation. In a sense they are thus interstitial to history in the two senses explained above. They deal with some matters that the professional historians must know about, but they scarcely touch on problems raised by the mere existence of history in the less restrictive sense, and they avoid or say little about the problems that the actual writing of history creates. They are rather concerned with the techniques of systematic study of the record of the past prior to the writing of any actual history. This interstitial area is an entirely appropriate subject of investigation, and the study of it is certainly a kind of study of history, raising interesting problems of its own which this primer touches only tangentially. The claim of the primer to uniqueness is with respect only to the restricted sense of the term "history" already made explicit.

History, Philosophers and Historians

In this book we have paid a good deal less attention to what historians have said about history, than we have to what philosophers have said on the subject and to what has been done in actual historical writing. The reason for this can be inferred from what we have stated earlier. The elegance and precision of the delusional systems of some philosophers about history is so superior to that of most historians that it is far more convenient and tidy to get at the rudimentary truths about history by dispelling the delusions of philosophers than by struggling with the confusions of historians.[5] We have concerned ourselves with what historians have said about history only where their commitments do, or threaten to, adversely affect their practice.[6] As we have already indicated, this does not happen very often because the commitments themselves are usually so vague, inconsistent, and contradictory as to hamper but little in the pursuit of his historical rounds the historian who professes them.

Focal Centers

As we proceed through this primer, we will try to organize the argument around what are ordinarily called examples or illustrations, but what in the present context might better be called focal centers. We will try to make the focal center a specific entity—if the past as such, an event or event-cluster; if the record of the past, a fragment of that record; if history as ordinary men every day present it to themselves and others, then a bit of history as it is daily spoken; if history as professional historians write it, then a bit of history as it is professionally written. These items are here designated focal centers to emphasize that they are not mere examples and illustrations of generalizations which are "really" history. It is the focal centers themselves that represent both the ingredients of history and its actuality. This point is worth making because the kind of person who writes the kind of book about history that this one will be must have a propensity for generalization and theory; otherwise he would not write it at all. But such a person stands in imminent danger of detaching himself from the actu-

[5] See especially Chapters 1, 5, and 6.
[6] See Chapter 5.

ality and soaring off into the theoretical wild blue yonder. There the living details of the past and of its history appear so small and so trivial that, in the interest of shaping much of the record of the past to fit a seemly theoretical structure, it becomes a venial sin to shear away the untidy jagged edges these details often leave. For historians, this, however, can never be a venial sin; for them it is the unspeakable sin, the sin against the Holy Ghost. Substantive philosophies of history have long tempted historians to this sin. In the past thirty-odd years historians have been subjected to more subtle temptations to make the rough places smoother in the name of analysis. To keep both the danger and its antidote to the forefront of the mind of readers and writer alike, the focal center and the general or theoretical issues in that order make part of the chapter headings. The order is that of priority, existential if not logical, or, in case those terms are vague and confused, of the priority that counts more in this primer against the one that counts less.

The sorts of focal centers chosen will depend mainly on which of the two related senses of "history" is at the moment of chief concern. Since most of the true and coherent accounts of the past that men render depend on memory rather than on public record, the focal centers for them will usually be accounts of the sort of thing that has happened often or is likely to happen anytime to almost anyone. In this very limited sense they are "contrived"; they do not, are not intended to, and cannot meet one requirement of written history: that it rely for evidence only on a record accessible to anyone who wants to check it. Such focal centers are intended to be fully representative of the kind of history we all constantly practice by speaking it. Focal centers involved in problems of writing history will most often come from the record of the past or from readily available historical writing. I will not, however, be puritanical in this matter. If it occasionally saves time and increases illustrative aptness to contrive a few fictitious bits of "the record of the past" or to improvise a smattering of historical writing for the occasion, I shall not hesitate to do so in the interest of economy. I shall always make it clear, however, that this is what I am doing.

The focal centers are often concerned with extreme cases of good and bad ways to do things in history. Consequently, they will at times be very good history and at times quite bad history. I shall not provide references to the sources of the bad history cited, except in cases where my own work is the source. I shall provide references to the sources of good history which I cite.

A considerable number of these references will be to history I have written. This would seem to imply that I think some of the history I have written is good history. It does, and I do. It also seems to imply that I think I can distinguish between good history and bad history. It does; I do; and in most instances almost any reasonably intelligent literate person can, because usually it is a very easy thing to do. The best history has been written by Frederic William Maitland. Very, very bad history is written in their first research seminars by students who flunk out of inferior graduate schools. I have had no trouble at all distinguishing between the two or deciding which is good history and which is bad. I suspect that most people likely to read history would have no trouble either. It is one of those things readily susceptible to experimental testing, on which, fortunately, no one is likely to be foolish enough to waste time. Once one considers the point in this way, it is hard to understand how any one could dismiss the obvious differences between good and bad history as "merely" relative, "merely" subjective, or "merely" a matter of taste. There is nothing "mere" about it. Confusion on this point probably has several sources. One confusion is between ability to observe a difference and ability to explain the grounds of a distinction. Some people who can distinguish between the music of Bach and Beethoven one hundred times out of a hundred are unable to say anything at all enlightening about how they manage to do it. It is similar although not the same with respect to very good and very bad history. Consistent incapacity to distinguish between Bach and Beethoven is usually ascribable to a defect in aural perception. If we would forego preconceptions about the total relativity of values, we would just as readily ascribe consistent inability to discriminate between Maitland and an incompetent graduate student to a defect of historical perception.

So I think I can tell good history from bad, and I think I have written some that is good. But there is no correlation between how good I think my history writing has been and how frequently I have drawn on it for focal centers. That has been determined by another consideration. Sometimes from what they wrote I can infer what other historians have had in mind when they wrote it. Sometimes I can remember why I wrote what I wrote. Although not extremely precise, my memory of what I had in mind is likely to be more accurate than my inferences about what other historians had in mind, and therefore in focal centers chosen out of my own work I can more readily and confidently relate the history written to the intent of the writer. It is this rather than any differential judgment as between the good history I have written and the good (and better) history other historians have written that leads me often to use what I have written as a focal center. The judgment here is one of convenience and efficiency, not of quality.

Description and Prescription

A critical reader of a draft of my first more or less coherent effort to come to grips with some of the problems which this primer tries to solve asked whether my observations were intended to be descriptive or prescriptive.[7] This question had not occurred to me before. On consideration it seems to me that it cannot be a matter of "either/or," descriptive or prescriptive, and that this is so of any primer, whether of spelling or quantum mechanics, which aims to instruct its readers. All such primers are explicitly descriptive; they are also implicitly prescriptive and normative; they aim to describe, *and* to lay down rules, *and* to set forth standards. A primer of spelling indicates how words are spelled by most spellers. It also aims to teach *orthography*, right spelling, not how to spell words wrong. A primer of quantum mechanics tries to set out the truth about quantum mechanics to help readers understand it. So a history primer necessarily aims to set forth true fundamentals of how history works and how to think about it, not false ones. There is another way to put the same point: in intent this primer is prescriptive for writers of history and people thinking about history; it is in intent at least descriptive of the practices of historians who write good history and of those who think clearly about it.

The Use of "Science"

In what follows I will say a good deal about the relation of history to the sciences and much less about the relation of history to the fictive arts. Like scientists and unlike fictive artists, historians accept a primary obligation to check their assertions against evidence or data about a world that is, or once was, "out there," evidence that is open to public scrutiny and criticism by reexamination of the respective records—for scientists, the records of observations and experiments, for historians, the records of the past. The trouble with my frequent comparisons and contrasts between history and the sciences is (or may be) that I know very little about the latter. My formal academic training in the "exact"

[7] The effort appears as "The Rhetoric of History" s.v. HISTORIOGRAPHY, *International Encyclopedia of the Social Sciences* (New York, 1968). The question was raised by Mrs. Sheila Ryan Johannsen.

sciences stopped thirty-eight years ago with a college course in organic chemistry. My formal academic training in the social sciences as most of their practitioners define them today never began. Since the end of my formal schooling I have read in the social sciences diffusely but not very extensively, in the philosophy of science a little, and in the substantive natural sciences scarcely at all.

If this confession of ignorance mattered much for the purposes of this primer, I probably would not have made it. Actually it matters very little. Neither scientists nor philosophers of science enjoy the blessing of complete intramural rapport on the nature or the methods of the "exact" and the natural sciences, much less of the social sciences. Quite to the contrary. I have not the ability, the time, or the inclination to interpose myself into their internecine squabbles, an ignorant army of one, stepping into an arena where larger armies, more or less ignorant, clash by night.

Instead I have adopted a strategy that may be less counterproductive. Suppose that stage directions for a play indicate that in order to put the central character in sharp focus for the audience he is to appear clad in bright orange against the background of a black brick wall. Then it would not be sensible for a director to worry about whether the bricks he used for the wall were real bricks. Indeed he might well prefer readily procurable black bricks of papier maché to hard-to-get real dark gray bricks. The papier maché bricks might after all better serve his purpose, which is that of maximizing contrast. In this primer my purpose is to render distinct certain traits of history and of knowing history. These emerge most clearly if they are juxtaposed to a sharply contrasting background of the distinct traits of science and of knowing science, as hard-line logical positivists have conceived them. For my purposes it does not matter at all that other scientists and philosophers of science have conceived these matters differently. My statements about science in this primer, therefore, are not to be taken as the latest and hottest scoop on the subject, but as what the Big Thinkers call a heuristic device.

Analytical Philosophers and History

Earlier in this Nonchapter it was suggested metaphorically that the apparent difficulties which some analytical philosophers seem to emphasize in the enterprise of understanding the human past and explaining things about it were largely a cloud bank of illusion. It was not thereby intended that all the problems of writing history are easy—far from it; if this were so the average quality of the historical product would be far superior to what it actually is. Nor was it meant that all the difficulties noted by analytical philosophers were illusory or irrelevant to the historical enterprise; some are serious and substantial. It was meant that many of the problems with which philosophers of history have struggled to deal have seemed so easy to many historians and have been solved by them with such habitual insouciance that they have scarcely recognized them as problems at all. Consequently from their point of view, philosophers have appeared to have little to say about history that is enlightening. In part this is indeed the case, for two very different reasons. For one thing, some of the problems about history with which philosophers have concerned themselves have been pretty strictly philosophers' problems, generated by and directed toward the solution of perplexities emanating from their own discipline. The substance on which philosophers have operated at this level of discourse has been statements about the past abstracted from the context of historical discourse and therefore only of tangential interest to historians. To say this is not to suggest that the philosophers' interests in this region are anything but wholly legitimate. The noetic valuation of sentences tensed in various ways, and the epistemological implication of such valuation may be a major concern of philosophers; at present it does not concern historians as such; nor does it seem likely to. It is not clear that the answers philosophers have given to such questions bear in any way on the work historians do or the questions they ask themselves in the course of that work. The second reason is that even when actual historical writing was presumably the substance with which the philosophers were concerned, they often seemed to abstract so ruthlessly from the actual structure of such writing and to so atomize it as to destroy the sense of its integrity as a significant form of human discourse.

This seems to have resulted from an adventitious circumstance: the earliest analytical philosophers to draw the intense attention of their fellows to history were by and large logical positivists, primarily concerned with the philosophy of science, and committed to the conception of the unity and the superiority of scientific knowledge to all other modes of knowing and understanding. In a number of ways this was most unfortunate.

In the first place, to order the modes of knowing hierarchically is to treat with condescension, implicit or explicit, conscious or unconscious, those modes least comfortable to the top ones. Since, of the intellectual activities to which logical positivists were willing to concede any serious noetic value, history bore the least resemblance to the foremost science—physics formulated in the language of mathematics—it was naturally at the bottom of the totem pole. Unintentionally no doubt in some cases,[8] the philosophers of science tended to adopt a somewhat condescending tone toward the discipline of history, some of which naturally came through to its practitioners. Being men of ordinarily sinful vanity, historians who paid any attention at all to what the philosophers were saying were somewhat put off by the low esteem in which their vocation seemed to be held by people whose limited qualifications to judge did not notably diminish their propensity for *ex cathedra* pronouncements. It is this easy dismissal which accounts for a certain slight acidity that permeates my own customarily bland manner in what I have previously written on these matters, and that despite my best efforts may occasionally creep into what follows.

Of more substantial concern is the bias that the preoccupations of logical positivists imparted to their perception of "the problem of history." They somewhat arbitrarily enthroned physics as the Queen of the Sciences, and the methodological problems of physics became for them the central problems of knowing. Rightly or wrongly (and on this point my ignorance simply makes it impossible for me to judge), the analytical philosophers decided that validating explanations of physical phenomena was the central philosophical problem of physics. By their very nature, however, physical agents are unresponsive; they offer no help, no readily accessible information at all to those who seek it. Coercing that help—formulating hypotheses about nature's laws, and devising the intricate methods needed to elicit answers from the silent yet simple entities that physics deals with—is hard work, and in physics it yields high rewards.

The Assimilation of History to Science

Given their bias the analytical philosophers were naturally predisposed at first to believe that to the extent it was worth its salt, history had to be like physics, to share its preoccupations and, as far as the odd materials and conditions of historical investigation allowed, to emulate its procedures and modes of explanation. This view of the situation may be fairly described as "assimilationist." Always implicitly and sometimes fairly explicitly, it assumed that the value of history for the advancement of knowledge and the enlightenment of the understanding was directly proportional to the assimilability of its structures of explanation to the ones that philosophers of science discern in physics. The

[8] Hardly unintentionally, though, in the case of Professor Brodbeck. May Brodbeck, "Methodological Individualisms: Definition and Reduction" in William H. Dray, ed., *Philosophical Analysis and History* (New York, 1966), pp. 297–329.

converse proposition also held: "explanation" in history that deviated from the physical-science norm was either an inferior or inadequate surrogate for "real," "complete," or "satisfactory" explanation, indicative of the inferiority of history to physics as a science, or it was not an explanation at all, and was therefore of no serious interest to philosophers concerned with the necessary conditions for the advancement of knowledge.

Once formulated in this rigorous way the difficulty of assimilationists with history grew preposterously. The trouble was that what historians wrote about the past did not meet the rigorous specifications of explanation that the philosophers had established. Yet intuitively much of what historians offered seemed to contribute to an understanding of the past and sometimes even to be explanations of what men had done and what had happened to them. At least historians intended them for explanations, and among historians and others many of them passed muster; they were adequate to their purpose. What was even more awkward, some of these "explanations," which did not conform and were by no means conformable to the physical science model, seemed a more appropriate response to the questions that elicited them than alternate and available explanations that did conform to the model. Between what the philosophers of science, starting from a physical science model, regarded as the proper concern of historians seeking to advance knowledge and what historians did that readers intuitively accepted as advancing it, the divergence was very large indeed. For nearly thirty years now talented analytical philosophers of various sects and persuasions have been seeking ways to cope with that divergence. Despite occasional patches of darkness and confusion of counsel, their effort has been by no means fruitless. From the many-sided debate there seems to emerge an awareness of history as a significant form of human knowing and understanding that in some respects is similar to the knowing and understanding of the natural sciences, but in other respects is markedly different from them. Intuitively or traditionally, historians have engaged in operations that fit poorly the conception of knowing and explaining most widely current among the historians themselves, a conception which is itself a vague and clumsy version of the natural science model. For many of these operations recent philosophical analysis of history has found solid raisons d'être in an enlarged conception of the nature and scope of historical knowledge and explanation, and it has done so without accepting the misty, delphic, and ultimately rather restrictive views of the historical enterprise expressed by writers like Croce and Collingwood.

The expository strategy of this primer is to start from the physics model of historical explanation and to demonstrate the deficiencies of both its primitive version and of assimilationist efforts to save that version through minimal emendation. In this way I hope it will become clear why the traditional structures of historical discourse, even when their rhetorical forms are furthest removed from those deemed pertinent or even tolerable in the physical sciences, are proper and appropriate for explaining, knowing, and understanding the past. In pursuing this course, I also hope to say a few things about history as a discipline that have not already been said by others and to provide more adequate support for some things that others have already said. In the latter case I shall necessarily be traversing ground that has already been covered in the philosophic controversy about history.

Unfortunately I will not be at all sure when I am being original, when I am lending effective new support to arguments elaborated by others, and when I am merely saying again less aptly what others already have said, and even what I already have read. Only too often in the gestation of this primer I have experienced profound satisfaction with a particularly bright inspiration or formulation of mine, only to run across the same inspiration or a far brighter formulation in somebody else's work. Sometimes I was fairly sure that I had not previously read the work, sometimes I was fairly sure that I had, and sometimes I simply did not remember. In matters that one has sporadically read about and pondered for more than a quarter of a century, memory plays odd tricks, hopelessly scrambling originality, simultaneous independent invention, and unconscious borrowing. All this is prefatory to an apology to any writer who finds that I have used his ideas without acknowledging the source of supply. It is not that I am refusing credit where credit is due; it is simply that often I do not know where or even if it is due.

Whatever my debts to analytical philosophers of history, this primer is mainly intended not for them but for readers whose center of interest is in history. Although by and large I have tried to translate the special language of these philosophers into language which might prove more congenial to literate men, such translation is fraught with difficulty. Some rigor and precision are likely to be lost in the process. The dangers of such translation are compounded when the translator is self-taught and late-taught and therefore probably ill-taught in the language he is trying to translate. Such inescapably is my situation. I can only hope that my errors will not be too frequent or too egregious. From those whose cherished notions I have more or less botched in translation, I also hope for a charitable forgiveness, which, not having earned it by my own charity, I can not reasonably expect.

Borrowing and Novelty

This primer will suffer from at least one defect of which its author is fully aware and which he has nevertheless made no effort to correct. How serious this defect appears will depend in a large measure on the expectations of the reader, and the expectations themselves will be a result of the context the reader supplies in his reading. In the context that I have mainly had in mind as I have written, I do not believe that the defect is disastrous; in another context of which I have become faintly aware in the past couple of years, it could be catastrophic. An old story illustrates the possibile dimensions of the catastrophe.

Toward the end of the nineteenth century a young Talmudic scholar in a Polish *shtetel* happened to come upon a copy of Euclid's geometry. It fascinated him; moreover, it had the effect of producing an expansion and an acute intensification of consciousness in a mind trained on the close legal argument of Talmudic scholarship. To the young man, however, it seemed that Euclid had not pursued far enough some of the questions his *Geometry* raised. For twenty years in all his spare time the Talmudic scholar thought about those questions, slowly working out his conclusions, of which he spoke to no one. Then one day he mentioned his efforts to a nephew visiting from Warsaw. The young man, more widely exposed to secular learning than his uncle, suggested that the latter bring his studies to the attention of a professor of mathematics at the University of Warsaw. By dint of much persuasion, he got his uncle to organize his findings methodically and send them to the professor. He also persuaded the latter to promise that he would see the uncle after examining the manuscript. Several weeks later the Talmudic scholar went to Warsaw to keep his appointment with the mathematician.

"Well," he said, after an exchange of civilities "What do you think of my studies?"

"I do not need to think," said the professor. "I know."

"And how have I done?"

"Under the circumstances," the professor answered, "you have done quite well. Indeed miraculously well. Two hundred years after Newton and Leibniz you have discovered the calculus."

On a far less grand scale, in this primer I may have done something similar to what the Talmudic scholar did. If so, I lack one excuse that he had, and I have an excuse that he lacked. He had no forewarning that his "discoveries" may have been anticipated, that he may have been discovering things the properly informed already knew. I have had such forewarnings. My "Euclid" has been Carl Hempel's "The Function of General Laws in History," and my subsequent reading in philosophy has been confined almost entirely to writings that have been glosses assenting to, dissenting from, or amending that work. Friends who have read early drafts of chapters of this primer—especially two to whom it is dedicated, Mrs. Sheila Johannsen and Mr. Quentin Skinner —have gently but firmly suggested that I undertake wider explorations in recent Anglo-American philosophy. I have occasionally wondered whether those suggestions implied that unless I did undertake such exploration I might be told by less kind critics that what I was pulling out of my sleeve with such grandiose flourishes was a series not of lively rabbits but of tired clichés.

Yet I have not entered upon the studies my young friends kindly and wisely suggested. I have scarcely glanced into the windows of those studies, over the mantel of each of which there appears to hang the hallowed icon of Ludwig Wittgenstein.[9] For this willful ignorance I can only plead, for what it may be worth, an excuse that the Talmudic scholar lacked. He began the intensive investigation that had so peculiar an outcome when he was young; when I began mine I was past fifty-five years old, and my mind had lost a good deal of the flexibility that enables the young to develop durable skill in the athletics of abstraction. Had I attempted to acquire such skill at my age and succeeded, I might have written a better primer. It is more likely, however, that I would have failed, and not written a primer at all. While the loss inflicted by such an outcome on the sum of human wisdom would have been miniscule, the loss to me would have been considerable, since no work I have ever undertaken has afforded me more (and more innocent, I hope) enjoyment.

I have already indicated the measures I have taken to limit the waste motion involved in rambling self-indulgently and slowly toward ends that other minds may have arrived at far more rapidly and skillfully by other and shorter routes. The route I have taken is the one I know best, that of the actual practice of thinking and writing historically. By the device of focal centers I have tried to keep myself both from straying very far from that low-level route congenial to historians and from soaring to the heights of abstraction, where because of the rarity of the atmosphere historians tend to cyanosis. For some philosophers, the places where the primer ends may be familiar terrain, and the labors of getting there by the route I have followed may seem unduly onerous. For historians—at least so I hope—it may be otherwise.

[9] I have read nothing by Wittgenstein and only a few pages about him.

CHAPTER I: The Cases of the Muddy Pants, the Dead Mr. Sweet, and the Convergence of Particles, *or Explanation Why and Prediction in History*

SUPPOSE one were to ask a professional historian purportedly expert on Napoleon's military career why Napoleon won and the Austrians and Prussians lost the Battle of Austerlitz on December 2, 1805. And suppose the historian were to reply, "You know, I haven't any idea." One might reasonably be somewhat surprised by such an answer, so surprised as to wish to press the expert a little further by way of seeking clarification. The next question might then be posed to him in terms of a choice between alternative hypotheses, or true/false questions like these:

1. "Austro-Prussian acceptance of General Weyerother's proposed disposition of the troops for battle had something to do with it."
2. "The color of Napoleon's uniform had something to do with it."
3. "The allegiance of the Austrian army to the principle of nonviolence had something to do with it."
4. "The high morale and state of readiness of the French army had something to do with it."

A historian claiming expertise on Napoleon's military career who checked "true" for options 2 and 3 and "false" for options 1 and 4 would wake suspicion of his expertise or of his mental equilibrium or of both. Of course that historian is himself a hypothetical figment. An actual historian of the Napoleonic period would not only array his true and false's in the opposite way; if pressed, he would be willing to defend his judgment. He would provide grounds for believing that the color of Napoleon's uniform was irrelevant to the French victory at Austerlitz and that the alleged addiction of the Austrian army to nonviolence was counterfactual. Moreover, from the surviving record of the battle he would infer the failure of the commanders of the Allies to reject the Weyerother advice and document the disaster that in consequence ensued. From other contemporary records he would offer evidence indicative of the high morale and state of readiness of Napoleon's army in 1805. For a man to say "he has no idea why" something happened or someone did something is to suggest that he believes himself incapable of rendering the happening or act intelligible at all.

All this is a rather elaborate way of making a quite simple point. Historians can and do answer "why" questions about past happenings and events. Explanations *why* about such happenings and events are a meat-and-potatoes part of their business, and in practice they do not doubt that they can carry on this part of the business with results a good bit better than are attainable by mere blind guessing. To test the foregoing assertions is easy; all one has to do is open a history book at random and see if one can formulate any questions beginning "Why did . . . ?" or "Why was . . . ?" or "Why were . . . ?" to which there is an answer on the page. For example, opening Professor H. R. Trevor-Roper's *The Crisis of the Seventeenth Century*, I find on page 222 the following brief passage:

> In monarchical countries with a developed, independent laity, the Calvinist Church could not prevail. Erastian princes—Queen Elizabeth, William of Orange, Catherine de Médicis—might use the Church at times, but would always prefer to be independent of it, and looked to the laity to provide that independence. In petty principalities or city-states the Church would be proportionately stronger—especially if such states were politically weak and vulnerable and needed to draw on a reservoir of fanaticism. In such states the lay power would still seek to be independent of the Church. In Geneva there was a continuing struggle between the Venerable Company of Ministers and the City Council. In the Palatinate princely patronage was independent of the Church. But, in fact, in both societies, since they lived in fear of conquest, the Church exercised great power. In backward countries, like Scotland or Navarre, where an educated, independent laity hardly existed, the Church was without a rival: the prince had nothing to balance against it . . . [1]

[1] H. R. Trevor-Roper, *The Crisis of the Seventeenth Century* (New York, 1968), p. 222.

Note how much in these few sentences can be reformulated and paraphrased as "why" questions and answers to those questions.

Question: Why did the Calvinist Church not prevail in monarchical countries with a developed independent laity?

Answer: In such countries Erastian princes preferred to be independent of the churches, and they found in the support of the laity the means of being so.

Question: Why was the Calvinist Church stronger in petty principalities and city-states?

Answer: In such states, especially if they were weak and vulnerable, the rulers had to rely for support on the reservoir of fanaticism that the Calvinist Church provided.

Question: Why did the Calvinist Church dominate Scotland and Navarre?

Answer: In such backward countries the rulers had no independent educated laity at all to balance against the church.

Oddly, some historians who will explain why this or that happened with unabashed confidence, thus answering "why" questions one after another, will go all skittish if they are asked about the causes of some event or happening in the past.

Among historians, sensitivity to "cause" and its derivatives "causation," "causality," and "causal explanation" has two sources. One is an awareness that for a long time now, those words have made trouble for philosophical scientists, philosophers of science, and philosophers in general. The other is an awareness that those same words have also given trouble to historians in their own work. At a quasiphilosophical level the trouble was made explicit by Charles Beard. His statement appeared in 1946 in Bulletin 54 of the Social Science Research Council which was entitled *Theory and Practice in Historical Study*.[2] The bulletin was the first of three experiments in subvented soul-searching undertaken by the professional historians in America, in their official and corporate capacity as one of the members of the community of social scientists.[3] To his fellow historians, however, Beard's abstract ruminations on the vagaries of cause and causation may have seemed considerably less cogent and disturbing than the concrete evidence provided by the longest contribution to the bulletin. This was an essay by Howard Beale, an account of what from the beginning (and indeed before the beginning) to 1945 historians had written about the cause or causes of

[2] Charles A. Beard, "Grounds for a Reconsideration of Historiography," *Theory and Practice in Historical Study: A Report of the Committee on Historiography*, Bulletin 54 (Social Science Research Council, 1946), pp. 1–14.

[3] For the second and third experiments, see *The Social Sciences in Historical Study*, Bulletin 64 (Social Science Research Council, 1954), and Louis Gottschalk, ed., *Generalization in the Writing of History* (Chicago, 1963).

the American Civil War.[4] The distraught tone of Beale's "few generalizations in conclusion" (actually seven pages of them) might be construed as the result of trauma incurred through the minute contemplation of the historiographic chaos that was the fruit of the eighty-year
quest by American historians for the causes of the war. As Beale saw it,
it looked less like a dispassionate course of inquiry than a continuation
of the war itself by other means. After all, it must have been distressing
to discover, as Beale believed he had discovered, that all the apparently
conflicting "general" causal explanations of the Civil War had been offered even before the fighting started. The moral that Beard elicited
from trying to cope with the problem of causation on the theoretical
plane was thus reinforced by Beale's empirical investigation of what
actually happened in a case where a host of historians had devoted
themselves to explaining the causes of a major historical event. It may
well have seemed that in the interest of ameliorating pandemonium it
was expedient to stop talking about causes altogether.

All this turmoil about causes, causation, and causal explanation in
history and elsewhere suggests the prudence of evasive action on the
issue at the beginning of this primer. We have seen that historians all
the time ask and answer "why" questions about what men did and
what happened to them in the past, and that they usually stand ready
to defend and support these answers. If the way historians answer such
questions sometimes affords satisfaction to themselves and others and
adds to the available knowledge and understanding of the past, we can
then look into their procedures and perhaps find out how they work.
We can inquire into explanation "why" in history, meaning simply
any statement of a historian about the past which answers a question,
explicit or implicit, beginning, "Why was . . . ?", "Why were . . . ?",
or "Why did . . . ?"[5] If our inquiry is reasonably fruitful, it really does
not matter much whether or not we describe what we have done as an
analysis of historical causation or of causal explanation in history. We
can with good conscience leave it to philosophers, scientists, and philosophers of science to decide how what we find out compares with their
views on causes, causation, and causal explanation in the sciences, in
general, and even in history.

The views of philosophers and scientists on these matters differ considerably and have done so for several centuries, so there are more than
marginal advantages in shunning undue involvement in controversies
only peripherally relevant to what this primer is about at the insignifi-

---

[4] Howard K. Beale, "What Historians Have Said about the Causes of the Civil
War," *Theory and Practice*, pp. 53–102.

[5] For the time being we leave aside a most interesting problem—that of the historical status both of answers "why" ("He may have . . .") and "why" questions
("Why might they have . . . ?") hypothetical subjunctive in form. See Chapter 9.

cant cost of initially avoiding terms like "cause" and "causation."[6] Since, however, the mesh of an inquiry on explanation "why" in history is pretty fine, it will probably catch a good deal of what both historians and philosophers have been wont to call causal explanation in history.

And now let us turn to our first focal center, a paradigm of historical explanation "why." Having earlier encountered on the bathroom floor the dirt-encrusted trousers of his highly intelligent and invariably truthful twelve-year-old son Willie, his father addresses him thus:

"Why did you come home all covered with mud, Willie?"

This is a "why" question about an event or happening in the past and therefore requires as an answer a historical explanation "why." Three possible answers follow.

1. "I was not actually 'all covered with mud.' There is indeed a sense in which I was not covered with mud at all, since there was no mud on any part of my body. There was, it is true, a certain quantity of mud on my outer garments, but it actually 'covers' or is spread over only about 20 percent of their total surface. I will assume, however, that it is this situation, which you inaccurately designate as 'being all covered with mud,' that you wish me to explain. I will now do so. First, 'mud' is a more or less homogeneous mixture of dust and water in proportions that roughly permit it to be distinguished by its consistency from 'dirt' which contains more dust to the point of being readily frangible and 'muddy water' which contains more water and is therefore liquid and of negligible viscosity. Mud has two characteristics relevant to the present situation: (a) it is an adhesive, or, as *you* might say, 'It sticks to things'; (b) it is a lubricant; that is to say, when it contains a certain percentage of water or other liquid the liquid so coats the dust particles in mud as to reduce friction when they move or are moved with respect to each other.

"Given this second trait, if a muddy area is entered at relatively high velocity by a perpendicular rigid or semirigid object long in proportion to its base at point of contact, the base will accelerate more rapidly than the entry speed of the object. Consequently the center of gravity of the object will move in a downward and backward arc. If this downward and backward arcing continues at such a velocity that measures to counteract it are of no avail, the object will move from a perpendicular position with respect to the mud to a horizontal position recumbent upon it. If that object is covered with any material to which mud ad-

[6] I suspect that a reasonably careful writer can use the term "cause" in a way that makes sense and leaves doubt only in resolutely opaque understandings as to what he has in mind. Given such caution, there seems to be no sensible objection to using the term. (On this point see my *Reappraisals in History* [London, 1961], p. 200.) What is feasible, however, is not always expedient. Here and now expediency eliminates the need for unnecessary effort and is therefore the more desirable.

heres, and it will adhere to most surfaces, the mud's adhesive character will cause it to cling in varying quantities to the surface with which it is in contact. I am a semirigid body, and, when erect, have a height long in proportion to my base. At 4:09 P.M., April 5, 1967, I entered erect into a mud patch in Plumber's Field, Waterbury, Connecticut, at the velocity required to produce the sequence of movements of mass above described. Given a few simple laws of classical mechanics, it follows that under the particular circumstances set forth I should end my motion recumbent in the mud and that some of the mud should adhere to the surface of my garments. The event in other words is predictable from the relevant boundary conditions and general laws, and the prediction is validated by the observable and testable state of my outer garments. O.K.?"

2. "I slipped and fell in a mud puddle. O.K.?"

3. "Well, I had to stay late at school for Group Activities today. So I was in a hurry to get home, because I was late, so I took a shortcut through Plumber's Field. Well, some tough big kids hang around there, and a couple of them started to chase me—boy, they were really big— and yelled that they were going to beat me up. So I ran as fast as I could. Well you know it rained a lot Tuesday and there are still puddles in the field, and I skidded in one that I didn't see and fell; but they didn't catch me, and—well I'm sorry I got messed up. O.K.?"

Certain dissimilarities among the foregoing answers to the same question may have obscured a similarity that we need to keep in mind: all three are in intent answers to a question "why" about something that happened in the past to a person. That is, they are historical explanations "why." Moreover, they purport to be explanations of the same event, and since *ex hypothesi* Willie never lies, they all are true. It is therefore reasonable to wonder and inquire which is the better explanation. From one point of view there is no doubt on the issue: the first explanation is better because it is more adequate than the others. This point of view carries with it a certain authority; it is the view of men who in recent years have struggled with the problem of historical explanation most persistently and most vigorously.[7] The position of these

---

[7] The classical formulation of this view is Carl Hempel's "The Function of General Laws in History," in Patrick Gardiner, ed., *Theories of History* (Glencoe, Ill., 1956), pp. 344–356. Hempel's argument has undergone modification and refinement in the years since its publication. For evidence of such modification see Sidney Hook, ed., *Philosophy and History* (New York, 1963), pp. 136–142; Carl Hempel, *Aspects of Scientific Explanation* (New York, 1965), pp. 333–489. There are also recent and detailed modifications and refinements in Morton G. White, *Foundations of Historical Knowledge* (New York, 1965), and Arthur C. Danto, *The Analytical Philosophy of History* (Cambridge, Eng., 1965), some elements of which will require further scrutiny in Chapters 6 and 7. See also C. G. Hempel, in William H. Dray, ed., *Philosophical Analysis and History* (New York, 1966), pp. 95–126.

philosophic gladiators in the arena of historical explanation may strike some readers as itself less than wholly satisfactory. Yet an argument that over so long a period has engaged so many nimble philosophical wits is necessarily of historical (or at least antiquarian) concern. The view of these wits is that (with certain minor modifications and saving clauses) adequate and satisfactory historical explanations are causal explanations of events (and therefore a kind of explanation "why"), and that the best and most satisfactory causal explanations of events do the following things: they (1) specify all relevant initial or boundary conditions of the event, and (2) specify all relevant general laws (3) such that the statement of the boundary conditions and the general laws would strictly entail the statement that the event happened. Or, what amounts to the same thing, the boundary conditions and the general laws taken together would render the event strictly predictable.

Hempel has formalized this explanation schema as follows:

$$\frac{C_1, C_2 \ldots, C_k}{E}$$
$$L_1, L_2 \ldots, L_r$$

"Here $C_1, C_2 \ldots, C_k$ are statements describing the particular facts invoked; $L_1, L_2 \ldots, L_r$ are general laws: jointly, these statements will be said to form the explanans. The conclusion E is a statement describing the explanandum-event . . ."[8]

Alternatively, Whenever $C_1, C_2 \ldots C_k$ *then* E, *because* $L_1, L_2 \ldots L_k$; or finally, *If* $C_1, C_2 \ldots C_k$, E is predictable, because $L_1, L_2 \ldots L_k$.

Although none of the three answers to the question about the muddy pants rigorously fulfills all the above conditions for satisfactory historical explanation, it is quite clear that the first comes far closer to fulfilling them than the others and is therefore the best historical explanation of the three from the point of view of the philosophers who have most intensely devoted themselves to the problem.

Of course it is true that the first explanation in the case of the Muddy Pants does come closer to what is called by its proponents the deductive or "covering-law" model than do the other two. It is also true that explanations "why" that come pretty close to conforming to the model are useful in history. Consider, for example, the following graphs of population change in five lands in the same region over an identical time span. The question "Why did population of Country II drop sharply while during the same interval the populations of I, III, and IV climbed?" is legitimate. It is answerable only by an explanation "why," which might go something like this:

8 C. G. Hempel, in Dray, *Philosophical Analysis and History*, p. 97.

1. Boundary conditions. At time t_0, II was a land (a) densely populated, (b) almost wholly agrarian, (c) with an extremely primitive transportation network. (d) The population subsisted on a diet almost entirely composed of a carbohydrate present in plant x, which was raised locally. (e) Other native agricultural products were locally consumed in such limited quantity that (f) means were lacking for the necessary processing of the most important ones. (g) Plant x is susceptible to a disease y which (1) suddenly, wholly, and without warning destroys the edible nutritive portion very shortly before it is ready for harvesting, (2) spreads very rapidly, and (3) lingers in the soil and infects plant x in successive years. Finally (h) disease y infected plant x in land II for several successive years between t_0 and t_0 plus ten years.

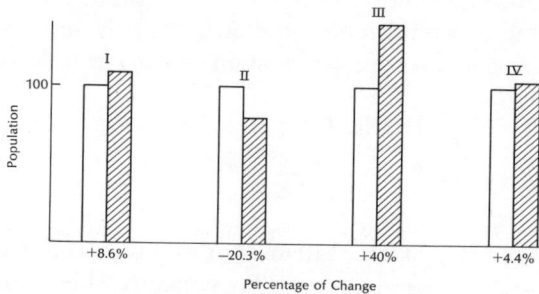

Figure 1

2. Covering laws. (a) A plant disease which acts as y does destroys the crop x in an area. (b) The almost complete destruction of the sole food staple in a densely populated area with a primitive transportation network and no means for processing other agricultural products reduces the available food supply in that area to a level far below the level of subsistence for the local population. (c) When the available food supply in an area is far below the minimum required by the population for subsistence, that population will decline through emigration and/or increased susceptibility to disease consequent to malnutrition, and/or starvation.

The statement of boundary conditions in (1) and of covering laws in (2) strictly entail the statement that between t_0 and t_0 plus ten years the population of III declined. In I, II, and IV boundary conditions in (1) were not present.

By now a good many readers will have recognized the particular demographic catastrophe that the explanation "why" above explains—the Irish Potato Famine. Indeed the foregoing explanation, although not its schematic structure, is derivable from Cecil Woodham-Smith's

[9] Cecil Woodham-Smith, *The Great Hunger* (New York, 1962). The other lands in the population graphs are Belgium (I), England (III), and France (IV).

account of the Famine—*The Great Hunger*.[9] Formally, this is a covering-law explanation "why." As such it should serve to quiet those who
insist that the nature of historical understanding is so divergent from the
nature of scientific knowledge that the explanatory modes of the two
never coincide. For here they clearly do; it would be simply perverse to
argue that anyone who had before him the evidence of population decline in Ireland between 1845 and 1849, given the explanation "why"
above, would not understand the decline better than he did before.

It is one thing to say that explanations in this genre are sometimes of
some use to some historians. It is quite another to say that they are per
se, intrinsically, and always superior to other forms of explanation
"why" in history. It was the purpose of the Case of the Muddy Pants,
to show that this is not so.

Particularly it was the purpose of the "o.k's?" with which Willie's
alternative explanations of the muddiness of his pants ended. Let us
try to imagine what the response of a male parent to each of Willie's
"o.k's?" would be. Since Willie's father is not an actual person but merely
a convenient fiction, we shall put in his place an actual male parent
with whom I am quite well acquainted, who a while ago had two sons
Willie's age. I can make a rough guess what his response would have
been to each "o.k.?"

To the one most closely conforming to the covering-law model, and
therefore the most adequate from the point of view of many philosophers of science (hereafter Muddy Pants I), his response would have
been, "No, *not* o.k., wise guy, and you know it." He would have fetched
Willie a sharp slap across his rear and sent him off to bed without supper to meditate on his sins. Of course my acquaintance is a violent man,
and other fathers might respond more mildly. They would, however, I
am sure, indicate in one way or another that they did not find satisfactory or adequate at all an answer to a historical "why" question in the
rhetoric of classical mechanics. Yet according to the theory of the philosophers that answer provides the best, the most satisfactory, the most
adequate historical explanation.

To the simple answer, "I slipped in a puddle. O.K.?" (hereafter
Muddy Pants II), my acquaintance's response would have been perhaps a little less irritable—something like, "Well, Willie, on a nice
bright day like this it must have taken a maximum effort for you to find
a puddle to slip in. Congratulations on your success." Connoisseurs of
the philosophical literature of historical explanation will recognize in
Muddy Pants II what is called an "explanation sketch." In this literature
an explanation sketch is deemed potentially true and correct as far as it
goes, with the reservation that it does not go far enough. Above, my
acquaintance seems to be soliciting a somewhat fuller account. An
explanation sketch is a truncated explanation "why," whose "general

outlines" can be supplemented so as to "yield a more closely reasoned argument based on explanatory hypotheses which are indicated more fully . . ."[10] But there, of course, is the catch; for to fill in the explanation sketch of Muddy Pants II in the way prescribed in the quotation would be to add those boundary conditions and general laws which would transform it into a deductive-nomological or covering-law explanation. This, however, will hardly do; it will simply get Willie back to Muddy Pants I and off to bed without supper and with something to remember his father by.

Muddy Pants II is indeed an explanation sketch, true and correct, yet inadequate and unsatisfactory, requiring to be filled in or filled out. *The filling in or out that will render it adequate and satisfactory, however, is not Muddy Pants I but Muddy Pants III*, the rendering explicit of the pattern of events and happenings that carried Willie from the place and time when school usually let out to the place and time of his disaster in the puddle in Plumber's Field. The historical explanation "why" in Muddy Pants III does not conform at all to the deductive model that is the most adequate form of a scientific explanation. It is hard to find any general laws to help Willie on his way from school to the puddle. It is not a general law that twelve-year-olds stay late at school for Group Activities, or that such activities make it late for twelve-year-olds to be getting home, or that twelve-year-olds try to get home on time, or that to do so they take shortcuts, or that tough big kids threaten to beat up little kids, or that little kids run when they are so threatened, or that they encounter puddles when they run, or that when they encounter puddles they slip, or that when they slip in puddles they fall. All these things may happen, but then again they may not; sometimes they do and sometimes they don't; and they do not appear to imply any general laws. Muddy Pants III looks like an answer to a "why" question that is all boundary conditions and no general laws. Even if it implies an unstated or perhaps unstateable general law, it is hard to see what force this somewhat special entity would add to an explanation that is already adequate to its purpose.

If Muddy Pants III is not clearly a deductive explanation "why," the strong form of scientific explanation, no more is it clearly a probabilistic or weaker form of scientific explanation. According to one of the most eminent authorities on such matters

probabilistic explanation . . . is nomological in that it presupposes general laws; but because these laws are of statistical rather than of strictly universal form, the resulting explanatory arguments of this kind *explain* a given phenomenon by showing that, in view of certain particular

[10] Dray, *Philosophical Analysis and History*, p. 107.

events and certain statistical laws, its occurrence was to be expected with high logical, or inductive, probability.[11]

Clearly this does not apply to Muddy Pants III at all. The circumstances it relates are far indeed from what is "to be expected with high logical, or inductive, probability." To the contrary. It is an account of a string of connected events, actions, and intentions, a few highly probable, most of low probability, thus rendering the full concatenation of very low probability indeed. The only high probability, amounting to near certainty, is that this quite improbable concatenation was what actually happened, and that it did happen simply follows from the given fact that Willie was a rigorously honest little boy. It follows, that is, not by deduction or induction but by definition.

Muddy Pants III then is not a scientific explanation "why" at all. But is it a satisfactory and adequate explanation "why"? Again we invoke the likely response to Willie's "o.k." What could a father, even the rather captious father referred to above, respond but "o.k."? What more could he want to know? What more did he need to know?

The obvious answer to all these questions is, "Nothing," but that is an answer which must give us pause, because by the standard accounts of such matters it is untrue. It is untrue for the best of possible reasons —because what it alleges is impossible. For if the answer to those questions is "Nothing," then Muddy Pants III, which is an explanation "why" of a unique event, is complete. But in the philosopher's vision no explanation "why" of a unique event can be complete.

> . . . the notion of a complete explanation of some *concrete event* . . . is self-defeating; for any particular event may be regarded as having infinitely many different aspects or characteristics, which cannot be accounted for by a finite set, however large, of explanatory statements.[12]

What this seems to imply is that the notion of a complete explanation "why" of an event is ambiguous.[13] In the sense that the set of relations in which a single event stands to all other events in any way related to it are infinite, complete explanation is strictly impossible, and since the gap between any finite set of relations however large, and an infinite set is still infinite, no explanation can be more nearly complete than any other. Yet in some sense some explanations are more complete than others. Thus, Muddy Pants III is more complete than Muddy Pants II because it wholly subsumes it. Moreover, the notion of an explanation being more or less complete than another is not merely useful but indis-

[11] C. G. Hempel, in Dray, *Philosophical Analysis and History*, p. 102.
[12] *Ibid.*, pp. 106–107.
[13] As we shall see later this is equally true of explanations "who," "when," and "where."

pensable for ordinary discourse and communication. So, for that matter, is the notion of an explanation being quite complete.

Which brings us back to that answer, "Nothing," to our question about what needed to be added to the explanation "why" in Muddy Pants III. That explanation was complete and therefore adequate and satisfactory because it provided Willie's father with what he needed to know and all he needed to know. Anything less would have been incomplete and therefore inadequate; anything more, unnecessary and dispensable, a waste of time and words. From this we can understand the likely responses of the father to Willie's "o.k's." He regards Muddy Pants I, II, and III as adequate and satisfactory *in inverse order to what one would expect if one's scale of adequacy for explanations "why" were the scientific one.* On the scientific adequacy scale the order would be

1. Muddy Pants I (deductive or covering-law explanation)
2. Muddy Pants II (explanation sketch to be filled in by Muddy Pants I)
3. Muddy Pants III (no explanation at all)

The adequacy scale based on what Willie's father needed to be going on with would be

1. Muddy Pants III (adequate and satisfactory because complete)
2. Muddy Pants II (incomplete, completed in Muddy Pants III)
3. Muddy Pants I (incomplete and a waste of time).

This very simple analysis may help dispel some of the trouble historians have had in dealing with causes. It may render intelligible the paradox with which this chapter started: that historians who answer "why" questions day in, day out, in the course of their professional work without qualm or misgiving as to the adequacy of their answers get all of a-twitter when they run athwart the term "cause" and its derivatives. In their piecemeal work they unconsciously accept the notion that an adequate explanation "why" is one that provides them with all the information and understanding they need in order to be moving along with their inquiry. The very moving along is a sort of "o.k." in action responsive to the query "o.k.?" that they tacitly posed before they moved along. Not, of course, that they are always right; but if they were not very often right, the history they set down would be a mass of nonsense, unintelligible because inconsequent—which for the most part it is not. When they tangle with "causes" and "causation" and so on, however, they think that adequacy demands complete explanation "why" in the other, "scientific" sense of "complete." But in that sense, as we have seen, no explanation "why" of an event ever is or can be complete, whether it be of the American Civil War or of Willie's muddy pants. They have made the mistake of committing themselves to completeness of explanation in a sense of the phrase in which such completeness is intrinsically unattainable. Thus they quite gratuitously inflict on themselves an unwarranted sense of the futility of their endeavors. They really need not pursue this chimera of completeness.

There is, however, in the father's response to Willie's "o.k?" in Muddy Pants I something beyond simple denial of the adequacy of the explanation, something revealed by his actions and by his "Not o.k., *and you know it*." In both word and act he is making it clear that Willie mistranslated his question, and that he suspects Willie of having done so willfully and maliciously. What Willie has done is to translate the question, "Why did you come home all covered with mud?" to be, "What series of physical conditions and of motions of bodies, taken together with the relevant physical laws, strictly entails the adhesion of a certain amount of mud to your trousers today?" The correct translation of the sentence, however, is "What series of connected intentions, decisions, and actions, your own or others, in conjunction with what situations and accidents brought you into contact with a lot of mud today?" It is the father's reasonable view that Willie, being a bright lad, knew very well what the right translation was, and chose the wrong one because he was a smart aleck.

Thus the "why" question under consideration can be translated into two "what" questions, each soliciting an answer or explanation quite different from the other. That is to say, the initial "why" question is inherently ambiguous. This is true of many "why" questions. The ambiguity of "why" questions is responsible for some of the ostensible difficulties of explanations "why." The difficulty is not that of providing an explanation, but of discerning or deciding what is to be explained. Much of the divergence results not from differences of opinion as to the correct version of what happened or how it came to happen but from differing and equally correct translations of the same "why" question. Historians sometimes think that they disagree as to the correctness of an explanation "why," when actually they are offering correct and appropriately different answers to different questions which correctly but unfortunately they have translated into the same "why" question. If all this is true, people who write history could save themselves a good deal of avoidable anguish and time-consuming controversy if they systematically practiced a simple regimen based on the following easy rules:

1. Before rushing to seek explanation, carefully examine the question that the explanation is supposed to answer.

2. Do this especially in the case of explanations "why," in order to be sure that you have not committed yourself to complete explanation in a sense of "complete" that makes your task impossible.

3. If possible translate "why" questions into some other interrogative form. To do this makes more explicit what you are trying to find out and thus reveals the conditions of proof of your explanation.

The salutary effect of these simple rules for the inquiring historian is worth illustrating:

The dead body of Mr. Sweet is discovered in his living room. Question: *Why is Mr. Sweet dead?*

Answer 1. Because of damage resulting in a massive hemorrhage, both due to the entry of a metallic foreign object into his cerebrum.
Translation of "why" questions answered by 1: What physiological dysfunction killed Mr. Sweet and what precipitated that dysfunction?

Answer 2. Because of the entry of a bullet from a Smith and Wesson automatic pistol No. XZ427906 into his brain.
Translation of "why" question answered by 2: What weapon was used to bring about and did bring about Mr. Sweet's death?

Answer 3. Because his wife shot him.
Translation of "why" question answered by 3: What human agent wielded the lethal weapon?

Answer 4. Because Sweet's wife executed a long-premeditated scheme for doing him in.
Translation of "why" question answered by 4: Was Smith's death at the hands of his wife accidental homicide, manslaughter, or murder?

Answer 5. Because Mrs. Sweet was driven to kill her husband by a consuming hatred of him.
Translation of "why" question answered by 5: What moved Mrs. Sweet to kill her husband?

Answer 6. Because the incredible brutality and bestiality with which her husband treated her drove Mrs. Sweet to kill him.
Translation of "why" question answered by 6: What made Mrs. Sweet hate her husband enough to kill him?

Note that each of the six answers is an explanation "why" to a question that can correctly be phrased "Why is Mr. Sweet dead?" All are historical answers. They explain why he is dead by reference to what some human being did or suffered or intended in the past: to what happened to Sweet (1, 2), to what Mrs. Sweet did or intended (3, 4), to what happened to Mrs. Sweet (5), to what Mr. Sweet did and what happened to Mrs. Sweet (6). Furthermore, each explanation is a *complete* answer to a question "Why is Mr. Sweet dead?" Each of the six questions "Why is Mr. Sweet dead?" however, is a different question, and one can only discover what the question actually is and in what sense each answer is a complete explanation by translating the "why" question into an alternative interrogative form. In "why" form the question does not suggest where to look for evidence to support a complete and adequate explanation. Each of the translations of the "why" question directs one toward the appropriate sources of evidence. Question by question, it suggests: (1) ask the medical examiner; (2) ask the police ballistics laboratory; (3) check fingerprints, and Mrs. Sweet's hands for gunpowder residues, look for eyewitnesses, etc.; (4) check the ownership and date of acquisition of the pistol, and examine the living room for signs of struggle, etc.; (5) make extended inquiries among neighbors, relatives, and acquaintances; (6) same as 5.

As the question in "why" form does not, the translated questions indicate clearly what sort of explanation "why" is called for. In the case of the first question, translated as "What physiological dysfunction killed Mr. Sweet and what precipitated that dysfunction?", the adequate explanation should be stated in the deductive or covering-law form. The boundary conditions are the actual condition of Mr. Sweet's cerebrum and the presence in it of a metallic object in a particular position. The covering-laws are those that deal with the movement and path of such an object through a less dense material, in this instance the cerebral tissue, and with the physiological consequences of the rupturing and maceration of cerebral tissue. From the conditions and laws the death of Mr. Sweet (or anyone else who suffers a like cerebral disaster) is strictly predictable.

The proofs of all the other answers or explanations "why" are what are usually called probabilistic. Thus it is extremely likely that a piece of metal of a particular shape, size, and weight was a bullet fired from a .38 caliber pistol and, if such a piece of metal bears certain markings, that it passed through the barrel of the Smith and Wesson pistol having the serial number XZ427906. Evidence from the record can or might be able to establish with quite high probability (or as the law insists "beyond reasonable doubt") that Mrs. Sweet fired the pistol, that the firing was a premeditated one, not an accidental one or something done in self-defense, that Mrs. Sweet passionately hated Mr. Sweet, and that he had given her every reason to do so.

And here we are brought up short. What we appear just to have done is to show that historical explanation is indeed formally identical with

one model or the other, deductive or probabilistic, of scientific explanation. For at each step, in providing proof for each answer to our translated sequence of "why" questions, we have made deductibility or
probability our criterion for acceptability. We seem indeed to confront
a paradox. Having asserted and (I hope) demonstrated in the Case
of the Muddy Pants, the irrelevance of the two forms of scientific explanation to some kinds of historical "why" questions, we appear now
to have performed a complete about face and in the Case of Dead Mr.
Sweet shown that the forms of scientific explanation are the only acceptable ones in history. In all this, however, there is no paradox: there
is only an illusion. If we juxtapose the two we see that the function of
the "scientific" explanations in the Case of Dead Mr. Sweet was merely
to get us to the point where explanation "why" started in Muddy Pants
III. In the latter instance, on the grounds of Willie's known honesty and
accuracy, his father took as given all the sorts of answers that we tested
so carefully and scientifically in the Case of Dead Mr. Sweet. What are
called "the facts in the case," provided *ex hypothesi* in the Case of the
Muddy Pants, had to be painfully sorted out and sifted from a fragmentary record of the past in the Case of Dead Mr. Sweet. Having performed this difficult operation in the latter case we are only now prepared to ask for the sort of historical explanation "why" that will enable
us to be getting on. That explanation goes very simply, "Mr. Sweet is
dead because he treated Mrs. Sweet so outrageously that she came to
hate him and finally got herself a pistol and blew his brains out." The
correct translation of the "why" question here is, "Who is responsible at
law for Mr. Sweet's death and to what extent?", and the "us" that needs
this explanation is the jury which has to decide whether to condemn
Mrs. Sweet to prison for a long term for murder or to free her under
the M'Naughton rule on the grounds that she was incapable of knowing "the nature and quality of her act."

The point to emphasize here, however, is that this explanation "why"
(Dead Mr. Sweet 7) is on the same footing as Muddy Pants III: it is
adequate, satisfactory, complete, and quite unassimilable to either form
of scientific explanation "why." It makes Mr. Sweet's death intelligible
and credible. It distinctly does not make it certain, or probable, or predictable. Since, however, our inquiry starts with Mr. Sweet's corpse it is
not altogether and immediately clear that *ex post facto* certainty, or
probability, or predictability of his death would be very helpful or
would enable anyone to get on with anything. The useful time for
assessing the probability of or for predicting a murderous assault by
Mrs. Sweet on her husband would on the whole seem to be before it
happened rather than after.

Since the matter of prediction and predictability in history has come
up, and since some analytical philosophers have suggested that predict-

ability is a criterion of adequate explanation in history as in the natural sciences, we will finish this chapter with a brief consideration of historical prediction and predictability.

The power of prediction is built into some scientific explanations "why." The word "power" is used advisedly here. The power, the control over nature, that the natural sciences have achieved accounts for much of their fascination and attractiveness, and for the prestige that they have earned and enjoy. For a physicist or a chemist to assert that prediction did not matter to him, and that he never aimed to achieve it, would be a wild eccentricity. A scientific explanation that leaves outcomes random, and therefore wholly unpredictable, is a contradiction in terms. Some historians assert that their discipline is a science and yet doubt that historians can predict future human events. This view is sometimes accompanied by a shamefaced, somewhat exculpatory confession that history is a rather backward and low-grade science and by an expression of the hope that when, if ever, it grows up, it will be able to predict future events. Given this outlook, a humble view of the status of history among the sciences necessarily follows. But is it true that historians cannot predict future events?

Actually historians predict future events with great frequency and high accuracy. But then so does everybody. Let us inspect a historian in the throes of predicting future events.

Mr. H., an historian, is seated at a desk examining and sorting out 450 encoded cards. When he finishes his task he will make and act on the following predictions:

1. At a specified moment in the future at a specified point there will take place a confluence of 600 particles ± 30.

2. That confluence will be repeated 30 ± 3 times in a specified time span and each time it will have a duration of 55 ± 5 minutes.

3. The set 600 ± 30 particles will overlap the 450 particles concerning which the cards provide H. with encoded information, but the entire 450 is not a subset of the 600. He predicts that 50 ± 10 of the members of the 450 set will *not* converge as predicted in (1), but 200 particles concerning which his cards afford him no information whatsoever will converge with the remaining 400 at the predicted point and moment.

4. He further predicts that sets of 20 ± 4 particles will converge at other specified points, that in the specified time span they will so converge 15 ± 2 times; that these sets of converging particles will not overlap; and that they will all be subsets of the 600 set.

To do full justice to the power of prediction historian H. is deploying, however, we need to specify some of the information he does not have at the time he makes his forecast.

1. He has no precise information about the current position of the 600 particles, although he knows they are currently scattered in a very irregular dispersion pattern between about 250 and a couple of million of their own lengths from their predicted point of future convergence.

2. He has no information about their current rate or pattern of movement, if any.

3. The time span between the moment of prediction and the moment of initial confluence is such that if they were in continuous motion throughout the span (which they certainly are not), at their normal rate of self-propulsion the particles would traverse 1^{10^7}, where 1 is their average length.

4. The region on which they converge will have an area equal to only 10 times the combined length of the particles ($A = 10 \times 600 \; 1$).

If one were to ask a physicist within what margin of error he could make such predictions in connection with subatomic or atomic particles, he would indicate that such predictions are impossible or that the margin of error is incalculably large, or both. Yet not only does historian H. make all the predictions indicated, but others have such confidence in his predictions that they make large investments of capital on the basis of them.

Actually what historian H. is performing is not some sort of black magic or scientific miracle, but an operation annually repeated by him to the amazed plaudits of no one. In June on the basis of preregistration cards he is setting up his large twice-a-week history lecture course for the following semester and "sectioning" it into once-a-week discussion groups, making allowance for additional later registrants and for "no shows."

Surely historian H. is predicting future events. A point in time, B, a hundred days subsequent to another point in time, A, is "future" with respect to point A; and at point A, historian H. is in effect preparing in advance for a highly specified event which he expects to happen at point of time B in a specified place. When the predicted event is due to happen he will be present with a large number of others to verify it, that is to observe the meeting of the lecture class, and teaching assistants will be present to verify the meetings of the sections. It would be hard to think of a meaning for the phrase "predicting future events" less ambiguous and less confusing than the one assigned here to it, or a prediction more readily verifiable.

So the historian H. has made a precise, accurate, and readily verifiable prediction of the future. But, one might object, anyone can do that sort of thing. That is certainly true. Indeed it is what I said was true a couple of pages back. All men predict events and do so with such regularity, frequency, and accuracy that they are unaware of doing it. Yet a subliminal awareness of the situation emerges occasionally in casual conversation. Consider the remark "I do not (or do) like Jones. He is completely unpredictable." In the first place the very singling out of unpredictability as a distinguishing trait indicates that the remarker, Smith, is comparing Jones with other people whose actions he is able to predict. But there is more to it than that. If one tries to discover exactly what Smith means when he says that Jones is completely unpredictable, one will usually discover he means that over the span of his time in Jones's presence he can predict approximately the sort of thing Jones will do next only 99 percent of the time, whereas with "predictable" people he can do it 99.9 percent of the time. That, of course, makes the frequency of Jones's unpredictable acts ten times as great as that of "predictable" people, but it hardly means that Smith has no notion at any moment what Jones will do the next moment; on the contrary 99 percent of the time he has a quite clear notion. He acts on such notions, and Jones's own actions regularly verify his judgment. Furthermore, Smith means that as between two responses or among a quite small number he does not know which Jones will choose. Since, however, the range of Jones's possible responses is very large, he has already performed quite a feat of predicting by reducing it to three or four. In fact, if instead of setting "Jones will do A and only A" as the standard of correct prediction one were to extend it to "Jones will do A or B or C or D," the predictability average of the unpredictable Jones would probably climb to 99.9 percent. Of course, not everyone could score so high an average on Jones. But then not everyone could score so high an average on predicting what the yield will be in a reaction in organic chemistry. In order to score high on the prediction scale one needs to know something of the subject one is predicting about, and as the organic chemist knows something about organic chemistry, Smith knows something about Jones.

But what about the professional historian? Can he predict the future better than other people? The answer to this question seems to follow fairly simply from what has gone before. If you know Jones a great deal better than I, a professional historian, know him, you will be able to predict his future actions a lot better than I will. Like Smith and organic chemists, professional historians do better in predicting the future in matters that they know more about than other people do.

In general, however, predicting the future is not the regular business of professional historians. They put in most of their time writing about the human past. The interesting questions about such historians, then, would appear to be: can they predict past events? What would one mean by saying historians can predict past events or past actions? What use to them would their ability to do so be? By the prediction of the past one might mean the statement of some outcomes of a past event by an historian who knows the event happened but does not know what the outcomes were. An example may be helpful here. I know that the Senate of the United States divided on the Civil Rights Bill of 1964. The only evidence before me is a list of the senators for the 82nd Congress indicating the states from which they were elected and their party affiliation, but I also remember that the bill passed and that Senator Everett Dirksen voted for it. I do not know but will now predict: (1) exactly which senators on the list were present for the discussion or were paired in their absence on one side or the other; (2) how many senators were present; (3) on which side each senator present or paired voted. Here are my predictions.

Prediction I. Every senator on the list not dead at the time voted or was paired;

Prediction II. Ninety-six of the senators were present;

Prediction III. They voted as follows:[14]

Aye

Aiken, Allott, Anderson, Bartlett, Bayh, Beall, Bennett, Bible, Boggs, Brewster, Burdick, Byrd (W. Va.), Carlson, Cannon, Case, Church, Clark, Cooper, Cotton, Curtis, Dirksen, Dodd, Dominick, Douglas, Edmondson, Engle, Fong, Gruening, Hart, Hartke, Hayden, Hickenlooper, Hruska, Humphrey, Inouye, Jackson, Javits, Jordan (Idaho), Keating, Kennedy, Kuchel, Lausche, Long (Mo.), McCarthy, McGee, McGovern, McIntyre, McNamara, Magnuson, Mansfield, Mecham, Metcalf, Miller, Monroney, Morse, Morton, Moss, Mundt, Muskie, Nelson, Neuberger, Pastore, Pearson, Pell, Prouty, Proxmire, Randolph, Ribicoff, Saltonstall, Scott, Simpson, Smith, Symington, Williams (Del.), Williams (N. J.), Yarborough, Young (N. D.), Young (Ohio),

Nay

Byrd (Va.), Eastland, Ellender, Ervin, Fulbright, Goldwater, Gore, Hill, Holland, Johnston, Jordan (N. C.), Long (La.), McClellan, Robertson, Russell, Smathers, Sparkman, Stennis, Talmadge, Thurmond, Tower, Walters.

We now turn to the record of the proceedings of the Senate on June 19, 1964, to check my predictions. Here are the results:

I. Every senator on the list either voted or was paired. Therefore, I was able to predict which senators voted or were paired with an error of 0 percent.

II. Every senator was present. Therefore I was able to predict how many senators were present with an error of 4 percent.

III. Ninety-five of the senators voted or were paired on the side I predicted. I was wrong about five senators: Byrd (West Virginia), Cotton, Hickenlooper, Mechem, Simpson. Therefore my error in predicting the side each senator took was 5 percent.

[14] See *Congressional Quarterly Almanac, 1964,* p. 696.

This is a pretty good instance of what it makes sense to call predicting the past, and a pretty accurate job of doing it. This is said with no pride at all. Any moderately regular reader of political news should be able to do nearly as well three years after the event. It happens that these particular predictions of the past, although demanding a good bit of complicated knowledge about how recent American politics work, are quite easy for the many who have it, of whom I am one. In crudest terms I was able to predict accurately the particular past events that I did predict, because I already knew a lot about their setting, just as in the preceding argument the organic chemist already knew a lot about organic chemistry, and Smith knew a lot about Jones.

So far, so good. But having given a sensible meaning to the expression "predict the past" and having shown that I, and by implication a great many other people, can do it, does predicting the past have any serious use for professional historians, or is it just a device that permitted me to make a reasonably spectacular grandstand play?

It seems to me that predicting the past is so useful to historians that unless they did it fairly often they would soon be talking insufferable nonsense. This does not mean that they often predict the past explicitly or consciously or that such predictions often appear in their written work. The following passage, however, is explicit enough to illustrate the usefulness of predicting the past to professional historians. The purpose of the inquiry to which the passage refers was to discern the party or factional structure of the House of Commons during the first year of the English Civil War.

> Now if a distinct cleavage separated war party from peace party, given the side a member took on one question involving war or peace, we should be able to predict his position in regard to any other question involving the same issue. For example, if a member voted against a treaty of peace in February, that would identify him as one of the war party. We should then expect that in July as well as in February he would oppose a treaty, that he would support the weekly assessment ordinance, that he would attempt to brand all petitioners for peace as potential traitors, and that he would refuse Charles's servant a pass to go from London to Oxford with fresh bed linen and nightshirts for the king. Let us try the powers of prediction with which this hypothesis endows us on the stubborn facts that we find in the *Journals* and in the diaries of the Civil War Parliament.[15]

The author then went on to test the hypothesis against the actions of six reasonably eminent members of the Long Parliament. In not one of the six cases did the hypothesis square with the patterns of voting or

---

[15] J. H. Hexter, *The Reign of King Pym* (Cambridge, Mass., 1941), p. 36.

action of the member. None of them followed a course that was distinctly "war party" or distinctly "peace party." The hypothesis was therefore not verified but falsified. Since from the outset the historian in question had been fairly sure that the then generally favored view which divided Parliament into two factions in the first year of the Civil War was wrong, the falsification of the hypothesis served his purposes very nicely. In the course of their work historians do this sort of hypothesis-testing very frequently although not very self-consciously. When views of the past that they seriously entertain are regularly falsified as a result of their examination of the record, they change their views. Or at any rate, they had better.

CHAPTER II: What Makes It So Easy and So Hard, *or the Language of History*

W HAT we have just said about explanation "why" and prediction leaves a good many questions open. An exchange that took place a few years ago between a professor of engineering and myself may provide a simple though slightly indirect approach to some of those questions.

I had just completed a lecture in which I had argued that although history could not be assimilated to the natural science model, still it was not a wholly contemptible or mindless activity. The professor of engineering in the audience did not at all share this rosy view of the discipline. In the question period after the lecture, he rose to ask me whether historians could predict the future. When I answered that of course they could, he challenged me to make a prediction. I offered predictions about the professor's own activities in the forthcoming weeks—that he would go to a room in one of the Engineering buildings 7 ± 3 times in the next week, that there he would offer instruction to groups of persons whose median age was between eighteen and twenty-two, that in each such group the males would be more numerous than the females, and that he would meet no classes at all between December 24 of the current year and January 2 of the following one. His response to these predictions was, if one considers the matter carefully, peculiar but instructive. He might have faulted my predictions on two grounds. He might have said they were wrong. The only thing that barred that course to him was his evident belief that they were right. His second line might have been that one did not have to be a historian to make that sort of prediction. He did not take this line either. What

he did was say, "Do you call *that* predicting the future?" and smiled
at me contemptuously and triumphantly. He believed I had failed
utterly to do what I had alleged I could do; his question was purely
rhetorical, intended to emphasize what he believed to be the fact: that
he had won the implicit argument hands down. Yet predicting the future was manifestly what I had just done. Moreover he did not even
suggest that events were likely to falsify my predictions. It is not
immediately apparent that the sequence of events had earned him his
overpowering sense of dialectical triumph.

It is quite perplexing that he should have felt he had won an argument which in fact he had lost. How could he have imagined this?
How could he have failed to see that he was simply mistaken about
prediction of the future? The triumph of the professor's demeanor is
rendered intelligible (though scarcely justifiable) only in conjunction
with the contempt of his tone of voice. What he meant to convey was
that what I had done was so trivial as to be unworthy of the name of
prediction. Yet the ability to predict the sort of thing I predicted is not
obviously more trivial than the ability to predict the rate of fall of a
brick about to be dropped from a fourth story window. True, the
second prediction marked a most important advance in the development of classical mechanics, while the sort of prediction I made about
the professor cannot be regarded as a major advance in anything at all.
Yet why this should be so is not at once perspicuously clear.

Wherein then lay the professor's mistake? What accounts for his
wholly inapproprate sense of triumph and air of contempt? Simply
that he regarded my predictions of the future, however precise and
accurate, as too easily come by to be dignified by the term prediction.
There is, of course, no reason a priori why all prediction of the future
should be hard rather than easy. And there is no reason, either, why
prediction should be deemed a particularly dignified activity. The
engineering professor's multiple mistakes were the result of his thinking
all prediction of the future to be an analogue of scientific prediction.
Scientific prediction and its verification are traditionally rather difficult
operations; they require specialized skills; and for these reasons they
are treated by scientists and philosophers of sciences as a pretty high-
class business. But there is no reason why all predictions should be altogether like scientific prediction, and in fact with respect to difficulty
and the requirement of special skills some prediction is, as we have just
seen, not at all like scientific prediction.

Second, the professor regarded what I predicted as so trivial as not to
be worth predicting; but then I did not say that everything that could
be predicted about the future was important. Anyway it was not actually the unimportance of the predictable events that bothered him, but
their *commonplaceness*, which is a different thing. Ordinarily in the

United States we can accurately predict that when we go to the grocery tomorrow the shelves will be abundantly stocked with food. The event predicted is certainly commonplace enough. That the event or its predictability are unimportant would be doubted by inhabitants of lands less fortunate, or in places in the United States struck by hurricane, flood, arson, looting, and other acts of God and man, where such a prediction of the future is not possible.

There is one further point, and it is psychological. The events about which men most yearn for accurate prediction are the ones that create the greatest anxiety and sense of insecurity. They create anxiety and insecurity because they combine a high level of contingency with a high component of catastrophe. I cannot predict exactly what vegetable my wife will serve with dinner tonight. What particular vegetable I get does not matter, as long as I get a well-prepared dinner, which I can predict. Therefore my inability to predict this bit of the future is wholly unimportant to me. On the other hand, who will be elected President in the next election matters a great deal not only to me but to millions and millions of other people. The fact that this future event, a source of general insecurity and anxiety, is immersed in irreducible contingencies, including the life spans of the more likely candidates, creates a particularly powerful psychological yearning for the impossible: that it should be exactly and precisely predictable, not merely that the President will be a native, white male Protestant or Catholic over thirty-five years of age, and quite likely one of ten identifiable men, but that he will be one particular individual out of several tens of millions of eligible persons.

What the erroneous notion of historians and others that prediction of the future is impossible boils down to is (1) that *total* prediction of the future is impossible; (2) that precise prediction of a great many future events is impossible; (3) that among the future events not precisely predictable are especially those that from a sense of anxiety and insecurity, itself a consequence of this unpredictability, men most desire to predict precisely; but (4) that prediction of future events is not only often possible but is often accurate, precise, and important; and (5) that historians and others have deluded themselves on this point not because such predictions are rare or unimportant, but because although very important indeed they are both easy and commonplace.

Granted then that prediction of future events is possible, what makes it so, and why is it so often easy and commonplace? Again the answer is easy and certain, but not very interesting. In the form of a platitude familiar to everyone, it has time and again been rejected as false. The rejected platitude is "History repeats itself." This old saw has often been misconstrued to mean that there are future events which in every conceivable respect will be absolutely identical with past events. This, of course, is an assertion that no sensible man would make; no event is ever absolutely identical with any other. Moreover, the platitude happens to use the term "history" as a synonym for the "past." This is a quite proper common usage, but for reasons indicated in our Nonchapter, we will avoid it in these investigations.[1] To avoid both present misconstrual and subsequent confusion we want to restate "history repeats itself" in language a little more precise and less ambiguous. So we say that tomorrow and tomorrow and tomorrow, stretching a considerable span into the future, are in many matters and in considerable detail likely to be much like yesterday and the day before and the day before that, both with respect to stabilities and to rates and directions of change. To the extent that this is true men not only will be able to predict the future with some precision and accuracy, but they will so predict it. Moreover, they will act on their predictions, and they will have their predictions verified by the occurrence of the events they predict.

Of course all predictions will not always be right, nor will they be right in every detail, and the further into the future we push our tomorrows, the less accurate our predictions will be, and the more often they will be mistaken. At this point our earlier investigations of explanations "why" in history converges with our investigation of prediction of the future. The Case of the Muddy Pants has evoked from auditors on whom I have tried it out a response almost identical to the response of the professor of engineering to my predictions of his future: "Do you call *that* history?" There are perhaps reasons for not calling it history. The rejection implied in the incredulous "Do you call *that* history?" however, rises from no legitimate objections. It results from the feeling that The Case of the Muddy Pants is unworthy of being called history, that as one usually perceptive historian recently said of happenings considerably less ordinary, they were "beneath the dignity of history."

What appears to be involved in such a view is an atavistic bit of snobbery that harks back to the days when History was about the Great Deeds of Great Men, and any account of human events had to have as their centerpiece the *res gesta* of the great. The centerpiece has been augmented and embellished considerably without changing the habit of thought implicit in its initial construction. A great many people still think of history with a capital "H." For such people, in order to be History, an account of the past must deal with Big Issues, Great Heroes, Main Trends, Underlying or Basic Factors, Seminal Ideas, or Key Events. To be History, such an account must be important, and to be important it must be about what was important in the past. To think about the problem in this way, however, is to build in a disaster which

[1] See Nonchapter, p. 4.

is sure to prevent any sensible discussion of general historical problems.

Each person calling himself a historian acquires a vested interest in asserting that the sort of thing he writes about is important and therefore worthy of the name of History. Being like all others of the human kind, a vain creature, he soon gets around to claiming that *only* the sort of thing he writes about the past or *only* the sort of thing in the past he writes about is History. Conservatives in the guild insist that only the sorts of things their predecessors have rendered important by writing about them are History; while radicals turn the conservative position upside down and reserve the honor of being "real" History for what their predecessors have not and they have written about. All this is not in aid of enlightening the understanding but of bolstering the ego. It is a short cut to logomachy, which unless they exercise extraordinary care, historians are likely to attain very readily anyhow.

The easiest way to avoid this sort of endless bickering is to make a fast withdrawal, to de-escalate "History" to "history." Just coming down from capitals to lower case makes it easier to accept the notion that history can be unimportant and trivial, can be about what is unimportant and trivial in the past, and still be history. The withdrawal itself may seem unimportant and trivial. It is nevertheless necessary if one is to avoid a stultifying problem in taxonomy. For if a coherent account of what happened to me a while back when I was rushing up and down O'Hare Airport in Chicago trying to book an early afternoon flight to San Francisco is not history, then what in the world is it? And if an explanation of how I finally managed to get a place on a United Airlines plane leaving at 12:55 P.M. is not a historical explanation, then what kind of explanation is it? Regardless of its unimportance, why is the account *not* history; why is the explanation *not* historical explanation? Later for tactical reasons we may want to narrow our conception of history somewhat, but at the outset, to avoid painting ourselves into a corner, it would seem the way of wisdom to be as ecumenical and nonsnob as we can about it. So when we talk about history, we do best to junk notions about dignity and worth and importance both in the past and in what we say about the past. If we do this, we can avoid a great deal of unnecessary difficulty and wrangling. We can then simply say that for our immediate purposes:

1. The human past is whatever happened to happen to people; it is whatever they have intended, and whatever they have happened to do up to now.

2. History is an attempt to render a coherent, intelligible, and true account of some of these events, intentions, and happenings.[2]

[2] This means leaving out all the past and all natural history before the coming of man on earth. There are good reasons for doing this since the human past has cer-

Now that we have got history out of the Capital Clouds and down to
the lower-case earth, we can cope with the perplexing fact that a great
many people, including some historians, feel that it is, or any rate ought
to be, terribly hard. The perplexity is brought home by another look at
The Case of the Muddy Pants, especially the contrast between Muddy
Pants I and Muddy Pants III. At the outset of the case we posited that
Willie was a very bright twelve-year-old. He did not have to be all that
bright, however, to come up with Muddy Pants III:

> Well, I had to stay late at school for Group Activities today. So I was in
> a hurry to get home, because I was late, so I took a shortcut through
> Plumber's Field. Well, some tough big kids hang around there, and a
> couple of them started to chase me—boy, they were really big—and
> yelled that they were going to beat me up. So I ran as fast as I could.
> Well you know it rained a lot Tuesday and there are still puddles in the
> field, and I skidded in one that I didn't see and fell; but they didn't
> catch me, and—well, I'm sorry I got all messed up. O.K.?

Indeed one might be justified in feeling that a slightly stupid six-year-
old would be quite capable of Muddy Pants III. We posited Willie's
brightness so that it might be credible that he was capable of the explanation of Muddy Pants I, the explanation "why" most readily assimilable to the scientific model.[3] The contrast between the two explanations "why" is illustrative of a contrast between most explanations
"why" in the sciences and a great deal of explanation "why" in history.
The former are much harder than the latter. There has been a considerable amount of propaganda disseminated to suggest that science is
really easy and just extended common sense, and the only serious
trouble with this propaganda is that it is palpably false.

The first requirement of science is that one jettison common sense,
abandon the obvious evidence of one's senses in favor of data provided
by complex telescopes, microscopes, gauges, meters, and other measuring devices whose very principles of operation are quite hard to explain
or understand. To save his faith in the devices a man must swallow
such nonsense or at least noncommon sense as that on the bitterest
winter day when he is chilled to the bone and on the fiercest day of
summer when he is suffocating with the heat, his body temperature has

tain traits and dimensions wholly absent from the past of prehuman nature. For
example, man alone leaves records, first oral and more recently both oral and tan-
gible, that he intends *as records*, and this trite fact makes a radical difference between the work of a natural historian and that of a historian *tout court*. This does
not mean that I think that history and the work of historians are somehow more
worthy and dignified than natural history and the work of natural historians. I
simply do not think this at all.

[3] See Chapter 1, p. 25.

not changed at all. To say that this is a mere extension of common sense demands an inordinate extension of the very meaning of "extension." One might perhaps say that science requires only that we *transcend* common sense; but one would have to add the codicil that to get anywhere in understanding science we have so to transcend common sense, get so far above it, that it disappears from view. Consider the absurdities that three great scientific revolutions—the Copernican, the chemical, and the Darwinian—required men to swallow. Copernicus proposed a notion of the earth's movement which required men to believe that the earth, the biggest heaviest thing of which they were directly conscious, incommensurably bigger and heavier than anything else they directly experienced, was tearing around in a circle at the rate of several hundred thousand miles an hour and simultaneously spinning at the rate of a thousand miles an hour, while they, standing on the surface of this outsize cannon ball, somehow did not notice that it was moving at all. And these absurdities were advanced on the grounds that by accepting them one could better explain the observed erratic movements of a few specks of light called planets. To accept the chemical revolution all that men had to swallow was the idea that the fire which reduced a heavy log to a handful of dust did so by *adding* weight to the log. After all, to believe that was easy compared with believing that a rabbit, an oyster, a great whale, and Uncle Eric, an insurance salesman, had as a common ancestor an organism so small as to be invisible to the naked eye. This is what the Darwinian revolution required one to believe. Given such heavy drafts on human credulity, given the increasing reliance of the most successful sciences on mathematics, the least commonsensical of all human intellectual activities, is it any wonder that men intellectually oriented toward the natural sciences found it hard to believe that explanation "why" in history could ever be as easy and commonplace as Muddy Pants III? As the twig is bent so the tree inclineth: under the circumstances outlined above it is no wonder that the scientific-minded expected explanation "why" in history to share the traits of such explanation in the sciences—difficulty, mathematization, rigor.

Muddy Pants III, on the other hand, is so easy and commonplace that a stupid child can do it. It is not, however, simple. It is far more complicated, for example, than Muddy Pants I. There by confining "the field of explanation" to a brief interval between the moment Willie slipped and the moment he landed in the puddle, the very construal of the "why" question drastically simplified the problems of answering it. The explanation thus takes place within a very small and simple time-and-space "container," in a system that is almost wholly closed. Operating in larger dimensions of time and space, Muddy Pants III enormously increases the number of items that may be necessary to complete the explanation "why." Yet out of this mass of items a stupid six-year-old can select those few which provides the appropriate, adequate, and complete explanation. Moreover, given the inherent ambiguity and openness of "why" questions, in order to come up with the right answer the stupid six-year-old had first to come up with exactly the right translation of the open "why" interrogative form. He not only had to pick the correct items to put into the container, he had to choose just the right container from the large stock on the open "why" shelf.

Surely, with the paradox of the stupid six-year-old who cannot perform very simple mathematico-scientific operations, but who can perform highly complex historical operations we come to a major crux, an evident difference between the natural sciences and history. This difference we need to drive home. For unless we grasp the stark contrast of the simplicity and difficulty of much science with the complexity and ease of a great deal of history, we will overlook a major difference between them. Then we will not ask the right questions about how they come to diverge so much from each other as significant forms of inquiry, because we will not be aware how vastly they do diverge. We will be like very clever men who have entered a maze at the wrong place. We will perform a series of extraordinarily clever maneuvers to get to the center, but we will never get there. And the more clever we are, the more fruitful our minds will be at dreaming up clever new maneuvers. Since the number of possible maneuvers are probably quite large, we will never satisfy ourselves that the next one won't work any better than the last three hundred did toward getting us to the heart of the maze. The one easy idea that we will instantaneously reject is that anyone as clever as we could have started in at the wrong place, and that until we back out and start all over again we are licked.

For those who prefer "worthy" and "dignified" History to the unworthy and undignified history of The Case of the Muddy Pants, the crucial point can be made again with respect to professional history. In one of the better historical journals an acute and hard-nosed critic of historical writing tried to state concisely just what it was that he admired about a historical study. This is what he fixed on: "*Each point about it has just that air of obviousness which everyone can agree to, but which no previous writer seems to have attained*" (italics mine).

The sentence seems to me to get right to the heart of the paradox. It fully implies the stark contrast between history and science. For can we imagine a work of science being praised mainly because every point in it was so obvious that everyone would immediately assent to it? This brings us to the substructure of our divergent appreciations of the natural sciences and history. The highest attainments of science give us a sense of discovery through innovation. What was hidden is suddenly uncovered by men who have done something radically new. The better works of historians impart to us a sense of recognition achieved through renovation. By clearing away some confusing rubbish, a good historian enables us to see clearly what we already dimly sense might be there. Great scientists proceed by rare and enormous leaps through a terribly simple trackless desert. Good historians make their way surefooted and steadily, day by day, on easy ground along a familiar but inordinately complex network of well-worn tracks. Between the scientists' "Is that a legitimate logical or mathematical inference?" and the historians' "Does that make sense?" there is a world of difference. To say this is not to depreciate the work of professional historians. They do what is appropriate to their calling.

And that brings us back to the heart of our mystery: if historical explanation "why" is complicated, why is it so easy as often to be in the reach of a stupid kid? In the first place historical explanation "why" is easy because we get so much rigorous training for it. From the time that we develop any facility at talking, we are flooded with "why" questions, particularly "why did you" questions, by parents, by teachers, by friends. All of them want not only an answer but a quick, clear, and accurate answer, and often they keep chivvying us until they get what they ask for. We are put through historical-explanation drills of considerable stiffness as well as other exercises in historical discourse long before we run into drills in reading, writing, and arithmetic; and we continue to practice, to perform historical exercises day in, day out, Sundays and holidays included, year after year. Moreover, in daily life if bad historical explanation is detected where there is a reasonable expectation of good historical explanation, it incurs heavy social penalties. It is like fielding under .950 in major league baseball; a very high absolute average is a low relative average. It is rightly taken to show that you are throwing the game for your own advantage, or that you are not good enough to be playing in that league in the first place. Since the league in which reliability of historical explanation comes under critical judgment is the league of daily living, the sanctions imposed on anything less than consistently good performance are in the nature of things extremely stiff.

A second reason why the historical explanations we are all called upon daily to give are easy is that they are usually limited to matters concerning which we may be reasonably supposed to have sufficient information, as it were, in stock. With respect to the historical explanations ordinarily demanded of him, each man is likely to be an expert; indeed most of the historical questions he has to answer are asked in the belief that with respect to them he is the most readily available expert.

Finally, historical explanation is often easy because it has at its command and for its use the instruments of common language—an extremely complex, marvelously supple, superbly nuanced, beautifully manageable means of communication—an interweaving of spoken words, gestures, intonation, and facial expressions. The common language of all great population groups is shaped by the recurrent and pressing daily needs of millions of men. To meet those needs, so numerous, so divergent, so intricate, men have to be able to communicate with one another fast, frequently, fully, and precisely. Matters about which men need to communicate day in, day out, often require them to make clear their historical explanations and their predictions. Any language inadequate for this purpose would shortly lead to such an accumulation of minor and major frustrations and disasters as to render common enterprise and then life itself unbearable and ultimately impossible. Such is the lesson of the Tower of Babel. Such is the common experience of anyone who enters a community whose level of life is approximately the same as that of the community he comes from, and tries to live there at that level. If he has no verbal means at all of communicating across the language barrier, he will soon discover that his enterprise is hopeless. The difference between the stultified life he will have to lead and the richer, more complex life led by those no better endowed financially and intellectually to whom the local language is native will measure for him how much difference the language makes, how beautifully and effectively it functions to render not only possible but rapid and easy that flow of negotiations and exchanges which alone suffices to sustain a highly organized mode of life.

We may make our point in another way. Every highly specialized activity requires and generates for its own convenience a specialized vocabulary which becomes indispensable for its smooth and efficient functioning; explanation is almost always an ingredient necessary for such functioning. To take part in the specialized activity a man will have to master its vocabulary and special language usages. History is such an activity. But in one essential respect it differs from all other specialized activities. Every man is not and does not have to be a poet, or an automotive mechanic, or an investment banker, so he need not master the languages of those activities. But every man must be a specialist in history, making historical explanations of the past and predictions of the future. Otherwise he shouldn't be running around loose.[4] So in the very nature of things the specialized language of history is and has to be for the most part common language. Or conversely *common language is usually adequate and satisfactory for historical*

---

[4] How complex the problem can be is illustrated by difficulties encountered by the first generation of peasants off the land when they come to the city, *even a city of the same speech*. Some, though by no means all of the worst of the difficulties of the nineteenth-century Irish in England, and of the Negro in urban America resulted from their ignorance of the common language of cities.

explanation, meeting most of its ordinary requirements, because it IS
the language of history, specialized for the use of that ubiquitous spe-
cialist in history who is Everyman.[5]

Everyman is a historian, a specialist in history, because he has to be.
He is not a mere amateur historian indulging himself avocationally in
what he enjoys doing, in the way some men are amateur painters, or
ball players, or carpenters. He works at history every day out of sheer
necessity. On the other hand, he is not a professional either; he does not
work at history for a living but only to keep alive. In the main, the rest
of this book is going to concern itself directly with historians who are
not only specialists in history but professionals, who earn their living at
it; it is most particularly going to be about professional historians who
write history and about the history they write. We started with Everyman, and indeed Everyboy, as historian because it is important early
to make clear the unique situation, different from that of every other
scholar, that this creates for the writing historian and for the history he
writes. We can now begin to consider how the writing historian's close
kinship to Everyman affects the way he writes history.

History has notoriously little in the way of a vocabulary of its own,
shared by all who write history and not shared by those who neither
read nor write it. This does not mean that historians use only words that
any literate man might be expected to understand. It means that when
they use words that literate men might well not understand, a good
many other historians will not understand them either. Those words
almost always (1) belong to the vocabulary of some other discipline or
craft—economics, law, mendicancy, Christian doctrine, draw poker; or
(2) are proper names of persons, places, events and periods immediately intelligible only to specialists in the history of a particular region at a
particular time, not to all historians—words like the Ridolfi plot, the
Casket letters, Lord Burleigh, Tilbury, Martin Marprelate, the Rising of
the North, Inigo Jones. Conversely, except for such proper names and

[5] By now some readers of this study will recognize that part of its purpose is to
drive home with a verbal sledge hammer points most of which were made with far
greater brevity, wit, and skill thirty-five years ago by Carl L. Becker in the first
part of his essay "Everyman His Own Historian," *American Historical Review,* 37
(1931–1932): 221–236. For this the author makes no apology. It was characteristic of
Becker, the keenest historical mind of his generation in America, that he deftly made
the easy, uninteresting, and important points, here reiterated and expanded on, in the
first few pages of his essay. He then went on to deal with his usual brilliance with the
far more difficult and interesting problem of historical relativism, falling into a number of fascinating errors that he would have avoided if he had paid more attention to
the uninteresting points he made earlier. As so often happens in such cases, a generation of disciples overlooked or forgot Becker's easy truths and lovingly adopted his
fascinating errors. Those errors have since become evident enough. It is time to return to and elaborate on his important uninteresting truths. That is what I have tried
to do here.

for imports from other disciplines, ordinarily competent historical discourse will be intelligible to any literate man, whether or not he has ever "studied history." [6]

Some historians have deplored this peculiar situation: some social scientists and philosophers have regarded it as the hideous mark of some sort of debilitating disease of history as a profession and a discipline.[7] Invariably, one of the concerns of social scientists who respond to historical discourse in this way is to work out for their discipline a special vocabulary and language-structure or rhetoric that is inaccessible to all but themselves or those who make a particular study of their specialty. Some of this sort of thing may be necessary and desirable and some of it may be unnecessary and undesirable. There appear to be two operative reasons for doing it:

1. In the course of his work as a specialist, an investigator comes upon a recurrent something—situation, process, relation, or what not—for which no precise, economical, unambiguous designation exists. For purposes of precision, economy, and clarity, he therefore creates what in effect is a new sign to designate the entity, either by inventing a new sound cluster (*telephone*), or assigning a special meaning to an old sound cluster and using it only with that meaning (*matrix* in matrix algebra).

2. The "hard" and therefore prestigious natural sciences all have special vocabularies and rhetorics. To achieve the status (and emoluments) enjoyed by the natural sciences, it behooves the social sciences to emulate them in this matter.

The first reason seems to be quite legitimate. As to the second, social scientists might consider that not only hard scientists but specialized groups of lesser status such as jailbirds, prostitutes, and pimps also have special languages, partly intended to frustrate those who would otherwise comprehend and inhibit their nefarious doings and felonious little plans. In any case the gratuitous creation of obscurity is an unseemly activity on the part of persons who allege that they are committed to the advancement of science. It is, however, for the social scientists to decide among themselves what particular items of their special lan-

---

[6] This view drastically differs from that of Morton White who seems to assume that *all* words "belong to" one discipline or another. He does not account for the multitude of words which antedate any discipline to which even implausibly they can be alleged to belong. Morton G. White, "Historical Explanation," in P. Gardiner, ed., *Theories of History* (New York, 1967), pp. 364–367.

[7] In the rather odd article just cited, because of its lack of a specialized vocabulary history is sunk without a trace into sociology; *Ibid.*, pp. 368–369. Since he has not reiterated this view in his recent book, *The Foundations of Historical Knowledge*, it may be believed (or at least hoped) that he no longer entertains it.

guages serve which functions and cooperatively to police their own delinquents. It is none of my business as a historian, except insofar as it frustrates my attempts to profit from their instruction. It is my business, however, to repudiate the suggestion that historians should model their vocabulary and rhetoric on that of the social or natural sciences. That they should not do so is a consequence of the paradox of historical discourse. Because as a life-or-death matter all men engage in such discourse at a considerable level of complexity, common language itself provides a marvelous and efficient rhetoric highly specialized for it. The suggestion that historians should wholly reject this splendidly viable instrument and attempt to emulate scientific discourse is not, alas! strictly unthinkable and unspeakable since intelligent men have both thought and spoken it; it is, however, evidence of how absurd such men can be when they resign their wits in an impassioned pursuit of the Higher Foolishness. Opposed to this Higher Foolishness stands the clear and certain rule: the model, measure, and ideal of historical discourse are common language; historians deviate from it at peril; every deviation should be so fully justified in the historian's mind that the grounds for it are likely to be transparent to those to whom his discourse is directed.

Having said this, we need to note that *good history writing does deviate frequently (although rarely very far) from common language;* and therefore we need to know the reasons for such deviation. There are several:

1. Occasionally historians have to explain precisely and accurately the operation in the past of an entity whose operation can only or best be so explained in the special vocabulary of another discipline—for example, the potato blight (floral pathology), the steam engine (elementary physics and engineering), the squeeze play (baseball), international balances of payment (economics). Even here good historians will balance the equities of brevity against those of ready intelligibility with some bias in favor of the latter in case there is a conflict.[8]

2. The best way to understand some of the doings of men of another era or place may be to use a few words of the common language of that era or place. Such a word, for example, is "polis," part of the common language of ancient Greece, not of present-day America. It did not just mean "city," its most obvious translation. Like "city," it was a value-

---

[8] In practice this means using every available technique for eliciting the best possible true accounts of the past. It also means conforming those accounts as far as possible to the historian's standard approximation of common language. I suspect that findings which a historian who puts his mind to it cannot bring within range of common language can often with little or no loss be stashed away in an appendix or arrayed in a set of tables.

packed word, but many of the values with which it was packed lay outside the range of *any* of the values present-day men commonly attach to "city." To avoid the ethnocentric and anachronistic perils of such a situation a historian sometimes will prefer not to translate a word like "polis" but to permit the fullest sense of its meaning to emerge from the contexts in which he uses it.

3. Written language sacrifices the fertile interplay of gesture, facial expression, and intonation with vocabulary and syntax, which frequently makes common language clear and unambiguous. The full load of communication thus falls on vocabulary and syntax alone. This can result in misunderstandings that would not happen in common language. Some years ago I was reading a piece by a historian with whom on most matters I usually disagree; and as usual I disagreed—until I came to the last sentence. It read, "After all, history [by which he meant, and I understood him to mean, "the past"] is not just one damn thing after another." I assented without reservation to the sentiment; it exactly expressed my sense of the past. But somehow so agreeable a conclusion seemed an odd thing to find at the end of a communication from which I almost entirely dissented. It appeared indeed dissonant with the communication itself as I understood it. I puzzled over the statement in context, and the light dawned, or at least I think it dawned. It seemed probable that I had misunderstood his last sentence, that it meant to him something quite different from what it meant to me. To him it meant that nothing of serious consequence in the past was a mere accident. To me it meant that, although important accidents sometimes happened, there was much more to the past than just accident. I suspect that if the author had been speaking rather than writing, something in his gestures, facial expression, and intonation (emphasis on "*not*," rather than on "*just*," perhaps) would have tipped me off and reduced or removed the likelihood of misunderstanding.

4. Moreover, if he had made the same statement in conversation and I misunderstood him, my response very likely would have revealed the fact, and he would have corrected my error. For common language is most often a dialogue, not a monologue; it involves an exchange of signals by means of which a speaker can detect and correct the misapprehensions of his auditors. But written history is a lonely monologue; the historian does not get the help of immediate signals from his public.

Because historians write without the help of dialogue and without the help of the elements complementary to words and syntax that common language usually provides, they use a modification of common language, common formal prose, to try to compensate for the loss. This is a sign system much stiffer, more formidable, and harder to manage than common language, and many who speak history quite handily in common language write it in common formal prose ineptly and with difficulty or, in the case of illiterates, not at all.

Some of the perplexing peculiarities of written history are explicable in the light of the foregoing discussion. For example, until he tries, almost everybody thinks he can write history and that to do it is easy. Experts on any subject one can name, who would modestly deny their expertise in other subjects to which they had not previously given systematic attention, boldly announce that they will preface a treatise on their own subject with a few paragraphs or pages of what they call "historical background." They then write the pages, and if they have recently read any good history, they become unhappily aware that even though they have "gotten the facts right," and have indeed written history, they have written quite bad history. Why should so many people think writing good history is easy? Why should writing bad true history be indeed easy? Why should writing good true history be quite hard?

Many people think writing history is easy because they sense that every man is indeed a historian, because they are aware that in their daily life and in common language, they do many of the things professional historians do when they write history, and do them adequately. If they try to read the best physics or the best chemistry, they realize at once that they could not write it at all without special training, because they neither understand nor can manage the language in which it is written. On the other hand, if they read the best history, much of it confirms their faith in their as yet untested ability, because such history usually seems so very similar to the historical discourse they engage in orally, day in, day out, with successful results. Indeed the better written the history is, the more marked this similarity will appear to be, the more deceptive it will be, and therefore the more it will encourage their illusions.

With care and diligence, most men can dig accurate facts out of the record of the past and set them down in some more or less orderly relation. It is not hard to find such facts about a good deal of the past. Nor is establishing some of the connections among them much harder than establishing connections among facts remembered. Yet although every factual statement of an unpracticed experimenter in the writing of history may be true and every connection he makes between the facts warranted, something palpably goes wrong in the writing process. Sometimes the proportions are off; he has gone on at excessive length elaborating the obvious and trivial. Or the arrangement is muddled; what he is (or should be) driving at is impossible to discover because he has not placed it conspicuously enough, so his point gets missed. Or like a man with unselective total recall, he himself loses the thread of his own discourse in the maze of his data.[9] Part of the trouble with true but unsatisfactory and inadequate history writing is that its perpetrators have little experience in finding in common formal prose verbal and syntactical substitutes for the gestures, facial expressions, and intonations of common language, and often are not even aware of the need for such substitutes. Nor are they always aware that much of the ease with which they provide everyday historical explanations depends on the signals given in dialogue which as they go along guide them in the suppression of the redundant and the superfluous, in the clarification of the ambiguous, and in the insertion of what they would have otherwise omitted. A writer of history who lacks these two kinds of awareness is capable of producing large quantities of true bad history.

A common experience of instructors in the freshman college course in history confirms this account of the matter. That course is likely to be the first occasion when most students have had to meet a serious demand for historical explanation in common formal prose. This happens on the first hour examination. After returning the examination, instructors have to confront the equivalent of the "good-field, no-hit" ball player—the "good-talk, no-write" history student, intelligent and vigorous in class discussion and an utter bust in writing history—who wants to know what he did to merit such a bad grade. The instructor points to a sentence and says, "What does that mean? I don't understand it." With little or no prompting, the student then provides a meaning for the sentence that would have served him quite well on the examination. "If you knew that," says the instructor, "why didn't you write it down?" "But," the student replies in bafflement and frustration, "that was what I *meant*." And there is a good chance that it was what he meant. More than that there is a good chance that in the context of a classroom exchange with its tonal, facial, bodily complements to words and syntax, the instructor would have known that the student meant what he later alleged he meant. The student was simply unaware of the need to translate common language into common formal prose, or incapable of such translation. As he reads further, the instructor comes to another sentence. "Why do you say that? I don't see how it connects with what you have written before." And without hesitation the student provides a quite satisfactory connection. "If you knew that," says the instructor, "why didn't you write it down?" The student replies in sad perplexity, "But I did know it. I just didn't think I needed to write it down." In effect the signals of perplexity from students and instructor that would have reached him in class and led him to supply the missing connection

---

[9] Needless to say, all professional writers of history make these kinds of mistakes some of the time; and unfortunately throughout their careers, some seem to make them all of the time.

could not reach him in an examination, and so he was not alerted to the need to supply it.

It is so hard to write good true history (1) partly because it is so easy to write bad true history and (2) partly because it is so hard to write good common formal historical prose. What I am getting at in my first point is illustrated by a peculiar standard difference between examination grades in compulsory mathematics courses and in compulsory history courses. On a hundred-point scale with failure set at sixty, failing grades in the range from ten to thirty are not at all uncommon in such mathematics courses; they are relatively rare in such history courses. Failing history grades below forty-five in a course where sixty is passing tend to be rare. What accounts for this difference? In mathematics a considerable number of students will simply not get it at all or will not get most of it. Their solutions to problems involving mathematics they did not get at all will simply be wrong from start to finish. Really bad mathematics, therefore, is the consequence of an utter failure of comprehension and results in answers that are simply and wholly false.

This sort of total disaster is far less likely in a history examination. The examiner usually requires the students to order data which they may reasonably be expected to command. If a student is extremely stupid or if his control of the data is very feeble, he is likely to mess up the answer. Still the instructor's questions are about how people acted sometime, somewhere. About this even an ill-informed stupid student is not likely to get everything all wrong. A slightly informed, intelligent student will do better. He may even pass. He will then say he "bluffed his way through." Nobody bluffs his way through a written mathematics examination; it cannot be done. What the bright ill-informed student has actually done on the history examination is to apply his intelligence to a situation which, because it is a human situation, is not wholly alien to him. If he controls a little relevant information, his native intelligence and his experience are enough for him to get by on. His bad history is not so obviously and disastrously bad as his bad mathematics would be.

Partly because writing bad history is pretty easy, writing very good history is rare. In other words bad history writing is so much better than bad work in almost any other reasonably rigorous discipline that a good historian has to rise above a far higher level of widely diffused competence than the able practitioners of other disciplines do. Good history is also rare partly because common formal historical prose looks so easy but is so hard to write. It looks easy because historians who are able to do so make it look very much like common language. This creates an illusion that does not exist in the sciences. No fledgling scientist thinks for long that he starts equipped to write in the language of his discipline. His first look at that language quickly tells him otherwise, particularly if, as is increasingly the case, considerable portions of it are mathematical. He becomes immediately aware that if he is going to engage in scientific work, he is going to have to learn a new language, master a new structure of discourse, and command a new rhetoric. This new language is in intent more rigorous than common language. By minimizing chances for blurring through slippage of meaning, it reduces the writer's chance of befuddling himself about what he is saying. Therefore, it provides better insurance than common language does against error in reasoning, confusion in communication, and the many other ills that thought is heir to.

Since, however, common language *is* the special rhetoric of historical discourse, writers of history cannot afford wholly to sacrifice its suppleness and flexibility for the meager exactness of a contrived "historical language." Yet they have to do without two major elements of common language—the gestures, intonations, and facial expressions which at once complement and economize on the flow of words, and the signals emitted in dialogue which warn a speaker that either has failed to communicate satisfactorily.[10] Without the support to discourse lent by the former element and without the early warning system lent by the latter the writer of history has to contrive surrogates for them in writing common formal prose. He has to be alert for places where the uncomplemented word structure of common language will fall short of communicating his meaning and then seek out word clusters to supply the deficiency. He also must in effect replace the running external dialogue of oral discourse with a running internal dialogue, so that he will generate within himself those signals of misconstrual, doubt, and perplexity which lead to modulations, revisions, and expansions of statement in the interest of clarity, emphasis, force, precision, and other desiderata of historical discourse. Even for historians aware of the need to do these things, they are very hard to do. For historians unaware of them, unconscious of the difficulties of adapting the language system of history-speaking to the language system of history writing, they are impossible to do. There are hundreds of reasons why hundreds of *specific* tasks that historians undertake are difficult. What I have tried to give an account of here is why *in general* the writing of good history is a particularly difficult skill to master.

We have already noted that in the easy commonplace complicated explanation "why" of Muddy Pants III, the most complicated operation of all was the process of data selection. Yet, as we have seen, and for reasons that we have noted, a six-year-old would have no trouble in making the appropriate selection. Moreover, except for the placatory

[10] All writers whose vehicle is common formal prose share this problem with the historians.

last few words, the data he would have selected are precisely those and only those relevant to the explanation "why" required by a contextually correct construal of the question. This remarkable yet commonplace achievement may help to solve a problem frequently raised in connection with written history, or better, to dispose of a pseudoproblem, or best, to distinguish between the pseudo and the serious aspects of the problem. It has frequently been said that in the process of explanation, writing historians have to select among large masses of data, decide what and how much of the data to use, and choose among the many words available the few that they actually set down. This, of course, is quite true. It has also been said that, this being the case, the judgments (that is, explanations) of historians about the past are necessarily subjective and biased. This is partly a trivial statement and partly just plain false.

The part about subjectivity is trivial. In the context above the term "subjective" means "biased," which is redundant, or it means that the decisions of historians on what to select from the record of the past for statement or consideration are based wholly on their own experience. This is entirely true and entirely trivial. Every word or action, not wholly reflexive, of everyone is subjective in this sense; and unless such "subjectivity" can be shown to have some special consequences for historians that it does not have for everyone else, the statement is not worth making. If the subjectivity of historians as such is supposed to have any special consequences it can only be to render them especially prone to bias which the universal subjectivity of men does not render other men prone to. Yet, this would seem to be the opposite of the case, since a great deal of the training of historians is directed precisely to the point of warning them of the *possibility* (not the necessity) that their experience will sometimes bias their judgments. It would seem that man's universal subjectivity would be less likely to bias the judgments of historians than those of men not alerted to the danger. The notion that the abundance of data and the inevitability of selecting from the abundance necessarily biases every judgment or explanation a historian makes is absurd. By identifying the very process of selection with bias, it renders impossible a distinction between biased and unbiased selection. In the end, however, one has to make such a distinction. The prosecutor selects and arrays evidence with a bias toward securing the conviction of the accused; the defense attorney selects and arrays it with a bias toward securing his acquittal. But what of the jury? It is supposed to come in with a *verdict*, a true statement about the legal innocence or guilt of the defendant. To say that it selects and arrays evidence with a bias toward speaking the truth simply destroys the utility of the term "bias," which always implies that truth is subordinated to some other end.

In fact our young historian Willie is quite capable of the unbiased selection of data both for explanation and for judgment. For example:

1. MOTHER: Why did you stop off at Jamie's this afternoon, Willie?
   WILLIE: I walked home from school with him, and he asked me if I wanted to see his new electric train, and I did. So I went up to see it.
2. MOTHER: Why do Jamie and his sister fight all the time?
   WILLIE: I think it's 'cause Jamie is always taking Linnie's toys away from her.

In both instances Willie is selecting from a considerable amount of data the items necessary for true historical explanation and a true historical judgment. What bias does he have? Why should he have any? One way or the other it is no skin off his nose. He simply selects evidence that enables him to give a true answer to the question. Why in the world not?

It is conceivable that mature men with special and rigorous professional training, from the age of thirty on become wholly incapable of performing in their vocation operations of which they were quite capable at the age of six, and of which they remain quite capable in their daily lives; but this hypothesis is not one likely to elicit immediate and unanimous assent. It is, however, the one that most writers who warn us of the inescapable liability of historians to subjectivity appear to be committed to.

The truth of the matter is much more credible; it is that usually historians—like Willie—select data on the basis of its relevance to giving adequate and satisfactory explanations. Indeed this is all the less surprising since often at the outset historians have as little reason for prejudice or vested interest in many of their explanations as Willie had. After providing such an explanation a historian does acquire an interest because he has invested his effort in it and committed himself to it; but ordinarily the simple desire to get some things straight as expeditiously as possible operates just as effectively in writing history as in writing science or in dealing with everyday problems. The very frequency with which historians provide adequate and complete explanations has paradoxically created the illusion that they never provide them at all. Like the steady rumble of traffic in a big city, such explanations are "gestalted" out; and people do not notice them unless someone calls them to their attention. Almost any competent piece of history writing will include a multitude of such easy adequate explanations. Of course, this is not to argue that any historian is always free of bias in all his judgments, or that historians never use data selectively to support one bias or another.

When I say that historical explanations are often not only without bias but also complex and easy, I do not mean that all such explanations are complex and easy. What mainly concerns me is the question of ease. The illusion that historical explanation is usually difficult may be due to the fact that history has become identified with written history, and especially with historical research. But in order to do research that demonstrates a high level of competence (1) a researcher must find unused records or deal with used ones that for his purposes present formidable difficulties of construal which he overcomes, and/or (2) what he *ultimately* aims to explain must be difficult to explain. No historian gets any medals for explaining that John Pym won his position of leadership in the House of Commons because he was a most adept political maneuverer. Every bit of available evidence testifies to this explanation. That assembling the evidence may be pretty time-consuming, and that the judgment is not a simple one does not matter. Historical researchers cannot and do not expect to get much credit for doing what any mediocre historian can do quite as well. It is like being a big-league infielder. Fielding easy chances calls for a very complex set of motions not vastly different from what it takes to field the hard ones; but no one becomes a big leaguer because he can catch an easy grounder and make the easy throw to first. A big leaguer may even make more errors than an amateur, but that is because he gets within reach of balls that an amateur would not get near to. The analogy is useful in throwing at least a ray of light on the difference between importance in the past and importance in history. *En masse* easy chances may be as important in determining who wins a ball game as hard ones. Indeed, this is almost sure to be so, since most chances in baseball are pretty easy. But in deciding who is fit to stay in the big leagues, the question is, "Can he field the hard ones?" [11] So, too, there are events in the past that are easy to explain. On a reasonable accounting some of these are considerably more important (have had, say, more evident large consequences) than other events and actions harder to explain. Yet the historian who makes a good try at explaining these harder but less important things in the past will almost certainly be regarded as a better historian than one who writes only about big, easy-to-explain events, and the history he writes will be judged more important. This situation insures that the best historians will often pose for themselves hard questions that they are likely to answer inadequately or wrong. "What kind of discipline is it," historians then ask themselves, "whose acknowledged ablest practitioners so often fail to get right the thing they try hardest to get right?" But, of course, these practitioners built a high probability of failure into their very act of selecting a

[11] In history as in baseball there may be a very few men who get some of the hard ones, but flub an undue number of easy ones. They do not last either.

problem. They went after the hard one. Consistently correct explanation is more likely to turn up in the work of mediocre historians who
intuitively go after only those easy problems that lie within their limited
reach.

Why should the fumbling and the frequent failure among the best
historians evoke surprise? Exactly the same situation prevails in the
sciences. In every discipline the askers of easy questions come up
regularly with easy correct answers, and the askers of hard questions
often fumble and miss. And in every discipline the practitioners are
rated not by a mere count of the number of questions they answered
correctly, but by a corporate judgment of how hard the question was,
how much worth answering, and how good a try the practitioner made
in his effort to answer it. The "unscientific" character of history is most
costly to historians not in the realm of explanation but in that of expectation. They have somehow stuck themselves with equally profitless
alternatives: absolute Platonic certainty about the Ultimate Truth of
History or absolute relativism about the possibility of knowing the past
at all. Thus, perversely, the very process of challenging and revising
older views in the light of new findings, which is rightly the glory of the
sciences, is taken by historians and their critics alike to be evidence of
the inadequacy or backwardness of history.

*C*HAPTER III: Points without Lines, *or the* Record of the Past

Up to now we have dealt with two kinds of historians and two kinds of history. The two kinds of historians are Everyman and the professionals; the two kinds of history are the kind that Everyman uses and talks everyday, and the kind that the professionals write when they can find time. Between the two kinds of history we have noted one significant difference—a difference in rhetorical structure. The first is couched in common spoken language, the latter in formal written prose. There is, however, another major difference between Everyman and the professional historian, a difference in the grounds on which they expect and receive credence.

Thus when Willie Everyman answers his father's "why" question he alleges that certain things happened in the past. He does not, however, offer any evidence in support of his allegation that what he said happened did happen other than the actual mud on his pants, for which he is trying to account.[1] On the other hand, to falsify the prediction of the past (or retrodiction or postdiction) that there were two and only two parties or factions in the English Parliament between September 1642 and September 1643, as a professional historian, I am not permitted merely to allege that certain members engaged in actions that were inconsistent with such a view.[2] Nor can I merely indicate that I once saw documents from which I legitimately inferred that the alleged actions were what I said they were, and demand that my readers take my word for it. If a reader chooses to challenge my statements I do not have the option of drawing myself up huffily and saying, "Don't you trust me?" If that question comes from a professional historian, the universally ap-

[1] See Chapter 1.
[2] See Chapter 2.

propriate answer is "No, I do not," or more tactfully, "Well, I just thought I'd take a look at the evidence myself." At that point, if I want to maintain my professional standing, I had better be able to direct my challenger to the sources of my inference. The evidence a historian offers must always include a record of the past from which his statements are derived by way of inference. To understand the way professional historians and the history they write work, we must examine some of the major traits of this record, the record of the past.

In the first place, if a historian puts a part of the record of the past in evidence, it ought to be publicly accessible to examination by others. Sometimes chance may render some part of the record a historian has used temporarily or forever inaccessible—a natural or a man-made catastrophe, like the flood of the Arno or the blowing up of the Record Office in Dublin, the arbitrary fiat of a bureaucrat, or the mere whim of a legal owner. This is hard on that historian, since thereafter part of his credibility will depend on evidence not available for examination and, so to speak, audit. And free public access to "the books" is the foundation of the credit and credibility on which the company of historians depends. In this we are rather like a bank. The public puts its faith and credit in us without checking up on all our operations. But to maintain that corporate trust we have to be ready to have any single transaction scrutinized at any moment and be ready with the record that will justify it. That is at least one good reason for the close and sometimes petty attention to which historians subject the evidence of each other's transactions. We do not want our joint enterprise to get a bad name and lose its credit in consequence of the petty larcenies or mere carelessness of a few clerks.

Another important trait of the record of the past is that in a sense it is fixed; once a day has passed no man can add an iota to the record that came into being that day. At most he can find some part of that record which historians have hitherto not found or use some part that they hitherto have not used. Thus the base of operations of the professional historian's history is different from that of Everyman's history. For his data Everyman can draw freely on his memory of past happenings and rest his credit on his general reputation as an honest man with good recall. For his data the professional relies only on the surviving publicly accessible record.

The professional historian's evidential base also differs from that of the experimental scientist's. The latter can add to the record of an experiment at will by replicating the experiment; no equivalent operation is possible in history with respect to the record of the past. This is a mere fact of life, not a measure of value or status. History and the natural sciences are not or should not be engaged in a futile status race. They are two significant, significantly different, and incommensurable forms

of human inquiry, and consequently no intellectually meaningful mea-
surement of their relative status is possible.[3]

At any given moment the record of the past comprises all items whatsoever publicly accessible to examination and evaluation, from which
any valid inferences can be made about the intentions, the doings, and
the sufferings of any human being in the past. Both the range and
number of the items which constitute the record of the past are enormous: the most recent recording of the Beatles, the headlines in today's
paper, the latest copy of the latest book fresh from the bindery on the
one hand; on the other, stone tools and animal bones deposited in
Eurasia and Africa several hundred thousand years ago.

With respect to this "total record of the past" it is worth noting several traits: (1) it is constantly in a process of simultaneous accretion and
attrition; (2) it is incredibly enormous; (3) it is equally incredibly exiguous. All three of these facts about the total record of the past are relevant to the task of the historian who writes history.

1. The accretion of the record of the past takes place actually or
potentially every time a newspaper adds an issue to its file or an item to
its "morgue," every time the television industry videotapes a quiz program, every time a new building goes up, every time anyone whoever
or anything whatever so acts as to leave, however briefly, some publicly
accessible mark on man's visible (or audible) environment. Attrition is
also a continuous process. For years a particular newspaper is daily
reading for a large number of families. If it is acquired by newsstand
purchase the fact that it was fare for those families is lost as day after
day for years they chuck the paper out with the day's rubbish. Frequently the very actions indispensable to the creation of what thereafter become (again potentially) new records of the past obliterate old
ones. The bulldozer prepares the ground for building suburban houses.
As it does so it annihilates every trace of the layout of the fields of the
abandoned farm on which those houses will rise; but, once built, the
houses themselves, become a new record of the past. The flood sweeps
down the valley of the Arno leaving behind in Florence a record of its
own violent impact on that city; but it destroys hundreds of documents
recording matters that will now never be known about Florentines of a
more distant past. In the mid-1940's a Nazi major in a fit of insensate
rage burns the archive which contained almost the entire surviving
record of the medieval Angevin kingdom of Naples. And in 1921, during their rising against the English oppressor, the Irish revolutionaries
annihilated the basis of whole centuries of their own national history,

[3] Historians and scientists are, of course, in competition for scarce funds. If success in this race is to be taken as a measure of status, however, they both stand
way below the operators of gambling joints.

when in a moment of unfortunate pique some of the patriots blew up
the Record Office in Dublin. Daily, without anger or malice, but only
because the weight and bulk of his office's files threaten to displace the
staff and buckle the floor under him, some official of government or of
a business concern consigns tons of what had been the record of the
past to the paper shredder.

While the simultaneous creation and destruction of the record of the
past is going on in these odd disparate ways, professional historians
and other seekers after information about the past discover methods of
finding records never before accessible, or of transforming what hitherto had been treated as records of one set of transactions into records
of another. Besides archivists and archeologists whose steady patient
work makes the written and the "artifactual" record available, there is
now the x-ray specialist. Between the stone face of an abbey wall and
the sixteenth-century painting which for hundreds of years it has presented to public view he finds a fifteenth-century painting that the later
one concealed. Suddenly the carbon-14 test transformed the charred
wood of very ancient fire sites from evidence *that* men were present at
a particular place to evidence of *when* they were present. And now it
seems likely that through no one's design future historians will not be
able to use carbon-14 tests for dating us, since the increase of radio-
activity consequent on atomic-weapon testing has reduced the accuracy
of the carbon-14 test as a chronometer of the later twentieth century.
It is never possible for a historian concerned with any segment of the
record to be certain that he has exhausted the historical uses of that
segment (one never knows for sure what is going to turn up). Nor is it
possible to be certain over any considerable period of time what part of
the record now accessible will be available in the future (one never
knows what is going to blow up, burn, rot, or be washed away).

2. The thought of how much of the record daily gets destroyed is,
however, slightly less appalling than the thought of how much accumu-
lates each day and is one way or another preserved. There have perhaps been times when (if such a conception makes sense) the absolute
quantity of the potential record of the past was diminishing. Such was
probably the situation between 500 and 1000 A.D., at least in Western
Europe; and, of course, this may happen somewhere and even everywhere again. But as long as modern industrial bureaucratic society with
its insatiable need for maintaining and extending its collective memory
survives, the likelihood of such a shrinkage is small. On the contrary,
the written, spoken, and visual record of the recent past proliferates at
a terrifying pace with each passing year. Meanwhile, increased skill,
increased interest, and increased historical piety secure the discovery
and the better preservation of records and monuments of remoter times.
In ages less addicted to finding out about and saving what time has

spared, these would have moldered into dust, tumbled into ruin, or carelessly been consigned to destruction.

The sheer bulk of the accumulated and accumulating record is enough to reduce to despair those historians who believe that it is their collective task to produce a steadily accumulating history that would ultimately exhaust the record of the past.[4] It is now evident that only a cataclysm of vast proportion is likely to destroy such a large quantity of the record of the past as to reduce a substantial number of historians to technological unemployment. Indeed the cataclysm would have to be of such dimension that it would be more likely to eradicate the historians themselves than the record that is the body on which they operate for a living.

3. The bulk of the whole surviving record of the past is therefore appalling and its growth since the invention of printing and especially since the industrialization of many parts of the world particularly dramatic. Yet that record reports but an infinitesimal fraction of the past words, deeds, and suffering of mankind. This is not due merely to the massive attrition of the record, of which we have already spoken: it is simply that very little of what men have said and done in the past ever became any part of the record at all. Even nowadays what gets recorded of and about men's actions stands to what they actually do and say as a grain of sand to Mt. Everest; up to quite recently it stood as a speck of dust to the whole Himalayan range.

Let me reinforce this point with an illustration. On June 1, 1954, I sat at home by the radio as I had done day after day since April 22, hypnotized by the engrossing monotony of the Army-McCarthy hearings. I heard the familiar sick-sweet, throaty, yet nasal monotone of the Junior Senator from Wisconsin:

> In view of Mr. Welch's request that the information be given what we know of anyone who might be performing any work for the Communist party, I think we should tell him that he has in his law firm a young man named Fisher, whom he recommended incidentally to do the work on this committee, who has been for a number of years a member of an organization that was named, oh years and years ago, as legal bulwark of the Communist party, an organization which always springs to the defense of anyone who dares to expose Communists. I certainly assume that Mr. Welch did not know this of this young man at the time he recommended him as the assistant counsel for this committee. But he has such terror and such a great desire to know where anyone is located who may be serving the Communist cause—Mr. Welch—that I thought

[4] The ideal of exhaustiveness still prevails among some historians as a residue of their positivist heritage from the nineteenth century. The problem of what constitutes a sufficiently intensive and extensive examination of the record of the past has no a priori answer, and can only be profitably discussed in particular cases.

we should just call to your attention the fact that your Mr. Fisher, who is still in your law firm today, whom you asked to have down here looking over the secret and classified material, is a member of an organization not named by me, but named by various committees, named by the Attorney-General, as I recall, and I think I quote this verbatim, as the legal bulwark of the Communist party. He belonged to that for a sizeable number of years according to his own admission. He belonged to it long after it had been exposed as the legal arm of the Communist party. . . .[5]

That ended the ennui for me. "How could he?" I thought, "how could any man do a thing so mean, so brutal, and so contemptible?"

There was a brief altercation as Joseph Welch, the counsel for the Army, raised a point of personal privilege and despite the chairman's grant of it, McCarthy's voice went droning on, ostentatiously paying no heed. When McCarthy at last quieted down, Welch's voice was gentle, low, reproachful, that of a great actor or of a deeply moved, profoundly shocked man; or was it the voice of a man who was both these things? "Until this moment, Senator, I think I never gauged your cruelty or your recklessness." Welch went on to throw light on Fisher's actions and situation quite other than that in which McCarthy had presented them. He concluded with respect to Fisher's employment in his law firm:

> It is true that he is still with Hale and Doerr. It is true that he will continue to be with Hale and Doerr. It is, I regret to say, equally true that I fear he shall always bear a scar needlessly inflicted by you. If it were in my power to forgive you for your reckless cruelty, I would do so. I like to think I am a gentle man, but your forgiveness will have to come from someone other than me.

Years later, in September 1963, I saw the film, *Point of Order*, a melange selected from the videotape of the Army-McCarthy hearings. After a while I saw McCarthy himself hunch forward and begin with a smug yet reckless smirk. "In view of Mr. Welch's request that information be given. . . ." And then next to him I saw Roy Cohn, his comrade-lieutenant. Cohn's eyes flickered with alarm, he sat bolt upright, and in something between repudiation and shocked wonder he abruptly shook his head. In that moment it was clear that, as the result of a foolhardy ruthless action, utterly irrelevant to the issues of the hearing, McCarthy had irretrievably damaged himself and in a large measure destroyed his whole position; and it was also clear that Cohn, his shrewd ally, in-

---

[5] *New York Times*, June 11, 1954. Note that the "record" of the hearing is either inaccurate or Senator McCarthy said the opposite of what he meant in speaking of a "legal bulwark of the Communist party, an organization which always springs to the defense of anyone who dares to expose Communists." All subsequent quotations are from the *New York Times* report.

stantly knew that this was so. When Welch spoke in *Point of Order*, I both heard and saw him speak; and his measured words took on a dimension of which I had not been previously aware. In addition to being a skilled actor and a sincerely distressed man of decency, he was also a remorseless judge passing sentence on a criminal at the bar, who had condemned himself out of his own mouth.

In the context of what went before there are a number of points about this account of my two confrontations with a substantively irrelevant yet ultimately decisive moment in the hearing and, perhaps, since he was never to recover from the blow he dealt himself that day, in McCarthy's strange career. The first point is one of fact: except for the quoted words and the dates, I am drawing on my memory. The second is that except for my own response to McCarthy's intervention, what I have tried to describe is part of the available record of the past. Insofar as, in what I have written, there are simple misstatements as to the course of events, they can be checked against the videotape of the hearing. Even my attempt to find words for the tones of voice, the facial expressions, and the body movements that I think I remember can be subjected to some checking for accuracy and aptness. To this end they can be placed in a wider context of record provided by videotape of earlier and later public appearances of Messrs. McCarthy, Cohn, and Welch. There is a record to check all these things against. Third, although Senator McCarthy was a very public man indeed, the total visual-audible record of his doings constitutes but a tiny fraction of the whole of his doings in his lifetime. Fourth, very very few persons alive today will leave behind them, when they die, any direct record whatever of any sound they uttered or any bodily movement they made, save, perhaps, as a voice and a speck in a roaring crowd. And finally, no men or women in the entire past up to the 1880's left any audible record whatever of any sound they ever made; no men or women up to the 1890's left behind any direct visual record of a gesture, a change of a facial expression, a bodily movement.[6] For any dates earlier than those, we have to rely on still pictures and portraits to judge what any man looked like and on the pitifully ill-adapted rhetoric of written language to hazard a guess at what he sounded like. What this means in loss of understanding of the past will immediately become clear to anyone who reads a hundred-odd crucial pages of the flat verbatim transcript of the Army-McCarthy hearings and then compares them with the nuanced videotape record.

This, of course, is only the beginning of the defect of the record of

[6] Dates for the earliest versions of phonographic and cinematographic recording. One must add another whole decade or more before material of this sort became plentiful for anything but the public performances, dramatic, musical, or political, of public figures.

the past. We have already referred to that constant demolition and attrition which completely destroys so much of the written and artifactual
record. Beyond a point in time 5,000 years back and stretching some
hundreds of thousands of years further there is no written record at all,
only artifacts. When the written record began it appeared very spottily
in a few, very small areas, and it spread with glacial slowness. Today
still, 5,000 years later, there are places on earth that the written record
has barely touched and a very few that it has not touched at all. Not
only was the geographical spread of literacy and therefore of the written record slow and irregular; its vertical penetration, so to speak, within a given society was equally or more so. What went into the written
record at all in any society depended on the will, the desires, and the
needs of those who controlled and could command a very scarce kind
of goods—the human instruments of redaction, the tiny portion of the
population that could write. Pharaonic tradition, which required permanent memorials, incised in stone, of the god-kings' relations with
other gods, imparted a particular character to the written record of ancient Egypt; the custom of Crete, which left its religious tradition to
oral transmission but called for the preservation in writing of palace in-
ventories and accounts, resulted in a written record of a drastically
different sort. Another contrast may dramatize even more sharply the
eccentricities and exiguousness of the surviving written record of the
past. For historical reasons three ancient peoples—those of Greece, of
Rome, and of Israel—have been of supreme interest to Western man;
they stand in a special relation to his own past. Of more than a millennium of their own past one of these people has left a curious record—a
most miscellaneous anthology of myth, legend, chronicle, legislation,
religious songs, love poetry, wise saws, romance, and prophecy. The
whole of it, the Protestant "Old Testament," plus the pre-Christian
apocryphal writings, however, has a wordage less than that contained
in the semiannual Sears Roebuck Catalogue, or the New Haven telephone directory, or one Sunday issue of the *New York Times* in the
year 1970. And to repeat, for almost the entire human past, "the short
and simple annals of the poor" of whom God made so many, were even
shorter and simpler than when Thomas Gray so described them in
the "Elegy Written in a Country Churchyard" in the middle of the
eighteenth century. Such "annals" were almost never the work of the
poor themselves, who up to very recently appear in the record of the
past most sporadically and indirectly through legislation; judicial proceedings; songs and complaints of their self-appointed champions and
defenders; birth, death, and tax lists; pictures and sculpture; the traces
of the movements of their plows through the field; the great monuments
with which they mixed their sweat; and the remnants of their tools,
their household utensils, and their pitiful hovels.

Perhaps enough has now been said to convey some sense of the paradox of the record of the past; its unmanageable immensity considered from the point of view of the capacity of all the historians on earth at any given time to comprehend it; and at the same time its appalling deficiency, its arbitrary imbalance, its long lapses into something near to complete silence. In view of this paradox most of the historical enterprise may seem hopeless. Given the record of the past as the indispensable prerequisite for writing history, given both the excess and the defect of that record, how can historians seriously pretend to write history? Surely if the object of the enterprise is a "universal history," a complete and certain account of the whole past, that object is utterly frustrated before it even starts; the question of whether it is desirable becomes futile in face of the clear evidence that it is impossible. Thus stated, the alternatives at least become clear: either give up on the historical enterprise altogether or in practice reject this hopeless conception of it.

Any variety of human inquiry can be stultified by insisting that it provide answers to questions that lie beyond the scope or possible limits of its means of knowing. The question "Where precisely were the atoms in this cluster last Thursday at seven P.M.?" or "What is it like to have the kind of awareness of this Chincoteague oyster?" are not on the face of them meaningless questions, since those atoms were presumably somewhere at that time and this Chincoteague oyster may have some sort of awareness. Yet no physicist would apologize for his inability to answer the first question, no biologist for his inability to answer the second. Nor would either be abashed if it were to be shown that because of the elusiveness of the data required it was highly improbable that any physicist or biologist would ever be able to answer questions of that sort. Neither scientist would consider writing off his mode of inquiry merely because it could never promise answers to every conceivable question about the entities with which it concerned itself, nor —one suspects—would the prospect of such lacunae much upset him. Against the business physics has not done, probably will not do, and may not be qualified to do, the physicist would set the business that physics has done, is doing, may do, and is or may become qualified to do.

To return now to the historian, we have seen that his ability to answer questions about the past is limited by the surviving record of the past, against which it must be possible to check in some way any positive statement he makes about what happened. Questions so framed as to insure that the records from which an answer might be elicited do not exist or have never existed—for example "What was the annual variation in tonnage of shipping in the Port of Marseilles in the twelfth century?"—reveal some irreparable defects in the record of the past;

but a historian need no more be abashed by his inability to answer such questions than physicists or biologists need be (or are) concerned about their inability to answer the kind of question we set for them above. Much less need historians be abashed by their inability, both individual and collective, to answer a question like "What is the *whole* story, the *complete* account of man's past?" To such a question historians can only respond by pointing to the record of the past and observing, "It does not say, and there are and can be no means of making it say; and therefore it cannot be the business of historians to answer such questions." This is so obvious that it should not be necessary to say it. It would not be necessary except that some historians have taken their inability to answer questions of this sort as a stigma upon their profession, a mark of its inferiority. But the limitation of any discipline by the data available to it, and therefore of history by the nature of the record of the past, is not a wailing wall on which practitioners are bound to lean and bemoan the inaccessibility of the emptiness beyond. It is rather a helpful boundary to enable them to define the areas in which they may fruitfully work and to warn them of the futility of seeking to step beyond.

Against the occasional hankering of some historians to do what, given the character of the record of the past it is impossible for them to do, stands the practice of almost all historians who have contributed anything to the enhancement of men's understanding. What do such historians do? How do they cope with the problem posed by the paradox of the record of the past, at once so overwhelming and so exiguous? In his study of some part of the record of the past a historian discerns, or believes he discerns, a clue or clues to some pattern of human activity that to the best of his knowledge other historians have not perceived or have misunderstood. For any of a hundred reasons he decides to follow up on the clue. In order to do so, he carefully studies or restudies that part of the record and looks into other parts of it that he thinks may provide him with additional evidence to enlarge his understanding. When he believes that he has gone as far into the matter as the subject is worth and understood it as well as his talents and the time at his disposal permit, he writes about what he found out. This is, of course, only a primitive sketch of what historians do, but as it stands, it is substantially correct.[7]

[7] Note again that here and elsewhere unless specifically or contextually it clearly appears otherwise, I use the term "historian" in the restrictive sense stipulated above (pp. 4–6). Here the statement itself needs to be qualified to say that sometimes a historian will perforce rely heavily on the study of what we called "secondary works," that is, on the writings of later historians about the event-clusters that concern him. This is especially true of histories of a very extensive time-span like Hajo Holborn's *History of Modern Germany* (New York 1959–1969), or a broad geographical span like R. R. Palmer's *Age of the Democratic Revolution* (Princeton, 1964).

As we have said, of most men who lived on earth and of the thick networks of relations that once bound them to other men there is no record
at all and therefore nothing for a historian to work with, nothing for
him to say. And on the written records men once made intentionally for
others to take note of, on the archeological records they unwittingly
created, nature and time and other men have laid capricious and destructive hands obliterating most of them forever and burying deep
much of the rest, where they still wait for men of the future in search
of the past to dig them out. Consequently within history's standard dual
framework of time and space the surviving accessible record of the
past is by no means evenly spread, nor is it spread in proportion to the
"importance" of what it records: to the earthly power of those who
made it or whose doings it recounts, to their number, their wealth,
their force of intellect, or their originality, or even to the relative importance they themselves attached to the part of those records about
them that do survive. Occasionally what survives embodies the ultimate
expression of their most profound aspirations; occasionally it is stuff
that with little reluctance they regularly consigned to the rubbish heap
or used to stop a hole in a wall. Chance, which preserves a considerable
record of a little backwoods community, almost wholly obliterates the
records of the great potentate who ruled the land of which it was a tiny
part. Historians cannot too frequently remind themselves that their
material is not the enormously dense networks of actual human relations in the past, but only the fragmented surviving record from which
they may be able to elicit some sense of some of the intelligible patterns
and structures that once were part of that network.

Right now, however, we want to deal with a peculiarity of the whole
record of the past and of every item constitutive of it. All historical
knowledge depends on the existence of a relevant record, but that
record is of itself passive and silent; taken alone it does and says nothing. Consider the following hypothetical item of the record:

ose Ids ated King C.: Wk, Bk, Nd.

Here are two alternative construals of this item.

1. Whose toads ate King Cole: Wynken's, Blynken's, or Nod's?
2. Those lords hated King Charles I: Warwick, Brook, Northumberland.

Even before the issue of the correct choice between the alternative
construals rises, we see that they imply a number of shared common
judgments about the document.

1. The marks on the paper that constitute the document are to be construed as words, not mere squiggles or doodling.

2. The separate words of the document are English words, not German or Swahili or any other.

3. The words are not random. Together they are to be construed as forming a coherent grammatical structure of meaning.

Having gone so far together, the construals diverge. Both emend the document in order to conform to it to the three preceding common judgments, but differ as to what constitute the appropriate emendations. In argument as to which emendation was correct one would have to make points about provenance of the record (seventeenth-century English State Papers? late nineteenth-century children's story book ms.? twentieth-century absurdist poetry manuscript collection?), intelligibility within the ascribed context, and so on. In either case it can hardly be asserted that "the passage speaks for itself." One way or the other it has been made to speak by those who construed it.

Suppose, however, that the document instead of reading as indicated in our example, read verbatim as in construal 2, without significant paleographic problems: "Those lords hated Charles I: Warwick, Brook, Northumberland." Even then it would be excessive to claim that the record was speaking for itself, for in the first place the historian would be making the three judgments listed above. He would also be judging that whoever set down the document made no significant scribal errors, that the information intended was not, for example, "Those lords *bated* Charles *II*, Wenwick, Brock, Northumberland." Of course no a priori assumption about the accuracy of any particular writer or transcriber is allowable; there are too many scribal errors for that. What is allowable is referral of the burden of proof to the historian who seeks to emend a reading about whose literal accuracy there is no dispute. Under this burden the proposal for emendation in the present case would collapse, since there is no record of lords named Wenwick and Brock in Charles II's reign. Supposing the text to pass for literal accuracy, a historian might still want to know a good deal more about it. He might want to know whether it came from a source trustworthy enough and knowledgeable enough to warrant credence for the statement it embodies. Or he might be quite indifferent to the truth or falsity of the statement, but powerfully struck by the mere use of the term "hated" to describe the response of great lords to their anointed king, since he had never seen such sentiments ascribed to a member of the peerage in a like context before.

What all this indicates is that the historian who stands by, waiting for the record of the past to speak for itself, will wait a long, long time. The record will indeed make noises, as it were; but even the decision to construe those noises as speech requires an act of the historian. The actual relation of historians to the record of the past cannot, I think, be better described than by paraphrasing and modifying a statement by Collingwood:

> The historian must put the record of the past to the question. This is to deny that the historian's attitude to the record should be one of respectful attentiveness, waiting upon its utterances, and building his theories on the basis of what it chooses to vouchsafe him. It rather asserts (1) that the historian must take the initiative, deciding for himself what he wants to know and formulating this in his own mind in the shape of a question. (2) He must find means of compelling the record to answer, devising tortures under which it can no longer hold its tongue, twisting a passage ostensibly about something different into an answer to the question he has decided to ask.[8]

In making this point about the indispensability of the activity of historians in transforming the points of the record of the past into the lines of connection that constitute history, and thus getting rid of the notion that a historian ever simply lets the facts speak for themselves, I do not want to lead readers to slip into the notion that in writing history historians are involved in some peculiar, difficult, and arcane activity that is beyond the grasp of men of ordinary good sense. The only trouble with Collingwood's account of the activity of historians paraphrased above is that it may suggest that there is always this kind of involvement. From exaggerating the singularity of historians' work it is an easy step to making out that there is some special mystique about history, that what historians do is so strange and exceptional as to be beyond the grasp of men without special training as historians. Given the perverse appetite of men of learning to exalt their particular form of activity above those of other learned men, this danger exists throughout the learned world. It leads to self-satisfaction, pomposity, and mystagogy. This danger is especially acute in history, because of all learned disciplines it is the least mysterious, the least removed from common human experience. It is noteworthy that the special kinds of knowledge that historians are required to command are usually lumped together as "auxiliary sciences" or disciplines—diplomatics, numismatics, paleography, statistics, and more recently economics, political science, demography and so on—and foreign languages. To deal with some facets of the record of the past, one or several of these auxiliary disciplines may

[8] In context here "twisting" must be understood to mean "forcing," not "distorting." It is what happens when historians use parish registers, left in conformity with church law, for the purposes of historical demography. For the unmodified original of this passage, see R. G. Collingwood, *The Idea of History* (Oxford, 1946), pp. 269–270.

be necessary. Still good history can be, and has been, written without recourse to any of them.

This is simply to reemphasize a point made in the previous chapter that perforce every man is in one sense his own historian, and is so every day of the year and every working hour of the day all his life. Scarcely an hour passes that he does not call upon his memory to provide him with a patterned true account of the past. Since he cannot cite his memory as a publicly accessible record of the past, he is not a historian in the rather restricted second sense in which the term is often used in this book; but so much of his daily activity is so like that of a historian that he has no difficulty in understanding what historians are most of the time up to, and, given their purposes as historians, why they go about their work the way they do.

So while insisting that the record of the past never speaks for itself, and that no historian ever merely lets the facts speak for themselves, it is also desirable to make clear that that activity is often not much more difficult than looking up a friend in the telephone directory and deciding that the number on the right of the column and in line with his name is his phone number. Indeed it is very often very much like doing just that.

Putting it another way, the surviving records of the past are a set of dimensionless points. As such they lie outside history. It is the work of historians to draw lines connecting records of the past, and thus bringing the dimensionless points within the dimension of history. But it is proper to add that some of this line-drawing is so easy that one has to be a special sort of idiot not to be able to do it.

The image of the historian, not as a passive channel for information which pours freely through him from the record of the past, but as the worker at the pump handle of the record supplying the energy which forces that supine apparatus to yield the actuality of the past, requires us to give further thought to the historians' part in the production of history. What is this "energy," indispensable to any historical work, that the historian supplies? Clearly it is not muscle power, as a literal application of the analogy of the pump would require. It is something other than that, but what is it? Once we pose that question we pin ourselves to the problem of a second record—a record that is individual, unique to each historian and partly private and personal. We pin ourselves so firmly to that problem that we can free ourselves to proceed about our business only by dealing with it.

Our previous dealings with the first record, the record of the past, have already so involved us with the second record that we are snared, and a mere drawing back will not free us from it, but rather tighten its grip, like a man so trussed up that his own straining at his bonds serves only to tighten them. On the other hand, the most cursory glance at what we have called the second record, which is everything that historians bring to their confrontation with the record of the past, shows that it poses not *a* problem, but problem after problem after problem, not neatly layered in strata but intricately interrelated. What we need is a strategy for dealing with the second record here in a way that will most expeditiously and efficiently free us from it, so we will not be *forced to* deal with it again and again but rather be able to use it at our choosing when it is convenient. The strategy hereafter adopted will be to try to understand how we got hooked on to the second record, to study the mechanism of our ensnarement closely enough to be able to disengage ourselves from it, and to hope that what we learn about it in pursuit of this limited purpose will suffice to keep us out of the traps and off the hooks in any subsequent dealing with it.

CHAPTER IV: The Sown and the Waste, or the Second Record

Each historian's second record, as we have said, is in some measure individual to him. Much of it is wholly personal and private, entirely inaccessible to others except insofar as he renders it accessible. It is everything he can bring to bear on the record of the past in order to elicit from that record the best account he can render of what he believes actually happened in the past. Potentially, therfore, it embraces his skills, the range of his knowledge, the set of his mind, the substance, quality, and character of his experience—his total consciousness. Since no historian is identical with any other historian, what each historian brings, his second record, differs in some measure from the second record of every other historian. As we shall see, by laying down restrictive rules as to what historians may properly draw on from their second records, it is possible to reduce considerably the effective and practical differences among historians in this respect. We will need to consider, however, whether in their effort to enlarge their own understanding of the past, and that of others, historians should welcome or reject inhibitory rules on their access to their second records. In any case the second record, so defined, is indefinite in scope, and much of it is, as we noted, personal, individual, ephemeral, and not publicly accessible. Many sorts of men—psychologists, poets, sociologists, theologians—have studied and sought to understand men's second records. Few, however, have concerned themselves with the second records of historians as such and with how historians utilize those records in their dealings with the record of the past. On this subject, historians, too, have been rather taciturn and diffident.

At the end of the last chapter we suggested a strategy to avoid the general entanglement and ultimate engulfment of this book in the uncharted bogs of the individual consciousnesses of all historians, to

disentangle ourselves from the second record and to delimit our subsequent entanglements with it. In keeping with that strategy, we are
now ready for the question: How did we get entangled with the second
record in the first place?

The answer is that, although we may not have noticed at the time,
we were entangled as soon as we began to discuss the first record, the
record of the past as given, as a *datum*. We did not pause at that point
to explain what was meant by "given" in that particular context. Had
we done so, we would have discovered that in treating the record as
given we were primarily trying to contrast it with the vast expanse of
human activity which has left no surviving record whatever—the part
of the past irretrievably lost, eternally *not given*, since it never reached
the record, or the record it reached is itself forever lost. On the other
hand it was not suggested, at least it was not my intent to suggest, that
the *datum* was so given as to require no activity on the historian's part
to possess himself of it. Indeed scattered remarks on the constituent elements of the first record all implied that to turn them to historical use
historians had to *do* something about them—at the very least to find
them, and recognize them *as* records of the past (not always easy to do,
for example, in the case of the tools of the early paleolithic or of old
field-systems).

The treatment of the record of the past in the preceding chapter implied in fact that it was "given" in both of the senses that Locke considered the goods of nature as given to man, given freely in the sense
that it existed and was there to appropriate (as the "lost past" is not),
given conditionally in the sense that in order to appropriate any of it at
all, the historian must mix a modicum, however tiny an amount, of his
labor with it. The very fruit that drops from the tree into a man's supine
hand he must think of and identify *as fruit*, and then he must raise it
to his lips, chew, and swallow it. It is the same with even those records
of the past of which it seems most just to say that a historian "blindly
stumbled upon them." Unless, after he has stumbled, he opens his eyes,
pulls himself together, and considers them, and does not just stumble
silently on, he may as well not have stumbled upon them in the first
place. If he is to be conceived as engaged in a historical enterprise at
all, the very minimum that he must do is to say to someone else who he
believes might want to know, "I think there may be some records
there." Even in doing so much (and so little) as "thinking there may be
some records there," he is bringing to bear on the record of the past
some bit or item of that second record which is private and personal to
him and not freely accessible to others. He renders it accessible by mix-
ing his labor with the record of the past that he stumbled upon to the
extent of conceiving of it as a record and imparting that conception to
someone else.

History, therefore, depends not only on the surviving record of the past but on what historians bring to it. And all any historian brings to the first record lies somewhere in his second record. Every time a historian moves explicitly or implicitly from the record of the past to a historical assertion *about* the past he is drawing on his second record, claiming that he has and, if necessary, can produce from his second record grounds for his assertion that the first record means what he says it means. In this way he makes some part of his second record, hitherto private and inaccessible, public and accessible, open to criticism and evaluation.

It will be well to pause and consider this a little further. The notion of the record of the past as an array of points turns out to be useful in this context. The points are nondimensional, and no number of them finite or infinite make a line, so every line is a leap from nondimensionality into dimensionality. With respect to history the whole record of the past is only a set of points. However closely arrayed they may be, all by themselves they do not make a pattern. The pattern is always the work of a historian or of someone acting in the capacity of a historian. It always involves an inference. The points themselves do not have the dimension of history and cannot alone legitimate the inference. To legitimate it the historian himself must supply something. Without that something there can be no history, and that something must come from the second record, since there is no place else for it to come from. So without resort to the second record there can be no history at all. Let us put the matter in its most radical form. Suppose a French historian in, say, 1700, was writing a history of English Civil Wars. In examining the record of the past he finds the following sentences in different documents: (1) "Today on January 30, 1648, the murderous rebels dipped their vile hands in the life blood of our martyr King." (2) "January 30, 1648, Today the people of England brought to justice at the hands of the public executioner, that Man of Blood, Charles Stuart." (3) "Execution of King—January 30, 1648."

If our historian simply quotes those sentences and draws no inference from them he is not writing history at all. To write correct history he will have to continue to write *as if* he inferred from the documents that *King Charles I* was executed in January *1649*, or he will have to make the inference explicit and write: King Charles I was executed on January 30 (old style = February 9 new style) 1648 (9).

Note that in doing so he is writing what none of the records explicitly say—that the "martyr King" of the first statement, "Charles Stuart" of the second statement, and the "King" of the third statement were the same man Charles I, and that the January 30, 1648, of all the statements was on the writers own calendar (as it is on ours) February 9, 1649. There is of course very little likelihood that anyone would challenge what he says. That does not alter the fact that his statement is something other than the record of the past. It is not a "mere fact" but an inference from the record of the past. By making an assertion about the past as he believes it actually was, he moves out of the point sets which are the records of the past and into the line sets which are in the dimension of history. Whenever any particular move of this sort is challenged, the historian who made the move must be able to defend it, and the only armaments of defense he controls are in his second record.[1]

By seeking out patterns and reconstructing connections among the records of the past, historians attempt and in part achieve accounts of the past as it actually was. In this seeking out of patterns, historians are sometimes bold and imaginative, sometimes rash and fantastical, sometime cautious and prudent, sometimes timid. In their dealings with the record of the past the very best historians display both imagination and caution, boldness and prudence, each at the right time and in the right place. Boldness and imagination are not traits of the record of the past or of any part of it; they are traits of men, as are prudence and caution. They are part of what a good historian brings to the record, part of what he draws on to elicit from it an understanding of the past as it actually was. They are elements of that second record, which is the sole equipage at his disposal, all that he is endowed with for meeting the demands of his vocation. On what he is able to find in that record and the way he uses what he finds depends his personal fulfillment or frustration in the way of life he has chosen for himself. And on the sum of the ways that all historians of a generation use their second records depends the health or the sickness, the welfare of history itself during that generation. One would expect, therefore, that historians would have devoted a good deal of systematic attention to this second record, so crucial to any understanding of the past that they may hope to achieve.

They have not done so. Most manuals for the instruction of historians do not meet head on the problems posed by the second record. They do not say, in effect, "There it is. It is all you have to work with in your encounter with the record of the past. You had better get to know a good bit about it." Of course if one presses the implications of some of the statements in such manuals, one will discover the second record underlying them. But it is scattered and hidden, discernible by inference only. By both scattering it and concealing it from others, writers of books on the historian's craft have also managed to conceal it from themselves and thus to minimize its importance in history and for historians. In the context of a study of the writing of history, this situation

[1] In a specific case a historian may reasonably decline to respond to a vague challenge on the legitimate grounds that the challenger is wholly without qualification, and that historians are not bound to waste inordinate amounts of time dealing with doubts unsupported by bills of particulars.

poses a difficult dilemma. The second record requires from historians a minute attention and a consecutive and coherent consideration which it has not received, but the problems that record poses, while related to the writing of history, extend far beyond it and beyond my competence. Yet the implications of the omnipresence of the second record for the writing of history require me to say more about it than most historians do when they write about their vocation.

How has it come about that historians concerned with understanding and explaining the mysteries of their craft and in instructing neophytes, have said so little systematically and explicitly about the second record? In all fairness it should be said that on the part of some of these historians the neglect was not conscious. Because of the habits of thinking about history that they inherited from their predecessors the second record came into their range of vision only at the periphery and in a most fragmented way, so it never got integrated into their gestalt of the operations of a historian. That gestalt had as its central and almost sole focus the records of the past and the carefully elaborated and intricate techniques for learning to read them, for identifying their provenance and for verifying their dating. The force behind this concentration of effort derived from the nature of records that most often concerned historians who wrote many of the earlier manuals— the issue of royal and lesser centers of authority in the Middle Ages, where documentation is very scanty, and the preliminary problems of paleography and diplomatics are very acute. The rather narrow conception of these historians was therefore a natural though not a legitimate consequence of their professional preoccupation.

In some writers on the historians' work, however, one senses a more than peripheral awareness of the second record and an almost instinctive cautious backing away from it, a sort of uneasy sense that it better not be confronted because it means Big Trouble. This response is interesting especially in what it may reveal about a widespread professional syndrome. This group of writers well may have turned their collective back to the second record because they felt that it jeopardized one of their most cherished beliefs—that history was a science and they were scientists. Their nervousness on this score was the result of their assumption that one of the indispensable virtues of science was its objectivity and that an overclose scrutiny of the role of the second record in history would reveal the discipline's appalling subjectivity and forfeit its claim to scientific status. Here again we encounter a recurrent concern of many historians—to lay claim to a place for their discipline among the sciences. It is not the first nor will it be the last time we will find historians frustrating their own development out of excessive respect for a line of argument that they have not fully grasped. In this particular instance in the interest of defending their "scientific objec-

tivity" historians have tried to maximize the role of what they misconstrued as pure object, the datum, the "given" record of the past, and to
minimize the second record—the reservoir of what they know, have
learned, and are—on which they must draw to force from the first record an understanding of what happened in the past and what the past
was like.

It is to this almost exclusive concern with the first as against the
second record that we owe the endless assertions catechetically reiterated that the only function of the historian is to dig the facts out of the
record, set them down, and let them speak for themselves. It is hard
to think of a better recipe for an utterly mindless human activity, and
those who tried to follow the prescription almost achieved mindless-
ness without achieving the purpose of the prefrontal lobotomy that they
inflicted on their discipline. They failed, they were doomed to fail, to
attain that elimination of the second record which was their object,
because as we have seen, the second record is radically uneliminable.
In the end they had to draw on it in every sentence in which they committed themselves to asserting any relation of anything in the past to
anything else, to passing from the dimensionless points of the record
to the dimension of history. All they insured was that the relations that
they did establish were of the most obvious and the least interesting
sort. So the effort was useless, failing to achieve what it aimed at.

It was indeed doubly futile since what it aimed at was not worth
achieving. For what historians were confronted with and what unduly
and quite unnecessarily panicked them was simply another one of those
meaningless definitional victories. If objectivity is so defined that it requires the emergence of truth and knowledge from the record with no
intervention of persons acting in relation to the record and drawing inferences from the seen and palpable to the unseen and impalable, then
not only is historical objectivity impossible but so is scientific objectivity, and perhaps any objectivity at all. To pass from the record of an
experiment to scientific generalization requires the scientist to bring to
bear on the experiment part of his second record, his knowledge of the
scientific corpus. It requires him to make inferences from the visible
movement of scaled devices like thermometers, pressure gauges, meters,
and scales to insensible entities like equal small increments and decre-
ments of temperature, pressure, voltage and amperage, and weight. Then
scientific knowledge is subjective by definition, and if the only real
knowledge is objective, scientists as such really know nothing about
anything. Scientists, or most of them, had the good sense to step all the
way out of an absurd position. They swiftly redefined "objectivity" in a
way that made at least a measure of sense, gave the term some degree of
usefulness, and did not cut them off from any part of *their* second record which might come in handy to their work. Historians were not so

wise; they still wanted to maintain tacit restrictive covenants a priori
on a great deal of their second records. By a sort of inexplicit agreement
among themselves they admitted that each other's historical writings
were a little bit objective: citation not merely to records of the past but
to the accounts other historians wrote of what had happened in the
past testified to the touching faith of historians in each other.

The bias of much of the historical profession in this matter in past
decades is reflected in what has become the pattern of selecting for
training those who are to be future members of the profession. In the
first place almost all applicants for such training take a very large
number of courses in history during their undergraduate years. Although they may study some of the record of the past from "the
sources," what they mostly do in those courses is read books by historians and listen to lectures by them. Their extensive selection of such
courses testifies to their intuitive judgment, probably correct, that what
graduate history faculties will most closely scrutinize in applications
for admission to graduate school will be the courses the applicant took
in history and his level of performance in them indicated by the grade
he received. Once in graduate school the successful applicant is pressed
even more firmly into the mold for which he previously opted. He
senses that the most prudent thing for him to do is to take *nothing but*
courses in history until he has completed all the requirements for his
doctorate except the doctoral dissertation. This is not to deprecate or
deny for a moment the importance in the training of historians of extensive reading in history. The notion that it is likely to be in any way
profitable to come to the record of the past with "an open mind"—
meaning a mind empty of any of the knowledge of the past patiently
accumulated and made available by hard-working and intelligent professionals over a long course of years—is absurd. It implies a brash
repudiation of the worth of the constructive efforts of all historians that
no historian who sets any value on his own work is likely to find reas-
suring or agreeable. Anyone who comes to the record this way will
surely spend much of his life rediscovering what has long been well
established, discovering what has long since been shown not to be so,
and failing to understand much of the record he examines for lack of
the clues with which knowledge derivable from the writings of other
historians would have provided him. As a historian he would almost
surely condemn himself to a life of nearly total futility, redundancy,
and error. The previous remarks therefore are not intended as a blanket
criticism of the way of training historians that they describe, although
perhaps there has been a bit too much of a good thing, and the accumulation of history courses by fledgling historians may have reached the
point of diminishing returns. Still the whole pattern of training of historians suggests that the only part of his second record of serious use to

a writer of history is what he has learned, taken notes on, and remembers from his earlier reading in the record of the past and from lectures and books by other historians. This implies that there is nothing else in the second record that is worthy of his attention or reflection, and that he need have nothing else in it.

Fairly frequently in recent years this parochial view of the second record has been challenged; but the challenge has come from a group which would only extend the boundaries of the parish somewhat and then all the more strongly enforce on historians an explicit rule against trespass beyond the new limits. Under the circumstances it is possible to be ambivalent about *lebensraum* offered on such exigent terms. For while the old bounds were very narrow, they were rather hinted at than precisely drawn, so that the more daring or vagrant members of the community of historians wandered beyond them without a great deal of compunction and with considerable profit. The new bounds though more generous are also more sharply defined, and ventures by historians into the second record outside the prescribed limits might come under the disapproving scrutiny of a sharp- and beady-eyed Big Brother. Big Brother in this case is the generalizing and/or quantifying social (or behavioral) scientist.

For about three-quarters of a century historians have been aware of a considerable amount of activity in shops in their neighborhood—shops previously so stodgy, so small, or purveying goods so sleazy that what went on in them seemed to be of little interest. The tale of the ambivalent and sometimes slightly hysterical attitude of historians during the past seventy-five years to what has been going on in sociology, anthropology, political science, linguistics, and psychology would be worth telling provided it was told by a historian with a sound sense of the ridiculous. By now, however, the returns are in, in the simplest and most empirical sense. In each one of the fields of investigation mentioned, and in economics,[2] scholars who identify themselves with that particular field have written works that some historians have found useful in connection with their own studies. And that really leaves historians no serious option but to admit that some of what goes on in the social and behavioral sciences is of concern to historians (although this is not true of everything that goes on in these sciences, and with respect to any particular historian's investigations many of these sciences may provide no enlightenment at all). The experience of many historians with the social sciences has considerably and on the whole desirably extended their view of what they might properly draw on from their second record to apply to the record of the past. Instead of restricting them to just so much as they learned by reading the works of other

[2] Economics has, of course, a longer career of intellectual viability than the other systematic social sciences.

historians, it opened up to them what they had learned by reading in the social sciences, and rather firmly implied that they would do well to take active measures to stock some knowledge of the social sciences in their second records for possible future use.

As far as it goes, this is all to the good. Having conceded so much, it would be well for historians to take heed. They need to be a little cautious about this particular set of Greeks bearing these particular gifts. The reason for this caution lies in the intellectual habits and general strategies of the social sciences. Because they have more fully committed themselves to being scientists and nothing else, they have also become more concerned than historians to determine whether their methods approximate the tests of rigor, precision, and testability that the natural scientists impose or appear to impose on themselves. To meet these tests they have ruled large tracts of the second record out of bounds by establishing rigid criteria of "adequate explanation." By defining what they mean by "knowing" both exactly and somewhat narrowly, they have become both aware of and somewhat inhospitable to conceptions and claims with respect to knowing and explaining more open than their own. After associating with them, historians learn in very short order that many of their own habits of thought are off-limits for social scientists. They also are made conscious that, protests to the contrary notwithstanding, their inexplicit assumptions have led historians to range more freely through their second records than the social scientists deem proper or even tolerable. The contempt of the social scientists for the "impressionistic" language and loose conceptual wanderings of historians should help alert the latter to their own vagrancy.

Indeed with more and more historians becoming knowledgeable about the social sciences and consequently aware of how far the historians' actual way with the second record diverges from the standards made explicit by social scientists for themselves, it is not at all unlikely that the historical discipline is headed for a crisis over method. The day may not be far off when a considerable group of historians will demand that the entire profession face up to the deviance of its ways. They may challenge it either to give up its illicit procedures and adopt the conceptions of knowing, explaining, and testing acceptable among social scientists, or to give up the claim that by such procedures they can or ever have advanced human understanding of the past. Forewarned of this possibility, indeed of this danger, of being brought up against an either-or dilemma, with manifold temptations to the sort of mutual anathemization and internecine warfare that have recently afflicted several of the social sciences and philosophy, historians may do well to be prepared to surrender or to defend their peculiar way of using the second record to elicit history from the record of the past. Already their contact with social scientists should have alerted them to the fact that the ways they actually use it have committed them to a conception of knowledge and the routes to it not acceptable to the disciplines in their neighborhood.

What then is the actual situation? How do historians make use of the second record in ways likely to put them in the bad graces of the intellectually more ascetic social scientists? What intellectual sins do historians casually and amiably commit that the purer scientists are likely to find either shocking or degrading? Historians can hardly decide whether to take the pledge or to continue to wallow in their customary vices until they make out clearly what those vices are. Perhaps at this point an illustration of a number of the ways a historian has actually used the second record in his ordinary pursuit of trying to understand something about the past and to advance knowledge of it may help define an important difference between historians and social scientists and make clear what is at stake.

During the past fifteen years I have spent what may have been an inordinate amount of time on historical investigation and writing that had as its focus one rather small book, *Utopia*, by Thomas More. Leaving aside judgments as to my wisdom in putting in so much time on that particular enterprise (a matter on which I have had serious doubts), historians would deem the attempt to explicate a book as a significant record of the past an activity appropriate to a member of their profession. What follows is a tabulation of a very small cluster of the historiographic problems I encountered in the course of this presumably legitimate activity. The first column in the table describes the problems in the form of questions; the second indicates the solutions offered; the third identifies the elements in my second record on which I drew in arriving at the solution; the fourth is my estimate of the grade on an A to F scale that the procedure described in the third column would earn from many social scientists (see pp. 90–91).

Our examples clearly appear to fall into three pairs. In the A–B pair my solution of the problems posed involved relating them to generalizations ratified by the consensus of one or more of the social sciences. It therefore represents a perhaps rather sloppy effort to make use of the elbow room within my second record provided by legitimization of the social sciences as a resource for the historians in their commerce with the record of the past. The C–D pair is more orthodox still. To provide solutions to new problems raised by my investigations into the first record, it draws on earlier deposits of knowledge of the past that I had banked in my second record.

Before we pass to the last and crucial pair let us note a couple of casual common traits of all four of the examples so far discussed. Several of the items in the third column were not acquired as a result of my research into More's *Utopia* or with a view to solving the prob-

	PROBLEM	SOLUTION	SOURCE IN SECOND RECORD	SOCIAL SCIENCE RATING
A	Why did More express such vehement revulsion in *Utopia* to taking office as a councilor to the king?	To treat More's views in this matter as a special case of awareness of the general problems that an intellectual is likely to encounter in the higher levels of government service.	Robert K. Merton, "The Role of the Intellectual in Public Bureaucracy," *Social Theory and Social Structure* (Glencoe, Ill., 1949), pp. 161–178.	B
B	Why did More provide *Utopia*, his ideal commonwealth, with economic institutions so defective from the point of view of an economist?	a. To "translate" some of his outlook into more recent economic language, i.e., opposition to "conspicuous consumption" and "conspicuous waste." b. To contrast his view of the function of an economy as the fulfillment of legitimate needs with the modern conception of its function as the maximum satisfaction of wants.	a. Thorstein Veblen, *Theory of the Leisure Class.* b. Desultory reading of nineteenth-century utilitarians and recent economic theorists.	B
C	Why did More ultimately decide to enter the king's service despite his reservations made so explicit in *Utopia*?	To link More's change with concurrent changes in royal policy that brought it nearer to More's views of what was desirable and possible within the bounds of the existing social order.	William Holdsworth, *History of English Law*; A. F. Pollard, *Wolsey*; general and reasonably extensive reading in English history in the reign of Henry VIII.	C

(continued)

	PROBLEM	SOLUTION	SOURCE IN SECOND RECORD	SOCIAL SCIENCE RATING
D	What are the peculiar and unique traits of communism as practiced by the Utopians in More's *Utopia*?	To compare and contrast Utopian communism with various communist conceptions and practices that More knew something about.	Plato, *The Republic*, The Benedictine Rule, statements about community of property in stoic and patristic literature.	B–
E	What accounts for More's enthusiasm, clearly expressed in *Utopia*, for measures to ensure future security for families in case of the premature death or disability of the breadwinner?	To point to More's situation in 1515 with a large young family for whose future security he had to engage in work he intensely disliked.	a. Data on More's situation from various sources. b. My own situation in 1950, when I encountered this problem in *Utopia*.	F
F	What accounts for the extremely harsh and repressive character of so many of the institutions that More provided for Utopia, his ideal commonwealth?	To show that Utopian institutions can be construed as primarily concerned with the containment and suppression of pride and that so to construe them makes better sense than alternative hypotheses as to More's purposes in structuring them as he did.	a. Evidence from *Utopia* itself of the coherence of Utopian institutions if construed as indicated. b. Biographical data bearing on More's religious ethic and reading in a considerable range of theological writers on Christian teaching about sin. c. My own understanding of the power of pride.	F

lems it raised. They had been in my second record for varying lengths of time and had been acquired and deposited there haphazardly or for other purposes. The principle "historical research" requisite for solving the problems, therefore, turned out to be not investigation of records of the past hitherto unknown to me but a rummaging through oddments that were already stashed away in my second record. Moreover, they are a miscellaneous lot of intellectual lumber, acquired for the most diverse purposes or, in the case of the Merton study, for no purpose at all, but merely to kill time in the periodical room of the Columbia University library while waiting for a friend. Lying around helter-skelter in my second record, they turned out to be accessible to me at least in part because of my general attitude toward the use of my second record for eliciting knowledge of history from the record of the past. That attitude, which according to taste can be described as ecumenical or raffish, may be summarized: cast about for and use anything you have got that will build up steam in the boiler and get you moving. The results of this methodological libertinism are sometimes idiosyncratic, but occasionally interesting.

And that brings us to the crux—the third pair of examples, E and F. I could reasonably hope for the restrained blessings of social scientists and historians on my exploitation of my second record in the first four instances because, however I came by them, the items in the third column were themselves respectable enough, consisting of tightly organized bodies of knowledge carefully structured within the bounds of rules established by the several disciplines; and they were incorporated into my second record, however haphazardly, by a structured activity of reading and study. They are all patches of systematic knowing in the enormously larger tract of the second record constituted by all that I have experienced, can remember, and have become. The last pair of instances, E and F, demands that we face the problem posed for the historian by the vast residue that remains when he subtracts from his second record all that either historians or social scientists would allow as systematic and structured knowledge, clearly and legitimately applicable to the record of the past for the purpose of the advancement of historical understanding. For in instances E and F I have drawn on parts of my second record that lie outside the bounds of systematic knowledge. The failing grade conjecturally assigned to these instances is intended to reflect the disapproval with which I assume most social scientists would view so unscientific a procedure. If historians accept this grading they submit to an injunction that would wholly bar them from access to the part of the second record I entered in instances E and F, on the ground that nothing properly called scientific knowledge is to be found there.

It seems to me that historians would be most unwise to accept such a view, that to do so would reduce the nourishment available for their enterprise and seriously stunt its growth. What is at stake may be made clearer by pairing this metaphor with another. Earlier I characterized those parts of the second record that historians might hope to use with the unstinted approval of social scientists as "patches of systematic knowing in the enormously larger tract of the second record." The issue is between two radically opposed views of the true relation between those patches and that tract. To many social scientists the patches represent the totality of what for their professional purposes can be properly certified as knowing. They are, as it were, bits of fruitful ground, wrenched from a desert of ignorance and confusion by excruciating labor-intensive methods, and the *only way* to advance knowledge securely is to apply further mass investments of labor to augment the patches of the sown. What is the alternative view? It is that what labor-intensive methods in the social sciences have yielded may indeed have repaid the cost of labor; but that what lies beyond the sown is not desert, it is what in the Middle Ages was called "the waste." The medieval waste had two important traits. (1) In the present-day sense, it was not waste at all; it was the grazing area, utilized by labor-extensive rather than labor-intensive methods. (2) From the point of view of the community the relation of waste to sown was not antagonistic; it was symbiotic. The economic welfare of the community depended on a balance between waste and sown. The metaphor of waste and sown as against sown and desert suggests the view of the second record I wish to maintain. I believe that historians must reject the idea that they may properly apply to the record of the past only what they can bring to fruition in the cultivated patches of systematically structured knowledge. Historians find support and sustenance for their work in these patches, but also can find such support and sustenance in the rest of the second record. If one is to maintain this position, one must be ready to argue that what lies beyond the sown in the second record is not desert, not mere ignorance and confusion, but "waste," rich in knowledge, yet knowledge in a sense qualitatively different from the knowledge in the cultivated patches and therefore to be exploited in a somewhat different way.

For the qualitative differences between the kinds of knowledge in the sown and the waste of the second record, there are good reasons. Up to less than two centuries ago what men knew about the atomic structure of matter was nil. Therefore any assumption at random that they made about it had the same value as any other assumption: all discourse on the subject was fundamentally speculative; and notions men may have had about it were nonprescriptive with respect to action. About this aspect of their environment, they possessed less verified knowledge on which they could act than an infant a month old has about his surroundings. If every adult in the world did not know a great deal more about the world around him than the greatest scientist two hundred years ago knew about the atomic structure of matter, he would be dead within a few hours, for the greatest scientist knew nothing of it and could predict nothing about it. By contrast, the assistance to living that the world provides for an adult is organized in a way that requires him each day to make hundreds of predictions about what others will do and what the effect of his words and actions on others will be. Unless he is right in almost all his predictions he is in bad trouble. Consider the following question and answer:

> JULES: "What are you going to be doing this evening?"
> JAMES: "I am going home from work and have a nice cold highball, and then sit down to the good hot dinner that my wife has cooked for me."

Such an answer given with almost complete confidence and with scarcely a pause for thought is based on an extraordinary network of predictions—that transportation from James' place of work to his home will be available, that access to the road network will not be blocked, that there will be whisky, water, and ice available when he gets home (that is, that the waterworks will have maintained operation, that someone will have seen to it that the ice trays in the fridge have been filled, that the electric company will have maintained service, that no one will have drunk up all the whisky without replacing it), that his wife will be home, that she will have been able to purchase the supplies necessary for dinner and will have actually done so, and so on. The ordinary daily life of even quite stupid men, as we saw earlier, is based on a dense and firm fabric of such predictions, and any one who cannot do a good job of predicting at this level has a very poor chance of surviving at all. A car slowly approaches the street crossing. If the driver slams down the accelerator as I step into the street, he can kill or maim me. Nevertheless, predicting that he will not slam down the accelerator, I cross the street. The man behind the counter is armed with a lethal weapon, a very big sharp knife. Without quailing, I say to him, "Let me have three thick loin pork chops." I tacitly predict that his response to my order will be to bury the knife into a loin of pork, not into my entrails. And so it goes with all of us day in, day out, year after year, as dozens of times each day we stake our comfort, our health, our hopes, our very lives on—on what? On our knowledge of ourselves and others. To deny the name of knowledge to what we are betting on seems to me to involve an excess of snobbishness and prudery about what we are ready to certify as knowing. In our society we cannot unpack all the connotations and implications of value from a word like "knowledge." Unless we recognize the processes described as a kind of knowing, we cannot investigate them as a kind of knowing; we cannot ask how we use them; we cannot know how historians can and do use them. In this situation it may be proper for testing purposes to invoke The Bet and The Rule of Random. To anyone who argues that what we have insisted on calling knowledge is not knowledge we propose a bet. We propose, for example, that in ten different bars with a view to getting a glass of beer he recite a sentence chosen at random, and that we be allowed to recite any sentence we wish (in this case, "a beer, please") with the same end in view, and that each time we make a large even money bet on which procedure actually elicits the beer.

The issue hardly seems worth pressing further. It is quite evident that as part of his second record every moderately viable adult knows a great deal both about others and about himself. It is also evident that whether or not all this knowledge could with great care be transformed into those systematically structured, intensively cultivated patches which the social sciences exemplify, or at least seek to exemplify, in the actual second records of most men most of the time it is not so transformed. It is also certain that a great deal of it has not been transformed at all by anyone, that daily men bet successfully on a mass and a kind of knowledge that has not yet been absorbed into the tidily structured patches of systematic knowing with which social scientists feel they can profitably deal. It is clear, too, even if social scientists were willing to guarantee that some day they would bring the whole of men's knowledge of men into the bounds of their disciplines, historians could not wait on the fulfillment of that promise; their pressing occasions require them to use whatever is at hand as best they can in their work, and not loiter about waiting for the millennium. And it is most unclear that the whole range of experiential and personal knowledge by which men live is actually reducible to the kind of knowledge with which social scientists concern themselves; it is at least conceivable that their very conception of scientific knowledge requires them to define it in a way that shears a dimension from knowing as men actually experience it. Nor is this imperfectly structured knowing by which men live a desert; indeed if a man is to survive in the world at all it must not be a desert.[3] It is a "waste," but waste very abundant indeed, since from it most men draw most of the knowledge they need to sustain them throughout their lives.

Once one recognizes that a very, very large part of each man's second

---

[3] For their safety and our comfort we remove from the world men whose cover of knowledge is very thin, though not absolute desert. In asylums they enjoy (or suffer) immunity from the dangers of ordinary life outside.

record consists of the knowledge of himself and of others that he uses
to steer himself through the daily dilemmas and difficulties of living,
to question whether in his struggle with the record of the past a historian should use knowledge so relevant to understanding human conduct and so regularly tried in the crucible of experience becomes
almost impertinent.[4] Why, indeed, should it be taken seriously? Why
in pursuit of knowledge of what men have done and suffered in the past
should a historian cut himself off from the most extensive and most
severely tested source of knowledge about men that he has direct
access to, the knowledge of others and of himself on which he daily
stakes his life and the welfare of those who are dear to him? Surely if
we ask whether a historian should nourish his powers of historical
perception in this abundant and rich range of his second record, the
record that by its very nature is his and his alone, since it is the
repository of his remembered and rememberable experiences—surely
if we ask that, we simply ask the wrong, the foolish question. It must
be clear that the question is not "whether?" but *"how, and how best?"*
How do we use what we know, how do we employ every accessible
relevant resource in our second record to draw out of the first record
the best possible account of the matters that concern us, to provide the
best answers we can to the problems we have raised?

To try to answer such a question once for all time and in general
is futile, for the very generality of the answer would make it empty.
To deal with the question by the way of specifics was the purpose of
the third pair of examples, E and F, drawn from my studies of More's
Utopia. That pair was intended to illustrate and demonstrate how one
historian made use of parts of his second record that were particularly
private, individual, personal, and inaccessible to others in order to
elicit or reconstruct from the first record patterns of the past as they
actually were, or (to remind readers of the larger framework of our
problem) to extend a nondimensional array of points from the record
of the past into the dimension of history. Let us now examine those two
instances more closely.

In the first example I related a particular passage in *Utopia* to More's
personal situation as it was when he wrote the passage. Here is the
quotation in praise of *Utopia's* social arrangements.

For what can be greater riches for a man than to live with a joyful and
peaceful mind, free of all worries—not troubled with his food or harassed
by the querulous demands of his wife or fearing poverty for his son or
worrying about his daughter's dowry, but feeling secure about the liveli-

[4] This is not to argue that it is to be used carelessly or mindlessly, or that it
is always adequate or that in some instances it may not be ambiguous and misleading. But all this is equally true of "the sown."

hood and happiness of himself and his family: wife, sons, grandsons, great-grandsons, great-great-grandsons, and all the long line of their descendants that gentlefolk anticipate? Then take into account the fact that there is no less provision for those who are now helpless but once worked than for those who are still working.[5]

More thought highly of a number of the social contrivances that he ascribed to Utopia, but this passage seemed especially lyrical. Might it not point to something beyond sheer delight in his own ingenuity at imaginative contrivance, to something personal perhaps? In the record of the past the points of evidence on his situation—his standards of consumption, his income, his own sense of being under financial pressure, his family situation—were widely scattered through a variety of documents. Taken together, however, the scraps of information readily combined into a picture of a man with a large family, high views on what should be spent on educating children, a generous standard of expense, several daughters to provide for, and a son to start in the world. He was moreover, at the moment he wrote, short of money, and his income was cut back to the bone by enforced absence from his law practice, a practice that he pursued ably but out of necessity and without joy. In such a context the outburst in *Utopia* acquired an added dimension. It became a cry from the heart.

But what made me raise the question in the first place, and sent me to the record of the past to gather the scraps that made the picture plausible? It was the precision with which the passage from *Utopia* spoke, as the theologians say, to my own condition at the time I was writing. On a meager salary I was supporting a wife and three children under six years of age. I had taken no steps to ensure their care or welfare in case of my death or disability; and with no other secure way of providing for them in sight, I was about to undertake a writing job I thoroughly disliked in order to meet my obligations to those who were dear to me. It was this flash from my experience, my second record, that fused a couple of the bits of information from the record of the past into an insight into More's dilemma and sent me back through the first record in quest of other bits that might confirm it.

The second instance is more complex. Scholars who had studied *Utopia* had made numerous attempts to understand why More endowed "the best ordered commonwealth" with the particular institutions he ascribed to it. I did not find any of the explanations altogether persuasive. Many of them seemed to reflect the ideological commitment of the men who proposed them rather than the known or knowable concerns and preoccupations of More around the time he wrote *Utopia*.

[5] *The Complete Works of St. Thomas More,* ed. Edward Surtz, S.J. and J. H. Hexter (New Haven and London, 1965), 4: 239.

98 THE HISTORY PRIMER

Others quite legitimately identified in earlier authors antecedents of this or that particular detailed arrangement in the Utopian commonwealth; but the men who made the identifications did not find (sometimes did not even seek) any integrative principle or set of related principles, logical or psychological, that would make the commonwealth what it manifestly was—the product of one coherent intellect and imagination. Finally it seemed to me that few scholars had been aware how austere and unabashedly repressive the institutional structure of More's ideal commonwealth was, and that those few had failed to provide a satisfactory explanation of what they had observed.

My dissatisfaction with the way previous scholars had written about *Utopia* [6] was not diminished by my uneasy sense that at the moment I could not come up with anything better. This uneasiness persisted until, as I reread *Utopia*, a brief sentence seized my attention:

> No doubt about it, avarice and greed are aroused in every kind of living creature by the fear of want, but only in man are they motivated by pride alone—pride which counts it a personal glory to excel others by superfluous display of possessions. The latter vice can have no place at all in the Utopian scheme of things.[7]

At that point I both thought and worked through *Utopia* again keeping in the forefront of my mind both an awareness of More's profound concern with Christian righteousness and of the place of sin, especially the sin of pride, in the moral economy of the Christian ethic. Seen in that perspective, the institutional structures More presented for his "holy commonwealth" [8] fell into a coherent pattern. In writing about what I thought I perceived, after some ground-clearing exposition, I concluded as follows:

> Once we recognize that More's analysis of sixteenth century society led him to the conclusion that pride was the source of the greater part of its ills, the pattern of the Utopian commonwealth becomes clear, consistent, and intelligible. In its fundamental structure it is a great social instrument for the subjugation of pride. The pecuniary economy must be destroyed because money is the prime instrument through the use of which men seek to satisfy their yet insatiable pride. It is to keep pride

[6] Especially Russel Ames, *Citizen Thomas More and His Utopia* (Princeton, 1949); W. E. Campbell, *More's Utopia and His Social Teaching* (London, 1930); Karl Kautsky, *Thomas More and His Utopia*, tr. H. J. Stenning (New York, 1927); R. W. Chambers, *Thomas More* (New York, 1936).

[7] *The Complete Works of St. Thomas More*, 4: 139.

[8] The term "holy" is not used casually here. I subsequently attempted a comparison of More's "constitution" for Utopia with John Calvin's ordinances for his City of Saints. The comparison indicated that in some respects Utopia was a good bit more repressive than Geneva.

down that all Utopians must eat in common messes, wear a common uniform habit, receive a common education, and rotate their dwelling places. . . . Above all idleness, the great emblem of pride in the society of More's time, a sure mark to elevate the aristocrat above the vulgar, is utterly destroyed by the common obligation of common daily toil. . . . More was a logical man; he knew that to bind up pride on all sides it takes a strait prison, and he did not flinch from the consequences of his diagnosis. As he truly says this "kind of vice among the Utopians can have no place."

. . . More draws . . . the whole Discourse of the best state of a com-mon-wealth to its conclusion [with those words]: "I doubt not that the re-spect of every man's private interest or else the authority of our Savior Christ . . . would have brought all the world long ago into the laws of this weal public, if it were not that one only beast, the princess and mother of all mischief, Pride, doth withstand and let it. She measureth not wealth and prosperity by her own interest but by the miseries and inconveniences of others; she would not by her good will be made a goddess if there were no wretches left over whom she might, like a scornful lady, rule and triumph, over whose miseries her felicity might shine, whose poverty she might vex, torment, and increase by gorgeously setting forth her riches. This hellhound creeps into men's hearts; and plucks them back from entering the right path of life, and is so deeply rooted in men's breasts that she cannot be plucked out." [9]

The immediate germane question here is not whether my solution to the problem I posed is right or wrong, better or worse than the alter-native solutions proposed by others, but how I happened to hit on such a solution in the first place. After all a great many scholars reading *Utopia* very closely had not hit on it, although they also had read the passage that triggered it off in my mind. There was no automatic trig-gering device; the record of the past was not, in a phrase we have already rejected, simply "speaking for itself." We are dealing not with one operative force but two, the passage itself and "my mind" the second record, private, personal, individual to me, inaccessible to others, that made me ready to perceive the passage as I did. In this case the second operative force was peculiarly private. Over the years I had read Scripture a good bit; I also tried to understand something of the teach-ing of Martin Luther and John Calvin, and recently I had had my first introduction to neo-orthodox Christian anthropology by way of Reinhold Neibuhr's *The Nature and Destiny of Man*. As a result of reflection on my reading about the Christian teaching on sin, and especially the sin of pride, I was partially inclined to accept the account of the human condition that it expressed. I had become acutely conscious of the harm that pride inflicted when it took command of men, and, especially when

[9] J. H. Hexter, *More's Utopia: The Biography of an Idea* (New York, 1965), pp. 80–81 (slightly modified).

it took command of me, of the ravages that it wrought both on me and on others. This is not to suggest that in order for him to sense a certain perspective or perception of life in the person or group he is studying, a historian must actively share that perspective or perception. In the particular case under consideration, however, it actually did happen to help. It does suggest, and I would like to insist, that in his work a historian is likely to find it highly profitable to keep his mind open to any hint of a clue to the actual pattern of the past that comes to him from any place whatever in his second record, no matter how he happened to acquire it. If he does otherwise, he gratuitously deafens and blinds himself in advance on grounds at once dogmatic and irrelevant. In other words, ruminating in the waste of his second record can be a profitable thing for a historian to do.

An examination of what I wrote about More as a result of my two unorthodox excursions into my own second record reveals a curious and significant fact. In nothing that I put into print is there so much as a hint about its relation to those excursions. The range of experience I draw on so heavily gets no credit line at all. This is not to be construed as reluctance on my part to admit to relying on my way of using my second record; to do just that, both to recommend and to defend such reliance, is precisely my purpose in this chapter. What the lack of overt reference to my private and personal experience in the examined instance implies and is intended to imply is that *my* personal experience is not viable evidence about anyone or to anyone but me. However fully persuaded I may be of the actual similarity of More's anxiety and mine about our families, about his perception of the dimensions of sin and mine, I cannot argue that my experience *proves* anything about his, because of course it does not.

This, however, poses a difficult problem for me as a writer of history, especially in my final example (F). Persuaded as I am that my understanding of the record of the past is the correct one, how do I convince others of what I believe to be true? I cannot offer new confirmatory data from hitherto unknown items in the record of the past; I have been quite unable to find any such data. All the data, all that I can cite, have been around since the day *Utopia* was published, and everyone who ever read *Utopia* has seen it. Yet no one who wrote about *Utopia* arrived at the particular conclusions that I arrived at, and many, many came to conclusions quite different from mine. Even more did not come to any clear conclusion at all. If in support of what I believed to be true about the fundamental aim of the imaginary commonwealth More created, citation to my second record is both inappropriate and useless, what is appropriate and useful?

I could, of course, simply array what I consider the relevant texts from *Utopia* and "let them speak for themselves." But this would be a feeble approach to the problem. Once I have persuaded myself of the correctness of my perception of what actually happened, to generate such conviction in others by all legitimate means is my job. What obstacles to doing the job stand in my way? The ineluctable obstacles are a host of second records, those of the readers I seek to convince, each record in many ways different from mine, most of them *terra incognita* to me. To readers of varied and unpredictable cast and habit of mind I need so to present what I believe to be true as to elicit assent.

Although I cannot be sure what the second record of any one of my readers will be like, I can at least classify them by dividing the whole set of readers into subsets:

1. There will be those who have never been aware of or given thought to the particular problem in understanding *Utopia* that I am concerned with.
2. There will be those dimly aware of it who have never felt strongly impelled to seek a solution to it.
3. There will be those already committed to some other solution.

These three subsets comprise the whole set of readers to whom I am adressing myself; but there is another way of classifying them which I very much need to be aware of:

A. There will be those who because of their own experience of and reflection on pride and its relation to the human condition will readily respond to the solution I propose to offer.
B. There will be those who have reflected little or not at all on the matter.
C. There will be those to whom the entire vocabulary of the Christian analysis of the human condition is foreign.
D. In this particular case there will be some who have developed over the years a strong resistance to the whole Christian anthropology, and especially to the Christian teaching on the sin of pride, which is part of it, readers who may be described as culturally or psychically conditioned against what I regard as the correct solution to the problem.

These four subsets also comprise the whole set of readers to whom I am addressing myself. If one thinks of the set of all readers of my book as divided into the first three subsets (1, 2, 3) my problem is to find and present the evidence in support of my argument logically and clearly, and to find counter arguments against the solutions already proposed. Every historian has to cope with this sort of problem when he writes history. If, however, one thinks of the set of the readers above specified as divided into the second subset (A, B, C, D), my problem assumes new dimensions. It can no longer be thought of as wholly responsive to the efficiency of logical argument. I am faced by nonlogical traits already imbedded in my readers' second records either supportive (A) or nonsupportive (B, C, D) to my solution. The only way I can secure the assent I seek from subsets B, C, and D is by effecting an entry into the second records of other men and somehow rectifying them. This is not impossible; in fact, historians have to attempt it all the time, and their attempts are often successful. What follows is a part of my attempt (linked to the passage quoted earlier):

. . . Men only of God's creatures are greedy out of "pride alone, which counts it a glorious thing to pass and excel others in the superfluous and vain ostentation of things." Here, I think, lies the heart of the matter. Deep in the soul of the society of More's day, because it was deep in the soul of all men, was the monster Pride, distilling its terrible poison and dispatching it to all parts of the social body to corrupt, debilitate, and destroy them. Take but a single example: Why must the poor in Europe be "wearied from early in the morning to late in the evening with continual work like laboring and toiling beasts?" What feeds the pleasure that men derive from luxuries and vanities, or to use the phrase of a modern moralist, from conspicuous consumption and conspicuous waste? It is pride. Many men drudge out their lives making vain and needless things because other men "count themselves nobler for the smaller or finer thread of wool" their garb is made of, because "they think the value of their own persons is thereby greatly increased. And therefore the honor, which in a coarse gown they dare not have looked for, they require, as it were of duty, for their finer gowns' sake." . . . The same sickness of soul shows itself in "pride in vain and unprofitable honors." "For what natural or true pleasure doest thou take of another man's bare head or bowed knees? Will this ease the pain of thy knees or remedy the frenzy of thy head?" It is to support [a] prideful "opinion of nobility" that men must be treated like beasts of burden to keep idlers in luxury. The great mass of wastrels bearing down on Christendom are maintained to minister to the pride and vainglory of the great. Such are "the flock of stout and bragging rushbucklers," "the great . . . train of idle and loitering servingmen," that "rich men carry about with them at their tails." Such too are the armies, maintained by those paragons of pride, the princes of Europe, out of the blood and sweat of their subjects, to sustain their schemes of megalomaniac self-glorification. Thus seeking in outward, vain, and wicked things an earthly worship which neither their achievement nor their inner virtue warrants, Christians lure their fellow men into the sin of sloth, or subject them to endless labor, or destroy their substance, their bodies, and their souls too, in futile wars; and over the waste and the misery, over the physical ruin and the spiritual, broods the monster sin of pride.[10]

[10] Ibid., pp. 75–76.

It is easy enough to abstract a structure of logical argument from this passage and the long one earlier quoted.

1. Whenever a man consistently ascribes negative value to a term, it indicates his own negative valuation of what that term represents.
2. Thomas More consistently ascribes negative value to the term "pride."
3. Therefore he set a negative value on pride.

But since the purpose of the passage was only very secondarily to present this simple-minded logical argument, such a reconstruction of it misses the point. Indeed, it misses it in three ways. In the first place, the term "pride" does not occur in all the places from which the quotations in the passage are drawn. Second, in More's description of Utopian institutions from which it is inferred that they are "a great social instrument for the subjugation of pride," the term "pride" itself occurs relatively rarely. And third, the formal logical argument about pride would not serve my whole purpose in any case, since part of that purpose is to establish, so to speak, a hierarchy of negative valuations, to argue that More subordinated the sins of avarice and sloth to the sin of pride. This cannot be done, however, by showing that More always set a negative value on pride, since he also set such a value on avarice and sloth; and it is hardly very revealing to point out that a professed Christian like More is, as Calvin Coolidge once said of a preacher, "against sin."

What is more to the present point than the immanent logic is the manifest vocabulary of the passage. Consider the following words and phrases: "the monster Pride distilling its terrible poison"; "outrageous slavery"; "conspicuous consumption and conspicuous waste"; "drudge out their lives"; "vain and needless things"; "sickness of soul"; "beasts of burden to keep idlers in luxury"; "mass of wastrels"; "blood and sweat of their subjects"; "schemes of megalomaniac self-glorification"; "outward, vain, and wicked things"; "the waste and the misery"; "the monster sin of pride."

If one compares this sort of language with the language of logical argument exemplified above, it does not seem likely that they serve the same or even a similar function. The first is a syllogism *about a particular term and a universal pattern of value assignment*. Its language is the language of logical demonstration, as neutral and nonaffective as care can make it. Its tonality, or rather nontonality, its minimization of affect, is what the literature of the hard sciences, physics and chemistry, achieve nowadays without even having to try (it was not always so), and what many social scientists aspire to in their discourse as an indispensable aid in their drive to approximate the *modus operandi* of the hard sciences. The list of phrases on the other hand is charged, perhaps supercharged; almost every phrase is heavily loaded with affect. For anyone to allege that he was using such phrases without imputation of value would simply be taken as evidence that he was spoofing. Words are a culturally and psychically conditioned means of communication, and one simply cannot discharge by fiat the emotive impact of a phrase like "schemes of megalomaniac self-aggrandizement." Indeed, a successful effort on the part of a reader to do so would utterly defeat the purpose of the writer in choosing the phrase in the first place, which was to select terms so heavily charged with affect that even the most apathetic reader could not slide past them without emotional response. The whole section in which the phrases are imbedded is constructed not on logical, but in a sense, on musical principles. It is not presented as a sequence of logical implications or causal connections but as theme and variations. It starts out after a brief introduction with an announcement of the theme *forte*: "Deep in the soul of the society of More's day, because it was deep in the soul of all men, was the monster pride." From that point the theme is carried through variation after variation; then at the end, "over the waste and the misery, over the physical ruin and the spiritual, broods the monster sin of pride"; a repeat *forte* of the initial theme.

Historians do this sort of thing often in their effort to communicate what they think they know about the past. The rhetoric used is by no means merely decorative; it is functional in relation to the second records of the readers to whom it is directed. Its aim is not mere assimilation of the thesis of the historian into the preexistent structure of those records, but the *modification and extension* of the records themselves to accommodate them to what the historian believes he has learned about the past. In this dimension of his work he has to go beyond the logical apprehensions of his readers, because, until he has prepared the ground for it, logical argument is rootless and footless. In terms of our earlier attempt at classification he is concerned not with subsets 1, 2, 3 but with subsets A, B, C, D, and particularly the last three.

How does a historian use language to overcome kinds of resistance to his views that render logical statement of them ineffectual? Consider again the list of phrases from the passage on pride quoted above. One stands out from and in a way jars against all the rest—"conspicuous consumption and conspicuous waste." This is not my language or Thomas More's; it is the language, familiar to many men, of a recent economic and social philosopher, Thorstein Veblen; he used the two phrases over and over in his *Theory of the Leisure Class* and in many of his other works. Its function in the contrasting setting of a passage heavy with theological overtones is to jolt a reader of one sort, the reader who resists thinking of pride (and perhaps of anything else) in a theological framework. To do so requires him to adjust his habitual set of mind to a set of terms that he is not habituated to or that he is accustomed to regard with suspicion. The introduction of the phrase may hopefully assist him to alter perceptions about human conduct that he readily fits into a pattern around the congenial concepts of conspicuous consumption and conspicuous waste in a way that fits them into a new pattern whose center is the sin of pride.

The function of the historian's language here may best be described as "translational"; it aims to assist the reader to translate his experience from a familiar accepted context into a context strange and perhaps initially repugnant. The *direction* of the translation is as important as its effectiveness. It is translation from the language of social analysis that he knows into a theological language which, given the structure of his second record, he is predisposed to misunderstand. If the rhetorical device used only teaches him to translate the other way, to replace the Christian anthropology of human pride with the modern anthropology of conspicuous consumption and conspicuous waste, it has failed badly. It has led him to apprehend More's sixteenth-century sensitivity to pride in terms of his own sensitivity to a present-day form of social analysis. Instead of augmenting his sense of the past, it has sealed his alliance with the worst enemy of historical thinking—anachronism. Failure of this sort actually extends its ill effects beyond the particular situation that evoked it. The example we are considering was part of a coherent effort on my part to link *Utopia* with its most evident matrix, the mind of Thomas More at the time he wrote the book, and this involved relating it to the kind of Christian humanist that More was in 1515–1516. If my recourse to the language of Thorstein Veblen leads some readers to translate the Christian anthropology of pride into the Veblenian anthropology of conspicuous consumption and conspicuous waste rather than the other way about, I will have done nothing to prepare those readers for the further interplay between what More wrote in his book and his concerns as a Christian humanist. On the contrary, I will have diminished the effect of a cumulative argument by diverting some of its force into an anachronistic channel.

Beyond the group (C) just considered, who have previously given thought to the kinds of human activity that More associated with pride, but who have already filed them in a different, more "up-to-date" filing system, lies another group (B in the preceding analysis) who have not given much serious or orderly thought to such activity at all. For whatever reason, the range of human experience that concerned More has not played much part in such reflection on the human condition as they have engaged in, or quite possibly they are not much addicted to reflecting on the human condition. This does not mean that they have had no scattered perceptions of the sorts of human response that More gathers together under the rubric of the sin of pride; what they lack is not the raw experience but an awareness of the force of More's Christian way of organizing that experience.[11] The highly charged affective language in which I set forth More's view and the whole rhetorical framework within which I expounded it, all aimed at creating in readers a kind of awareness that they may not have had before or at extending and expanding an awareness hitherto rudimentary.

In view of its intent to expand the consciousness of the reader, this use of language by a writer of history may be described as "psychedelic." Here again as in the translational use of language, the aim is to induce in readers a temporary receptivity to a pattern of human response; but it is more than that. The effect of one success in this matter carries over to the next occasion. A reader who has expanded his awareness enough to encompass the idea that More's Christian view of pride led him to reject the whole institutional structure of the European states in his day is more ready than he was before to expand that awareness again to encompass the idea that More felt morally and religiously bound to weigh a call to serve as councilor to his native prince against the obligation of the Christian *literatus* to the Christian commonwealth, the whole church of God on earth. Again hopefully, the language in which I present what I believe to have been the pattern of More's thought, implicit in *Utopia*, in some measure effects this sort of permanent increment in the historical awareness of others. And this sort of intensification of the resources available to them in their second record improves the quality of the judgments on which historians rely for the validation of their efforts to reconstruct historical accounts from fragmentary records of the past.

This last sentence raises in acute form the question of the validation of the statements historians make about the past. For such validation they often or always rely on the judgment of others. Having applied to the record of the past whatever resources they can draw upon from their own second record, they write about what they believe they found out and thereby solicit the assent of others to their views. In a sense, of course, this is like what everyone else attempting the advancement of learning does, because there is really nothing else to do. If we substitute something like "the record of experiment or observation" for "the record of the past," it describes the procedure of scientists as well as historians. The troublesome difference appears when we examine this quest for assent in relation to our analysis of the second records of those whose

---

[11] This, of course, does not mean that all instructed Christians will be disposed to organize that range of experience as More does. It does probably mean that they will find it easier than others to grasp the appropriateness of More's response to his own perceptions.

assent is sought into two sets of subsets. All those second records lie both in the rational-logical subsets (1, 2, 3) and in the alogical-affective subsets (A, B, C, D).

Scientists and would-be scientists ostensibly confine their appeal to the second record to subsets 1, 2, and 3. The very efficacy of such an appeal depends on logical argument, and the efficacy of logical argument in turn depends on the standardization and stabilization of the terms of the argument. Within the logical structure those terms must be "sterilized," made exact and universal, cleared of any affective infection.[12] Historians also appeal to subsets 1, 2, 3. Thus from the whole section in which I set forth the grounds for my judgment about the relation between More's conception of the ideal commonwealth and his convictions about the social destructiveness of pride, it is easy to extract an argument whose formal structure would satisfy the demands of a fairly rigorous logician.[13] The argument would get nowhere, however, with readers in sets B, C, and D. They withhold their assent not on logical grounds but because they remain untouched by the existential minor premise. The notion that an intelligent civilized man could get all that wrought up about the sin of pride is alien to them. Until they can make sense of the notion that a very intelligent, highly civilized man *could* make the sin of pride the active ingredient in his social analysis, they cannot in any way be persuaded by a logical argument which depends on his actually having done so. So if not logically or chronologically prior, the assent of readers in subsets B and C, and D, must be psychologically prior to their assent as members of subsets 1, 2, and 3. And therefore except for the A's who will enjoy the benefit of immediate conversion, the translational and psychedelic use of affective language in this particular instance becomes an indispensable condition of validation of a historian's statement about the past.

Historians then use language translationally and psychedelically not merely because "history is an art," but as an indispensable means for communicating knowledge about the past, as an integral part of the proof of their statements about it. As a result of the impact of the translational and psychedelic language on their second record, readers indeed learn things about what happened in the past that they could not learn otherwise; that impact actually achieves an expansion of the reader's understanding.

Nor is the kind of learning involved strange, mysterious, and mystical; it is a familiar phenomenon in all the areas of human understand-

---

[12] Note that this is what was done with the word "pride," ordinarily heavily charged with affect, in the "logical" argument above (p. 103). It is reduced to a "term" and thus becomes *formally* interchangeable with any other term with which one chooses to replace it; for example, in this instance with "love" or "curds and whey."

[13] Hexter, *More's Utopia*, pp. 74–81.

ing where the extension of understanding does not depend entirely upon logical discourse and proof—the understanding of music, for example, or painting, or one's friends. We speak of learning to appreciate, to set the right price or value on, a particular quartet or even a whole musical style like the Baroque, a painting by Monet, or the whole school of Impressionism. What goes on in effective instruction in music and art appreciation is the expansion of the consciousness of the learner so that he can take in an experience hitherto alien to him because of its strangeness; what he will, hopefully, have achieved at the end is not only a *reception* of that experience but a *receptivity* to a whole range of new experiences and perhaps a permanent alertness that will enable him to respond to experiences even beyond that range. In the same sense the psychedelic and translational language used in the passage we have been analyzing may have extended the consciousness of some readers to a point where they not only became aware that a man like More might well have pivoted his social thinking around the sin of pride but also found themselves prepared to accept the idea that he was likely to have been impelled in all the crucial decisions he faced to refer to his Christian commitment.

In all this there seems to be nothing especially strange or perplexing. What is perplexing and has, I think, created a good deal of the perplexity about history, is that those who write it well have often maintained relatively high standards of rigor in their vocabulary, in their testing of evidence, and in the structure of their discourse in some parts of what they write while resorting freely to heavily charged rhetoric, highly affective and emotive, in others. Moreover, they do not keep these rhetorical modes neatly compartmented; on the contrary they often shift between the two from paragraph to paragraph, and even in the same paragraph from sentence to sentence.

One final point. We have just analyzed what historians sometimes do in order to reach into the second records of those whose assent they require to validate their accounts of the past. Several times in that analysis I used the word "hopefully" about their own expectations as to the effectiveness of their rhetoric. The word was intended to suggest that when historians deploy their rhetoric translationally or psychedelically rather than for logical discourse they cannot be certain of the result. What historians fear in these circumstances is not only what the scientist fears when he presents his work for validation or rejection by his public. The scientist may be concerned about the accuracy of his experimental results, the design of his experimental procedure, or the logic of his inferences from his results. He is not much afraid of being misunderstood but of being understood only too well and found wrong. Historians may fear this too. More than this, however, they are, or well ought to be, uncertain about whether their translational and psychedelic rhetoric communicates what they intend for it to communicate. This uncertainty is inherent in the very nature of the enterprise. In both kinds of rhetoric, scientific and translational-psychedelic, the targets lie in the second records of the readers, since in fact, except for the mind of God who presumably already knows the answers, no other target exists. But on the appropriate forms of rhetoric for logical discourse there is a high degree of public consensus. The second records of each mentally competent reader may therefore be presumed to be uniform and ready formally, if not substantially, to assign to the language the writer uses precisely the values he intended his sign system to convey. The historian's elaboration of his argument will also take place within the boundary rules of logical discourse which he can reasonably expect his readers to know or recognize as *the* rules. He may even properly demand such knowledge as a sort of price of admission, a prerequisite for the further knowledge that he stands ready to impart.

With respect to matters for which he uses language psychedelically and translationally, however, he can feel no such confidence as he does in the former case. He is aiming not at a target sharply defined in the second record of his readers, but at a blurry area differing in dimension and arrangement from one reader to the other. Precision firing under such circumstances is meaningless since there is no precise common target to fire at, self-defeating since an arbitrarily restrictive definition of the target area by the historian may result in his missing in the second record of others the very communication centers he is trying to reach. In such a case his proper rhetorical tactic, therefore, is not to fire rifle shots through telescopic sights. Rather he needs to lay down a rolling verbal barrage of high-explosive words with a very high fragmentation component. He can only hope, but cannot know, that some of the fragments will find lodgment in the second records of people he is aiming at, and force on those people the reorganization of their thinking that will achieve his purpose. His choice of language is governed by his experience of previous good and ill fortune in like situations and by his sense of the sort of rhetoric that would affect his own second record in the particular case that concerns him. To call such a procedure uncertain and scatter-shot is accurately to describe both the situation and the only effective means a historian has for attaining his purpose in that situation. God help him; he can not do otherwise and still do justice to his own understanding of the past.

CHAPTER V: Galloping Gertie and the Insurance Companies, *or Analysis and Story in History*

Argument over history, what it is, and what historians do or ought to do has taken a somewhat different course among historians than it has among philosophers. As we have seen, in recent years philosophers have mainly occupied themselves with the problem of explanation "why" in history. During roughly the same period historians have been trying to measure up the relative value and status of what they call analytical history against what they call narrative history. The "new wave" historians mainly pride themselves on what they describe as their analytical approach, and tend to regard those whom they describe as narrative historians as fuddy-duddies.[1] Paradoxically at the very same time analytical philosophers of several varieties discovered that historians tell stories which make things about the past more intelligible. They then tried to discover the structure of "narrative explanation," regarding it as the characteristic mode of explanation "why" in history. Since instead of engaging in dialogue with each other, philosophers and historians at least in the English-speaking world have long had the habit of simultaneous monologue, the noncommunication between them is neither surprising nor new. It does, however, confirm an occasional impression of mine that some leaders of fashion in history have a rather special gift for leaping aboard intellectually sinking ships and drawing their innocent followers along with them.

---

[1] In France a similar assault has been mounted against what are there called *"historiens historisants."* One can but admire the *panache*, or just plain brass, of a school of historians ready to take up arms against their colleagues who indulge in *"historizing."* See J. H. Hexter "Some American Observations," *Journal of Contemporary History*, 2 (1967): 5–21, esp. 18–21.

All historians who use the term "historical analysis" do not use it in the same sense. Moreover, it is by no means always clear that every historian using the term "analytical" has a very good notion of what he himself has in mind. The enormous choice in modes of analysis that the combination of variation and vagueness has left open has made the whole business of analysis an enormous smorgasbord at which only the most primitive writers of history, composing improving tales for readers in their nonage, could fail to find a mode of procedure suited to their taste that would pass one or another of the not very exacting tests for analysis.[2] As long as theoretical obeisance to analysis does not actually prevent a historian from doing what he needs to do with the portion of the record of the past that concerns him, as long as it does not prevent him from asking whatever questions are likely to elicit the best account of the past he is capable of rendering, it matters very little how he chooses to label his work; and if to label it "analytical" affords him spiritual consolation, he is to be congratulated on the sweet simplicity of his beatitude.

The trouble is that one cannot be at all sure that such a blessed state of nomenclatural-*cum*-methodological innocence will continue indefinitely. At some point it may occur simultaneously to a good many historians that their common commitment to analysis should have common consequences in practice and method, not merely in interstitial declamation. Indeed there are signs that a crisis of this sort may not be far off. For several years *History and Theory* has been publishing the pasquinades of philosophizing historians and historizing philosophers, and some historians have been reading them. A few years ago philosophers and historians lived together for several days in a common symposium during an assignation arranged by Professor Sidney Hook. The brief cohabitation produced a mutual rapport no greater[3] than the more protracted but less intense intercourse under the covers of *History and Theory*. Nevertheless the danger now exists that sooner or later some eager beaver historian who likes to gnaw away at timber along the section of the intellectual stream where history and philosophy converge will bring together the utterances of historians in support of historical analysis and analytic history. Then he or someone else will notice that they are not uttering the same or similar statements, that the objects of their discourse (historical analyses) lack formal common traits, and that

[2] C. V. Wedgewood with gentle and demure obstinacy has insisted that she writes narrative history and does not think it necessarily a bad (or even terribly inferior) thing to do. But for her mild intransigence, just a little semantical maneuvering could have brought her book, *The King's Peace 1637–1641* (New York, 1955), into the broad shelter and sanctuary of analysis.

[3] Rather the contrary. See Sidney Hook, ed., *Philosophy and History* (New York, 1963) and especially the remarks of Leonard Krieger, pp. 136–142 and Bernard Bailyn, pp. 92–101.

therefore discussion of analysis hitherto has produced some noise but
little communication.

From this point on, the fat will be in the fire. The quest will begin
for a common conception of analysis as against story, and if that
happens the course of development is predictable to a point close to
certainty. A few years of discussion will produce a pained awareness in
analytical historians that, like so many ad hoc allies, they have been
bound together solely by repugnance to a common enemy—"narrative
history," or history as story; that analytical history has hitherto been but
a residual category like "anti-Catholic." Then, since analytical history is
"essentially" or "basically" antistory history, they will first have to discover the common substantive traits of stories in order to make out
what analytical historians object to. The most obvious common trait of
historical stories is that often their coherent connections depend on precise collocations of times, places, and persons: "On October 14, 1066,
William the Bastard's army of adventurers encountered the Anglo-
Saxon force led by Harold at Hastings"; "While James I was off hunting, on April 2, 1604, the members of the House of Commons produced
a defence of their privilege that made things difficult for him and his
advisers." "In France the crown had ceased effectively to be elective
and become hereditary by the end of the eleventh century."

Such being the way history as story often works, analytical history,
being what stories are not, must depend minimally for its coherence on
the collocation of persons, places, and times. On this view of matters, it
is desirable to avoid explanations that point to things happening sometime, somewhere, to someone because he was who he was, where he
was, when he was, with whom he was. The collocations survive in the
record of the past. If one breaks history down into historical explanation, historical explanation into explanation "why," explanation "why"
into causal explanation, and causal explanation into explanation by
"factors," however, one can render quite negligible the impact on one's
own perception, of such collocations.

To the extent that historians enamored of analysis have not already
arrived intuitively at this reduction, the logic of their position must
drive them to it. For the historian who takes his commitment to historical analysis seriously "factor analysis" is where the action is. It most
effectively breaks up the most common bases of coherence and order in
stories—orderly sequence of time,[4] stability of place or intelligible
movement among places, continuity of identifiable persons. Factor
analysis presupposes and breeds subfactors without stated limit. Sup-

[4] This of course does not mean that in telling historical stories historians maintain a strict chronological sequence from the beginning of the story to the end,
with each statement falling further along the time axis than the preceding statement. Such rigidity is as rare as it is disastrous in storytelling.

pose one is engaged in an analysis of the factors that caused the French Revolution. Clearly it will not do merely to say that the French Revolution was caused by social, economic, political, military, religious, etc., factors. One has to specify something or some things under each of those rubrics, so that one gets at least:

I. Economic factors
   A.
   B.
   C. etc.
II. Political factors
   A. etc.

But one can surely press analysis further than this. Example:

I. Economic
   A. Demographic
      1. Rural
      2. Urban
   B. Industrial
      1. Large scale
         a. Extractive
            i. Owners
            ii. Work force
         b. Processing
      2. Small scale etc.
   C. Mercantile

If one commits oneself to an analysis by factors of the causes of the French Revolution there seems to be no *prima facie* reason why the breakdown into subfactors should not be pushed to the fifth degree or even beyond. And if one measure of the excellence of analysis is its difference from a story, the more degrees the better, since each degree further dissolves connections among and through persons and times and places, which are the sinews of history as story. This analytical procedure in fact involves those who adopt it in a further commitment of which they may not be aware. They have bound themselves to produce not only *a* causal explanation, but a particular kind of causal explanation, one whose standard of adequacy derives from the notion of sufficient cause or sufficient conditions.

There is a strong tradition identifying causal explanation with the eliciting of sufficient cause or causes. Some philosophers and more historians tend to regard the setting forth of sufficient causes as the standard for wholly adequate and satisfactory causal historical explanation "why." Such a standard is quite unnecessary and quite arbitrary; it is in hopeless conflict with what any historian (Everyman or the professional) well knows about explanation "why" in history. By sliding into the sufficient-cause syndrome, historical analysis makes the satisfactory explanation "why" of some explicable things about the past appear impossible. This illusion of impossibility leads some historians to throw up their hands in a humiliated *"ignoramus,"* in the face of problems of explanation of a kind that they themselves have managed quite competently for a long time. In justice to themselves they might do well to avoid so stultifying a commitment.

If it is to be more than empty verbiage, factor analysis requires a historian to set out the factors that made the phenomenon to be explained precisely what it was, and to do this the factors must be not only necessary but sufficient to make it precisely what it was. This is an invitation to explanatory disaster. The historian will have to ask whether all the causes or subfactors under each rubric, taken together, constitute a sufficient cause or the sufficient conditions for the event. But such conditions are ordinarily so generalized that they can be shown to have been present before the event that they are supposed to explain happened. Thereupon one is stuck with the question why the event waited to happen beyond the time when the sufficient conditions were all there. Or to put the matter another way, any time interval between the presence of the factors and the occurrence of the event for which they are supposed to be the sufficient conditions simply demonstrates that, as they have been stated, they were *not* sufficient during the interval.

Historians stuck with a sufficient-cause form of historical explanation in a situation where it will not work conceal their confusion from themselves as well as others. Factors like rise (or fall) of rents, pressure of population, persecution of the opposition, repression of dissent imply quantities. The difficulty, remember, is to explain why an event sat around *not* taking place immediately, although all the necessary factors were present. Historians escape it by saying that until the event happened the factors were not present with sufficient force or in sufficient quantity.

Instead of getting historians out of their trouble with sufficient-cause explanation, however, this only gets them in more deeply. Often they have to admit that they do not know what the statistics on these matters actually were in the crucial series of years, months, and days. Moreover, it is hard to define overpopulation and poverty, much less oppression and persecution, in a way that makes those terms useful in explanation by factor analysis. It tempts historians to talk about the "weights" to be assigned to the various "factors" and about the increased weight of this or that factor, when there is not a single hard statistic at hand to cover the nakedness of their argument. Paradoxically, the situation is some-times still worse when there are statistics available. By draping the statistical veil skillfully over an argument, it is possible to conceal its distortion and pitiful thinness. The effort to bring statistical support for sufficient-cause explanation by factor analysis in history does, however, get to the heart of the problem of such explanation. With respect to it the philosophers like Hempel and historians who insist on statistics and quantification are simply right; the whole argument reposes on the supposition of quantification. The language of sufficient-cause expla-nation is shot through with terms presupposing quantities. The terms are not merely metaphorical. Sufficient-cause explanation is structur-ally a rigid balance between quantities of factors and the event. Until all of the factors are present in sufficient quantity, presumably the event does not pop up; when they are so present it must pop up pronto.

To offer a very crude example, suppose one were to analyze the factors in the outbreak of the French Revolution into a political, a religious, an economic, and a social factor; and to specify the factors for example: political, the incompetence of Louis XVI; religious, the monopoly of high church office by the aristocracy; economic, the poverty of the peasantry; social, the disaffection of the privileged orders from the monarchy. The trouble with the analysis, not in terms of sub-stance, but formally and functionally, is that Louis was a political idiot, the nobility had a corner on bishoprics, the peasantry was down at the heels, and privileged bodies were cutting up rough before 1789 or even 1787. Therefore the factors specified may perhaps be necessary to explain the Revolution, but they are not sufficient because, if they were, the Revolution would have happened before it did. Note that no in-crease of the mere number of factors (or subfactors) will break through this bind, because the added factor will suffer from the same defect as those previously listed; they will have been present before the Revolution began, and will therefore leave an unintelligible gap, a sort of historical vacuum, between the time when they are all present and the outbreak of the Revolution.

It is this awkward situation that accounts for the equally awkward expedient that historians committed to factor analysis sometimes adopt to overcome it—the division of causes into "underlying" and "immedi-ate." Usually, their historical tact or intuition provides them with the message decoded above. They sense that somehow their factors do not "add up" to the event they are trying to explain. They then throw a bridge across the unfortunate interval or gap that their factor analysis leaves in their explanation by turning from "underlying" to "immediate" causes. But given their tacit commitment to analysis, the immediate-cause ploy will not do. For on scrutiny the "immediate causes" turn out to be a story.[5] The "narrative history," driven out the front door with appropriate anathemas, exorcisms, and warnings never again to profane the Temple of Clio, is surreptitiously smuggled in the back window, and the pretense is somehow maintained that it is really not there.

In theory this is all that needs be said on the matter of underlying and immediate causes; the distinction does not make it actually feasible to supplant story by analysis in history and it does not rescue analytical historians from the trap of sufficient-cause explanation latent in factor analysis. In practice, however, the distinction is helpful though ambivalent. On the positive side it serves as an inelegant but useful fiction. Some historians have a penchant for making theoretical commitments without quite understanding their implications. The distinction between underlying factors and immediate causes affords such historians the harmless comfort of feeling that they are out there doing factor analysis in the pioneering vanguard of their profession without tempting them in their daily work to do anything particularly foolish, anything that a historian in fair command of his senses would not do anyhow. This is all to the good. It does obscure, however, a truly serious historiographic problem: how best to intermesh story and analysis in historical discourse. That is one drawback of the fiction of immediate causes; it gives historians an excuse for quitting just when the going gets hard.

There is a danger too that historians will identify the fiction for what it is—a fiction. When an unduly solemn analytic historian, trapped by the notion that sufficient-cause explanation is the only adequate sort of explanation "why" in history, identifies the fiction, he teeters on the brink of recognizing that sufficient-cause explanation intrinsically requires quantification. The obvious inference from his two premises is that for most sensible historical "why" questions historians will never have adequate answers. If one is under the illusion that causal explanation is all there is to knowing history, and that all causal explanation requires the statement of sufficient conditions, the whole historical enterprise takes on a vesture of excessively laborious futility. Rightly persuaded that sufficient-cause explanation has to be quantitative, some historians convince themselves that the quantities they can find in the record or can reconstruct from it are the ones that are required to provide a sufficient-cause explanation of what they want to explain. On the face of it this is merely a hallucination, an unwarranted act of faith, since especially up to very recent times there is not a reason in the world why the absurdly erratic operations that have determined the recording of retrievable quantities and their survival in the record of

[5] For a classic example of this maneuver, see S. B. Fay, *Origins of the World War* (New York, 1928).

the past should have converged in just the way that suits the needs and convenience of present-day historians dedicated to historical explanation by factor analysis.

Some of the perplexity about the inadequacy of historical explanation "why" for events like the outbreak of the French Revolution promptly vanishes if we simultaneously abandon sufficient-cause and factor analysis in the places where they are inapplicable. In some instances there are good reasons for doing this on theoretical grounds independently of any empirical testing of the failure of sufficient-cause, factor-analysis explanation, although, of course, in those instances an empirical test will always confirm the conclusion based on theory. There are two interdependent reasons for the theoretical deficiency of this sort of explanation in history.

First, although sufficient-cause explanation by factor analysis is a quantitative form of explanation and implies mathematical operations, the only operation it ever actually contemplates in the ultimate step of explanation is the conjunction of positive quantities. It rarely gets as far as a simple casting of accounts, which would indicate the need for subtraction.[6] In causal-historical explanations purportedly analytical in mode, what historian has ever systematically taken into consideration all the factors that weighed *against* the event—the French Revolution, the American Civil War—happening, arrived at a quantitative determination, and tried to figure whether at the time of the event the determined quantity underbalanced or overbalanced the factors on the other side of the ledger? A certain intuitive sense of possible disaster has doubtless discouraged historians from so rash an experiment. For think how embarrassing it would be if, after striking the balance, it came out that the French Revolution did not get underway in 1789 or the American Civil War in 1861! Suppose on striking the balance of factors they did not happen at all or happened five years earlier. Surely some effort of this subtractive sort seems almost a prerequisite of factor analysis. For if the mere presence of all the factors necessary to cause the French Revolution are not sufficient to cause it, it is conceivable that they were counterbalanced by other factors that inhibited their operation—prejudice against social upheaval, for example, or the attractions of a fairly well-defined social pecking order, or the restraints of habit. And then one would want to inquire by what quantities these factors diminished to tip France over into the Revolution.

Those who practice factor analysis in the wrong places in history might well consider extending their repertoire to include the weighing factors that worked against the event happening, and striking a balance. To do so might have considerable tactical advantages. It

[6] Econometric history is, as far as I know, a unique and partial exception to this rule.

would permit them, Pooh-Bah fashion, to "add a touch of artistic verisimilitude to an otherwise bald and unconvincing" analysis. Because he already knows that the events which concern him actually did happen when they happened, all the historical practitioner of factor analysis needs to do is dump additional loads of fictitious nonquantative "weight" into a few of his do-it-yourself factor boxes until the balance tips the way he already knows it has to go. Since most of his weights have been of this nonquantitative sort all along, and are available to him in limitless though imaginary supply, this should not occasion him serious malaise. Given his knowledge that the event indeed did take place when it did, he is playing a game he cannot lose, though it may give him some slight pause to realize that he cannot win either without actual cheating.[7]

The form of causal explanation in history we are considering has a further deficiency. Because of its very form, sufficient-cause factor analysis destroys just those connections by means of which historians can and often do transcend a merely incremental conception of causal explanation. The connections are those provided by the interrelations of times, places, persons, and circumstances. These interrelations make possible the often extremely intricate connectings of bits of the record of the past into what in a deceptively simple-sounding term is called a "story." The whole tendency of analysis, is, as we have seen, to dissolve and destroy these tendons and ligaments that hold historical stories together. The consequences of this dissolution and destruction, of this emancipation of explanation from story is, as we have also seen, the not unusual consequence of emancipation: the freed explanation refuses to work for its emancipator, the analytical historian. Theoretically freed, actually bound rigidly into the analytical sufficient-cause mold, time after time explanations of events simply will not "add up," which is just what the mold requires them to do if they are to count as explanations at all. An Historian who has accepted historical storytelling as a worthy professional activity and who does not deem it inherently inferior to historical analysis for the purpose of explanation "why" does not worry about things adding up. His outlook gives him a chance to sense the force of the togetherness of events. He knows that they do not always just add up; sometimes they sort of multiply or build up. That was the way it was with Galloping Gertie.

Gertie committed suicide on November 7, 1940. In the end that had to be the verdict. Of course there were extenuating circumstances. She was under very considerable tension from the outside world. The likes

---

[7] That this is precisely how I would shuffle out of any explanatory bind that a misapplied factor analysis got me into occurred to me in a flash of inspiration engendered by alcoholic imbibition seventeen years ago. I have avoided the terms "factor" and "causal analysis" ever since.

of her often are sooner or later, and sometimes they break under it. Then it is fair to say that the outside tension destroyed them. But not Gertie. At the outset, the men most intimate with her (and there were a good number of such men) believed and thought they had good reason to believe that she was strong enough to bear the outside stresses and strains she was called on to endure. When she began to show signs of serious instability some of these men tried to help and to give her strength and support; but they were too late. Still it would not be true to say that she was simply a victim of her environment. Her environment alone did not destroy her; in the end she destroyed herself. So when she plunged into the turbulent waters of Puget Sound years ago, it was her own act, even though it was not an act of her will. Strictly, it could not be an act of will, because Gertie had no will. Gertie was a bridge.

The Tacoma Narrows Bridge linked the city of Tacoma to the east with the Olympic Peninsula on the west side of Puget Sound. On November 7, 1940, in a high and gusty wind of about forty miles an hour, the roadway of the bridge was undulating in that up-and-down wave motion which already had given the span the nickname, Galloping Gertie. Just before 10:00 A.M. the undulation suddenly stopped. A few moments later the roadway began to twist. Very soon it was writhing irregularly up to forty-five degrees on either side of its "normal" horizontal position. No concrete paving could long bear the stress of oscillation of such magnitude. The twisting continued. In half an hour a small section of the roadway slab dropped from the center of the bridge. Still the structure's contortions continued undiminished. At 11:00 A.M. a quarter of the suspended deck plunged into the sound. Ten minutes later almost all of the rest of the pavement of the central span, two thousand feet of it, followed. Such was the end of the Tacoma Narrows Bridge.

From the time she began to take customers on July 1, 1940, to the time of her fall, Galloping Gertie survived for just 130 days. She was longer in gestation—almost two years from the beginning of construction to opening. Much longer than both was the period of inquiry and inquest into her precipitate and dramatic demise. This was inevitable. From bridge designers to structural steel workers the time and energy of many men had gone into her construction. Millions of dollars went to the bottom of Puget Sound with her in her suicidal plunge. Moreover, her dark doom gave one pause to think about other suspension bridges, members of Gertie's family. There were older ones of long-tried stability, such as the spans across the East River from the Williamsburgh Bridge south to the Brooklyn Bridge, and young ones such as the Golden Gate and the Cross Bay Bridges in San Francisco, the George Washington and the Triboro in New York. There was also Gertie's

beautiful sister, the Whitestone Bridge, brainchild of the same engineer
Moiseeff. Several of her near contemporaries, notably the George Washington, had displayed a solidity under all stresses including enormous
live loads (traffic) and high winds (the hurricane of 1938), that commanded the utmost confidence. In immediate retrospect, what happened
to Gertie, however, gave an ominous cast, in the outcome unwarranted,
to a slight tremulousness of the Golden Gate Bridge and especially to
some early skittishness of Gertie's sister, the Whitestone. Finally, to be
considered was the generation of suspension bridges yet unborn, and
the interest of the members of the public in not crossing bridges likely
to kill them. (By an almost incredible stroke of fortune, in engineering
terms the "live load" on the Narrows Bridge when it failed was one car.
Its human occupant had managed to make his way off the center span
to safety after torsional oscillation began. The sole living creature that
went with Gertie on her death plunge was the car owner's dog.) [8]

The inquest on the Tacoma Narrows Bridge began even before it was
open to traffic, *in ovo*, as it were. The deck had early manifested that
inclination to undulate (oscillate in the vertical plane, as engineers put
it) that was to make a trip from Tacoma to the Olympic Peninsula
uncomfortably like a brief sea voyage on dry land. From that time early
in 1940 concerned engineers began systematically to keep an eye on
their ward. The record of the behavior of the Narrows Bridge remained
under close scrutiny until 1952. The first preliminary report on the
bridge failure, to the administrator of the Federal Public Works
Agency, appeared in March 1941. The third and last part of the final
official report appeared in June 1952. Professor Farquharson of the
University of Washington, who was on hand with a movie camera on
November 7, 1940 and recorded in film the last catastrophic hour of
Galloping Gertie's life, wrote most of the report's third part. That part
also contains a chapter by Professors von Kármán and Dunn of the
California Institute of Technology. The former had previously produced what ultimately came to be accepted by engineers as the correct
explanation of the failure of the Tacoma Narrows Bridge. What follows
is a modified engineer's explanation. It is modified to render it intelligible to those who, like me, are not engineers. The modifications, therefore, are all in the direction away from what an engineer would regard
as an optimum explanation, that is the explanation one engineer would
offer to another. [9]

[8] He refused to leave the car despite the courageous effort of Professor
Farquharson, the most dedicated of all Tacoma-bridge-watchers, to save him.
[9] I am indebted to Professor Gjelsvik of the Department of Engineering and
Applied Science of Yale University for aid and advice on the explanation. I
elicited a first approximation of it from him by asking him how an engineer would
answer, if he were asked by another engineer, "Why did the Tacoma Narrows
Bridge fail?" Tempering his answer to the shorn lamb, he immediately turned his

In three sentences the engineers' explanation goes this way. The failure of the Tacoma Narrows Bridge was a consequence of its aerodynamic instability. The bridge was carried over the threshold into self-excited torsional oscillation by wind vortices which the upwind or leading edge of its stiffening girders shed. Beyond that critical threshold the movement of the members of the structure that generated torsional oscillation were self-excited and increased indefinitely in amplitude until they passed the capacity of the parts of the system (especially the paving of the deck) to bear the stresses they created. Put in crude terms Gertie indeed destroyed herself, not by galloping or undulating as she had been doing without peril for several months, but by going into an uncontrollable convulsive twist.

Most readers will be as ill-versed in the inner workings of bridges as I was until recently. To make it clear to them what happened to the Tacoma Narrows Bridge during its last hours, some elaboration is necessary. First, the common structural members of suspension bridges are: (1) two cables, (2) two towers, (3) the suspenders or stringers, and (4) the deck (pp. 122). The two spun wire cables carry the dead weight of the deck which hangs from and is held to them by wire suspenders. The cables, anchored into concrete bases on both banks, pass through openings at the tops of the towers and sag parallel to each other on both sides of both towers. The shoreward sags carry the side spans of the deck or bridge floor. From the water side of both towers the cables sag in parallel curves, the lowest points of which lie at the midpoint of the center span of the deck.

All bridges should be so designed as to be capable of bearing the stresses and strains of their own dead weight plus any additional stresses and strains that external forces are likely to impose on them.[10] Traditionally, engineers used to take three external forces into consideration: (1) water pressures on the bases of the towers, (2) wind velocities on the bridge surfaces, and (3) "live load," that is, the traffic that moves over the deck of the bridge. Under these stresses a suspension bridge must remain stable within the limits necessary for its use. It is therefore constructed to resist stresses (rigidity) or to yield to them

---

language away from the mathematical formulations he actually would have used if he had been indeed explaining to an engineer, and without taking all the technical thrust from his explanation, he tried to bring it within the range of my uninformed grasp. Professor Gjelsvik further referred me to the reports on official inquiries into the bridge failure. From these two hard sources I quarried whatever my poor technical equipment enabled me to and used it to give additional support to the initial understanding that I gained from Professor Gjelsvik.

[10] Obviously, the "are likely" here is a loose term. Bridge designers do not take into account stresses imposed by direct bomb hits on the deck or by explosions of dynamite on the towers. Yet both "are likely" in times of war.

only within acceptable limits (flexibility). The system of moving or dynamic forces of a suspension bridge affects all its members; that is to say, all four members move. The movements that most concern those who use the bridge are the ones perceptible to them as they cross its deck from end to end—that is the movements of the deck itself. Engineers distinguish three kinds of movement, or as they say, three modes of oscillation, in the deck—horizontal or lateral, vertical, and

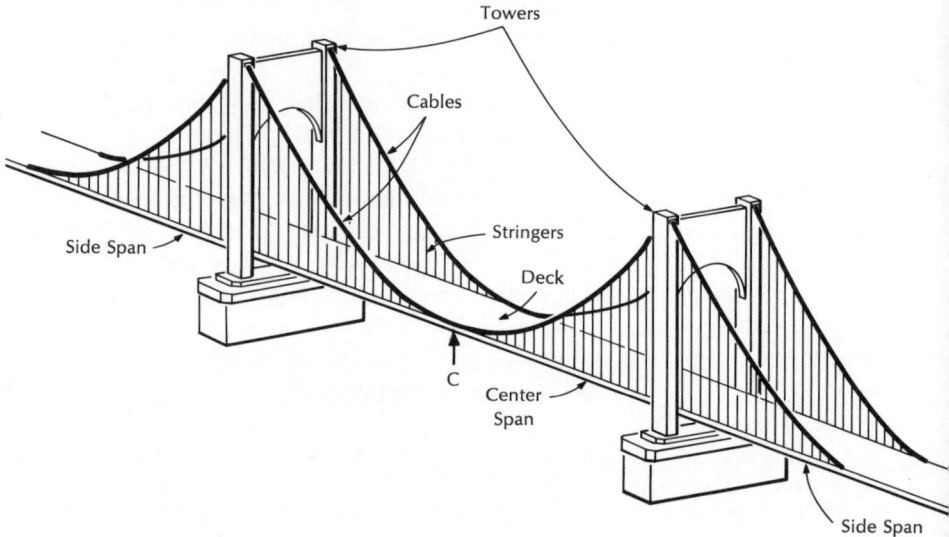

Figure 2

torsional. A high wind will press on the surfaces of a bridge in the direction in which it is blowing and will impart a bend to it in that direction. This is the horizontal mode of oscillation. Live loads unevenly distributed over the deck of the bridge from end to end will depress the areas of the deck where they are concentrated. Moreover, they will send waves of movement along the deck as it adjusts to the progression of live loads across it. These are in the vertical mode of oscillation. Finally, on any suspension bridge carrying two-way traffic the live load may be distributed unevenly on the opposite sides of the deck's roadway. If for example jobs are on the north end of a bridge and homes on the south, the stream of traffic will be heavy on the east side of the roadway in the morning and on the west side in the late afternoon.

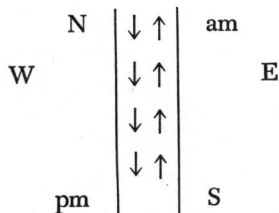

```
            N   │ ↓ ↑ │  am
      W         │ ↓ ↑ │        E
                │ ↓ ↑ │
                │ ↓ ↑ │
          pm    │     │  S
```

Figure 3

This imbalance will twist the deck somewhat on the side of heavy loading. This twisting of the bridge engineers call oscillation in the torsional
mode.

On the Tacoma Narrows Bridge it was uncomfortably evident, as it
had been less uncomfortably evident on earlier spans, that wind did not
just bend bridges in proportion to its velocity in the direction it was
blowing. It also caused them to oscillate in the vertical mode. The
windstream slipped unevenly under and over the deck, bearing down
on the paving at some points, pressing up at others and setting it into an
up-and-down motion. That was why even before it carried a live load,
Galloping Gertie galloped. On some suspension bridges these wind-
impelled oscillations were dampened by the sheer dead weight of suspended structure. On other lighter bridges, engineers had floored the
deck with open-lattice metal which they left unpaved. The uneven
windstream therefore, passed freely between the upper and underside
of the bridge floor, as it would pass through a sail made of fish net,
automatically equalizing its own vertical force. When they put solid
paving on the decks of light bridges, engineers added stiffening
members to dampen vertical undulations. These added members were
either deep, heavy, and open-lattice trusses or lighter narrow plate
girders running in a band along each side of the deck. On the Narrows
Bridge the girder sections were too light to produce much dampening
effect.

The relation of these girders to the wind was, however, more complex than that. Bridge engineers had always treated wind as a static
load although not a constant one. That is to say they conceived of the
wind as a force increasing uniformly with its velocity. Therefore they
computed wind stress on bridges as a smooth curve.

They were wrong. When it bounces off surfaces, especially off flat
and angular surfaces a steady windstream ceases to be smooth and
becomes chaotic. Especially it forms vortices, in effect miniature cy-
clones or whirlwinds of rotating air. On subsequent impact with a solid
bridge deck, the force of such vortices is of a magnitude radically

different from the overall velocity of the windstream, and variations in vortical points of impact result in highly variable rather than steady stresses. The leading edge of the stiffening plate girders of the Tacoma Bridge, flat and angular, were especially likely to generate and shed vortices in intricate patterns. Those patterns did not vary smoothly with the velocity of a free moving windstream but with its angle of attack and the angularities of the structure at the points of initial impact.

From the aerostatic model of bridges as engineers hitherto had conceived them, none of this irregularity entered into the stress estimates in bridge design. It did enter into the aerodynamic estimates of designers of airplane wings. So did an occasional catastrophic consequence of vortex shedding by the leading edge of a plane wing—"flutter." Once the torsional oscillation, the twisting under vortical stress, or flutter, of a wing reached a critical amplitude, it might continue, self-excited, to increase without limit, until the wing tore itself apart. The continuous shallow steel band of girders used to stiffen the Tacoma Narrows Bridge turned it into something like an extended ill-constructed airplane wing. The girders were too light effectively to dampen oscillation of the bridge in any mode. Their design tended to maximize the irregular shedding of vortices on to the top and the bottom of the narrow deck, imparting to a "wing" 2,800 feet long and only 39 feet wide an erratic lift and drag pattern. Given both the lightness of the center span and its extreme length in proportion to its breadth, it was only a matter of time until that span was carried across the threshold into self-excited twisting, and thence to self-destruction. The time was November 7, 1940.

In structures less fragile than Galloping Gertie, yet capable of some equivalent of self-excited torsional oscillation of amplitudes increasing without limit—and I suspect that almost all structured interrelations of men are analogues to such systems—questions of where and when particular "factors" made an impact on the structure become crucial to an explanation of "failure." Yet as we have seen, in the interest of specious generality and gross quantification, rigorous analysis into factors tends precisely to obscure collocations and synchronisms, the "merely historical" in the past. Finally, the quest for factor "inputs" of a magnitude equal to the "output" of change is not profitable, if what the factors are put into is a dynamic system with a potential for self-escalation into self-destructive torsional oscillation. This clearly applies to Galloping Gertie's last hour during which she was supplying all the energy necessary to achieve her own disruption. It is equally applicable in such ordinary human situations as family quarrels, as is commonly said, "over nothing," and perhaps of revolutions.

That last common phrase, "over nothing," raises a question worth some pondering. A "quarrel over nothing" lies in the range of experience of almost everyone. There can be few people who have never been involved in such silly brawls. So the notion of a quarrel over nothing is likely to have a place in everyone's second record, and one man's notion of such a quarrel is likely to be reasonably congruent with another's. All of us have had the experience of a quarrel over nothing getting out of hand. We understand both the event and the common language used to describe it, and we do not imagine for a moment that "nothing" is a mathematical expression to be equated with zero. Given the peculiarities of the record of the past with which we have previously dealt,[11] and given the inherent instabilities of many human relations, is it not conceivable that such relations are more readily explained by means of the plasticities, complexities, and sublteties of common language in which one can write, with no fear of misunderstanding, about "a quarrel over nothing" than in the rigorous but also rigid and fragile language of mathematics? To me it seems not only conceivable but probable.

So far we have considered only what engineers regard as the most satisfactory available explanation of the failure of the bridge across Puget Sound. I will repeat it here:

> The failure of the Tacoma Narrows Bridge was a consequence of its aerodynamic instability. The bridge was carried over the threshold into self-excited torsional oscillation by wind vortices which the upwind or leading edge of its stiffening girders shed. Beyond that critical point the movement of the members of the structure that generated torsional oscillation were self-excited and increased indefinitely in amplitude until they passed the capacity of the parts of the system (especially the paving of the deck) to bear the stresses they created.

The appropriate extension of that explanation is not on the pages that immediately follow it. Those pages are strictly for laymen, not for engineers. The appropriate extension is Chapter 7 of Part III of the inquiry published in 1952 by the University of Washington Engineering Experiment Station. The principle investigator and author of the chapter was Theodore von Kármán, an eminent expert in the field of classical mechanics and aerodynamics, the discoverer of von Kármán vortices. Certain divergences of the earliest report, that of 1941, on the bridge failure and the subsequent one completed in 1952 require our attention. Some of them become evident if one juxtaposes corresponding items from the reports (see pp. 127–132).

Before attempting to construe these divergences we simply call atten-

[11] See Chapter 3.

tion to their conspicuous presence. The illustrations do not look alike nor the languages sound alike. The pattern of contrast into which they fit will emerge sharply if we consider four points less conspicuous visually. (1) In the report of 1941, the names of individual persons abound; by 1952 except for those of the authors of the report, such names do not appear. (2) One symbol present in the early report vanishes completely from the latter—the dollar sign. So do the series of whole numbers that ordinarily follow dollar signs. (3) Although both reports abound in numbers, another kind of number series present in the first report is missing from the second—the one that conventionally represents the year of the Christian era. (4) In the report of 1941 the word "bridge" almost always refers to the span over the Tacoma Narrows or reference to that bridge is implicit in the syntax. In the report of 1952 "bridge" is preceded by "proposed" seven times, while often the word appears with reference not to any span, past or planned, intended for human use, but to a scale model of a bridge section. (5) A fast leafing through of the reports reveals a density of graphic representation and of equations in the later report far in excess of that in the earlier one.

Now we can refine our sense of contrast in the gross visual representations from the reports of 1941 and 1952 previously reproduced.

The first photograph in the report of 1941 is a shot of Galloping Gertie in all her proud, frail, and slender beauty during the happy days when she was just undulating and not twisting. The first photograph in the report of 1952 is a shot of a scale model of a section of the Tacoma Narrows Bridge. The pattern implicit in the first photos is carried on throughout the two reports. The subsequent photos in the first report are shots of Galloping Gertie on November 7, 1940 from her first entry into torsional oscillation to the plunge of her deck into Puget Sound. The subsequent photos in the report of 1952 are shots of members and parts of the scale model. In the 1952 report there is not a single photo of Galloping Gertie.

The first page of the 1941 report is an introduction to what follows. What follows is a faltering and inept historical account, history of the sort that engineers without special interest or training in writing history are likely to produce, of the failure of the Tacoma Narrows Bridge. The first page of the report of 1952 is mainly taken up with a table of the symbols that are to be used in the mathematical formulations spread heavily through the rest of the study. The title pages of the two reports confirm what all the foregoing evidence suggest—only on a very loose construal of synonomy do the reports concern themselves with the same subject. Broadly speaking, the first report is about the Tacoma Narrows Bridge, what happened to it, and why; it is mainly history. The second report is about suspension bridges in general. It focuses on the probable aerodynamic response of the central spans of such bridges, propor-

THE TACOMA NARROWS BRIDGE

CHAPTER I

HISTORY, ORGANIZATION, DESIGN, CONSTRUCTION
AND BEHAVIOR OF BRIDGE

The northwest portion of the State of Washington is divided in
a north and south direction by the waters of Puget Sound which, extending southerly 90 miles from the Straits of Juan de Fuca, separate
an area of land 80 miles in width from the rest of the State. This
area, the Olympic Peninsula, is provided with local highways, but the
Puget Sound forms a barrier between it and the rest of the State to
the east. Previous to the construction of the Tacoma Narrows Bridge,
all travel to and from the peninsula was by ferries in the vicinity
of Seattle and Tacoma, or by highways around the southern end of the
Sound. (Drawing No. 1)

At the Tacoma Narrows, the Sound is restricted at its narrowest
point to a width of 4600 feet. The bridging of the Sound at this
location as a means of more ready access to the Peninsula had long
been proposed. However, because of the great depth of water and the
swiftness of the tidal currents, the cost of a bridge was an effective
barrier to its financing, and all efforts of private individuals in
this direction failed. Its construction became feasible only when a
considerable portion of its cost could be financed by means other than
as a charge against anticipated revenues. Even under this condition,
it was considered necessary to keep the cost of construction as low as
possible. However, after the opening of the bridge, the traffic and
the resulting revenues exceeded all estimates.

CHAPTER VII

WIND-TUNNEL INVESTIGATIONS CARRIED OUT AT THE CALIFORNIA INSTITUTE OF TECHNOLOGY[1]

THEODORE VON KÁRMÁN
Emeritus Professor of Aeronautics

LOUIS G. DUNN
Director of the Jet Propulsion Laboratory

I. PRELIMINARY REPORT ON THE AERODYNAMIC INVESTIGATIONS[2]

NOMENCLATURE

A_{max} = maximum half amplitude
C_D = coefficient of drag
C_F = non-dimensional coefficient
C_L = coefficient of lift
C_M = coefficient of moment
F_0 = impressed force
f = sag
l = length of main span
l_1 = length of side span
m = mass
m_r = reduced mass
N = frequency in cyc/sec
S = area

V = wind velocity
w = weight of bridge per foot
W = kinetic energy
α = angle of attack (for static tests)
$\alpha = l_1/l$ (in part II of this chapter)
β = damping constant
δ = logarithmic decrement
$\mu = \dfrac{\rho b^2}{w/g}$ = mass density ratio (part I of this chapter)
$\mu = \sqrt{2f/g}\,\omega$ (part II of this chapter)
ρ = density of air in slugs/cu ft = 0.002378
ω_0 = circular frequency of the system

The aerodynamic investigations carried out to date deal with three groups of problems—namely:

1. Vertical oscillations
2. Torsional instability
3. Drag, lift and moment characteristics of the proposed section, especially the reduction of lateral forces produced by the wind.

The investigation of these problems has not yet been completed. However, certain important conclusions can be drawn from the experiments completed to date. The results of these experiments are briefly discussed in the following sections.

31. Vertical Oscillations[3]

Scale models corresponding to sections of the original Tacoma Bridge and the proposed design were

investigated in the wind tunnel. The main objective of these experiments was the determination of the damping effect of the aerodynamic forces. It was found that these aerodynamic damping forces could be represented as a function of the velocity ratio V/Nb, where V is the wind velocity in feet per second, N is the frequency in cycles per second and b is the width of the bridge in feet. Instability corresponding to negative aerodynamic damping (as has been suggested by some authors in connection with vertical vibrations of the original Tacoma Bridge) was in no case observed. In all cases, the aerodynamic damping was positive.

The results of these tests are indicated in Figs. 61 and 62.[3] In Fig. 61, δ/μ is plotted as a function of V/Nb for the original Tacoma Bridge, where δ is the logarithmic decrement, and $\mu = \dfrac{\rho b^2}{w/g}$, in which ρ is the density of air in slugs per cubic foot, b is the

[1] These investigations, an extension of certain studies mentioned in "The Failure of the Tacoma Narrows Bridge; a Report to the Federal Works Agency," by O. H. AMMANN, TH. VON KÁRMÁN, and G. B. WOODRUFF, March 28, 1941, were conducted under the joint auspices of the Public Roads Administration and the Washington Toll Bridge Authority, at the request of the Board of Consulting Engineers for the New Tacoma Narrows Bridge.

[2] A Report to the Board of Consulting Engineers, May 30, 1942.

[3] In reproducing Chapter VII, numbers of sections, figures, tables, and symbols for quantities elsewhere employed, have been changed to conform to the general practice of this report. (Ed.)

THE FAILURE OF
THE TACOMA NARROWS BRIDGE

A Report to the
Honorable John M. Carmody
Administrator, Federal Works Agency
Washington, D. C.

●

BOARD OF ENGINEERS
Othmar H. Ammann
Theodore von Kármán
Glenn B. Woodruff

MARCH 28, 1941

AERODYNAMIC STABILITY OF SUSPENSION BRIDGES

WITH SPECIAL REFERENCE TO

THE TACOMA NARROWS BRIDGE

A REPORT OF AN INVESTIGATION

CONDUCTED BY

THE STRUCTURAL RESEARCH LABORATORY
UNIVERSITY OF WASHINGTON

UNDER THE DIRECTION OF

THE WASHINGTON TOLL BRIDGE AUTHORITY

IN COOPERATION WITH

THE BUREAU OF PUBLIC ROADS
DEPARTMENT OF COMMERCE

PART III

THE INVESTIGATION OF MODELS OF
THE ORIGINAL TACOMA NARROWS BRIDGE
UNDER THE ACTION OF WIND

BY

F. B. FARQUHARSON

WITH A CHAPTER BY

THEODORE VON KÁRMÁN AND LOUIS G. DUNN

JUNE, 1952

tioned in various lengths, widths, and deadweights, to wind variable with respect to velocity and angle of attack on their leading edge or windward side.

In its main thrust the report of 1952 is not about the failure of the Tacoma Narrows Bridge at all. As an engineering study it is excellent. It is not and does not purport to be history. The report of 1941 is not an excellent engineering study. It identifies the structural fault in the bridge responsible for its general instability—the unprecedented length of the center span in proportion to its width and deadweight. It is noncommittal, however, on what generated the forces that carried the bridge over the threshold into self-excited torsional oscillation, and thence to failure. Only subsequent investigation was to reveal the sinister effect of the leading plate girders in producing vortices chaotically under the impact of gusts of wind. Consequently the report of 1941 is of little or no interest to engineers. As engineers they now care nothing about a bridge that plunged into Puget Sound thirty years ago. They are properly interested in a class of contingent future events called "bridge failures" and in building bridges that will not fail through lack of knowledge and foresight on the part of the engineers responsible for their design and construction. The trajectory of investigation and explanation we have just examined, the trajectory from the report of 1941 to the report of 1952, is the appropriate trajectory for engineers to follow. It is away from historical formulation and the rhetoric of history; it is in the direction of scientific formulation and the rhetoric of one of the hardest of the hard sciences, classical mechanics.

By contrast the report of 1941 is a potpourri of inadequate engineering investigation and inadequate historical discourse. Its inadequacy is the consequence of haste in preparation. The authors were trying to answer an open "why" question, "Why did the bridge fail?" that concealed at least three divergent though related questions:

1. How does one build a suspension bridge secure from excessive torsional oscillation? (This is the question to which the report of 1952 seems to have given a provisionally adequate answer.)

2. What errors in engineering design resulted in the failure of the Tacoma Narrows Bridge? (This question received a firm answer in the report of 1952, although providing that answer was no longer the primary purpose of the investigators.)

3. How did a bridge as unstable as Galloping Gertie come to be built the way it was?

The authors of the report of 1941 sporadically addressed themselves to the third question. They had to. With several million dollars worth of government funds sunk in the sands of Puget Sound or dangling crazily from cracked towers and frayed cable across the Narrows, with not only a bridge but human hopes destroyed and careers in jeopardy, a lot of people were looking for someone to pin the rap on.

The third question is a historical question, and the answer in the report of 1941 is a historiographic catastrophe commensurate with the disaster which it sought to "explain." The catastrophe is the result of ignorance as well as of haste. In 1941 the engineers did not know the answers to the engineering questions indispensable to even a provisional allocation of responsibility for the failure of the bridge. More to the point, faced with one of the most difficult of historical tasks, the allocation of responsibility in a complex situation, they were wholly innocent of any of the skills professional historians are expected to acquire in the course of their training. In fact they were not aware that it requires skill to deal with an event coherently in a way that takes account of its historical context—time and place and persons and circumstances. The time and place—the United States still in the toils of its longest and most agonizing economic depression, with funds in short supply. The persons—a complex, interknit, and sometimes conflicting group. The Federal Works Administrator, Carmody. The local promoters. The members of the State of Washington Bridge Authority. The on-site engineer, Eldridge. The scholarly Professor of Engineering from the University of Washington, Farquharson. The designer of the bridge, Moiseeff, a New Yorker and one of the most brilliantly innovative engineers of his day with more than thirty years of experience in bridge design.[12] The circumstances—limited funds and a low projected estimate of probable traffic, both pointing toward lightness of structure to achieve economies in construction and thus toward Moiseeff's bold and disastrous extrapolation from his beautiful and successful design of the Whitestone Bridge. For the experienced historian all these ingredients powerfully suggest a mode of explanation at odds with the instinct of engineers—an explanation by historical storytelling.

This is not the place to tell such a story, nor has my inquiry into the suicide of Galloping Gertie been thorough enough to equip me to tell it. Clearly, however, to tell it one would have to deal with evidence that, long before the publication of their "definitive" report in 1952, the investigating engineers had come to regard as irrelevant to their explanatory purposes.

It might be said that historical explanations and engineering explanations are on different levels. It does not quite do, however, to describe an explanation by historical storytelling as being on a different level from the "definitive" explanation of the engineers. In common language

---

[12] Not to mention the official who deposited to his personal bank account the premium check for insuring the bridge, in the reasonable but erroneous belief that the span over the Narrows was there to stay.

in which "high" and "low" are value-bearing terms, the metaphor of
levels tends to slip into a misleading pejorative-honorific pattern with
one level above or below another. But a historical story about the
suicide of Galloping Gertie is per se neither better nor worse than the
explanation of the engineers. It is simply different, performing a different function, appropriate in a different context. Moreover, the notion of
levels also suggests parallel and therefore nonintersecting planes. But
the actual data-sets in question are not wholly discrete. A historian of
Galloping Gertie's suicide needs to acquire some understanding of the
findings the engineers in their 1952 report, that is, of how suspension
bridges work. And the scale-model bridge sections on which the
engineers performed their wind tunnel test was not just a model of any
old suspension bridge or of the Idea of a Suspension Bridge. It was a
model of the bridge that failed on November 7, 1940.

What insight relevant to historical explanation by analysis has our
inquiry into the suicide of Galloping Gertie afforded us? The yield is
monitory rather than prohibitive. With respect to such explanation it
does not say, "Do not step." It says, "Watch your step!" Two warnings
seem to come through. One speaks to the danger of conceiving intricate
constellations of past human activities, loosely labelled for convenience
—for example "the French Revolution," or "the American Civil War"—
as if they are inert receptacles into which inputs of "factors" or "causes"
enter and from which outputs of results or consequences commensurate
with the inputs flow.[13] Such constellations are far more complex than
Galloping Gertie, with her four standard components of cables, towers,
suspenders, and deck. Yet she was so far from being inert that she
converted an input, the wind, previously conceived as static, into a
dynamic chaos. Moreover, she absorbed that chaos into her system in a
way that started a twisting motion in which she alone produced the
energy which destroyed her. The over-simple image or model of cause-
and-effect relations to which historical analysis sometimes conforms itself does scant justice even to the relatively simple dynamic interplay of
the components of Galloping Gertie.

The second warning speaks to the fallacy of misplaced abstraction.
The historical analyst who disjoins his abstractions or generalizations
from the actualities of the past—the "when," the "where," the "who,"

[13] The form implicit here goes like this:
a, b, and c are causal inputs
d, e, and f are results
E is the "event" constellation

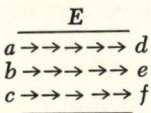

$$\frac{E}{\begin{array}{l} a \rightarrow \rightarrow \rightarrow \rightarrow \rightarrow d \\ b \rightarrow \rightarrow \rightarrow \rightarrow \rightarrow e \\ c \rightarrow \rightarrow \rightarrow \rightarrow \rightarrow f \end{array}}$$

the "how many"—moves in the direction taken by engineers' inquiry between 1941 and 1952. He is likely to sacrifice understanding of the past
to his purpose of control or power over the future. In so doing, he is
also likely to win himself the worst of both worlds—to lose his ability to
advance understanding of the past and never to achieve that increased
control over the future at which he aims. He may cease to be a historian
without recognizably becoming anything else.

What then do analytical historians find attractive about the
engineer's way of explaining "why" as against the way that involves
telling a historical story, the way of explaining "why" that historians
have long practiced professionally, the way that has its roots in the
habits of explanation of that ubiquitous historian Everyman? Perhaps it
has to do with the triviality of many of the stories professional historians have told. Here, however, the prophets of historical analysis
have made a sad and most human mistake. They have ascribed to the
mode of discourse the defects of the men who resort to it, and they are
doomed to disillusionment. No historian who has suffered the aridity of
innumerable dreary volumes of storytelling history, as they stretch end-
lessly over the past century with only the rarest oases as a refuge for the
wanderer, can fail to understand the revulsion of the analytical historians and even to sympathize with it. Yet the triviality that rightly
appalls them is not the triviality of storytelling as a way of explaining
"why" in history; it is the triviality of so many of the storytellers—a
triviality of intellectual power sometimes, but quite often a triviality of
concern, of commitment to their vocation, of zest for inquiry, of spirit.
And disillusionment is certain because no mode of discourse whatever
insures against the triviality of those who deploy it. Aside from any
questions as to the theoretical and practical limits of the viability of
analysis in history, if it becomes the fashion, like other historical
fashions it will attract its fluttering cloud of sterile moths, and the
history they write will be quite as trivial as in the bad old days of storytelling.

If many historians are impelled to analysis from the rear by the
fatuity of so much history as it has been—"A tale told by an idiot, . . .
signifying—nothing,"—they also are drawn toward it by a dream, a
dream of what history can and ought to be. Much of the burden of
what has gone before and of what will follow in this primer is a variation on the same refrain: the dream itself is a nightmare, not too well
disguised; not very much history can, not very much ought to conform
to the simple analytical model. To attempt so to conform much of it will
not be to realize a dream but to achieve a disaster. We have already
tried to make clear some of the implications of reliance on that model;
here we wish to examine them somewhat more closely.

First let us note a correlation: the historians who have invested most heavily in the enterprise of analytical history correspond very closely with the historians committed to the notion that history must be, and must be nothing else but, a social science. But to turn history wholly toward the social sciences is to fix its goal, its ideal, its Holy Grail, on a point that lies outside the social sciences. For the ideal of most social scientists, at least until very recently, has been the "hard" sciences; it has been physics and chemistry. Indeed that ideal may be something even more illusory. It may be the model of the hard sciences as envisaged by the philosophers of science a decade or two ago, but now itself on the way to obsolescence. If so, it will not be the first time that historians and social scientists wholly oriented toward the natural sciences have wasted much energy in pursuit of a mirage. Social scientists have rarely attained or claimed that they can attain their ideal. They have tended, however, to measure the achievement of their disciplines against achievement in the natural sciences as a goal and ideal—and so measured they do not and cannot find their work good. For what they discern in the hard sciences is high precision and accuracy in the predictions that those sciences undertake, and social scientists find themselves rarely able to make equally precise and accurate predictions in the matters they want to make predictions about.[14] Analytical historians whose inclination turns them directly toward the social sciences and indirectly toward the natural sciences often do not have a very clear understanding of what the pursuit of their ideal entails.

For us, one route to that understanding lies through a scrutiny of the last phase of the investigation of the collapse of the Tacoma Narrows Bridge, the phase most satisfactory to the engineer as scientist. As we have seen, it consisted, first, in the construction of ingenious small-scale models of the bridge or sections of it. Then the models had to be encapsulated in a wind tunnel where they could be subjected to controlled aerodynamic stress. For the analytical historian, if he would understand his own ideal, the point on which to zero in is not the difficulties of replication that the engineers, Professors von Kármán and Farquharson encountered, but the relative ease with which they achieved encapsulation. Encapsulation was the heart of the matter. The kind of explanation "why" that the engineers aimed to achieve required that they subject a structural system (the bridge model) built of materials of known strength to a variety of measured aerodynamic stresses of varied intensity and duration from a variety of angles, and that they observe the effect of those stresses, and those alone, on the system. They therefore had to shut out all stresses but the ones they could control. They had to shut

---

[14] As I indicated in Chapter 1, the sense of failure is not the consequence of the difficulty of predicting what people will do, which in fact we all predict quite frequently and quite accurately.

out the stresses that the natural uncontrolled wind might generate, and the ones the little Farquharson and von Kármán boys (if there were such boys) might impose, if they were seized by the amusing idea of dropping a jolly little brick on Daddy's jolly little toy.

What the engineers' experiment makes clear is that encapsulation, closure, lies at the very heart of the exact sciences. The exact sciences aim at maximizing encapsulation at three levels—the level of rhetoric, the level of theory, and the level of experimental design and testing. Concerning the level of rhetoric we have already written briefly in Chapter 4, and will write further in later chapters. At the level of theory there are some observations both in Chapter 1 and in this chapter. We wish to draw the closest attention here to encapsulation at the level of practice, that is, experiment and testing, and to its implications at that level for historians inclined to a purely analytical and social-science view of history.

In connection with the workings of that practice in the past, note that the very first predictive activities of men which had in them some of the rigor and precision of modern science had as their object the only completely closed natural system readily accessible to easy observation, the solar system. Because of the cosmic isolation of that system, every movement of any of its components, visible to the naked eye or indeed with the most powerful telescope, is intrasystemically generated. By almost any standard the solar system was an incredible bit of luck. It has only eight components visible to the naked eye.[15] Systemic motion measurable within the limits of naked-eye observation and even of sophisticated instrumentation is wholly a function of the interrelations of these few components. No other natural system has such sweet, visible, and built-in simplicity.[16] The advance of the exact sciences in modern times has in part depended on inventiveness in devising "spy glasses" and measuring devices of ever-increasing intricacy and sophistication to enable scientists to observe systems inaccessible to naked-eye examination. It has also depended upon the ingenuity and cunning of experimental scientists in contriving containers for the systems they have under observation. Within the context of the experimenter's purpose these containers are presumed to be impermeable for the relevant period of the experiment. This presumptive exclusion of uncontrolled external forces from a system under investigation is necessary in order to insure that the only changes observed are either intrasystemic or are injected under systematic control. One of the classic instances of such a contriv-

---

[15] The sun, the moon, Mercury, Venus, Mars, Jupiter, Saturn, and the earth.
[16] With respect to closure the nearest thing to it is perhaps the avian egg, on the development of which Aristotle was able to make a series of very shrewd, but limited, observations.

ance of closure enabled Lavoisier to demonstrate that combustion was an additive rather than a subtractive process, and thus to initiate the chemical revolution. The apparatus—a model of thousands of like contrivances—is illustrated below. As the environmental problems en-

Figure 4

countered by natural scientists increase in difficulty and complexity, the contrivance of effective containers becomes more difficult and complex—and more expensive. The apparatus with which Lavoisier initiated the chemical revolution probably cost less than $100. The capital cost alone of the Stanford linear accelerator, the use of which hopefully will someday make an important contribution to an as yet unattained subatomic-particle revolution was over $100,000,000. This escalation of cost indicates that the advance of science demands capsules more and more expensive in order to achieve the sophisticated closures necessary to seduce nature into exposing her inner secrets.

The situation of the historian contrasts starkly with that of the natural scientists just in the matter of experimental closure. The paradox of the historian's situation is neatly set forth by the well-worn lines of Fitzgerald's Omar Khayyám:

> The Moving Finger writes, and having writ,
> Moves on; nor all your Piety nor Wit
> Shall lure it back to cancel half a line,
> Nor all your tears wash out a word of it.

In one sense, the past of which historians try to retrieve some conception, and to which through the surviving record they seek to do justice, is utterly and absolutely closed: what happened, happened; what men did, they did; what they thought, they thought. Nothing that any man can do now can change the past a jot or a tittle; time is irreversible. But just because in this sense the past is closed, every event, every human action in the past is as open as it actually was; no contrivance of closure, no container, however ingenious or costly, can cut off one past event from the relations it actually bore to prior or subsequent events in the past.[17]

Historians, then, work in the presence of, and bounded by, two encompassing paradoxes. One we examined in an earlier chapter: the inordinate richness and the meager poverty of the record of the past. And now we have become acquainted with the second paradox: the indefeasible closedness and the equally indefeasible openness of the past itself. In practice historians not oriented to the exact sciences by way of the social sciences have long since shaped their methods and goals in a way that enables them to deal with the inherent paradoxes of their situation. Historians oriented to the exact sciences have pursued three lines of action. Some have leaped in where angels fear to tread, attempting gross application of "scientific method" to their data, and ended up, as one might expect, with a terrible fall. Some have made resounding proclamations of their ideological commitment to the scientific nature of the historical enterprise, and then have gone on to do useful work quite unrelated to the fulfillment of their impossible program. Finally and rather recently a few have begun a gingerly systematic exploration of possible means of attaining their ideological goals. This last enterprise, or rather cluster of enterprises, can perhaps most aptly be described as the quest for the methodological equivalents of tight containers with which to deal with the record of the past. Such equivalents are necessary for these historians. Otherwise, when they try to work with porous capsules, they discover that a sort of historical osmosis has rendered it impossible to separate what is inside the container from what is outside, or in current jargon the signals within their containers are drowned out by random external noise.

Within reasonable bounds it is occasionally possible to devise methodological equivalents of tight containers in the social sciences, and where the record of the past is full enough, it is possible to make use of these equivalents in some explanations "why" in history. A history primer, however, is not the place to examine the intricate and sophisticated forms of container-equivalents with which analytical historians have tried to work.

A useful approach to the problem of effective container-equivalents in human affairs lies via the activities of men who have long been seriously committed to creating such equivalents. One of the surest

---

[17] Past events are even more radically open than we have indicated, for they open not only on to their past futures but on to our own present future in two ways. First, they will have an impact on what is to come as, for example, the past consumption of the iron ores of the Mesabi Range will probably long affect a number of decisions of the United States government on foreign policy. Second, they will have an impact insofar as the recollection and reconstruction of them, through memory, or tradition, or the systematic study by historians of the surviving record keep them in or bring them before the minds of men in the future.

means of inducing such seriousness is to impose a heavy pecuniary mulct on those whose container-equivalent leaks too badly. Money is very serious stuff. Men legally responsible for the custody of a large amount of money, systematically required to bet it on their own predictions of human events, and accountable for their bets, need to take special care about their container-equivalents. Responsible executives of insurance companies have to build reasonably tight container-equivalents into their rate structures or the companies will go broke. How do insurance companies build container-equivalents which enable them to avoid the unpleasant and likely consequences of too many bad bets in an enterprise that is nothing but a prediction business?

In the first place, sometimes premiums (the inputs) are adjusted to location, differing from city to city, or state to state. This is the case with driver-liability and fire insurance. Moreover, policies on most insurable items are duration-limited, and their renewal can be and often is accompanied by changes in premium rates. Insurance policies, depending on what they insure against, also include "exclusions." The exclusions turn out on examination to be the kinds of incalculable, unpredictable, and irregular natural or human catastrophe of which the insured entity may be a victim—flood, tornado, wind-driven rain, and earthquake; riot, civil insurrection, and war. As a further precaution, companies impose differential premiums on different populations—in the case of driver-liability insurance, higher rates for the population in the male age group, eighteen to twenty-five years old; in life insurance, higher rates for the population of structural steel workers. Then there is the insurance-company procedure of reinsurance, equivalent to that of "laying off" in other betting industries. At the margins of insurance lie the assigned risks, the persons on whom and/or the situations against which insurance companies will offer to bet only under carefully hedged arrangement, and the uninsurable risks against which they will not offer to bet at all—car insurance for the man who has had sixty convictions for drunken driving; life insurance for the man whose vocation is lone exploration in the territory of the headhunting tribes of the Upper Amazon.

What do these specifics tell us about characteristic traits of the container-equivalents built by those who habitually bet on the outcome of human activities—the insurance companies? First, that their model is never deductive; it is always inductive. At its foundation are not the rigid structures of general law, but (according to taste) the flexible or shaky structures of statistics. The model does not stand firm on immutable rules, but shifts its ground, that is, changes its rates, to adjust to changes in the insured category. At the very least this might suggest to all but the most sanguine analytical historians a quiet de-escalation of their scientific aspirations from the nomological-deductive model of explanation "why," sometimes applicable in the exact sciences, to the inductive-statistical model more appropriate to the softer ones. Closer consideration may even further dim hopes for an impending analytical millennium in history. For we have seen that before they set the odds on which they will back their predictions, the insurance companies want to know when and where, they prescribe how long, and by adjusted risks, uninsurable risks, and exclusions they determine under what circumstances and who. They thus avoid or reduce to manageable proportions casual conjunctures of times, places, persons, and circumstances that are likely to play havoc with the odds. The container-equivalents of insurance—when? where? how long? who? under what circumstances? —allow the companies to make predictions on which they can bet (fix premiums) within acceptable margins of error. For the purposes of analytical history, however, the insurance analogy is not a solution but an evasion of the paradox of the past—its ineffaceable closed-openness. Taken as the sole model of historical discourse, analytical history, in its attempt to construct container-equivalents to approximate the containers of the natural sciences, requires that in writing about the past its practitioners minimize in their "history" what was ineluctably there in the past —the contingencies of times, places, durations, conjunctures, catastrophes, and persons. And this means refusing to write about the past as it often happened; it means not writing history but prescinding from it. For that is the implication of the insurance model. It is the most detailed and inclusive attempt ever made by man to create practicable container-equivalents to deal with the contingencies of human life. It does so not by grappling with "the historical," but by building in limitations on its betting that sharply restrict or eliminate "the historical."[18]

Let us now turn back to two ways of answering "the same" question, "Why did the bridge fail?"—the one a historian might give and the one the engineers gave in 1952. Hypothetically or potentially, both might be adequate and errorless. What then would account for their drastic incommensurability, their divergence in mode?

The engineers' answer is governed by an overwhelming concern that no bridge built in the future should ever collapse as a consequence of the kinds of stresses that destroyed the span over the Tacoma Narrows. Historians, however, would be ordinarily concerned to render as credible and intelligible an account as they could of what happened to Galloping Gertie and how it came about, from conception to suicide. As we look at these two statements of purpose we can see that they indeed are answers to two very different questions: the engineers were rightly concerned about a safe negative future prediction ("How can we be sure that under reasonably anticipatable circumstances no suspension

---

[18] This is one of the rare occasions on which I have used the term "the historical," to mean the ongoing processes of men's lives in time.

bridge will do what the Tacoma Narrows Bridge did?"); historians would be just as rightly concerned about the credibility of a sequence of past happenings ("How does the story of Galloping Gertie help us make better sense of her ultimate fate?").[19] The divergent "translations," both quite correct, of "Why did the bridge fail?" render intelligible the differences between the engineers' answer and the historians', and makes evident the reason for and reasonableness of their divergence.

By now the term "credible" has popped into the immediately preceding paragraphs often enough to suggest my view of what constitutes one standard of adequate and satisfactory causal explanation in history. It offers an alternative to the sufficient-cause standard when, as is so frequently the case, that standard would simply strike historians dumb, and leave them with nothing to say about questions concerning which they could actually say a great deal, most of it to the point. I suggest a standard of credibility. If we accept the credibility standard, however, we discover that to meet its requirements analysis often must make room for, if not give way to, historical story, because credibility will often heavily depend on the conjunctures of times, places, persons, and circumstances, and attention to these conjunctures will be unduly distracted if, in our enthusiasm for analysis, we permit the bonds that they create to be analytically severed.

It would be vain, foolish, and dangerous indeed to imagine that the conscious and explicit acceptance of the credibility standard as an alternative to or replacement for the sufficient-cause standard of explanation "why" in history "solves" all the Big Problems about history and history writing.[20] What it does is what such changes usually do. It forecloses some questions which seem to have become at once pressing and insoluble by making them into nonquestions or downgrading them. For example, *how do historians find necessary and sufficient causes of an event?* Answer: *They usually do not, but it does not matter.* Often it reopens wide some questions which seemed to have had fairly satisfactory answers that lay within the capacity of the preexisting structure of notions, without more than (or even) the pretense that it affords means for their solution. For example, *what should a historian look for when he seeks the causes of an event?* On the other hand, it opens up ranges of inquiry that carry promise of intellectual excitement, ranges that by their indispensable assumptions the older notions

[19] It is not my intention to insist that everything that has happened in the past is "credible" in the sense of being amenable to being placed in an account that renders it intelligible to a person with a reasonably lively imagination. Although I am a fairly hard-bitten elderly man, I still find the atrocities of the Nazis incredible in this sense. More on this point in Chapter 6.

[20] Replacement is possible through a subsumption of the sufficient-cause standard, so that it becomes *one kind* of "credibility" explanation.

foreclosed. For example, *what place does the rhetoric of history have in establishing the credibility of an account of the human past?* And finally, at a few cruxes, it provides answers to questions (or at least hypotheses that can for the time being be treated as answers by reasonable people) which emancipate men from what had become hopeless entrapment in an increasingly futile word game. For example, *do historians ever provide credible explanations "why" of past happenings that are also adequate, appropriate, and satisfactory; and if so, how?* Answer: *Yes, they do, and often they do it by telling a story.*

I will not attempt to cope with all the serious questions that the adoption of a credibility-standard of historical explanations raises. At least one major positive gain accrues from the adoption of that standard. It legitimates a common procedure to which very able historians are often irresistibly impelled in their quest for adequate explanation; it justifies what they actually very often do; tell the best historical story that their knowledge of the record of the past, their command of subsequent studies of that record, the use of their second record, and their control of common formal prose permit them to.

The last bit above has gotten a little abstract and drawn us further than we like to be from the actual activities of historians. It may be well, then, briefly to illustrate how the credibility standard actually works in a matter closer than the collapse of the Tacoma Narrows Bridge to the conventional conception of what professional historians bother about—the collapse of an empire, specifically the first British Empire on the American continent. The causal explanation for the revolt of the thirteen colonies that was taught me in my youth went something like this:

> Liberty-loving men fled England and came to America in search of freedom. Then later the English and especially the King of England, George III, tried to establish tyrannical rule over them by taxing them and otherwise crushing their liberties and subjecting them to despotism. Except for a handful of cowardly traitors called Loyalists, the Americans, with love of liberty in their hearts, then rose in arms and declared their independence from their oppressors.

Even in the early 1920's many historians in America had settled on a somewhat more sophisticated historical story to explain why the American Revolution broke out. Still this is the way I remember it. Since I also remember that in my youth a man named "Big Bill" Thompson successfully campaigned for mayor of the Second City by promising to keep King George out of Chicago, the George in question apparently being the late George III (1760–1820), I may have remembered it right. The narrative does have somewhat "1066 and All That" overtones; yet it is possible to find in the record of the past statements which lend support to the above story. It was on the basis of precisely such statements that historians like Palfrey and Bancroft constructed that larger story of which the above is a condensed and rather primitive version. Given such support, their story comes fairly close to fulfilling the requirements of the credibility standard. One may, however, strain a little at the notion of people being quite as villainous as the British under King George III appear to be in the supporting record. One may also entertain certain reservations about the likelihood of any large number of men being so consistently noble, virtuous, and brave as in the foregoing account our (adopted) forebears are supposed to have been.

The "fairly close," the "straining at a notion," the "certain reservations" are the very stuff of which are made the improvement of historical explanation and the extension of historical understanding under the aegis of the credibility-standard. For these good purposes it matters hardly at all what the genesis of the straining and reservations is. Sometimes their source is an ideological commitment of sorts, like mine to the Judaeo-Christian anthropology or of a Marxist to dialectical materialism; but only someone hopelessly addicted to the sociology of knowledge could imagine that such an ideology is the only source of such strains and reservations. They may come from almost anywhere. Sometimes they emerge by processes which no one has successfully made intelligible from an unkempt corner of one's second record. Or they may just happen because, reading desultorily, one accidentally lights a bit of the record of the past that seems not to fit the currently accepted story. What is important here is not why the strains and reservations happen, but that they happen, and once they have happened, what one does about them.

What used to be said was that one took the ostensibly conflicting evidence, "weighed" it, accepted the true, rejected the false, and thus arrived at a judgment as between alternative historical stories. Although some men, historians and others, sometimes misconstrue it, the metaphor of "weighing" should not be misconstrued here. Its referent is not the physicist with his superaccurate scales, but blindfold Themis with her rough balance; and the purpose is not to elicit or test a generalization, but to do justice. The law with its concern for and rules of evidence is a more satisfactory and safer source of analogy for history than the physical sciences are. The categories "true" and "false" are not the most useful ones for describing a historian's way of classifying items from the record of the past in order to make clear why things happened the way they happened, and why men did what they did. Rightly construed any and every line in that record, even a forged line, will tell historians something true about what happened in the past. The unresolved question is: *what* does it tell? When an inquirer, driven by difficulties rising from whatever source, turns back to the record of the past and elicits from it information that will not precisely fit the currently accepted historical story about the events or actions under consideration,[21] he faces the crucial decision for a historian: what to do about it? It turns out, for example, that before the American Revolution the Loyalist, Thomas Hutchinson, was not a coward and not in his own view of the matter at all treasonous; that on the other side a good many patriotic lovers of liberty had solid vested interests in opposing British taxation, and that some who were expert and prompt at making patriotic noises, were not especially hasty to assume serious personal or financial risks in their resistance to tyranny. And far from being shamed by the accusation of tyranny, the English, and especially George III, were simply startled that the American colonists, the most lightly taxed people in the European world,[22] should make such a fuss about contributing to their own defense. Here the conception of weighing the evidence on the scales of justice seems to go awry. As a historian, my first priority is not to declare Hutchinson or George III innocent or guilty as charged: they have long since passed beyond the reach of any punishment that could be inflicted on them here below. My initial concern is to do justice not to them but to the record of the past. That I thereby happen to do better justice to Hutchinson and George III is a sort of windfall, although an important one.

Often the process by which a historian does justice to the record of the past goes something like this. Some part of that record which he has not hitherto known, or a historical study of parts of that record that looks solid to him comes to his attention. Unfortunately, that study or that part of the record of the past appears to contradict the historical story he had hitherto accepted to explain why something happened. At that point a historian is impelled to reexamine the record he formerly used and check his construal of it. The purpose of the checking is to decide how much damage the new evidence has done to the story he previously told or accepted and to make the appropriate repairs and modifications, if necessary, if any, and if possible. For a historian this means accepting one of about four general alternatives: (1) that the story he started with at the outset is not at all adversely affected by the items encountered in the record, which at first sight seem to diminish or destroy the credibility of some part or all of it; (2) that the story's credibility is totally destroyed by these items; (3) that the items indicate that some parts of the story need to be changed to maintain its credibility; (4) that they indicate a situation in which two equally credible but irreconcilable stories emerge from equally acceptable

---

[21] If new information does wholly fit the story, it needs at least be noted in the "literature" that this evidential confirmation of the current view exists.

[22] See Robert Palmer, *The Age of Democratic Revolution: The Challenge* (Princeton; 1964), p. 155.

construals of the available record of the past. Each of these alternatives prescribes a different course of action to a historian. In the first instance he must find for the new items a place in the old story that enables him to preserve the credibility of that story from their ostensibly adverse effect. In the second he must order the newfound items from the record of the past and reconstrue the items of that record, which once led him to different conclusions, in such a way as to replace the old story with a new and radically different one. In the third he sizes up the extent of the soft and weak parts in the old story, clears them out, and rebuilds the cleared area in a way that both takes the new evidence into account and maintains or strengthens the credibility of the story. In the last case, he either accepts the situation as given, or he goes hunting for further evidence to confirm one story or the other or to provide him with material for constructing a third story more credible than either of the alternatives.

Clearly none of the four general alternatives can be excluded a priori; only examination of each particular story in detail will suggest to a historian which course he needs to follow. Still on the face of it, it would seem that the two former situations, those requiring no recasting at all of the widely accepted story or its total recasting, are likely to be the exceptions, the latter two situations the rule. One would also imagine that historians might prefer it so. The notion that one's predecessors were always absolutely right about everything and the notion that they were always absolutely wrong are equally disturbing. For if they were absolutely right one is left without much to do but repeat exactly what they said, which would be pretty tiresome; and if they were absolutely wrong, it does not afford much hope for our own effort when, with the passage of time, we have become predecessors ourselves, as all of us are doomed to do. Yet historians sometimes act as if the second were really the normal outcome of the efforts of members of the profession. The clamor of revisionists (of whom I have often been one) suggests that all their predecessors were absolutely wrong. It is not wise to take such noises too seriously; they often represent a combination of propaganda and aspiration rather than actuality; and they engender an amplitude of fluctuation in historians' judgments of the past that is sound neither intellectually nor in respect to the collective mental hygiene of the profession. The current cultural situation is partly responsible for such noises. It is one that treats innovation, almost *any* innovation, honorifically. The new is assumed to be good simply because it is new. This puts a high premium on "bold pioneering work," "daring new outlooks," "completely fresh viewpoints," and so on. Serious iconoclasm— iconoclasm that so shatters some major aspect of the current image of the past as to require historians to repattern almost the whole accepted account of the record bearing on that aspect—is really quite hard work and, besides, it demands a more than ordinary allotment of native intelligence. There are simply not enough brains or energy around in the profession to produce the amount of serious novelty, pioneering, and originality that the undue pressure for innovation requires. Unfortunately, the supply of dubious and frivolous innovation then rises to meet the inflated demand for instant intellectual revolutions in history, the area of systematic inquiry in which by its very nature they are least likely to be achieved legitimately. For historians this results in a quite uneconomical but, in the circumstances, inescapable expenditure of time on tidying up intellectual messes that need not have been made in the first place. It also occasions an inordinate and embarrassing amount of flip-flopping from one point of view about a past era to its opposite. If historians could persuade themselves of the desirability of flipping less often they would flop less frequently.

CHAPTER VI: The Pennant Race and the Baseball Season, *or Historical Story and Narrative Explanation*

Having written about historical storytelling and historical analysis in the last chapter, we wish to pursue the matter somewhat further in the next three, first within and then beyond the bounds of historical explanation. We will start by reiterating an earlier observation and making a second and new one. We previously noted the curious propensity of historians, especially historians addicted to general meditations on the problem, "Whither history?" to leap aboard philosophically sinking ships. (There may, of course, be a similar propensity among philosophers to board historically sinking ships.) The current fashion of analytical history among such historians confirms our observation. For—and this is the second observation—concurrently with the vogue of analytical history among avant-garde historians, whole shoals—or schools—of philosophers were discovering to their astonishment and perplexity that historians often explained things by telling stories.

Because of their precommitments the acceptance of the explanatory function of stories created a special and acute set of problems for a particular group of analytical philosophers. This group is the same one to which we have already given some attention. Their precommitments were as follows:

1. All adequate and satisfactory explanation coincides in form with scientific explanation.
2. All scientific explanation is explanation "why."

3. All explanations "why" express or imply laws, either deductive-nomological ones or statistical-probablistic ones.

4. All adequate and satisfactory historical explanation is a kind of scientific explanation.

5. Therefore, all adequate and satisfactory historical explanation is in form deductive-nomological or statistical-probablistic.

The crucial problem is that most historical stories do not look and sound at all like deductive-nomological or statistical explanations "why," or even like run-of-the-mill explanations in physics or chemistry.

Analytical philosophers dealt with this conspicuous anomaly in one of two ways. Those not committed to the five points just set forth simply threw Point 4 to the sharks, with Point 5 chained to its leg. They argued that all storytelling including historical storytelling was a kind of explanation different from scientific explanation, that it followed a different "logic." The problem, as they saw it, was to discover the logic of storytelling as it relates to history. They applied themselves to the project with considerable energy and zest and to considerable effect.[1]

Philosophers committed to the full five-point package had no such easy out. They were prepainted, so to speak, into a corner best described as assimilationist, with painfully little room for intellectual maneuver. Somehow they had to persuade themselves (pretty easy) and others (a good bit harder) that, gross appearances so much to the contrary notwithstanding, explanation by historical storytelling really was scientific in form, or at any rate as near to being so as made no serious difference, or, at worst, as near as so odd a discipline as history could get. The assimilationist undertaking is a bold but necessary venture. The five points being what they are, there is no place to hide. There are only three options: (1) to recognize historical storytelling as an extra-scientific explanatory procedure; (2) to deny that storytelling performs any explanatory function in history; (3) to reduce storytelling to, or close to, a form of scientific explanation. For the philosophers in question the first option is revolting; the second requires the affirmation of obvious nonsense; so it is the third, or bust. The instrument—the blunt instrument, as it were—of assimilation of historical storytelling is a device called the logic of explanation by narration.

Of course, the enterprise is doomed from the word go, as we shall see, and as the assimilators might have seen had they looked hard in the right place; that the field is full of booby traps is conspicuous enough in all conscience.

[1] John Passmore, "History and Sociology," *The Australian Journal of Politics and History,* 3 (1958): 218–228; Walter Bryce Gallie, *Philosophy and the Historical Understanding,* (New York, 1964).

The first move of the assimilationist is to point out that if historical stories do not look much like scientific explanations, neither usually do scientific explanations. In fact, actual scientific explanations are not ordinarily adequate and satisfactory scientific explanations. Nor do they need to be. They are "explanation sketches," which do not state all the relevant boundary conditions or all the relevant covering laws. Nevertheless such laws and conditions are implicit in scientific explanations. All that has to be done, although no sensible scientist would waste his time doing it, is to fill in the sketch with the missing laws and conditions. Then the conformity of the sketch to deductive-nomological or statistical scientific explanation will be evident. And, of course, as it is with actual scientific explanation sketches, so it is with actual historical explanation sketches—except, except . . .

Except, of course, that patently it is not so at all. In one most conspicuous respect historical stories are quite unlike scientific explanation-sketches. The latter are *thin*; they have to be filled out with missing words and sentences formulating the missing implied laws and boundary conditions. But although historical stories omit a good many laws and conditions, too, and although some laws are rather hard to find even when one looks for them, those stories are not thin; by scientific standards they are often fat, egregiously obese, stuffed with unessential words quite useless for the purpose of adequate and satisfactory explanation. Unlike actual scientific explanations which need to be fattened up, historical stories need to be trimmed down to meet the philosopher's standards. And when trimmed they reveal the lineaments not of full explanation, not of an adequate explanation, but merely of a series of explanation sketches. And what is one to do with all those wasted words? What are they doing there in the first place? The problems of explanation by historical storytelling thus have not been solved by assimilative strategy; they have simply been at once evaded and rendered embarrassingly conspicuous.

To see more clearly what the trouble is with substituting explanation by narration for storytelling as a form of historical explanation, let us see what results from examining the problem in the context of a focal center—in this instance, actually two such centers, a primary one, the National League baseball pennant race of 1951, and a secondary one, selected for purposes of contrast, the American League baseball season of 1939. I have chosen the pennant race of 1951 partly because it raises so effectively and clearly a number of the questions to which we need to address ourselves, and partly because I am more than ordinarily well-informed about it.[2]

[2] A good many of the finer points of information shortly to be put on display I owe to the assiduous and meticulous labor of Mr. Tim Bannon, my bursary assistant at Yale University, 1967–1970.

Let us first ask a "why" question in the standard form: Why did the New York National League baseball team win the National League baseball championship in 1951? Here is an answer to that question:

A. The particular facts or boundary conditions.

1. In 1951 the New York Giants were a baseball team in the National League.

2. In 1951, during the official National League baseball season, the New York Giants won more games from the other teams in that league and lost fewer to them than any of the other teams in the league won or lost.

B. The covering law or general rule.

Until 1969, whenever a National League team won more games and lost fewer than any other team during the official National League season, it was the league champion.

We are now familiar with the form of this explanation. It is nomological-deductive. It therefore conforms to the most rigorous form of scientific explanation: the only relevant "covering law" and the only two relevant boundary conditions are precisely stated in language wholly denotative and univocal, and the statement that the event happened is strictly entailed by the statement of the conditions and the law, and hence is predictable.[3]

The explanation therefore is true, adequate, satisfactory and, as it stands, complete.

Much earlier we proposed a far looser notion of explanation. We suggested that we might want to think of an adequate explanation as whatever in a given context someone needs to know to be going on with. It is not hard to think of some contexts and persons relative to whom the foregoing explanation would be in this looser sense adequate. Suppose an Englishman wanted to know how major professional team-sports championships were decided in the United States in 1951. It happens that, then as now, general rules determining such champion-

[3] The explanation may even be "scientific" within the bounds of Hempel's rigorous statement of the conditions of scientific explanation. The only obstacle I can see to regarding it as such is that the source of the "covering law" in this instance is the official rules of baseball, and therefore human fiat, that of the Professional Baseball Playing Rules Committee. This means, of course, that this covering law is also changeable by fiat of the same authority. In fact, it has been changed. It does not appear to me, however, that Hempel's stipulations refer to the *sources* of law at all, and therefore they do not rule out laws that owe their universality to human fiat. Hempel, *Aspects of Scientific Explanation* (New York, 1965), pp. 264–70. Nor does he specify immutability as a condition of universality. On mere logical grounds it is hard to see how he could. For example, if tomorrow, rather improbably, all masses started attracting each other as the cubes rather than the squares of their distances, it might be a considerable cosmic nuisance, but it would be hard to deny the new law of gravitation the status of universality hitherto accorded to the one it superseded. I may, however, have incorrectly apprehended Hempel's argument as to what he would count as a law.

ships differed among the National Football League, the National Basketball Association, and the National Hockey League; and they all differed from the rules of the two major baseball leagues, which were identical one with the other. To a person seeking the kind of knowledge specified just above, the foregoing would surely provide him with the explanation he needed—but only briefly.

If, for example, he happened to look at the end-of-the-season standings in 1951, he would notice that while all eight teams in the American League and six of the eight National League teams played 154 games, the first and second teams in the National League played 157 games. This might strike him as an anomaly and perplex him. And so the initial explanation, still true and still complete by the "scientific" standard, would remain true but cease to be complete by that looser standard of explanations which we may here christen pragmatic, or, better, processive.[4] In effect, what looked like enough to be going on with for a while quickly ran into a blockade. The trouble is easy enough to cope with. We simply add a second covering law and another secondary boundary condition.

Covering law 2. Before 1969, when at the end of the *regular* National League baseball season the two leading teams had won and lost the same number of games (a tie), they continued to play each other until one of them had won two games (the playoff); the said team thereby winning the championship.

Boundary condition 3. In 1951, having ended in a tie for first place with the Brooklyn team at the close of the regular National League season, the New York team won two games against one for Brooklyn in the playoff.

So without moving beyond the limits of the covering-law model we have provided a processive explanation "why" for the historical question, "Why did the New York National League baseball team win the National League championship in 1951?" Again it is worth stressing that the question is indeed a historical question and the response a historical explanation, and that therefore there is no reasonable doubt that occasionally explanations in the most rigorous scientific form are useful in some contexts for assisting processive explanations, for providing someone with the knowledge he needs to continue with the work of explaining in history.

With our amended explanation "why," however, given the context, the process really does stop; it is indeed complete, it has no further to go. In the context of an inquiry into the formal rules for winning championships in major professional team sports in 1951, the questioner

---

[4] Hitherto, oddly enough, the English language has had but made very little of an adjective meaning "in the nature of a process." For remedying a patent deficiency in the common vocabulary there is no time like the present.

knows all about the National League baseball championship he needs
to know. And although we have perhaps disclosed and separated out
a significant genus of explanations, processive explanations, we are
scarcely any closer to historical storytelling than we were when we
started. The notion of a story is a very flexible one, but there are limits.
Anyone who can believe that the foregoing explanations are historical
stories is likely to mistake a stock market report for a Homeric ode.

In order to elicit an explanation "why" in the form of a story, we
have to set our question in a different context from the one above. Suppose a quite young baseball fan is leafing through a collection of baseball statistics. He comes on a section giving end-of-season standings in
the National League. His eyes light on the standings for 1951:

	Won	Lost	Average
New York	98	59	.624
Brooklyn	97	60	.618

His eyes light up. He says, "Wow, some pennant race!" and then with
the charming courtesy and deference which in this generation youth
shows to age and experience, "Hey, Pop, you know why the Giants
won the pennant in 1951?" And then unless his father has completely
lost his memory, or unless he suffered frightful cultural deprivation in
his younger days, his eyes, too, will light up, and he will say, "Well,
son, that was quite a story." And willy-nilly the young man will have to
listen for the next half hour, at least, to the story of the National
League pennant race of 1951.[5]

Consider now the two questions, "Why did the New York National
League baseball team win the National League baseball championship?" and "Why did the Giants win the pennant?" They are logically
synonymous, the same question in the sense that $\sqrt{4}$, $\dfrac{-64}{32}$, $3-1$, $-6+8$,
and 2 are mathematically the same number. The referents of the "New
York National League baseball team" and "the Giants," of "the National
League baseball championship" and "the pennant" are the same two

[5] That quite devoted social scientists resort to explanation by historical storytelling is nicely illustrated in that long New Covenant of those scientists with analysis, *International Encyclopedia of the Social Sciences* (New York: Macmillan, 1968),
2: 41–45. The illustration appears—of all places—in the article "Behavioral Sciences"
by Bernard Berelson. The problem is to explain why there are *behavioral* sciences.
Berelson's explanation "why" is so clearly a processive explanation by historical storytelling that I shall reproduce part of it as an appendix to Chapter 8, after I have
dealt more fully with the character of that kind of explanation. Placed there, it may
serve to persuade the otherwise skeptical that the discussion in the three chapters
that precede it is not just an aberration of a loose-thinking historian afflicted with
a passion for the antiquities of major league baseball (see pp. 221–224).

entities. Why then does the young man's "why" question elicit a historical story, when the earlier "why" question, logically identical to it, elicited a nomological-deductive explanation? What accounts for the difference? I suggest that the difference is clear, unmistakable and nonlogical. It is the rhetoric, not the logic of the questions, that solicits the divergent answers. Rhetorically in context "the New York National League baseball team" and "the National League baseball championship" belong together. Together they mark an inquirer who, to be getting on with whatever he seeks to get on with, may need to know the official major league rules for winning a league championship. "The Giants" and "the pennant" also belong together. The very use of the latter terms by anybody over the age of ten is a better than average indicator that such a one already knows the appropriate rules. To answer the question "Why did the Giants win the pennant in 1951?" with a statement of rules and boundary conditions is to offer an explanation that will probably turn out to be correct, true, and wrong—true because it contains no false statements, correct because it involves no logical missteps, wrong because to judge by the rhetorical elements of the question, it answers a question that is not being asked. Moreover, if in construing the question one takes into consideration the exclamation "Wow, what a pennant race!" that is, if one pays attention to the context, the "why" question looks as if it must be translated, "How come that . . . ?" or "How did it happen that . . . ?" both of them ordinary incipits to story-soliciting questions.

We now must find out how the group of analytical philosophers whom we have selected for background contrast [6] cope with a "why" question or a "why" question-equivalent soliciting an explanation "why" which is a historical story. This group of philosophers has been especially concerned to assert the underlying unity of all sciences and by extension, the unity or solidarity of all truth, including historical truth, with scientific truth. Therefore, we anticipate, as before indicated, an attempt to assimilate or rope in historical storytelling to the models of explanation already certified as scientific by the group.

The assimilation of historical storytelling to scientific explanation proceeds through the following seven easy and simple steps to its predestined conclusion.

Step 1. Historical storytelling is narration.

Step 2. Historical narration has as its base a chronicle, a sequence of true but nonexplanatory facts.

Step 3. "A narrative is a conjunction of explanatory statements." [7]

---

[6] See Nonchapter, p. 14.
[7] Morton G. White, *Foundations of Historical Knowledge* (New York, 1965), p. 14.

Step 4. In historical narration, the succession of true facts of a chronicle are or can be explicity conjoined by words like "because" into chains of causal explanation.

Step 5. Such explanations are deemed true only on the assumption that there is a deductive argument in which the alleged cause will appear as a premise and the alleged effect as its conclusion.[8]

Step 6. All the truth of historical narration is either in the facts of the chronicle or in the logic of the explanations "why."

Step 7. Therefore all the words of a historian's story that do not function as indispensable elements of factual statements or of explanations "why" are irrelevant to the discovery and ordering of historical truth.[9]

Note how quickly at Step 1 this argument shuffles off the scene the historical stories that historians actually write by speciously equating them with narration, thus enabling the shuffler to deal thereafter with what he defines as narration. Note how the stories reappear in Step 7, with their actual structures little further investigated than they were at the outset, and with a good excuse built in for never investigating them further, if one's interest is in historical truth.

By assimilationist standards, then, all that we need for the truest possible historical story answering the question, "Why did the Giants win the pennant in 1951?" is a historical narration conformable to the requirements of Steps 2 through 5. For this purpose it is to our advan-

---

[8] Step V is an effort to summarize what White calls "existential regularism" without becoming snarled in the convolutions of analysis that he deemed necessary for his particular purposes. White, *Foundations of Historical Knowledge*, p. 60. I have used White's discussions in preference to possible alternatives because he makes explicit implications of the assimilationist strategy that are present but less conspicuous in other assimilationist arguments, for example, that of A. C. Danto, *Analytical Philosophy of History*, (Cambridge, 1965), pp. 251–256.

[9] ". . . The historical narrative, the extended story, is so large and rambling by contrast to the single sentence treated by the logician that any effort to treat it as a repeatable and identifiable pattern of language may give an impression of remoteness and distortion well beyond what might be felt by the historian who finds his causal statements cast in a single syntactical mold. On the other hand, the very qualities of narrative which might lead a historian to think that logical analysis distorts it are those that might inhibit a logician from trying to discern its structure. The complexity and variety of narrative, the fact that one story seems so different in structure from another, may give both the romantically minded historian and the classically minded logician pause. Yet the vast differences that human beings exhibit do not prevent us from X-raying them in an effort to discern the skeletal structure that each of them possesses. . . . History is a literary art as well as a discipline aimed at discovering and ordering truth, and if we neglect some of the narrative's literary qualities in order to clarify certain epistemological problems connected with it, our procedure is like that of the sane roentgenologist, who searches for the skull without denying that the skin exists and without denying that the skin may vary enormously in color, texture, and beauty." White, *Foundations of Historical Knowledge*. In passing I might note that I do not regard the categories "romantically minded historian" and "classically minded logician" as exhausting the set "historians and logicians." Rightly or wrongly I consider myself a classically minded historian. Whether any logician is or deems himself romantically minded I do not know.

tage that the official rules of baseball provide us with a vocabulary almost as purely denotative as that of the sciences. In that vocabulary we can produce a narrative explanation of why the Giants won the pennant in 1951. Here are the National League standings as of September 30, 1951:

	Won	Lost
Brooklyn Dodgers	96	58
New York Giants	96	58

Because of the tie at the end of the regular season Brooklyn and New York were required to play additional games, the first team to win two games to be designated as the National League entry in the World Series.

First additional game, October 1, 1951: final score, New York 3, Brooklyn 1; games won, New York 1, Brooklyn 0.

Second additional game, October 2, 1951: final score, Brooklyn 10, New York 0; games won, New York 1, Brooklyn 1. Because neither team had won two games a third game was played.

Third additional game, October 3, 1951: inning-by-inning score to second half of the ninth inning:

| Brooklyn | 1 0 0 | 0 0 0 | 0 3 0 |
| New York | 0 0 0 | 0 0 0 | 1 0 |

Score to second half of the ninth inning, Brooklyn 4, New York 1. New York at bat.

The first batter singled. The second batter singled. Because the first batter was a reasonably fast runner, he advanced to third base. Because the third batter hit a short fly ball which was caught, he was out. Because the fourth batter doubled, the first batter scored a run, and the second batter advanced to third base. He was replaced by a substitute runner because he had hurt his leg. The Brooklyn pitcher was replaced because the manager of the Brooklyn team ordered another pitcher to replace him. Because the fifth batter hit a home run the substitute runner, the fourth batter, and the fifth batter scored runs. Because New York scored four runs in the second half of the ninth inning, making the score 5 to 4, they won the game. Because they won two games of the playoff before Brooklyn did, they won more games and lost fewer than any other team in the National League. Because of this they were the National League champions.

About the preceding explanation by narration a number of instructive points are worth noting.

1. It almost perfectly conforms to the proposed structure of narrative explanation outlined above; that is; it is a series of sentences in which the causal connections between the events mentioned are explicit or clearly implicit, and into which the relevant possible general laws may

readily be inserted. Any number of such laws are not merely possible but actually available; for example, if the two leading teams in the National League have won and lost the same number of games at the end of the regular season, the rules require that they resolve the tie by playing against each other until one of them has won two games.

2. All the facts as stated are verifiably true and all the causal inferences are valid, and therefore the whole narrative explanation is historically true and accurate in every respect.

3. As it stands, the explanation is historiographically pitiful, and the historian who offered it would immediately lose the historian's moral equivalent of a union card.

But a philosopher might object to such a characterization; indeed he might feel somewhat hurt by it. He has gone to great pains and as far as possible to assimilate narration, an evidently common form of historical explanation, hitherto unassimilated, to the standard forms of scientific explanation and thus to legitimate the truth-values of narration as they had not been legitimated before. Instead of being duly grateful for this earnest effort, the historian [10] takes a look at what is offered, sniffs contemptuously, refuses the offer, and then sinks his fangs into the hands of the offerer. Little wonder if the offerer shows some pique at what has the look of rank ingratitude, sharper indeed than the serpent's tooth.[11]

From the point of view of historians and of Everyman, who, remember, is also a historian, what is wrong with the explanatory narrative above? We will need to examine it closely to say what is wrong with it in detail, but can we start out by saying what is wrong with it in general? Not perhaps in terms appropriate to the logic of scientific explanation. We can, however, diagnose the trouble in the rhetoric proper to historical storytelling. The trouble is that the explanatory narrative in answer to the question "Why did the Giants win the pennant in 1951?" is couched in a rhetoric that would be appropriate only if the question were "Why did the New York National League team win the National League championship in 1951?" and perhaps not appropriate even then. The answer disregards the rhetoric of the first question and of the context: "Wow, some pennant race!"

A closer look at the explanatory narrative draws our attention to two kinds of defects in it. The first and more simple are those that cluster about the conception of the logic of historical narration as set forth above. Consider the "explanation" of the substitution of one Brooklyn pitcher for another in the ninth inning of the third game of the playoff.

[10] Well, anyway, *one* historian—the present author.
[11] This is a reasonably fair summary of an unfortunate exchange of nonamenities between Morton White and the author, *New York Review of Books*, February 9, 1967, pp. 24–28; March 23, 1967, pp. 28–31.

According to one view of the matter this is an explanation sketch readily expandable into an adequate "scientific" explanation of the most rigorous sort. We herewith expand it:

Covering law: "A player, or players, may be substituted during a game at any time the ball is dead.[12]

Boundary condition: The Brooklyn manager called for the substitution of one Brooklyn pitcher by another in the second half of the ninth inning on October 3 when the ball was dead.

The statement of the covering laws and of the boundary conditions strictly entails the statement that the Brooklyn pitcher was replaced by another, or, given the laws and the conditions, the event is predictable. This explanation is not only satisfactory, it is the only sort of historical explanation that satisfies the requirement of scientific completeness. Complete explanations of particular events are in this view impossible; what is possible is the complete explanation of *kinds* of events, and of a particular event only as an instance of a kind. So we have achieved something quite remarkable—a bit of historical explanation by narration that is scientifically true, complete, and adequate in every respect, and that is also trivially true since less than 1 percent of the crowd at a ball game do not understand the rule.

Suppose that to avoid this waste of time one seeks a sort of intermediate position. Instead of saying the Brooklyn pitcher was replaced because the manager ordered another pitcher to replace him, we say he was replaced "because he was hit safely by three of the four batters to face him in the ninth inning." The lot of a historian who tried this one for size would be devastating—the lot of all men who try to achieve compromise between incompatibles. His well-intentioned attempt would be ground to bits between the upper and the nether millstone. From the assimilationist point of view it is hopeless. There is simply no general rule or covering law at all behind the ascribed cause, sufficient to entail the statement that the event happened or to render the event predictable. All there is is the judgment or guess of a particular manager in a particular situation that a particular pitcher should be replaced by another particular pitcher. That the three hits were indeed among the considerations of the manager who made the decision is just about certain, but what is the general rule? Is it that in a close baseball game three safe hits against a pitcher will always cause a manager to remove him? Certainly not. To consider removing him? Usually it will; but always . . . ?

And that brings us to the nether millstone—the historical storyteller and his story. From his point of view the compromise "explanation by narration" is almost as far removed from his concerns and as useless as

[12] *Official Baseball Guide and Record Book, 1952* (St. Louis, 1952), p. 516.

the one that starts with the Official Rules of Baseball. If he is worth his salt, if he is not a wholly incompetent historical storyteller, his attention will immediately focus on the particular manager, Charles Dressen, the particular pitcher he relieved, Don Newcombe, the particular pitcher Dressen called in, Ralph Branca, and the particular batter Branca pitched to, Bobby Thomson, who hit Branca's second pitch for a home run. And what he will tell about are Dressen's decisions, so disastrous in their outcome, to substitute Branca for Newcombe and to order Branca to pitch to Thomson instead of giving him an intentional base on balls. Hopefully, what will move him to do this will not be the belief that Big "H" History is concerned *only* with the Particular and *never* with Generalization or General Laws. If he is encumbered by any such belief, the sooner he disencumbers himself of it the better. Hopefully, as a small "h" historian he will take the right course, because he will recognize that in context it is this course that any moderately informed reader will want and expect him to take, because he will know that this is the *only* adequate and appropriate response of a historical storyteller to this bit of the record of the past, that anything less, even if it is true, is not enough. *How* he knows this it may be hard to say. *That* he does not know his business unless he knows it is beyond reasonable doubt. That he will be able to provide an entirely satisfactory explanation for Dressen's decision is not at all certain; that he must wrestle with the questions it raises is certain. He cannot simply default.

If no regularity, rule, or law appears relevant to the historical narration of the penultimate moment of the pennant race of 1951, even less does any appear relevant to the ultimate moment—Thomson's home run. It is true that given the velocity and trajectory of Branca's pitch, the velocity and path of Thomson's bat, the distance between home plate and the left-field stands, the ground rules of baseball, and a few special cases, mainly ballistic, of the general laws of motion, it follows that Thomson hit a home run off Branca's second pitch. It is true but beside the point, since the one thing that every one concerned with these matters would agree to is that, in the context of the pennant race of 1951, citation to the laws of physics at this point is an intrusive irrelevance.[13]

If the foregoing explanation is irrelevant, what of the explanation of Thomson's decision to swing at Branca's second pitch? Why did he do

[13] In special cases citations to the ground rules might not be irrelevant. For example, the empty lot on which I was introduced to the game of baseball at the age of six had a very short left-field fence. On that lot the rule was, "Over the fence is out." To anyone who thought the only ground rules of baseball were those in force on that lot it might be necessary to explain why Thomson was not out but credited with a home run when he hit the ball over the left-field fence in the Polo Grounds.

it? His own answer to this question is particularly awkward: it was, he said, a bad pitch; a good batter would not have swung at it at all. What possible general law or regularity principle is operative here? That bad batters always swing at bad pitches? False. That Thomson always swung at bad pitches? False. Actually even batters bad by Big League standards do not usually swing at bad pitches. And, of course, all batters, even the very best, sometimes swing at bad pitches. Actually, there is no need to invoke either a rule or a regularity principle. Anyone who has played or watched baseball has seen hitters, good or bad, swing at bad pitches and usually miss them or hit them weakly, but once in a while hit them hard. And Thomson happened to hit the one Branca served up to him hard, and that is all there is to it. Terms like "usually," "once in a while," and "sometimes" do not and cannot assert or imply a universal rule; on the contrary, they signify that no universal rule is intended. It appears then that we can and must make sense out of much that has happened in the past without reference to any general laws and without assuming such laws at all, and that even in the context of the logic of explanation by narration, we are sometimes going to have to get along without such laws.

Beyond the bounds and limitations of explanation by narration as conceived by assimilationist philosophers lie another set of problems. The view of those philosophers about what is to count as truth and explanation in history prevents them from seeing these problems. Yet from the point of view of truth and explanation in historical storytelling, and therefore from the point of view of this primer, the issues raised by what assimilationist philosophers prevent themselves from seeing may be more worthy of attention than what they do see. To identify some of these problems let us go back to the question we started with: "Why did the Giants win the pennant in 1951?" In the context of this question and before answering it, a historian would, I like to think, ask himself another question: "Let's see; where should I begin the story?"

The first thing to note about this question, which the historian himself raises, is that it conceals an implicit affirmative answer to yet another, albeit implicit, prior question: "Shall I explain why the Giants won by telling a story?" Now there is no a priori reason that questions of the form: "Why did the—win the pennant in—?" should call for a story. Suppose we fill in the blanks with "Yankees" and "1939."

Figure 5 is constructed on uniform scales for each axis, plotting day-by-day games won by the New York Yankees against the games won by the team in the league that was in second place.

On considering the situation revealed by the graph, no competent historian would answer the question with a story. The graph shows that

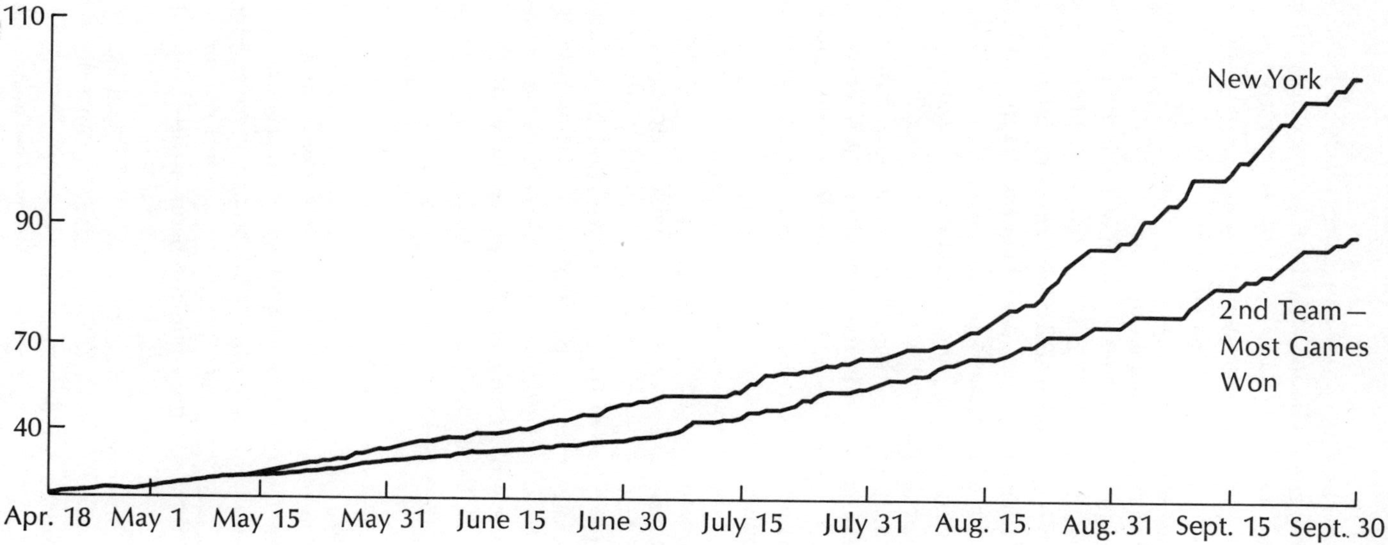
110
90
70
40
New York
2 nd Team —
Most Games
Won
Apr. 18
May 1
May 15
May 31
June 15
June 30
July 15
July 31
Aug. 15
Aug. 31
Sept. 15
Sept.. 30

Figure 5

as early as June 1, the Yankees led the American League by seven games, that thereafter the minimum gap between them and their nearest rival was six games, that by the end of the season the Yankees led by seventeen games. In short, for more than the latter two-thirds of the season there was never a moment when it even looked like a pennant race in the American League in 1939, so that on the face of the record, to answer the question "Why did the Yankees win the pennant?" with a historical story would be a historiographic error: the even-paced, dull, and trivial chronicle which the effort would yield would itself demonstrate the inappropriateness of such a rhetorical response. Given the question "Why did the Yankees win the pennant in 1939?" any historian worth his salt would translate it, "In 1939 what gave the Yankees a superiority over their nearest rival, the Boston Red Sox, so great that they turned competition for the pennant into a dull joke?" The answer calls not for historical storytelling but historical analysis. The analysis is elegantly simple: the Yankees won handily because they were the best team in the league in both offense (batting) and defense (pitching and fielding), significantly better offensively than Boston and far, far better defensively. The excellent statistics of baseball enable us to support this judgment —universal at the time among all competent observers—with quantitative evidence. (See Table 1.) The ultimate yield of these statistics is that, combining offense and defense, on the average against their opponents, the Yankees were two runs per game better than their closest competitors, the Boston Red Sox. The statistics are a surviving and presentable record of the symptoms of what was going on in the American League during the 1939 season.

Table 1

	NEW YORK	BOSTON
A. Offense:		
1. Batting average	.287	.291
2. Slugging average	.451	.436
3. Runs per game	6.46	5.96
B. Defense:		
1. Opponents earned-run average	3.31	4.33
2. Complete games pitched	87	52
3. Percentage of complete games pitched	56.6	34.6
4. Opponents run average per nine innings played	3.71	5.17
5. Opponents run average per official games completed	3.75	5.23

Source: *The Official Baseball Guide* (New York: 1940), pp. 111–122, provides the statistics for A.1 and B.1. All other statistical items are computed on the basis of statistics provided in the *Official Guide*.

But the analytical mode of explanation that we intuitively recognize as appropriate to the American League season we intuitively reject for the National League season of 1951. Why do we do so? Well, what good would such analysis be? It would either reveal a marked overall superiority of one of the teams to all the others or it would not. If it did, it would simply be wrong. If two teams play each of the same six other teams twenty-two games and play one another twenty-two games, a total of 154 games per season, and end up by winning and losing precisely the same number of games, as the New York Giants and the Brooklyn Dodgers did that year, then overall neither team is markedly superior to the other over the whole season, whatever the other overall statistics suggest to the contrary. And, of course, if the statistics show that the teams were about evenly matched, they just say again what the won-and-lost record has already said far more persuasively: they are not supporting or confirmatory to that record, merely redundant and superfluous.[14]

Figure 6 is a graph of part of the National League season of 1951. It begins on August 12, when the regular season was nearly three-fourths over. Only two teams are plotted, and one of them, Brooklyn, is not plotted in motion but is simply drawn as a horizontal constant upper zero or goal-line. Only the New York Giants are plotted as if in motion. The graph also varies several times in scale on both horizontal and vertical axes. The vertical axis incorporates three scales: (1) a unit scale from 13 games to 4½ games behind, (2) a two-unit scale from 4½ games to the second tie, (3) an exponential scale for runs behind or ahead in the last game of the playoff. The horizontal axis, in semilog units, incorporates four scales—a unit scale of calendar days from August 11 to September 21, a two-unit scale from September 22 to October 3, a unit scale by innings for the first six innings of the game of October 3, and a three-unit scale for the last three innings of that game.

Figure 6 is not a graphic alternative to an explanation by historical storytelling: when the record of the past requires a historical story to do it justice, a graph can supplement but not replace the story. Nor does the figure prescribe the disposition of the parts of the story, which is one of the main problems of historical macrorhetoric. It does not, that is, prescribe to the historian that he begin his story with the situation as of August 11, 1951, and pursue it in chronological order to October 3. A story, after all, can begin at the beginning, go to the end and then stop in conformity to the King of Hearts' injunction to the White Rabbit, or it can begin in *medias res*, in the midst of things, as Horace prescribed in his *Ars Poetica*. Or in the case at hand, because of an oddity of the

[14] Actual calculation of the sort that shows the Yankees playing ball superior to the Red Sox at a rate of two runs per game in 1939 shows the Brooklyn Dodgers playing ball at a rate .2 runs per game superior to the New York Giants in 1951, a figure as conspicuously as it is demonstrably insignificant.

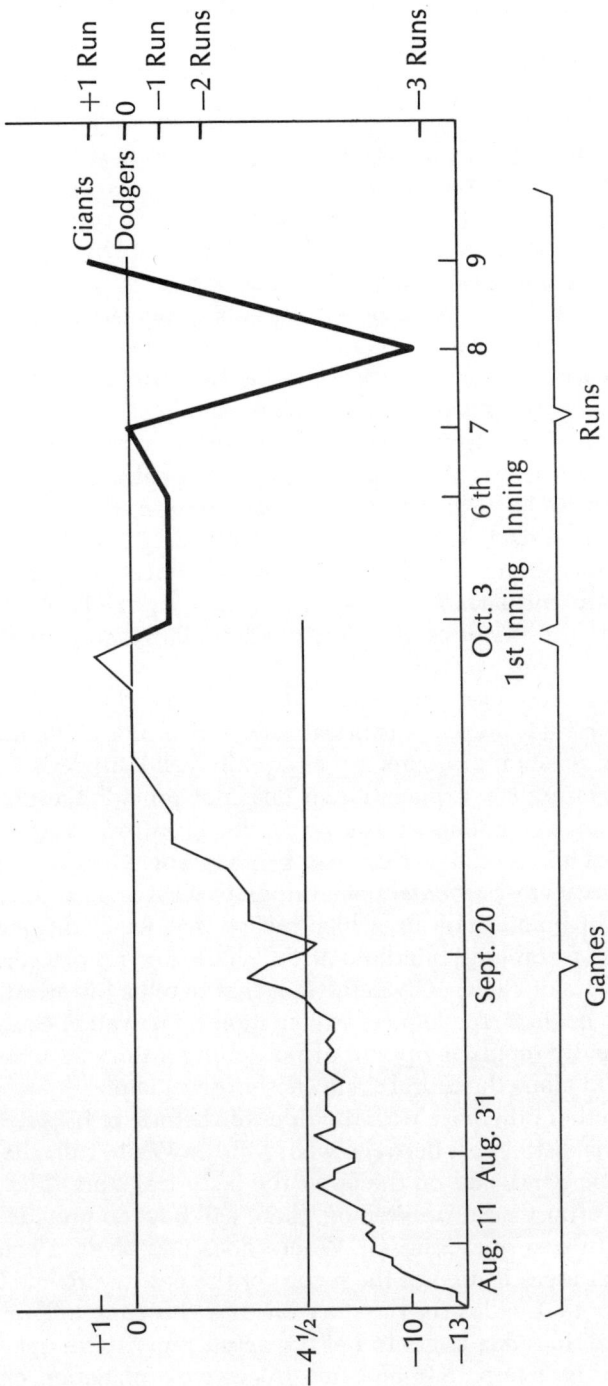

Figure 6

record of the past, a historian may, as we shall see, decide to begin his story at a point beyond the end of the graph.[15]

The purpose of the figure is to put before the reader certain items from the record of the pennant race of 1951 and to indicate graphically a few judgments that an examination of that record seems to imply. The peculiarities of the graph in structure and scale are a sort of memo to a historical storyteller, reminding him of points of interest that he will need to keep in mind in telling his historical story.

Figure 6 thus serves to bring out traits of explanation by historical storytelling obscured by the assimilationist's leap from historical story-telling to explanation by narration and his leap back.[16] Both leaps are an unintentional bit of *trompe l'oeil*. The assimilationist never got himself into the perilous position of taking historical storytelling seriously. He did not start with it at all, but with an artifice called historical narration, so of course he never had to cross back to it. And a good thing for him, too. Had he started there, he would have faced a rush of questions that every storytelling historian has to answer, questions that the logic of explanation by narration avoids answering by declaring them off limits, denying to the rules of historical storytelling and to the rhetoric that they are rules of, any truth value.

Let us consider a question we have already touched on: Where do we begin the story? The logic of historical narration affords either no answer at all to this question or an infinity of equally valid answers. Unlike its *Ur-vater*, covering-law explanation, it does not provide the grounds or means of its own containment. It is avowedly a *continuous causal chain*, and within its inherent logic there can be no reason whatever for breaking that chain at any *particular* point or points. That logic affords us only the options of infinite regress, which means that we could never start the story, or of grabbing blindfold at the chain any old place, since we have no criteria of choice. Given the fact that to tell a historical story at all one must begin it, the logic of explanation by narration confronts us with the equally repulsive options of not telling a story at all or beginning at a point along the causal chain chosen at random.

It is altogether otherwise with the rules of rhetoric of historical story-telling. Let us distinguish between what Morton White calls the chronicle on the one hand, and on the other the historical story. The rules of the rhetoric of historical storytelling, then, will have to provide us with the answer to two questions. (1) Where does one begin a continuous chronological investigation of the record of the past to provide the substrate of data that will carry the story one has chosen to tell, or most of it, and where does one begin to tell the actual story? The qualification "or most of it" is an important one. In a processive explanation, one some-

---

[15] See pp. 155–156.
[16] The leaps occur between steps 1 and 2 and steps 6 and 7.

times encounters phenomena for which exploration of the "continental" chronological continuum affords no explanation. Then in quest of data for solving the problem one has identified, one may well turn to what we may call record islands or record archipelagoes, chronologically discontinuous with the main record and with each other.[17]

In the case of the National League pennant race of 1951, the rules of the rhetoric of historical storytelling enable us quickly to identify a sensible point for our investigation of the chronological continuum. It is August 11–12, 1951. The premature obituary notice of the pennant race in *The Times* on the morning of August 12, just before the Giant winning streak of sixteen games, underscores that date like a bright red line.

> Knocked completely out of sight as a pennant contender by the Dodgers earlier in the week, the Giants yesterday found themselves in danger of being evicted from their long-time tenancy of second place in the National League standings.[18]

What of the actual starting place of the historical story? We have already pointed out that the story could begin at the beginning of the chronological continuum, or in *medias res*, or in this particular case after the ending. If one selected the second alternative, one would have to consider a few subalternatives—the end of the Giant's long winning streak on August 27, or the beginning of their seven-game drive to tie the race on September 21, or the interval between the Giants' victory over Philadelphia on September 30 and the moment a long hour later when the Dodgers defeated Boston in a fourteen-inning game to drag themselves back into an end-of-the-season tie. The third possibility, that of beginning after the end, is supplied by the story of an Old Timers' game that the New York Mets, a then new National League team, put on in the early 1960's. Old Timers' games are usually played for laughs by former players, most of them retired from baseball. Baseball is a sport that thrives on nostalgia, and the Mets' management knew that New Yorkers were still homesick for the days when the Giants, long since moved to San Francisco, and the Dodgers, who had moved to Los Angeles, were rivals for the heart of New York. So they invited the players from the Dodgers' and the Giants' teams of 1951 to play against each other. And as expected the old boys clowned it up. Then suddenly one of them was not clowning it up at all. The Brooklyn pitcher was throwing the ball hard and fast to a Giant batter. He even

[17] For an example of such an exploration of off-shore record archipelagoes, see Hexter, "The Structure of the Middle Group," *The Reign of King Pym* (Cambridge, Mass., 1941), pp. 63–99.

[18] *New York Times*, August 12, 1951. This is not to assert, what is not true, that all such points are always so clearly marked in the record of the past or so unequivocal.

threw one close to force the batter back from home plate. In the end the batter popped up an easily caught fly ball. Later he said of the pitcher, "He was throwing harder than when I hit the home run." The batter's name was Thomson; the pitcher's name was Branca—and the historical story could start there.[19]

The rules of the rhetoric of historical storytelling do not therefore point to one and just one place where we could begin our historical story; they point to several alternatives. This should not surprise historians or occasion them any excessive worry. Yet because many of them suffer from what might be called the positivist-idealist syndrome of expectations, it is likely to do so. Off and on in this primer we have already had occasion to touch glancingly on this syndrome; it is now time to identify it, describe it and, one hopes, dispose of it once and for all, since it leads historians erroneously to believe that the ways they go about studying the past fail to yield the truth about it.

Suffering from this syndrome historians have often erred in identifying its source. In effect they tend to believe that it results from something they have done wrong in rendering their accounts of the past; actually most of the time it results from their *thinking* something wrong about what they are doing right. Because of this mistake historians search for an error in their ways in the place where it is not, instead of where it is. They never find it and consequently their attempts to correct it usually fail. Consistent failure leads them into the fallacy of misplaced humility. They come to believe that they are doing their business badly and are very humble about what they do, when in fact they are often doing their business reasonably well and have nothing (or at least not terribly much) to be ashamed of. Humility is a major intellectual virtue, and historians have plenty to be humble about, but the economics of moral resources suggest that they deploy their humility on what they have to be humble about and not on what they do not have to be humble about. Instead of taking a low view of their practice of their vocation, and sometimes even of their vocation itself, they need to take a low view of their way of thinking about their vocation; then they can correct their error instead of being enmeshed in it. And this brings us back to the syndrome which underlies the error. Its components, positivist and idealist, are interlocked in practice, but they can be separated for examination. The positivist component goes as follows:

1. History is a collocation of statements of facts about the past.
2. All such statements are either true or false.

---

[19] Jocko Conlan and Robert Creamer, *Jocko* (Philadelphia and New York, 1967), pp. 128–129. Mr. Paul Fechheimer, a serious student of baseball history, called to my attention this passage and another that will be referred to later.

3. Unless the statement can be shown to be true, it is false, or if one does not know whether it is true or false, mere opinion.

4. What is false or mere opinion has no place in true history.

5. Much of what is alleged as true statement of fact in history turns out to be false or mere opinion.

6. Very little history is true.

The Platonic idealist component runs as follows:

1. Truth is one, certain, and eternal.

2. Therefore what is really true is immutable, beyond doubt, and uniquely correct.

3. What is not immutable, beyond doubt, and uniquely correct is false or not true; it is unreal, or a mere matter of opinion.

4. Every statement about the past is subject to change and doubt, and none totally precludes alternative possibilities.

5. Therefore all history that is not simply false is a mere matter of opinion.[20]

To this positivist-idealist syndrome of propositions, which results in a wrong, debilitating, inconsistent, and counterproductive way of thinking about history one alternative would go somewhat as follows:

1. Potentially history is a credible, coherent, and patterned construal of the record of the past.

2. Properly conducted historical investigation and properly constructed historical discourse usually result not in "mere opinion," but in close approximations to the truth about their objects of inquiry.

3. Sometimes the evidence available in the surviving records of the past will satisfactorily sustain two or more divergent yet credible conclusions about what went on in the past; and although an omniscient God could eliminate all divergencies, historians are not and are unlikely to become omniscient gods, so some divergent historical conclusions will be almost equally credible.

4. The rhetoric of history frequently permits two or more divergent alternative structures of discourse, and the alternatives are sometimes

[20] To foist so elaborate and specific a set of subconscious views on historians without a decent display of evidence may seem rash and is certainly bold. At best it involves stating with some coherence and precision opinions and even "feelings" that historians actually hold unsystematically and imprecisely, and some of which they would reject in the above precise formulation and systematic juxtaposition. I am nevertheless fairly sure that a search for the appropriate evidence would reveal fragments of belief strongly suggestive of the above-stated pattern. In any case the argument is the most plausible and economical one that I have been able to construct to account adequately for the phenomena. It is otherwise hard to understand the diffidence of so many intellectually nonmoribund historians about the way they do the very things that they actually do quite well.

irreducible in principle either (a) because they equally maximize the truth values that they achieve or (b) because each maximizes sets of incommensurate truths values that cannot be maximized simultaneously within any single structure of historical discourse.

5. Proposition 4–a should cause neither historians nor anyone else any discomfort or wonder, since the existence of several equally valid solutions to a problem is far from being unique to the rhetoric of history. It is a phenomenon familiar to everyone who got as far as quadratic equations in algebra, which have two equally correct solutions. It will also be familiar to anyone who considers the innumerable ways of bringing about chemical reactions of which water will be an end-product. In neither the algebraic nor the chemical case does the duality or multiplicity of correct solutions imply that there are no rules or that what counts as a correct solution is merely a matter of opinion. What is true of algebra and chemistry is also true of the rhetoric of history.

6. On the other hand position 4–b may present considerable difficulties since it may imply and be symptomatic of a fundamental difference between history and the natural sciences rooted in differences between the two aspects of reality that are their respective objects—"the past" and "nature." If this is so, it is of great importance, and it will be worth close scrutiny later.

In the case under consideration that elicited the foregoing detour it is hard to see enough difference among the three alternative ways of starting the story of why the Giants won the pennant to make one clearly preferable to the other two. But on this ground to argue that the rules of historical storytelling afford no guidance to historians and puts them under no constraints would be absurd. Those rules have got us out of the situation created by the logic of historical explanation by narration where A, B, C, D, . . . N are equally right or wrong places to start the narration and to a situation where A, B, C, and D are the only right places to start the historical story. To assert, "There is a rule," is not to state the rule or even to assert that the rule is discursively and clearly statable. It is not my intention here to attempt to work out fully the rules of the macrorhetoric of historical storytelling, but only to make clear in the context of a focal center that something far more reasonable than individual whim or random choice defines the starting place, the sequence, and the proportions of an explanation by such means.

This brings us to our next point. In Figure 6 the scale-expansion points on the graph for both the vertical and the horizontal axis are strikingly sharp and precise as the indicated starting point of the chronicle. The successive vertical expansions are story-tension expansions. They take account of the fact that absolute numbers of games behind have different meanings at different points along the horizontal axis. To be five games behind on August 27 with twenty-eight games to go after having been thirteen behind scarcely two weeks earlier gave the Giants grounds for reasonable hope and jubilation. To be still fiive games behind almost three weeks later despite having won two-thirds of their games in the interval and with only ten games to go should have been the end of hope. A gap of five games had become a chasm of five games.[21]

The expansions along the horizontal axis graphically illustrate a further crucial point about historical storytelling. Considered as interval measurements they are quite arbitrary. One twenty-four-hour day is of precisely the same duration as any other. But for the historical storyteller these considerations are quite irrelevant. The clock and the calendar provide no guidance to the appropriate dimensions of a historical story. Between those dimensions and mere duration, measured in homogeneous scaled increments, there is no congruence. The historical storyteller's time is not clock-and-calendar time; it is historical tempo. The problems involved in reasonably accurate determination of historical tempo have never been systematically studied, although results of the disaster of not studying them strew the historiographic landscape. But two points are clear. (1) Disproportions in historical stories induced by failure to appraise historical tempo correctly result in the telling of distorted stories about the past. To that extent they diminish, and correct perception of tempo increases, available knowledge of the past. (2) Correct determinations of historical tempo and the appropriate correlative expansions and contractions of scale in a historical story depend on the examination *in retrospect* of the historical record. When the historian tells a historical story, he must not only know something of the outcomes of the events that concern him; he must use what he knows in telling his story.

And this both brings us to and is the final point in our investigation of the rhetoric of explanation "why" in historical storytelling. The chronicle of the assimilationist philosopher investigating the logic of historical explanation by narration and the continuous chronicle of the historical storyteller, both assembled with the purpose of answering the question, "Why did the Giants win the pennant in 1951?" have the identical terminal point—Bobby Thomson's home run in the last half of the ninth inning of the last game of the playoff. But there is a difference; for the philosopher that event is an end-point; for the historian it is also an observation point, the place where he takes his stand and

[21] From the point of view of accommodating the rhetoric of graphing to the historical record it might have been preferable to represent the change as an inverse logarithmic expansion. But there is a limit to the refinements of rhetoric that are graphically expressible at a reasonable cost in time and labor.

from which he surveys the record of the past in order to make the indispensable decisions on a sound rhetorical strategy for his story.

Unless the writer has the outcome in mind as he writes his historical story, he will not know how to adapt the proportions of his story to the actual historical tempo, since that is knowable only to one who knows the outcome. For example, the decisive point for transforming the proportions of the historical story of the 1951 pennant race was entirely unobserved, unpredictable, and unpredicted by any contemporary observer. On August 11, at the point of maximum distance between Brooklyn and New York, no one foresaw or could have foreseen that New York was on the point of beginning a sixteen-game winning streak that transformed the baseball season into a pennant race in which New York was the ultimate victor. Indeed, the perspective of the historical storyteller throughout should be double—that of a contemporary observer and that of one who knows about Bobby Thomson's home run; but it is from the latter perspective, not the former, that the historian can perceive the historical tempo and thus determine the appropriate proportion of the historical story.[22]

We are now in a position to summarize what has resulted from the application of the rules of the macrorhetoric of history to a problem in historical storytelling. We can most effectively do this by comparing it with the parallel outcome of the application of the assimilationist logic of historical explanation by narration to the identical problem.

1. The assimilationist logic does not tell us whether to tell a story at all. By failing to do so, it leaves the choice between analysis and storytelling wholly indeterminate. The rules of the rhetoric of history on the other hand are decisive. They prescribe telling a story about the National League pennant race of 1951 and analyzing the American League season of 1939.

2. Assuming that explanation by narration is appropriate, the assimilationist logic offers no hint to the inquirer as to where in the past his continuous chronicle should start. It offers only a blind choice between infinite regress and complete whim. In marked contrast to the anarchy of assimilationist logic, the rhetoric of historical storytelling enables us to fix within a determinate twenty-four-hour limit where on the record to begin our continuous investigation in search of the chronicle.

3. The assimilationist logic is equally indeterminate about where

---

[22] In the case of writers of history, Gallie's interesting analogy between historical understanding and following a game or story breaks down. Gallie, *Philosophy and Historical Understanding,* (pp. 22–50). It applies to consumers of history, the readers, not to its producers, the writers. The readers need not know the outcome of the story; and it is well if, at least, they do not know the writer's construal of the outcome, since not knowing it whets their curiosity and intensifies their engagement and vicarious participation in the story, thus augmenting their knowledge of the past.

to begin the story itself. Any point in time antecedent to Thomson's home run is apparently as right or wrong as any other such point. On the other hand, the rhetoric of historical storytelling offers us four but no more than four quite precise options of approximately equal desirability, and these options are readily justifiable by evidence from the record.[23]

4. With respect to the proportions of the historical story—what data from the record should go in, what be left out, what be abbreviated and compressed, and what be given the full treatment—the assimilationist logic has nothing to say. Since any fact in a causal chain is in principle equivalent to any other, the incapacity of that logic in the matter is not incidental but inherent. Our earlier illustration, in the case of the pennant race, of the results of applying the logic of narration to the problem of historical storytelling is anything but a caricature; it is a beautified version of what the result of a strict application of that logic would actually yield. In that illustration the expansion of the narration in the ninth inning of the game of October 3 is actually gratuitous within the parameters of assimilationist logic. It was a sort of free gift from the rhetorical rules of history writing that expanded the narration for the Giants' half of the ninth. Those rules, however, would prescribe not the single expansion of scale that I smuggled in, but the series of expansions of scale visually but inadequately represented in Figure 6.

What then is one to say of a logic of explanation which when confronted with a historical question and with the record from which the answer to it must be derived cannot propose anything useful about what to put in or what to leave out, or where to start either our intensive investigation of the record or our explanatory answer, or even what form the answer should take? And what can we say of the claim that this logic enables us to exhaust the truth values of history? What, indeed, but that on the face of it the claim is absurd. And what can we do with the assimilationist claim that the rhetoric of history which enables us to deal effectively and in an intelligible and orderly way with all these fundamental difficulties, before which the logic of explanation leaves us paralyzed, is irrelevant to the truth value of history? What, indeed, but reject it as manifestly false.

Hitherto I have been reluctant to assert that anything said in this primer was both important and new. I do, however, believe that the inescapable inference which follows is both important enough and novel enough to warrant heavy emphasis.

The logic of explanation by narration does not exhaust historical truth values, and the rhetoric of history does not transcend historical truth,

[23] On the assumption that they would be quite evident to any historian Everyman who knew anything about baseball, we did not draw out our exposition by detailing the arguments in support of each option.

nor is it irrelevant to it. On the contrary, historical truth depends on at least three components: fidelity to the record of the past, simple formal logic, and the rhetoric of history. Therefore historical truth is not illogical or antilogical; it is translogical. For its maximization, the rhetoric of history is not irrelevant; it is indispensable. That rhetoric is far from being a mere garnish on history, like parsley or watercress on a steak, rendering it more attractive but in no way affecting its nutritive or truth value. To neglect the rhetoric of history, therefore, is not merely to choose the plain, dull, nourishing fare of historical truth in the legitimate interest of saving time in its preparation. Instead it cuts out a necessary component of history, and thereby risks acute malnutrition of historical truth.[24]

[24] Charles Harding Firth offers an interesting testimony to the point in his piece on Samuel Rawson Gardiner in *Dictionary of National Biography*, Supplement I s.v. Samuel Rawson Gardiner (London, 1912), pp. 75–78, Gardiner was the great pioneer narrative historian of Stuart England from 1603 to 1656. In 1856 he set out at his starting point. With heroic patience and immaculate scholarship he worked through a mass of surviving records and ground out the story of that era year by year. He continued to do this for forty-five years of his own life and fifty-three years of the period up to 1656. After many volumes had appeared and many years of his own life had passed, he surveyed his work from the point in the past he had by that time reached. He told Firth then, that had he known at the outset what he had learned in the interval, the proportions and emphasis he gave his work would have markedly differed from the proportions and emphasis it actually had.

CHAPTER VII: The Last Game, *or Processive* Explanation in History

Readers with an especially acute ear for words may by now have noticed that in the preceding chapter an initially long and unhappily cumbersome phrase underwent irregular and gradual shrinkage: The "rhetoric of explanation 'why' by historical storytelling" became simply "the rhetoric of history." They may properly wonder whether the verbal slimming was intentional, and whether it does not have as its correlary a considerable conceptual expansion. It was, and it does. The change has important implications for thinking about history as a significant form of human intellectual activity. To make clear those implications, however, the author will have to get his feet wet. Having gone on and on about writing history he is going to have to write a small piece of it himself. In the present context the obvious choice is the game of October 3, 1951, between the Brooklyn Dodgers and the New York Giants.[1]

The Last Game

On the morning of October 3, 1951, the National League race was down to the wire. Losing 2–1 to Philadelphia on September 28, the

---

[1] The acute readers mentioned above may perhaps suspect that the writer has been itching to try his hand at that story and is now seizing on a specious excuse for doing so. Granted provisionally that this may be true, he hopes for a happy symbiosis between his own gratification and the edification of his readers. His account will have to make the contrafactual assumption that all his readers have a rudimentary understanding of baseball and of its terminology. Unfortunately, no historical account, not even the most primitive, can proceed at all without assuming some knowledge on the part of the reader. I will try at least to avoid assuming any specific information on the pennant race of 1951 beyond what has dribbled out so far in the preceding chapter.

Brooklyn Dodgers had slid back into a tie with the New York Giants, after leading the league since early May. The teams held even for the next two games, finishing the regular season still tied for first place. In the first two games of the playoff, two wins to decide, the Giants and Dodgers broke even. They could not break even or tie on October 3; whoever won that day won all. The day was clear and warm.[2] Before the sun set on October 2, a few of the enthusiasts began to queue up at the ticket window for the sale of the unreserved bleacher seats for the next day's game. As the night passed the line lengthened. Fortunately the temperature dropped only to sixty-two degrees that night.

In the American League the New York Yankees themselves had had a close squeak in 1951. They had clinched the lead only two days before the season ended. In most years, so close a race would have focused the attention of all lovers of baseball. But not in 1951. That year the American League race was a bad second best to what happened in the National League. In two astounding surges, sixteen victories in a row from August 12 to August 27 and twelve victories in thirteen games from September 14 to September 30, the New York Giants had hurled themselves from a seemingly hopeless position, thirteen games out of first place, in mid-August to an end-of-the-season tie with the Dodgers. On October 3, which team was the more likely to be the winner?

Going into the last game the margin of difference between the Dodgers and the Giants was minute. In their last forty-four games the superiority of the Giants was evident. Brooklyn had won twenty-six games and lost twenty-two since August 11, giving them only a .542 average over the time span; meanwhile, the Giants had taken an astonishing thirty-seven out of forty-four for an average of .840. Yet the disparity in games won and lost somewhat exaggerates the difference between the performances of the two teams. What the Giants had displayed was a rare talent for taking the close ones: losing only two of their last forty-four games by one run, they had won thirteen. Despite the Dodgers' mediocre showing since early August, their competent defense had held up.[3] It was their offense, overwhelming for most of the season, that sloped off.[4] In those games just by maintaining the pace it had all season, the Giants' offensive moved out in front of Brooklyn's, from a slugging average forty points behind to one thirty-five points ahead.[5] But against Brooklyn's commanding lead of thirteen games the

[2] The *New York Times* described the weather for October 3: "Fair and warm today and tonight. Increasing cloudiness tomorrow."

[3] Opponent's runs per game: April 17 to August 11—4.2; August 12 to September 30—4.3.

[4] Brooklyn slugging average: April 17 to August 11—.457; August 12 to September 30—.382

[5] New York slugging average: April 17 to August 11—.417; August 12 to September 30—.417.

altered balance in hitting would not have been nearly enough to bring New York even, had it not gone hand in hand with an extraordinary tightening of the Giants' defense, and especially of their pitching. In its final forty-four-game onrush, the New York team allowed its opposition only 2.9 runs per game. This was a defensive improvement of more than 50 percent over its record up to August 12. In those games the opponents of the Giants had a run average scarcely higher than the run average earned against the best pitcher in the National League during the 1951 season.[6]

Baseball, however, is often a game of streaks, in which long-run averages may paper over what on close inspection turns out to be an uneven series of spurts and halts. And in the games played since the Giants and Dodgers slipped into a tie on September 28, it might have seemed that the trend since August 11 had gone into reverse. In those recent games, both on offense and defense, Brooklyn averaged out better than New York.[7] But in the last analysis, there was no analysis. Any player, manager, coach, or supporter of either team who said he believed his team had the better chance of winning on October 3 was perpetrating an act of faith, not talking sense. When Jorda, the home plate umpire, called "Play ball" at 1:30 P.M. on October 3, the odds were so even as to make no difference. Here is the starting line-up.

BROOKLYN	NEW YORK
Furillo, right field	Stanky, second base
Reese, shortstop	Dark, shortstop
Snider, center field	Mueller, right field
Robinson, second base	Irvin, left field
Pafko, left field	Lockman, first base
Hodges, first base	Thomson, third base
Cox, third base	Mays, center field
Walker, catcher	Westrum, catcher
Newcombe, pitcher	Maglie, pitcher

It surprised no one. All eighteen players on both sides were just the ones everyone expected to see. Manager Dressen of the Dodgers fielded seven of the eight starters he had been fielding since the season began.[8] It was evident in May that he had a winning combination and even dur-

[6] Although not supportable by any statistics, the generalization that a change of this dimension in defense is to be ascribed mainly to improvement in pitching not in fielding would, I believe, be ratified by all students of major league baseball.

	Runs per Game	Opponents Runs per Game	Slugging Average
[7] Brooklyn	5.8	3.2	.440
New York	2.8	3.4	.315

[8] Pafko, the player (except the pitcher) with the least number of games played, had appeared in 133, only twenty-three short of the maximum possible number.

ing the slide after August 11 he did not change it.[9] An injury left one of Brooklyn's best players out of the last game. Roy Campanella was a first-rate catcher and a powerful hitter. A painful bruise on his hand kept him out of the second game of the playoff. He would not be playing on October 3.

The Giants had their full complement of regulars ready and able to start. Since August 12, except for the catcher, Westrum, who on rare occasions was given a rest, only one of the regular players had missed as much as one game. Managers do not tamper with a line-up that comes through with sixteen straight wins and goes on to take thirty-seven games in forty-four.

The pitching choices of October 3 had almost the same inevitability about them. All season the Giants had run on three steady pitchers—Jansen, Hearn, and Maglie—with a few others to piece out the rotation with occasional starting assignments. During the pennant drive the three had gone on to a nearly steady four-day rotation, a donkey-work load at the end of a long season.[10] Maglie had taken his turn on September 29. Now on October 3, it was his turn again.

Manager Dressen had a fuller array of starting pitchers than the Giants—Branca, Erskine, Newcombe, and Roe. And late in the season a newcomer, Labine, had pitched magnificently. But just at the end disaster struck. Roe had a phenomenal record of twenty-two wins against three defeats. He started on September 30 with only two days of rest. He was hopeless, batted out in less than two innings. Brooklyn's best pitching arm had gone lame. Roe was out for the playoff. With Branca used up in the first of the playoff games, Labine in the second, and Roe out, Dressen's choice lay between Erskine and Newcombe. It was not a hard choice. During late September Erskine's performance had been erratic. In the final wild fourteen-inning game against Philadelphia on September 30 he did well enough, holding the Phillies scoreless for two innings. In that Donnybrook Newcombe had done even better, allowing only one hit in 5⅔ innings. And he had done this superb job of relief pitching after turning back Philadelphia without a run the day before. On October 3 he had had only two days of rest after pitching nearly fifteen innings the previous two days, but he was a big, very strong man. It was not much of a choice; Dressen had to go with New-

---

[9] Actually he did not have much to change it for; even when they slumped somewhat, the men in the line-up were a good bit better ballplayers than any of the reserves available to replace them. Only one of the available reserves (Abrams) had a batting average as high as any of the regulars, and all the regulars were very skillful in fielding their positions.

[10] The three did more than half the Giants pitching over the entire season, and more than two-thirds of it after August 11. Maglie and Jansen together pitched the inning equivalent of two full games in every five for the whole season.

combe. For the first eight innings of that final game he had no reason to regret the choice that baseball calculus forced on him.

Finally there were the managers, Charles Dressen of the Dodgers and Leo Durocher of the Giants. Statistics which provide extraordinarily good indicators for measuring many kinds of performance in baseball are particularly poor measures of managerial acumen. The fortunes of a manager depend on matters beyond his control, especially on the quality of players over whose acquisition he often has no decisive voice. Perhaps the best indicator of a manager's quality comes over the long run in the consensus of the baseball community. And the best statistical index of that judgment is the staying power of the man, his ability over the years to hold positions in which his acumen is regularly put to the test as manager of a major league baseball team. By that rough measure Dressen and Durocher have been among the best managers of the past thirty-odd years, and there was little to choose between them.[11]

If anyone could have thought of the game of October 3 as just another ball game in the season of 1951 and forgotten what was at stake, then for the first six innings it was not a particularly exciting game. Maglie got off to a shaky start. After striking out, the Dodgers' lead-off hitter, he gave bases on balls to the next two batters. Then Jackie Robinson, second baseman, drove Maglie's pitch to left field for a long single and a run scored. With a man on first and second and only one out, Maglie settled down. The next batter dribbled a ball down the third base line, forcing the man on second, and the last out came on an easy infield foul.

Maglie settled down and stayed out of trouble for the next six innings. During that time the Dodgers reached him for three hits and he walked one man; but no Brooklyn batter got past first base. If Maglie gave the Dodgers a hard time, the Giants were even less happy with Newcombe. In the first six innings they threatened Brooklyn's defense only twice. In the second inning, Lockman, first at bat, singled and Thomson followed with a single. The threat, however, turned out to be self-extinguishing. Thomson did not notice that the third-base coach had signalled Lockman to hold at second. In a fine display of head-in-the-bucket baseball, without looking or stopping at first he charged

	Dressen		Durocher	
[11] 1932–1934:	Manager-Nashville	1939–1946, 1948:	Manager-Dodgers	
1934–1937:	Manager-Cincinnati			
1938:	Manager-Nashville	1948–1955:	Manager-Giants	
1950–1953:	Manager-Dodgers	1966– :	Manager-Cubs	
1955–1957:	Manager-Washington			
1960–1961:	Manager-Milwaukee			
1963–1966:	Manager-Detroit			
1966:	died			

for second base. There, in a bleak moment of truth, he discovered that Lockman already occupied the berth. Thomson was easily trapped on his scurry back to first. In the Giants' pennant rush, Thomson had looked like a special hero; now he looked like a special clown. He tried to redeem his mistake in the fifth inning when he drove a two-base hit into left field with one out. But his teammates failed to hit behind him.

Newcombe was pitching superbly. In four of the first six innings he put the Giant batters out in order without a man reaching base. His control was excellent: he gave two bases on balls, one intentional. And he only gave four hits. In all six innings he had faced only twenty-one batters, just three more than if he had been pitching a perfect game. The run that the Dodgers owed to Maglie's momentary loss of control in the first inning did not look very large at the moment they got it. In 1951, going through a whole game without getting a run was not commonplace;[12] in the 154 games of the regular season the Giants had been held runless only seven times.[13] But the Dodgers' one-run lead that at first did not appear to amount to much to the Giants or their supporters loomed larger and larger, inning by inning, as Newcombe systematically and with evident ease mowed the Giants' batters down. By the end of the sixth inning, the game two-thirds over, it had become a horror. It looked as if the Giants might be shut out on October 3 as they had been on October 2. To blow the championship that way after their headlong pennant drive would be a painful, bad joke. It would be bitterer still to blow it on a double fluke—Maglie's momentary wildness in the first inning and Thomson's stupid baserunning in the second.

As the Giants came to bat in the last half of the seventh inning Monte Irvin, the left fielder, stepped into the batter's box. Day in, day out, all season long he had been the Giants' most consistent hitter, but in the past few days he had done poorly. In his last eighteen times at bat he had just three hits for the wretched average of .166. This time was different. He drove Newcombe's pitch into left field for two bases. Lockman was next. With no one out, a man on second, and one run needed to tie the game, the mythical "Book," baseball's name for the standard strategies in standard situations, calls for a bunt, a controlled shove with the bat to roll the ball to a quick stop on the infield grass. If properly executed, preferably between third base and the pitching mound, the bunt will permit the man on second to make it safely to third, at the probable cost of the bunter being thrown out at first. The

---

[12] The earned-run average of pitchers dropped sharply a few years later. For the very greatest of pitchers of 1951 the average of 1.14 of Bob Gibson of the St. Louis Cardinals in 1968, was simply unthinkable. In the National League in 1951 of 48 pitchers who pitched the equivalent of a dozen nine-inning games only three had ERA's of less than three runs, the lowest being 2.9

[13] In this respect the Dodgers were even more remarkable; in the regular season they suffered but four shut-outs

baserunner can then score a run on the feeblest of safe hits or on a long outfield fly by the following batter. The Dodgers knew the Book, too. The third baseman and the first baseman moved a few steps toward home plate, ready if it came their way, to charge Lockman's expected bunt. They hoped to make a fast throw to the shortstop covering third in time to cut down Irvin advancing from second. For the Book that tells the offensive to bunt in this situation also tells the defense, if there is any chance to do so, to try to get the runner heading for third and let the batter reach first. The main thing is to protect the one-run lead. It is better to play to get the advanced runner than to let him reach the easy scoring position at third base, even though a throw to first will almost certainly yield an out. The play is called a fielder's choice.

In the last half of the seventh inning the Book played itself out like a perfectly contrived bit of choreography. Lockman pushed a pretty bunt toward the pitcher's mound. The catcher pounced on it and threw to third—too late. Irvin beat the ball. The next Giant batter hit a long fly to center field. Irvin stayed on third until the ball was caught, and headed for home, arriving comfortably in advance of the throw. The next man hit into a double play, and the inning was over. The batter who lofted the fly that enabled Irvin to score the tying run was Bobby Thomson. In part at least he had redeemed his earlier misplay.

As baseball writers like to say when, in the late innings, a team comes from behind to tie, "It was a new ball game,"—but not for long. In the first half of the eighth inning the Dodgers unloaded on Maglie. He struck out the first man he faced. Two hits, a wild pitch, and an intentional pass later, the Dodgers were one run ahead again with runners on first and third. The next batter drove a hard ground ball to Thomson. Never a very adept third baseman, he knocked the ball down but could not handle it fast enough. All runners were safe, and the second run of the inning scored. A long single drove in a third run before Maglie, for the third out, disposed of the eighth batter he had faced in the inning. The Dodgers' one-run lead had loomed large as the last half of the seventh inning began; when Maglie walked dejectedly from the pitcher's mound an inning later, the Dodgers' three-run-lead looked like Everest. For Maglie at least it was all over. Manager Durocher's strategy that had kept him in the game too long would send him out for a pinch hitter in the last half of the eighth.

Six outs later the three-run lead looked more like infinity than Everest. Newcombe had faltered in the bottom of the seventh, but he came back strong next inning against the weak end of the New York batting order. No one got to first base safe. Jansen, pitching in Maglie's place, had no trouble in putting the Dodgers down in order in the ninth, but what difference could that make? The top side of the Giant batting order would lead off in the bottom of the ninth; but what difference was that likely to make either? All over the great city in houses, and flats, and offices, and bars, men, women, and children crowded around television sets and radios. Dodger fans relaxed joyfully at last in reasonable anticipation of a happy ending after a long anxious time, a month of hope too often and too long deferred. Sorrowfully or stoically, with little hope and less grounds for it, the supporters of the Giants waited for the ending, too. A weary lull settled over the spectators at the Polo Grounds. In the Dodgers' bullpen, where the relief pitchers warm up, Branca and Erskine and Labine threw the ball to their receivers unhurriedly, almost listlessly.

To begin the last half of the ninth inning Alvin Dark, the Giants' lead-off man, stepped into the batter's box. He hit a single off Hodges' glove. Don Mueller's single to right sent Dark to third. Up to the ninth inning only three men had given Newcombe any trouble. Now, with none out, he faced them in order—Irvin, Lockman, and Thomson. With men on first and third, the ordinarily reliable Irvin could do no more than pop a high easy foul to first base that got him out without advancing the runners. Then Lockman transformed a bit of trouble into a crisis. He doubled to left, and Dark scored. Mueller twisted his ankle going into third base and had to be replaced by a substitute runner.

The Dodgers had only a two-run margin now; with just one out the tying run was on second base. The possible winning run waited to go into the batter's box, taking a few warm-up swipes at the air. The Dodgers' manager, Dressen, had to make some hard decisions and make them very fast. A baseball manager's life is not a happy one. In a crisis if he makes a decision and in the outcome all goes well, the armchair strategists figure that he only did what they or any sensible person would have done anyhow, and he gets little credit for making the right choice. It is quite otherwise when in the outcome things go badly. Then what he did is sure to look more stupid than what he might have done.

In the situation as it stood after Lockman's double, the decisions that Dressen had to make were inordinately difficult. First, should he keep Newcombe in, or should he relieve him? On the side of keeping him in was Newcombe's masterful performance not only in the game of October 3 but in his last three pitching efforts. In twenty-three innings of pitching up to the moment he faced Alvin Dark in the bottom of the ninth, he had allowed twelve hits, six bases on balls, and only one run. It is hard for a pitcher to do much better than that. But those twenty-three innings of superb pitching had their dark side. Newcombe had done all of them since September 29. After a long season during which Roe and he had borne the brunt for the Dodgers, he had pitched the equivalent of $2\frac{1}{2}$ nine-inning games in the past five days. No pitcher's strength is limitless. In the hurly-burly of the last game with Boston, the danger signal had already gone up. After 5⅔ innings of almost perfect relief pitching following on a nine-inning stint the previous day, Newcombe himself asked to be relieved; his arm was simply used up. And now with only two days of rest he had taken another eight innings of pitching out of it. The three sharp clean hits of Dark, Mueller, and Lockman in the ninth seemed to speak clearly and to the point: that strong arm was gone; there was nothing left to take out of it.

If Dressen was driven to this hard conclusion then he would have to pick the man to take Newcombe's place. It had to be Branca or Erskine or Labine, the only pitchers he had warming up for relief.[14] On the basis of recent performance the best bet appears to have been Labine. On two counts, however, the record was a little too recent. Labine was a rookie who had only come up from the minor leagues in mid-season, and the situation at the moment was a very rough one indeed to thrust a rookie into. Moreover, he had pitched nine full innings just the day before. Under the circumstances he must have appeared a shaky risk. But then so were the other two pitchers warming up. Since August 12, Erskine had only broken even, four wins, four losses; and he had lost his last two games. In relief on September 30, however, he had held Philadelphia scoreless, allowing two singles in two innings. If on the record Erskine did not look altogether satisfactory, Ralph Branca looked worse. He had won nine games and lost only three as of August 12. On October 3, his record was 13–11. In the interval he had won only four games and lost eight. Since September 9 he had not won a game, and he had lost four. In three of his four starts the opposition had pounded him mercilessly and early.[15] On the other hand, although he had lost in his last start in the first game of the playoff, he had seemed a good bit more like the Branca of the days before the Giant flood. He had pitched eight innings and allowed only three runs on five hits, walking two, one intentionally.

Such was the sum of Dressen's live options in choice of pitchers. There remained the question of what any pitcher he chose should do next. With first base open and men on second and third, that again

[14] Conlan and Creamer, *Jocko* (Philadelphia and New York, 1967), p. 128. In 1951, Brooklyn had one good short-stint relief pitcher, King. His season record was fourteen won, seven lost. He had not fared well on September 30 when he lasted less than two innings and, with Labine, was responsible for the last two Philadelphia runs. Where he was on October 3, and why Dressen did not have him warming up, I have been unable to determine.

[15]

Date	Opponent	Innings	Runs	Hits
Sept. 15	Pittsburgh	3	4	7
Sept. 18	St. Louis	5⅔	7	10
Sept. 25	Boston[a]	0	4	3

[a] Branca was removed in the first inning with none out.

was strictly a managerial decision. Almost always a good manager will make his decisions by the Book. Every once in a while, however, the Book comes up with an ambiguous oracle; it speaks with equal clarity out of both sides of its mouth. And that was what it was doing just at this moment: the Book says:

> With men on second and third, first base empty, and only one out, do not pitch to the batter at all; give him an intentional base on balls. Then with a force at second, third, or home plate almost any ball hit to the infield is a sure out, and a ball hit sharply to an infielder is likely to yield a double play and retire the side.

The Book also says:

> When the batter represents the winning run, do not give him an intentional base on balls, especially with only one out in the last half of the last inning. For then an unintentional base on balls and a long single, a long fly ball and a single, two singles, a double, and several other combinations can bring home that run, and it will be all over.

At the crucial moment, however, the batter did represent the winning run, *but* there were men on second and third, first base was empty, and there was only one out. What to do then, the Book deposeth not.

The man waiting to step into the batter's box, and be pitched to or walked, however, was not a Book abstraction called The Possible Winning Run. He was very much flesh and blood, and as such a special and singular problem. He was Bobby Thomson, the Giants' third baseman. On his overall season record he was a pretty good hitter, with a batting average at the moment of .292. But pitchers do not pitch to seasonal batting averages, they pitch to the man in the batter's box. Since August 12, the man ready to enter the batter's box had raised his season's average from .256 to .292. To do that he had hit at an average of .369 in the last forty-six games. More than that, in his last sixteen times at bat Thomson had hit safely eight times, and of those eight hits, two had been home runs and two had been doubles. At the moment, then, Thomson was not just a good hitter and not just the Giants' best batter. Over the short run, which was the run that counted, he had a batting average of .500 and a slugging average of 1.000. In the playoff he already had four hits for nine bases in nine times at bat, with a base on balls, a sacrifice hit and run-scoring long fly thrown in for good measure. In fact at the moment that was, Bobby Thomson was the most formidable batter in professional baseball. Every time he came to bat, it was close to even money he would make a hit and even money that the hit would go for extra bases. On October 3, Thomson had not looked as if he was going cold. Up to the last of the ninth six Giant batters had scarcely seen Newcombe's pitching, and two others had just got their sights on it:[16] but Thomson had it right in the cross hairs. He had come up to the batter's box just three times; in the second inning he singled, in the fifth he doubled, in the seventh he delivered the long fly ball that allowed Irvin to score the tying run. That was when Newcombe was mowing Thomson's teammates down with the greatest of ease. Now Newcombe was tired.

All this is in the record. How much of it was in Dressen's mind as the injured Mueller was being helped off the field is a matter of conjecture. Of the ambiguity of the Book in the current situation he was surely aware. And of Newcombe's deep trouble. And of the shaky options available to replace Newcombe. And of Thomson's alarming recent record of effectiveness at bat. Did he also remember that over the season Branca had been a considerably more effective pitcher than Erskine?[17] Or on the other hand that Erskine had two wins over the Giants and no losses to them, while Branca's season record against the Giants was two won, five lost? And did it fully register in his mind that Mays who followed Thomson in the Giant batting order had hit a miserable .242 during the Giants' upward surge? That in the playoff games, he had managed to collect just one single in the ten times at bat? That in the last game, with men on base in the second, fifth, and seventh innings, he had not only failed to hit but had been unable to advance the runner at all?[18]

Walker, the Brooklyn catcher, Reese, the team's captain, and Newcombe were huddled at the pitcher's mound. Dressen made up his mind. As he walked toward the cluster around Newcombe, so did Conlan, the umpire at first base, to prevent any improper delay of the game. Dressen was not trying to stall. At once he gave his decision to Conlan. Never was a manager more quickly second-guessed or from a more unlikely source. Here is the way Conlan recollected it in tranquility fifteen years later.

> I did something that day an umpire should never do. I did it when Charlie Dressen came out to change pitchers before Thomson batted. Charlie was taking Don Newcombe out, and he had Carl Erskine and Clem Labine and Ralph Branca in the bullpen. I walked in to the mound and I said, "Who are you bringing in?"
> "Branca."

[16] Lockman with a single and a sacrifice, Irvin with a double.

[17] Among twenty-nine National League pitchers who had pitched 154 innings or more in 1951, Branca rated ninth in earned-run average, just two notches behind his teammate Roe who had won twenty-two and lost three for the season, and two notches above Newcombe. On that scale Erskine rated twenty-eighth, one from the bottom. Earned run average: Branca 3.26, Erskine 4.45.

[18] In the second Pafko had caught Mays' long hard drive to left field. In the fifth Mays struck out and in the seventh he hit into a double play.

"Branca!" I said. "A *fast-ball* pitcher?" Charlie had two curve-ball pitchers warming up, who Thomson couldn't hit. But Bobby could murder a fast ball. I shouldn't have made the remark because it wasn't any of my business, but I was really surprised.

"Yes, Branca," Charlie said, and I caught myself.

"Okay," I said, and called, "Branca."

I don't want to be a second-guesser, but in the Polo Grounds when the other team had the tieing runs on base you *had* to have a curve-ball pitcher. I never thought he'd bring in a fast-ball pitcher at a time like that.[19]

Branca joined the cluster on the mound. A moment later the group broke up, the Dodger players back to their positions, Conlan to his place behind first base, Dressen and Newcombe to the bench. Dressen's call for a relief pitcher at that moment implied his other decision. If he had intended to give Thomson an intentional base on balls he could have left Newcombe in to do it and thus allowed Branca an extra minute or so to warm up in the bull pen. Branca was on orders to pitch to Thomson. He took the eight warm-up pitches from the mound that the official rules allowed. Thirty-four thousand spectators watched, all silent. Umpire Jorda issued the command, "Play ball," and the Dodgers moved into their defensive positions. Thomson stepped into the batter's box.

Fifteen miles from the Polo Grounds in the catalogue room of a college library the staff gathered around a radio during coffee break. That day the break had already lasted a bit longer than usual. "Well," said someone a little fatuously to no one in particular, "a home run would do it." The Director of Library Services, a hopelessly addicted Dodger fan, flicked his eyes toward the speaker, a Torquemada measuring up a newly suspected Marrano for an *auto da fé.* ". . . The wind-up, the pitch, strike one." It was the voice of Russ Hodges, who did the broadcasts for the Giants. He was of the "cool" school of sports announcers, understating and thus allowing the play of the game to speak for itself. Branca had thrown one through the strike zone, and Thomson had watched it go by. None of the background noises that usually come through the loud speaker during a baseball game—the murmur, the rustle, interspersed with a distant shout or two—was coming through now. For a few seconds it was as if the radio had gone dead. Then Hodges, "Branca takes the signal from the catcher. He winds up. He p——." The noise of the crack of the bat against the ball. A fraction of a second of silence—and then pandemonium. And over the pandemonium, Russ Hodges' voice, suddenly a banshee shriek, "The Giants win the pennant. *The Giants win the pennant!* THE GIANTS WIN THE PENNANT!!"

It was over. Branca's pitch had come through high and inside.

[19] Conlan and Creamer, *Jocko*, p. 128.

Thomson nevertheless swung, and met the ball squarely, pulling it toward left field where the Polo Ground fence was short. Carl Furillo, the Dodger left fielder turned to race toward a ball he would never lay hands on. Before he got to the ten-foot barrier, 317 feet from home plate, Thomson's shot had cleared it with about a foot to spare—a home run. "Good Lord!" the Chief of Circulation croaked. The Director of Library Services said nothing. He had the stunned look of a pole-axed steer. Then in bewildered disbelief, "It can't be, it can't be!" But it was. At the Polo Grounds the uproar of the crowd went on—and on, a blend of despair and delirious joy. The Giants poured out of their dugout to greet Thomson as he touched home plate for the winning run, the pennant-winning run, and to carry him off the field triumphant on their shoulders.

The record does not tell about Ralph Branca's long lonely walk to the Dodger dressing room. Perhaps no one noticed it. It does not tell what anyone said to him. Perhaps no one said anything. After all, there was not much for anybody to say.

That then is my story of the last game of the pennant race of 1951. It is therefore a historical story told by a historian with about thirty-five years of experience as a professional writer of history. In all those years I have never learned to judge accurately the quality of my own work, so I cannot gauge how successful I have been in doing what I set out to do. As a historical story, "The Last Game" suffers from one limitation that I imposed on it: it stands on a more exiguous base of the record of the past than I would ordinarily deem acceptable.[20] However, given my purpose of providing a usable focal center for demonstrating several traits of the rhetoric of historical storytelling, the base was adequate. My selection of an umpired, rule-bound game as a focal center also blocked from consideration a number of important traits of the rhetoric of history with which I wish to avoid dealing at length.

For my present purpose, "The Last Game" has two merits. I cannot measure my success in achieving my intent; but from paragraph to paragraph, almost from sentence to sentence, much better than I usually do, I know what that intent was. I was constantly aware of what I had in mind. Second, "The Last Game" is clearly history with a small "h" about the past with a small "p." It is not an important piece of history writing, nor is the episode that is its subject of any great importance in a cosmic view of human affairs. For that very reason, whatever we may learn from it should have wide rather than restricted application.

[20] For almost all its data it relies on two readily accessible sources—the daily sports section of the *New York Times* from August 12 to October 4, 1951, and the *Official Baseball Guide*. Except for Umpire Conlan's reminiscences, I did not explore the considerable literature generated by the pennant race of 1951.

Hitherto we have encountered two philosophical views of what constitutes satisfactory historical explanation yielding true knowledge of the past. One, associated with the analytical philosophers Hempel and Popper, is usually described as covering-law explanation. The other, most fully propounded by White, attempts to adjust the Popper-Hempel argument derived from their conception of scientific explanation to the "story" form of much history writing; it propounds a logical schema of explanation by narration. We have also seen that these views of philosophers coincide roughly with two looser conceptions, current among historians, on the one hand that they explain the past analytically, on the other that they do it narratively. Narrative historians regularly confront the complex rhetorical problems of storytelling. Consequently, they are likely to be keenly aware of what those problems are. But because they are not by temperament analytically inclined, they have not paid systematic attention to the relation between their concern with historical rhetoric and their concern with historical truth. On the other side, most analytical historians, if pressed, would probably admit that history cannot wholly dispense with narrative, with its concern about the conjunctions of specific persons at specific moments in specific localities. They would, however, regard analysis, which obliterates or at least obscures such conjunctions, as the place to go for high octane historical truth.[21] Analytical historians tend to orient themselves toward what they imagine the sciences to be, and to conceive of rhetoric as an unseemly concern with mere tricks of language rather than as it is—the concomitant to any coherent discourse that aims at persuasion. To them the notion that the truth-attainment of history is linked at all with the rhetoric of history is repugnant; for them, as for the analytical philosophers, truth resides only in the "facts" and their logical adumbration. Two common assumptions seem to provide the common ties, such as they are, among the four groups—two of them philosophers of history, two of them practitioners of history—that we have identified. One assumption is that historical explanation has only two forms—a covering-law form and a narrative form—there is no *tertium quid*; the other is that explanation in history deals solely with why things happened.

It was my intention, one of my intentions, in telling the story of "The Last Game" to show that neither of these common assumptions does justice to historical storytelling and its appropriate rhetoric. The last game was decisive in determining which team won the pennant. Until one team won, any explanation of why it won would be premature. But the

---

[21] In a curious emulation of the Trojan horse, Christopher Hill, a proponent of analysis against narrative, begins each section of his *Age of Revolution* (Edinburgh, 1961), with a narrative so jejune that the subsequent chapters of what he calls analysis can scarcely help but look good by comparison.

structure selected for the first part of the story of "The Last Game" is functionally dependent on the way that game actually went. Suppose that instead of going inning by inning:

	1	2	3	4	5	6	7	8	9
Brooklyn	1	0	0	0	0	0	0	3	0
New York	0	0	0	0	0	0	1	0	4

it had gone:

	1	2	3	4	5	6	7	8	9
Brooklyn	0	0	0	0	0	0	0	0	0
New York	12	0	0	0	0	0	0	0	0

and that the Giants had made all their hits as well as all their runs in the first inning. Then although the description of the excitement in anticipation of the last game and the data on the performance of the two teams that precedes Umpire Jorda's "Play ball!" are quite accurate, in an account of the game they would both be inappropriate. In a way both the description and the data involve promissory notes. Because they imply excitement ahead, they justify the reader in expecting it. To lean so heavily on the excitement generated by the tied playoff, to stress the close balance in performance between the Giants and the Dodgers would be a sort of rhetorical fraud on the reader if the Giants had wrapped up the pennant in the first inning of the last game. Indeed the notion of "The Last Game" as a whole chapter in *The Story of the Pennant Race* would require skeptical scrutiny.

Does this mean that one suppresses facts just for the sake of a good story? Before shuddering at such a notion, let us recognize that only a madman would try to include all the facts in the story. The surviving record of the pennant race of 1951 tells us for every game played during the season who came to bat each inning, whether he made a safe hit, whether that hit was for one, two, three, or four bases, whether he received a base on balls, whether he struck out, whether he was put out by an unassisted fielding play or as the result of an assist. And this is merely the beginning of the surviving record of this fragment of the past. Only by judicious omission can we avoid submerging our story and our readers past hope of revival in a suffocating swamp of detail. Whether to omit is a pseudoproblem; given the dimensions of the record, in all good sense we *have* to omit. The problem is not whether but what to omit, and what to include, and how, and where.

Consider our contrary-to-fact hypothetical of a Giant victory of 12–0 on October 3 with all runs scored and all hits made in the first inning. If that had been the way it came out, in the introductory section on the excitement in anticipation of the game the author at the very least would owe the reader a hint of the impending bathos, of a decisive game that was effectively decided twenty minutes after it began. And under such circumstances surely the careful balancing out of the strengths of the two teams would scarcely be appropriate. In the story of the pennant race one still might want to strike just such a balance, but somewhere else, not at the beginning of the last game.[22]

In the actual case the excitement and the tension that preceded the last game held throughout, mounting rather than declining to the moment when Thomson swung at Branca's second pitch. It is this outcome that warrants the substance, the structure, and the tone of the introductory section of "The Last Game." In other words, the outcome defines the appropriate historical macrorhetoric, and the macrorhetoric in turn dictates the selection of "facts" or more accurately data to be drawn from the record. Or to put it more bluntly, amid a mass of true facts about the past too ample to set down, historians choose not merely on logical grounds but on the basis of appropriate rhetorical strategies.

The section of "The Last Game" that precedes Jorda's "Play ball!" is part of the story; but is it historical explanation by narration? Some of it surely is not, in any sense. The bits about the response of the baseball fans to the situation both at the beginning and elsewhere in the story have nothing to do with explaining why the Giants won the pennant. Just what they are doing in the story at all is a problem we will need to consider later.

When the story moves from the consumers of baseball, the crowds in the Polo Grounds and around radios and television sets all over New York City, to its producers, the players of the game, its structure remains perplexing. It does not plunge directly into the game at hand, but slithers back to a brief recapitulation of the pennant race since August 12, strictly unnecessary, explaining nothing really by analytical standards, since the tie on September 30 and the resumption of the tie on October 2 are quite adequate to explain why the game of October 3 was being played. And what of the rapid run-down of statistical evidence on the performance of the Dodgers and the Giants since August 11 followed by sketchy and highly selective observations on the starting line-ups of the two teams? Are they explanation by narration? They do not seem to fit the pattern of consecutive chronological ordering. Are they analyses? Surely not in the rigorous sense, not in any sense acceptable either to tough-minded philosophers in quest of the structure of scientific explanation or to tough-minded analytical historians on the lookout for necessary and sufficient causes. From any rigorist point of view the whole thing is too half-hearted. There is not even a

---

[22] Perhaps, for example, at the beginning of the playoff.

constant "universe of discourse," but three universes muddled together
—the overall team performances of the Giants and Dodgers for the
whole baseball season, their performances since August 11, their performances in the last few games before October 3. And scrambled with
these sketchy "analyses" are bits of "narrative" with its characteristic
specification of time, places, and persons—the recent misadventures of
catcher Campanella and pitcher Roe, the glance with shifting time per-
spectives at the two pitching staffs. And what is this suspension of the
ongoing narration in aid of? What function does it perform? What does
it explain? That in the wan slouching words of the author "in the last
analysis, there was no analysis?" We seem to have gone off on a mighty
long tack to get so little further forward.

And when at last the game of October 3, that promised, long-delayed
Last Game gets started, the pattern is almost as mixed-up and inde-
cisive as before. Ultimately we do get through the last game in a not
very reasonable facsimile of explanation by narration—but with what
detours! What arbitrary expansions and contractions! Not to speak of
the matters that do not by the furthest stretch of the imagination have
anything to do with why the Giants won the pennant—the detours into
the crowd at the game and to the fans in the city. And what of the last
eleven sentences, all of which have to do with what happened, and with
a thing or two that may not have happened, after the pennant race was
over, when there is nothing left to explain? Even setting aside these
obvious irrelevancies, and sticking to what happened on the ball field,
by the standards we have invoked the account of what went on is odd.
For six innings the Giants did not score a run. No runs in any of
these innings is equal to no runs in any of the others as far as the explanation of the outcome of the game is concerned, yet the author almost disregards four of the innings to dawdle about with two of them
the second and the fifth. Then in the last half of the seventh inning—
and about time, too—comes an almost classic bit of nomological-
deductive explanation with everything more or less deducible from
general rules—the Book—except, alas, that the Event, the scoring of a
run, was neither deducible nor predictable at any point before it
happened. And finally in the last inning, that painstaking elaborate
weighing up of the situation after Lockman's double! To what explanatory purpose? To indicate what Manager Dressen had in mind? The
author does not quite say that Dressen had all those details in mind. To
explain Dressen's decision? He does not claim to have done that either.
To show that Dressen made a mistake? He does not even quite get
around to doing that. Evidently then, from the point of view of either
explanation by narration or of explanation by analysis, historical or
philosophical, "The Last Game" is simply a mess.

Yet it seems to me that it is not a mess. It provides a better historical account of why the Giants won the pennant than either the covering-law explanation, or the explanation by narration previously outlined. The former is true and complete, but vacuous in context. The second is true and incomplete. For example, an explanation by narration would have to explain narratively the sequence in which the Giant players came to bat in the last half of the ninth inning. But the complete narrative explanation of that sequence depends on the prior sequence of New York batters from the beginning of the game. To be complete within the terms of its built-in requirements, explanation by narration would then have to provide an account of the whole last game similar in scale and form to the explanation, previously offered, of the Giants' last time at bat.

The explanation by storytelling offered in "The Last Game" avoids the vacuousness of the covering-law explanation and the *arbitrary* incompleteness of explanation by narration. It, too, is incomplete but it is *selectively* incomplete. That is, both omissions and inclusions can be justified on principles implicit in the kind of explanation that is going on. What is going on is a processive explanation. All historical explanation by storytelling is processive, but all processive historical explanation is not storytelling.

In the last game nine New York players went to bat a total of twenty-five times during the first seven innings, and there are approximately equal amounts of "factual" information on the performance of each man each time he batted. Yet in the account of those innings in "The Last Game" only three Giant batters are named at all, Irvin, Lockman, Thomson, and no one else. By the standards of historical explanation by narration neither all the exclusions nor all the inclusions make sense. At best the three players belong in an elided narrative explanation of the seventh inning when their collaboration produced the tying run for the Giants. Or for a complete narrative explanation they belong in every time they came to bat, as do the other seven Giant players. How do the rules of processive explanation justify Lockman's and Thomson's appearance in the account of the second inning and Thomson's in the account of the fifth, when the Giants did not score? It made no difference in the outcome, no more difference than the bases on balls, unmentioned in "The Last Game", that put Westrum on base twice during the first seven innings.

Where covering-law explanation and explanation by narration have a logical purpose, processive explanation has a historical purpose. The first two seek to fulfill conditions of causal explanation predefined as adequate on grounds of the logic of causal ascription. Processive explanation seeks to do justice to the record of the past as given (which does not of course mean merely accepting it as given). The first two start with a fixed E, what philosophers call an *explanandum*, something that happened that is to be explained. They mine the record for the antecedents of that E which will come closest to conforming to their rules for logically correct causal ascription. The E is a stable inert entity, one of a class, that remains identical from the beginning of the explanatory process to the end. Historians seeking to do justice to the record of the past start with an unstable active E. "Winning the pennant" is not just a homogeneous class of events; winning the pennant in the National League in 1951 was different from winning the pennant in the American League in 1939, and just what it was is ultimately determined not in advance but only in the course of an examination of the record.

An examination of the record of the game of October 3, 1951, reveals that the story of it has a pivot point, Bobby Thomson's home run. The processive explanation therefore needs to keep that point in focus. It requires the selection from the record of that game and other games of data compatible with or effective for guiding the reader's attention toward the pivot point. Some data are omitted from those included in the story of "The Last Game," in order to sharpen the reader's perception of the circumstances when the pivotal event occurred. The first, third, fourth, and fifth innings, in each of which only three Giants batted and none made a hit, are compressed into a single sentence that calls attention primarily not to the Giants' feebleness on the offense but to the defensive power of Newcombe's pitching—a useful contrast to what is to take place in the ninth inning. Westrum's two bases on balls in the third and fifth innings are not mentioned both because they did not result in any change in the situation at the time, and because Westrum did not figure in the climactic rally in the ninth. On the other hand Irvin, Lockman, and Thomson figure in scoring the tying run in the seventh and again in the ninth-inning rally. So when the latter two also appear in the fouled-up second inning and Thomson again as a threat with his fifth-inning double, even though "nothing comes" of these two episodes, in processive explanation they are useful as preparations for the climax.

The same attention to the pivot point determines the reverse disposition of the performance of another Giant batter, Mays. He failed to hit in each of the three innings treated in detail, and twice he failed with a man on second who could have scored on a single. But his failure has greater rhetorical, and therefore processive explanatory force, if the evidence of it is not dispersed among its particular instances but is brought to focus at the moment in the ninth inning where Manager Dressen had to choose between pitching to Thomson or passing him to bring Mays to bat. Here, as elsewhere in telling stories, historians do not allow themselves to be bound rigidly to consecutive temporal sequences in the way that White's causal linkings of a chronicle of "facts" suggest. And here as elsewhere no intelligible account of the actual explanatory procedures storytelling historians use—their partial adherence to a chronological framework *and* their occasional deviations from it—is possible within the bounds of any of the logics of explanation that philosophers have propounded.[23] It is, however, feasible within the scope of processive explanation.

One more point before we review the implication of our inquiry into the story of "The Last Game." We have earlier noted that often the objective of "historical analysis," the discovery of the necessary and sufficient conditions of any *explanandum* or outcome E is foredoomed to frustration. The trouble is that given a myriad of conceivable analyses, a closed E does not provide historians with sufficient clues as to what analyses to attempt. When, as in baseball, the data are abundant, the number of conceivably valid analyses becomes impossibly large.[24] They provide a plethora of riches. Again covering-law and analytical models of explanation dump us into the middle of an informational quagmire and provide us with a poor notion of where to go or how to move. And again in contrast, processive explanation keyed to the rhetoric of storytelling and to our pivot point and its related fragments of the record guide us to the appropriate "analysis."[25] The National League season of 1951 is a set of series of diminishing magnitude—(1) the whole season, (2) the pennant race since August 11, (3) the games since the Giants and the Dodgers went into a tie, (4) the playoff games up to the ninth inning on October 3, (5) the final half of the last game.[26] A review of "The Last

[23] This seems to be the case even with respect to Gallie's interesting "following a game" as a model of historical explanation. Because a game is followed precisely in temporal sequence, Mays' batting failures would have to be noted in chronological order instead of being reserved for introduction at the point of maximum effectiveness in storytelling. That is to say because it is spectator-orientated the model does not permit retrospection occasionally to take command of storytelling strategy. Only processive explanation with its acceptance of the involvement of truth value in the rhetoric of history can offer an intelligible account of this peculiarity of historical writing.

[24] From the printed record of the box scores of single games alone, statistics can be retrieved that will give individual performance records of every player for the 154 game season *and for any consecutive series of such games that one chooses.* For every batter one can derive his record of times at bat, runs, hits, singles, doubles, triples, home runs, stolen bases, total bases, sacrifice hits, and (approximately) bases on balls; for every fielder his total fielding chances, putouts, assists, and errors, for every pitcher the number of runs, hits, and bases on balls he allowed, the number of men he struck out, the number of innings he pitched, and the number of games he won and lost over any consecutive series of games.

[25] I use the term "analysis" loosely here, as it needs to be used in processive explanation. In context it involves going beyond the particular events or action at a particular time and place to the Book and/or to the performance record of a player or a team over a consecutive span, whether a span of innings or of games.

[26] This is not to argue that the five exhaust the possible interesting or relevant series. It is to argue that, except with respect to pitching, those series provide quite enough data for analysis to be getting on with. In records of the past where retrievable statistics are thick on the ground, one of the virtues of processive explanation is that in the interest of a sound rhetoric of historical storytelling it bridles the impulses of some historians toward statistical-analytical overkill.

Game" will show that one or another of these consecutive series is the base for most of the data put to analytical use. While other models of explanation fail to make sense of the story of "The Last Game," and make pitifully bad sense of the record of the past that it incorporates, processive explanation by historical storytelling makes good sense of both.

Earlier I argued that it was an error to believe that because a historian selected evidence from the record of the past he was biased. When a historian selects from the record only the evidence that will support his view or contention, of course, he is biased, and there are probably few historians who have never done this. There are probably fewer who have only done this. Yet this has not been immediately apparent. The two types of historical explanation propounded by philosophers have a rationale for selecting data that eliminates bias. The rule is to select from the record only those data pertinent to the explanation, that is, to select the boundary conditions or the appropriate chronicle. But most historical accounts include data that do not meet this test, and they often omit data that do. Because some of these data are sometimes selected to support biases, it has been supposed that mere act of selection is sufficient evidence of bias. Unless principles of all of them are always selected for that purpose and therefore that the selection can be identified that have nothing to do with bias, the supposition is at least plausible. In "The Last Game," however, we found one such principle. Data were selected for their bearing on the pivotal point of the historical story. What was involved was not bias but judgment. Independently of the logic of causal explanation, independently of bias, a rule of the macrorhetoric of historical discourse accounted for the selection of almost all the data that were included (and excluded) from the processive explanation of "The Last Game" by means of a historical story.

The philosophers of science whose views on explanation have provided us with useful background contrast throughout this primer have dismissed other philosophers of science who reject their views on the ground that the latter have concerned themselves with the psychology of scientific discovery rather than with the formal conditions of adequate scientific explanation.[27] Whether this dismissal is warranted I do not know. I do know that it is not warranted with respect to processive explanation in history. Processive explanation may—and I hope it does—throw some small light on the mysteries of the psychology of historical discovery. But that is not its primary intention. Its intention is precisely that of the philosophers: to deal with the form and condition of satisfactory historical explanation. It is just on this crux, where

[27] On the utility of background contrast, see the Nonchapter, p. 14.

covering-law explanation and explanation by narration fail, that I believe processive explanation in some degree succeeds. If it does so, it is because it takes the conditions and the form of a great deal of historical explanation seriously. The conditions are set by the surviving records of the past, their existential givenness, and their brute limitations. The form is very often a historical story. By one means or other— arbitrary rejection of its adequacy or equally arbitrary reduction of it to what it actually and manifestly is not, a collection of causally linked sentences—analytical philosophers have prescinded from the very problem they needed to face: how actual historical stories do achieve satisfactory explanation. Under such circumstances it is hardly surprising that the enterprise in which they have so heavily invested appears to be insolvent. By taking historical storytelling quite seriously as the form in which both Everyman and professional historians often explain the past, our account of processive explanation avoids the pitfalls of an unwarranted inattention to the explanatory efficacy of storytelling. That historical storytelling is translogical, that its truth values are dependent on its rhetorical as well as on its logical adequacy is just one of those facts that regardless of its consequences philosophers, and historians as well, will have to get used to and come to grips with.

In what precedes I may have inadvertently given the impression that I think this chapter or this book up to now has offered a complete, adequate, and satisfactory account of the form of historical explanation that I call processive. I do not think this at all. Moreover, I do not intend to offer such an account; if I tried, I doubt that I could do so; and I am far from sure that anyone will be able to do so now or in the near future. It will be a hard and complicated business. The accounts of other forms of explanation that we have had in view—covering-law explanation, for example—are as such adequate, complete, and satisfactory. The only trouble with them is that in many historical contexts they are irrelevant. They simply do not come to grips with historical storytelling. Since elements of storytelling penetrate a great deal of what historians call analytical history, this means that in the interest of rendering a satisfactory account of *forms* of historical explanation, the philosophers have rendered those forms too rigid to account for a good deal of explaining that history does. Like perfect numbers, the forms are pleasant to contemplate, but like the lilies of the field, "they toil not, neither do they spin," or at least they do not toil or spin enough. Processive explanation toils and spins, all right, but at the sacrifice of that mathematico-logical simplicity that makes the other forms of explanation pretty and neat. All that can be said for it is that it works when they do not. The difficulty of giving a full account of processive explanation is a correlate of its efficacy and virtues. It works by closely molding itself to the actual contours of the record of the past and to the varieties of the appropriate rhetoric of history; but since the former are very irregular and the latter quite complex and numerous, processive explanation may inherently be so irregular and complex as not to be fully describable.

What I have done so far then is:

1. To identify and label as processive a form of explanation which, as far as I know, has not hitherto been identified or labelled.

2. To demonstrate *that* it works by writing the historical story "The Last Game" as a focal center in which it works and other forms of explanation do not work, or at best work unreliably and sporadically.

3. To show by examining closely a few event-clusters in "The Last Game" how it works where no other form of explanation works.

4. To emphasize its capacity to make sense of the rhetoric of history as a component of historical explanation by storytelling instead of denying the relevance of that rhetoric to the attainment of historical truth.

To put the matter another way, because I doubt both the feasibility and the fruitfulness of such an enterprise, I have not attempted to present a "model" of processive explanation, but only an example of it, or a focal center embodying it. Thus the identification of Thomson's home run as the pivot point in "The Last Game" is essential to the processive explanation in *that* historical story. It does not, however, warrant the inference that every such story has a single pivot point. It only implies that when there happens to be a pivot point, failure to identify it frustrates processive explanation by obscuring the alternatives for organizing the story and disposing its parts and by misdirecting the historian in the necessary task of selection, omission, compression, and elision of data derived from the record. Such a failure thus produces an account, which, false in no detail, is of diminished truth value.

CHAPTER VIII:
Aristocratic Education and Beneficial Leases, *or Beyond Explanation Why and Beyond Explanation in History*

I n the preceding chapters we have identified the processive character of historical discourse as it applies to historical explanation "why" by storytelling. We have not rigorously analyzed the form of processive discourse and we are ready both to doubt whether it is reducible to a single form and to suspect that the discovery of such a form would be intellectually fruitless and vacuous. The notion of processive discourse points toward rules of rhetorical strategy in history that are relevant to enhancing knowledge and understanding of the past. In this chapter we wish to show that processive discourse opens the way to historical understanding beyond explanation. Since the tight ring that during the past few decades historians and philosophers in England and America have drawn around the activity of being a historian has unduly limited the conception of what historians ought to be doing, a breakthrough may effect a desirable emancipation of the historical imagination. It need not, and I hope it does not, lead historians to exalt themselves to the position that they occupied (or now imagine they occupied) in the nineteenth century, the position of grand panjandrums, gurus, and beneficed super-soothsayers to the greater human communities of which it behooves them to be reasonably humble members.

The first mental block we have already given a casual shove to, but perhaps it requires somewhat more systematic attention. It is the obsession of some historians with "why" questions, the gratuitous assumption that causal explanation is the only "real" explanation in history. In historical storytelling this uniformitarian bias is evidently inappropriate. There is a whole class of stories in life as well as in fiction called "whodunits." In such stories the ultimate processive explanation "who," depends on subsidiary explanations "why" (motive), "how" (method), "when" and "where" (opportunity). In "real life" the operative inquirers, the jury, often take the subsidiary explanations "how," "where," and "when" as sufficient to indicate "who." They find there enough to proceed with, so that they can arrive at their verdict, their statement of their view of the historical truth (*vere dictum*) without going into the explanation "why" or motive. But the murder trial is only one form, and a highly stylized one, that historical inquiry takes in the construction of historical stories. The emancipating trait of processive explanation is that it is in no way committed to a permanent evaluative hierarchy among explanations. If what needs explaining at the moment in the process of storytelling is who the man coming to bat after Lockman was, *that* is what needs explaining *then*, and is the most important thing to explain because it is needed to continue the story. Unless that explanation "who" is presented in the form of a past-performance sketch of Thomson, one dimension of Manager Dressen's dilemma will be missing from the story, and the story itself will be to that extent impoverished.

More than most human activities baseball is rule bound, both by the Official Rules and by "The Book." Since processive explanation has general if not universal application to history, it may be well to deal with it in a focus provided by a more varied and less fully controlled activity—education.

Some two decades ago, broad though loosely connected reading about the fifteenth and sixteenth centuries in Europe persuaded me that the most widely accepted accounts of what was going on at the time had a number of defects. Their correction would entail a fairly drastic restructuring of views long current and then still modish about early modern Europe. Of a half dozen or so defects three are especially relevant here.

1. Because of the influence of Jacob Burckhart's great work, *The Civilization of the Renaissance in Italy*, historians saw through Italian spectacles too much of what happened in trans-Alpine lands from 1450 on. I thought that a more serious consideration, politically, culturally, and socially, of the Netherlands-Burgundian principality from the accession in 1419 of Philip the Good to the abdication in 1555 of Arch-

duke Charles (since 1519, Emperor Charles V) would provide some correction of this overly Italianate perspective.

2. Middle-class French historians since The French Revolution and Marxist historians later had deemphasized the role of the aristocracy in the Western European monarchies during the period that concerned me. From what I could make out, socially, politically, and perhaps even economically, the aristocracies of the Western European lands were not having such a bad time of it in those days.

3. The traditional picture of the relation of the aristocracy to rulers of the countries of Western Europe was actually two pictures, radically divergent one from the other. One portrayed the nobleman as a tame, cowed courtier, financially dependent on royal favor and ever subservient to the prince's whim. The other portrayed him as a treacherous feudal magnate ever in search of a chance to revolt in order to diminish the royal power and enhance his own. This Jekyll-Hyde character suffered from inherent incredibility. Moreover, it ran counter to what my reading suggested: that between rulers and aristocracy the ordinary relation was a symbiosis, ambivalent and shaky on both sides, and that this actuality was reflected in contemporary theories of monarchy and nobility.

I had these notions fairly firmly in mind when I came upon a letter on the future education of his only son that a great Netherlands-Burgundian nobleman, Jean de Lannoy, had written in 1465. It advised that infant to go at the age of twelve to a "Latin school at Louvain, Cologne or Paris," to learn to speak German, to continue his reading in the books he would inherit from his father, especially in books on ethics, politics, and economics.[1] In his letter Jean explains:

> Those who have learned and retained much, and who have the greatest desire to learn and know, attain great good, honor, and riches . . . This has often caused me deep displeasure not for envy of them, but because of my simplicity and slight knowledge and because I was never put to school. I therefore know and can know nothing. I realize that for me this chance is lost and gone, never to be recovered, for I do not see or expect any remedy as to Latin or other studies. No day passes that I do not regret this, and especially when I find myself in the council of the king or of the Duke of Burgundy, and I know not nor dare not to speak my opinion after the learned, eloquent legists and *ystoryens* who have spoken before me. For I do not know the order or manner of speaking and can say nothing, but "Master John or Master Peter has spoken well, and I am of his opinion." Whence I have often felt deep shame and humiliation in my heart.[2]

[1] "Economics," as is evident from the context, means household management, as it did in the pseudo-Aristotelian treatise of that name.

[2] Quoted in J. H. Hexter, *Reappraisals in History* (London, 1961), p. 63.

The letter comes at the right time—three decades before the beginning of that extensive exposure of the aristocracies of the North to Italy and its humanist studies which is said to have followed the French invasion in 1494. It comes from the right place, Netherlands-Burgundy, and it comes from the right sort of person, a magnate-nobleman-courtier. And it hints, at least, at some of the right things—the self-image of the aristocrat and his conception of his relation to the prince. It pointed Louis de Lannoy toward an education at once rigorous, "intellectual," and in the medieval tradition "clerkly," for a churchman, which the sole heir of a noble magnate like Jean de Lannoy was most unlikely to become. Finally it indicated why the young man should want such an education—for honor, riches, and the opportunities it would afford him to rise in the service of his prince.

Considered as an E, an explanandum, something to be explained, the plan for Louis de Lannoy's education raises a problem of explanation so trivial as scarcely to be worthy of attention: the *explanans*, the sentences explaining why Jean wanted his son to get this sort of education, are either in the record, that is, in Jean's letter, or readily inferrable from it. But as a fragment of the record possibly indicative of historical processes surrounding it at the time, it was certainly from my point of view *ben trovato*, almost too pat. But was it *vero*? Was it an indicator of such processes, or just a symptom of a peculiar eccentricity on the part of Jean de Lannoy? To find that out required an inquiry into aristocratic education in the fifteenth and sixteenth centuries in the Netherlands-Burgundy principality, in France, and in England. Unfortunately, aristocratic educational performance evoked no such focused interest in those times and yielded no such tailor-made statistical records as interest in baseball provided in 1951 for "The Last Game." I could not refer readers, after referring myself, to two compact sources like the *New York Times* sports pages and the *Official Baseball Guide*. Instead in an article of twenty-five pages I had to refer my readers to sixty-five different sources after referring myself to about four times as many, three-quarters useless. I caught a bit here, a bit there. Occasionally one bit lead me to places where a few other bits turned up. Usually I proceeded almost scatter-shot just making half-educated guesses where I might find something. That I cannot reconstruct the process of my search, however, does not matter. Processive explanation is *not* intended merely as a description of the pattern and method of historical search and discovery; it is intended to signify a form of historical discourse directed toward rendering the past intelligible. What concerns us then is how the completed discourse incorporates a processive explanation. The completed discourse in this case is an article with the title "The Education of the Aristocracy in the Renaissance." [3] Readers who

[3] *Ibid.*, pp. 45–70.

wish to follow the path of a processive explanation in detail may do so in that article. For those who do not, a precis of the movement of that explanation may suffice.

A brief introduction leads into the following questions:

What, then, was the education of the aristocrats during the Renaissance, how many of them received it, when historically did they begin to receive it, and what did they want with it? [4]

Then a series of denunciations of the willful ignorance of the aristocracy from early modern English and French sources is followed by a further question:

"What is the meaning of this denunciation?" It *appears* to confirm from the contemporary record that view of the ineptitude of the early modern European aristocracy current among historians, when the article was written. Without explicitly doing so, it serves to point up the fact that historical views, long current and widely held, are usually not baseless; they almost always rest on some information in the record of the past; but as a result of deficiency or misconstrual their base may turn out to be inadequate. In any case, the criticism of ignorance among the aristocracy raises several questions.

Was the complaint new or of long standing? The situation—was it old or new? And, finally, was the situation real or unreal; to what extent was the sixteenth-century aristocrat actually an ignorant man? [5]

A quick survey of the educational ideal of the aristocracy from the late twelfth century provides a context for those questions. During three or four centuries, for the lay aristocrat that ideal had comprised rearing and training in courtesy and chivalry. But it was not for defect in that kind of education that sixteenth-century critics were berating the aristocracy. It was for indifference to a kind of education that medieval aristocrats neither had nor were criticized for lacking—bookish learning, the domain of the clergy rather than of the laity in the Middle Ages.

So much for the first two questions. The third requires reformulation to incorporate the improved orientation which the processive explanation has yielded up to this point.

What educational reality underlay the mass of exhortation and criticism directed at the aristocracy in the sixteenth century? Were the English gentlemen, say, of that age as innocent of and indifferent to school learning as Chaucer's squire was, and as the squire's contemporaries felt that he had a perfect right to be? [6]

[4] *Ibid.*, pp. 45–46.
[5] *Ibid.*, p. 47.
[6] *Ibid.*, p. 49.

This leads to a fairly detailed inquiry as to which English aristocrats, if any, were getting clerkly education in the sixteenth century, and when, and how many. The inquiry indicated that most aristocrats who got that sort of education got it where the clergy did—in the great schools and the two universities established in the Middle Ages primarily to train men for the church. The education of the aristocracy in book learning appeared to begin its increase somewhere during the reign of Henry VIII and to extend to larger numbers and downward in the aristocratic hierarchy as the century passed. By the end of the century a very large part of the English aristocracy, the sons of peers and of the upper gentry, were being exposed to the sort of learned Latin education that they had earlier been charged with avoiding.

The account of aristocratic education then swings from England to France. There the pattern turns out to be similar, but the evidence for it appears thinner, probably because the change in the pattern of education was itself more restricted. One of the earliest critics of the ignorance of the French aristocracy was the chronicler-historian Philippe de Commines.

"They are raised," he said of the nobles, "only to be fools in dress and words; they know nothing of reading French and they do not have a single wise man around them." [7]

A contrast is here seemingly implied between the French nobles and some other nobility. This raises a question. "Where had Commines come into contact with such a nobility?" [8]

In the 1480's when he made his critical observation the only other nobility he knew was that of his native land, the nobles of Netherlands-Burgundy. "Could it be those lords whom he is contrasting with the French nobles?" [9] According to the notion fashionable twenty years ago the idea was odd not only because of the date, but because Burgundy was then regarded as a sort of obsolescent antithesis to Renaissance Italy where newfangled notions about a learned laity were fairly common currency. Yet a search of the records, all from the reign of Philip the Good (1419–1467) turns up a surprising amount of fragmentary evidence of noble involvement in the bookish sort of education that became common among the English aristocracy a century to a century and a half later—names in university registers, a noble "board of directors" for the ducal library, special encouragements offered by the duke to students of noble families at the university, lay chroniclers of noble

[7] *Ibid.*, p. 56.
[8] *Ibid.*, p. 58.
[9] *Ibid.*, p. 59.

descent who previously attended a university, advice on education offered to their sons by great lords, especially the advice of Jean de Lannoy to his son Louis . . .

And thus by a circuitous movement in space through England and France and by a most erratic movement in time as far forward as the early seventeenth century and as far back as the late twelfth, the account of aristocratic education, three-quarters finished, reaches Burgundy under Philip and the fragment of the record that started us on our investigation, a fragment that now neatly fits in as the pivot point of a processive explanation. The pivot point, but clearly not the end point chronologically. And not the end point of the processive explanation either. That explanation moves on to explore the hint in Lannoy's advice about the reasons for the shift in aristocratic education. Again the account moves through the lands of Western Europe from Netherlands-Burgundy to England, to France, and even to Spain. Everywhere the results are similar. Renaissance rulers are laicizing governmental services hitherto largely staffed by clerics, but insisting that the services be competent. To gain the honors and emoluments that those services afford—in a recent colloquialism to "get themselves a piece of the action"—aristocrats are acquiring a kind of education that their forebears neither sought nor needed. Ideally, the goal of that education is neither the armed service a warrior-vassal owes to a feudal lord nor the unbounded service a mere pensioned courtier-dependent must render to an absolute monarch by divine right. It is the service, willingly rendered but not blind or limitless, that a Renaissance aristocrat owes through the prince to his native commonwealth. So the account ends:

> What we have already said may be enough to show that a revaluation of our whole conception of social ideas, social structure, and social function in Europe in the age of the Renaissance is long overdue. It may also suggest that we start our revision by thinking in terms not of the decline of the aristocracy but of its reconstruction.[10]

The processive explanation we have just followed raised and answered (more or less correctly as the case may be) a number of questions. Among them "why" questions and explanations "why" enjoyed no pride of place, no special paramount position in some imaginary value-hierarchy of explanation. The processive explanation moved from one question to the next in response to the exigencies of the rhetoric of history in order to array the relevant fragments of the record of the past in relation to the pivot point in such a way as to render the patterns they implied perspicuously clear. Processive explanation thus broadens

[10] *Ibid.*, p. 70.

the problem of what constitutes adequate or satisfactory explanation, because to the question "why?" it adds, "What constitutes satisfactory explanation 'when?' 'where?' 'how?' 'who?' " and so on and so on.

I doubt that the "adequate" or "satisfactory" form of processive explanation is abstractable from the rhetoric of historical discourse which is its vehicle. If it were abstractable, I doubt that it would be much more relevant to an account of viable historical explanation than the covering-law and narrative forms have turned out to be. Issues of the adequacy of such explanation are resolvable only in a context that takes account of the exigencies of the rhetoric of history. Consider explaining "who." Who, for example, was Jean de Lannoy? An adequate and satisfactory explanation of who he was might be one sentence long or it might run on for fifty pages. And two such explanations each entirely true might have not a single fact in common with the other. To arrive at an adequate and satisfactory explanation in a given instance one must relate it to a prior question: "What do you want to know for?" And the answer to that question can emerge only from the overall context—the whole processive explanation into which both the extent and the content of the explanation who Jean de Lannoy was must fit. The problem lies in the area of macrorhetoric.

By setting before us the operation of two processive explanations, the two focal centers employed in this chapter and the one preceding have helped us break out of an excessively constrictive view of what counts as explanation in history, the view that such explanation is confined to answers to "why" questions.

Those two centers may further broaden our conception of history, each in a different way. We first discerned the processive form of explanation in our attempt to account for the explanatory force of a historical story. But is "The Education of the Aristocracy in the Renaissance" a historical story? Surely not as unmistakably so as "The Last Game." A reasonable latitudinarianism in our views as to what counts as a story still should not do too much violence to the bounds of what passes for a story in the ordinary use of the term. And to apply that term to the history of aristocratic education might well evoke legitimate surprise or even indignation: "You call *that* a story?" Perhaps better not; yet it is a historical *account*, and the conception of processive explanation does better justice to the organization and structure of its truth values than do the other conceptions of historical explanation we have given attention to in this primer. Processive explanation, then, has generic application to history, not just specific application to historical storytelling. If it is not the sole form of historical explanation, it is surely the most comprehensive, rendering intelligible for extensive historical accounts their appropriate structures and some of their standards of relevance, enabling us to make sense of their direction of movements through the records of the past, and of the variations in their tempo.[11]

The story of "The Last Game" broadens our conception of history in a different way. Or rather it may help revive interest in aspects of the general conception of history that professional historians have allowed to become moribund in recent years. Consider a few bits of that story— the parts about the baseball enthusiasts who lined up after the game ended on October 2 to stand about all night in order to be sure that they would have a seat in the bleachers for the last game, about the alternations of hope and despair among the crowd at the Polo Grounds and at the radios and television sets in the city, about the cluster of listeners around the radio in the college library, about Russ Hodges' wild outburst, about the responses of the Chief of Circulation and the Director of Library Services, and about the long walk of Branca when it was all over. Obviously, they play no part at all in the explanation of why the Giants won the pennant. Just as obviously the author regarded them as useful in some sense and for some purpose. Since similar items appear in many historical stories, they raise a general question as to their function.

In historical accounts such items may be divided into three categories: antirelevant, irrelevant, and relevant. Antirelevant items are simply a mark of historian's ineptitude. They indicate the triumph of his diligence as a collector over his competence as a selector. Having gone to the trouble, often quite considerable, of acquiring certain information, he cannot resist including it in his historical account, even though its inclusion perceptibly diminishes by dilution the effectiveness of the account and thus frustrates his own defined historical intention, supposing he ever got around to defining an intention. This sort of thing, throw-in-the-kitchen-sink history, is most characteristically an infantile disorder among apprentice historians; but as a consequence of laxity among the trainers of the craft, it is sometimes permitted to become a chronic disease. It does so particularly among more advanced historians who, lacking any viable claims to merit, base their hopes for professional status or advancement on the demerit of logorrhea.

Irrelevance, the interjection of items, which without seriously diluting an historical account do nothing to improve it, is usually the consequence of extrahistorical commercial motives, the desire of the writer to enhance not historical understanding but sales. It is regulated by estimates of the current public taste, and until very recently often has

[11] The conception of processive explanation may usefully apply to disciplines other than history. Lacking any depth of understanding of any discipline but history, I can make no judgment on this point. The very flexibility of the conception, as of the conception of credibility, which recommend both of them to me as a historian, may render them obnoxious to practitioners whose disciplines commit them to greater rigor, and to historians with a similar commitment.

taken the form of the tutti-frutti method, the deployment of scandalous or scatalogical details calculated to titillate the more naïve prospective purchasers and enlist them into the army of word-of-mouth advertisers. Awareness that sexual activity is not highly variable in sensual yield, though delightful in itself given an appropriate level of interest by both participants, is relatively recent, the consequence of earlier, easier, and more open and frequent access to that activity by the literate and talkative classes. Until recently, then, while the essentially simple operation was surrounded by a thick padding of sacred-profane mystery, reference in historical stories to the priapic athleticism or deficiencies of the male characters, the ready accessibility and mammary endowments of the females, might win praise from reviewers of a certain sort on the ground that the writer was "bold" or "frank" or that he "made history come alive," apparently on the view, largely delusional, that the most significant and interesting things in the past happened while the people they happened to were in bed.

In historical stories there remains, however, a large residue of items that are nonexplanatory yet relevant to the story. They serve to remind us of a most important fact that some professional historians have recently tended to forget, disregard, or reject to their own detriment and to the consequent desication and dehumanization of history. It is that *history is not necessarily and not always directly concerned with explanation even in the broadest tolerable sense of that term.* A quite legitimate concern of many historical accounts is, within the bounds of the rules of the discipline, to confront the readers with a human situation and to enhance their awareness of it. Since this is not a concern of the natural sciences as such, no knowledge of those sciences is of any use at all, no analogy to them is in the least helpful to historians when they undertake to perform this function.

Consider the last few sentences of "The Last Game." From the moment that the story got Thomson's home run safely tucked into the left field stands, explanation was over. Given the rules of baseball, there was nothing more to explain. But there were two things left—the victors and the victim, triumph and tragedy. Triumph for the victors, the Giants and Bobby Thomson; tragedy for the victim, Ralph Branca. To say this, to render it explicit, explains nothing that the story set out to explain, and in the story it was not made explicit. It was not my aim to make it explicit; on the contrary, it was my aim not to make it explicit. Why? It is a hard question. For the same reason perhaps that one does not finish a joke by saying "That is a joke." If it is a bad joke, labelling it as a joke does not make it better. If it is a good joke, labelling it as a joke diminishes it. If the very last sentences of "The Last Game" convey to readers no sense at all of the coexistence and correlation of triumph and tragedy in the fabric of human life, I have simply failed as a historian, and no bare explicit statement about that coexistence and correlation will serve to paper over my failure, since to convey that sense without explicit statement was my purpose.

The step beyond explanation "why" and beyond explanation to the nonexplanatory ways that history extends human knowledge and enhances human understanding is at once dangerous and necessary. Unless one takes care one is suddenly plunged from the sometimes bare and sterile but at least hard rock of painstaking reasonable inquiry and argument into a slough of mystagogy. Because of the unfortunate preoccupation of most of the more rational and competent historians with problems of explanation, until recently this whole area of nonexplanatory history has in the main though not entirely been resigned to verbose declaimers, obscurantists, and excessively precious intellectual weaklings. Such historians fastidiously avoid tough problems, and they bring shame rather than needed succor to the humanities which they profess to defend. For them to use the phrase "historical rhetoric," the most useful term around which to construct a conception of the historian's work in its final written form, renders the phrase repulsive to those who work at history and do not just fool around with it. Here I wish to indicate what some of the problems of historical rhetoric are. In doing so I hope it will be evident that my interest is not in fooling around with history but in working at it and making it work.

The task of a historian is defined for him by two primordial archetypal questions: (1) what explains what happened, and (2) what was what happened like? The questions are archetypal and primordial in the sense that they are both the questions that Everychild raises and the questions that others ask him time and again on his way to becoming Everyman. The first question solicits enhanced intelligibility; the second vicarious experience; both solicit an advancement of the understanding, a conquest of knowing against the unknown. In history, we have suggested, the first question is usually dealt with by means of the form of explanation we call processive. It is with the second question that we pass beyond the bounds of explanation. The moment we examine the historical question "What was it like?" it crumbles into fragments before our eyes. Even when asked about a single entity or event in the past, although that event was instantaneous and experienced by only one person, there is no single answer. A thunder clap at night on a deserted hillside where there is one man only to witness it is to him like one thing at the moment of immediate perception and no longer quite like that a moment later. "The Last Game" was like one thing to the Director of Library Services, another to Leo Durocher, another to Charles Dressen. That game was like one thing to Bobby Thomson when he made a stupid misplay in the second inning, another as he cantered around the bases in the ninth; like one thing to Ralph

Branca when he wound up for his first pitch in that ninth inning, another a minute later as he began his long walk to the Dodgers' dressing room. And if the question, "What was the last game like?" thus fragments itself, much more so does such a question as "What was the Reformation (or the French Revolution) like?" What-was-it-like questions about such large event-constellations as the Reformation will always mean what was it like to someone, usually to someone there and then;[12] and it will always imply that the constellation referred to or some elements of it were perceived by the person in question, though not necessarily perceived as "the Reformation." Thus to ask what the Renaissance was like for citizens of Florence in the later Quattrocento makes a modicum of sense, because they could scarcely have failed to perceive something about it. To ask what it was like for Calabrian peasants in the fifteenth century is a waste of time; nothing about it passed the threshold of their consciousness. To ask what it was like for Jacob Burckhart, a nineteenth-century historian, is also appropriate, because he perceived it indirectly in the record of the past. The point is not an idle one. A great deal of bad history has gone into detailing how large collectivities —medieval man, the French bourgeois—viewed certain historical abstractions—the code of chivalry, the Cartesian world-view—without any persuasive evidence that most of the constituents of the collectivity were more than peripherally, if at all, aware of the abstractions.

Since "What was something like?" questions are always and necessarily "What was something like for someone?" questions, since they always imply a perceiving and responding person or group, they can always be translated "In such and such circumstances what was it like to be such and such a person or kind of person?" To ask "What was it like for Luther to burn the books of the canon law?" is equivalent to asking "What was it like to be Luther when he burned the books of the canon law?" Whether he knows it or not, every historian who has ever ascribed a purpose, a sentiment, or an intention to any person or group he has written about implicitly claims that he can know what it was like in some circumstances to have been someone else, to have been an Other.

At this point a curious divergence occurs between the proper purposes and limits of the natural sciences and history. The vocabularies of the natural sciences do not incorporate words to enable practitioners to communicate what it is like to be the objects of their study, or they do so at considerable risk. Physicists seek to know what a neutron or an electric charge is in terms of what it does; the question what it is like to be a neutron or an electrical charge does not make sense to them, nor is

[12] Not always or necessarily, however. The question, "What was the Reformation like for Bishop Bossuet?" who lived a century and a half later is an appropriate (and answerable) historical question.

there any reason why it should. Only in the vocabulary of animal psychology do words that seem to suggest what it is like to be an Other appear. It is doubtful, however, that the scientist who describes as "comfort seeking" the huddling together of several paramecia in a slowly evaporating drop of water is likely to claim that he is conveying or trying to convey to the reader what it is like to be a paramecium, or that he really has any notion what it is like to be one. Indeed terms such as "comfort seeking" seem like unfortunate humanized metaphors. In context animal psychologists protect themselves from the misconstrual of such metaphors by a closed frame of reference made up of the paradigmatic terms—"stimulus," "response," "function," and "behavior." These terms carry a warning from the scientist to those to whom words like "comfort" and "care" suggest what it is like to be an Other: check all such notions at the door before entering our frame.

Consider by way of contrast a historian's rhetoric. Lawrence Stone is one of the ablest historians of this generation, and one of the historians most firmly committed to the view that history will be better only as it becomes more scientific. In *The Crisis of the Aristocracy* he seeks at one point to render intelligible an idiosyncrasy of early seventeenth-century English agrarian life—the beneficial lease. The peculiarity of this arrangement was that although it had serious drawbacks for landlord and tenant alike, at the time both landlords and tenants positively preferred it to alternative options that would have been economically more rational and mutually advantageous. According to Stone, among the things that rendered the beneficial lease acceptable to seventeenth-century tenants was the tenants' "vision of life on earth." Into that vision fit the most irrational features of the beneficial lease, a very large initial payment and a small annual rent.

> When man is at the mercy of disease and the weather, in health today, crippled or dead tomorrow, gorged today and starved tomorrow, with money to burn today from the sale of a bumper crop, plunged into debt tomorrow because of harvest failure, the human condition is one of perpetual flux. The beneficial lease was just one more card in a large pack of jokers, and leaseholders and the customary tenants positively preferred a few years of misery and hardship while the fine was being paid, followed by a long period at a low rent, to the regular payment of a reasonable annual sum.[13]

This remarkable passage deserves close examination. Lawrence Stone has been successively an English public school boy, an Oxford undergraduate, an English army officer, a Fellow of Wadham College, Oxford, and a professor of history at Princeton University. He has never

[13] Lawrence Stone, *The Crisis of Aristocracy, 1558–1641* (Oxford, 1965), p. 316.

been an English peasant holding land by beneficial or any other kind of lease in the twentieth much less in the seventeenth century. Yet he claims to understand "the vision of life" of such peasants three hundred years ago. To claim this is to claim to know a good bit about what it was like to have been such a peasant. It is a considerable claim, and I am not very well informed about those records of the past on which it must rest. Still given the little I do know, and given Stone's accomplishments as a historian, I am not at all inclined to challenge his claim. It is no different in kind from the claim I would be ready to make that I have a good notion what it was like to be an unlearned courtier-magnate surrounded by fast-talking lawyers in the council of the Duke of Burgundy in the mid-fifteenth century. If after reading Jean de Lannoy's letter to his son, I had no idea at all what it was like, I would be pretty stupid.

This point calls for some emphasis because one set of writers about history makes something of a mystique of the historians' claimed ability to know what Others are like, while a second set seem to think that historians can carry on all their proper business of explanation without claiming or possessing such knowledge. There is certainly no sense in making a big thing of the claim of historians to know what it is to be like some person or group in the past. It is no way different in principle from Everyman's assumption that he knows something about what some people are like in the present. Everyman watches closely what such people do, listens closely to what they say, and his observations coalesce into his notion of what they are like. If he is a terrible incompetent at the job, he gets very little that he wants from his association with others, and a lot that he does not want, a lot that fills his life with unpleasant surprises. We have a useful adjective to describe people who do a consistently bad job of knowing what others are like; we call them naïve.

A professional historian pays close attention to the record of what the people who concern him said and did in the past and he pieces his observations together into his notion of what they were like. As additional information about them comes to light, if it never fits with his previous notion of what they were like, then either they were very peculiar people or he is a very bad (because naïve) historian. Since not many people are all that peculiar, the second alternative seems the more likely. To say that both professional historians and Everyman know what Others are like does not, of course, mean that they know exactly or everything about what Others are like. No man even knows exactly what he himself is like. All of us are occasionally surprised at what we find ourselves doing and saying. Only if we equate knowing with total and continuous certainty, however, will we make our occasional errors about ourselves and others the ground for a complete skepticism as to

our ability to know something about what it was like to have been
Another.

The process of understanding what it is like to be Another is sometimes easy, sometimes difficult, but certainly an everyday affair. Hard-
headed philosophers have sought to minimize its place in explanation,
even in historical explanation,[14] to the point where it ceases to have
any explanatory function, conceived in the narrow sense of explanation
"why." They find its vocabulary of "empathy" and "intuitive understanding" confusing and opaque. Yet in treating the beneficial lease, a
quite hard-headed historian glides smoothly from telling what it was
like to envision the world as seventeenth-century peasants did to explaining why those peasants found the beneficial lease attractive. And
Stone's ability to envision the world as they did is entirely relevant to
his explanation, which would be impossible to achieve without it.

Again it is not at all hard to understand why this should be so. To
provide the best accounts they can of what men have done in the past is
a major part of the task of historians and such accounts are most of
history—Catholics massacring Huguenots in France on St. Bartholomew's Day, 1572, seventeenth-century English peasants entering into
beneficial leases, German Communists in the early 1930's doing what
they could to destroy the Weimar Republic, trade unionists in 1968
voting for George Wallace.[15] What people do is intelligible in terms of
their "vision of life," of what they think things are like and how they
feel about them, and therefore of what those people themselves are
like, and what it is like to be them. Note that what things are actually
like and men's vision of what they are like may stand in the most
varied sorts of relation to each other. The views of statesmen as to the
pressure of population on food supply in their homeland may be
accurate or wildly inaccurate. Accurate or not, it is their notion of the
extent of that pressure, of what should be done about it, and of what
can be done about it that defines for them their course of action. To
understand these notions is to understand in this particular context what
those statesmen were like, and to understand what they did we need to
understand what they were like. In general to understand what men
have done and why they have done it, it is necessary to understand, not
perfectly or totally but in some measure, what they were like, or alternatively what it was like to have been them.

This is all so obvious, so evidently the way that both professional

[14] Carl Hempel, *Aspects of Scientific Explanation* (New York, 1965), pp. 161,
163, 239–240, 257–258.

[15] The list of examples has been especially chosen because all of them require
of the kind of person likely to be a historian, a special effort to understand what it
was like to be their subjects.

historians and Everyman ordinarily go about understanding why people do what they do and what people are like that it seems little
short of babytalk to put it down in writing.[16] I put it down only because the familiar simplicities of the case have been almost wholly
blocked from view on both sides—on one by a rhetorical curtain rendered unnecessarily and inconveniently opaque by the infusion of the
vocabulary of German idealism, on the other by the impenetrably fine
mesh of analytical apparatus of logicians, which seems designed to keep
light out rather than let it in.

Looked at in one way the passage from *The Crisis of the Aristocracy*
that we have examined can be regarded as explanatory. So regarded,
the question "What was it like to be a seventeenth-century English
peasant?" appears subordinate to the question "Why was the beneficial
lease the most common form of agreement for letting land in England
three centuries ago?" The first answer then becomes instrumental in the
work of historical explanation, a mere though necessary means to a
superior end. There is no need, however, to look at the passage that
way. In principle it is equally appropriate to look at it the opposite way,
to think of Stone's investigation of the beneficial lease as a mere means
to the superior end of finding what it was like to be an English tenant.
Why, indeed, not think of it this way? Obsession with and excessive
exaltation of explanation "why" is probably due to the belief, not always true, that once we know why something happened we can do
something about it, can control it in the future. The obsession seems
especially inappropriate in historians. Surely it would be odd to
imagine that once we knew why men entered into that obsolete agreement, the beneficial lease, in the seventeenth-century, we could do
something about such leases in the eighteenth century—a "future" long
since past.

Clearly then, in the quest of historians for knowledge, understanding,
and truth there are no intrinsic or a priori grounds for asserting the
absolute superiority of either of our archetypal historical questions,
"What explains it?" and "What was it like?" Just as clearly, historical
discourse itself achieves extension of knowledge and intensification of
understanding while passing from one archetypal question to the other
in patterns prescribed by the exigencies and strategies of its own
macrorhetoric. We first noted as characteristic of historical explanation
"why" by storytelling, and then of historical explanation as a whole
the trait of processiveness, of giving the reader both enough to be going
on with and the sense that the path he is being led along is going some-

---

[16] For a general note on the contrast between the actual easiness of the operation
of being a historian and the excessive and unnecessary difficulty of the discourse
about the operation, see the Nonchapter, pp. 7–9.

where, not just rambling aimlessly about. That trait now appears to be a significant characteristic of historical discourse in general.[17]

It is tempting to leave it at that, which is, indeed, to leave history poised and in balance between the sciences and the humanities. Such has been a traditional view of history, sanctioned by both experience and common sense. Inclined toward the sciences, history seeks explanations of the things that happened to men in the past; inclined to the humanities, it seeks to know what it was like to have been the men to whom those things happened. This is, or used to be, the conventional wisdom. But an author writes at a time and in a milieu. Unless he is quite emphatic, what he says gets misconstrued to suit the prepossessions current at that time and in that milieu.

At a time when so many professional historians are so wrapped up in achieving satisfactory explanation "why," it is all too easy to foresee how the foregoing will be misconstrued by those in control of the instruments of misconstrual. Granting that in order to achieve explanation "why," it is usually necessary to know what some persons or groups of persons were like, it will be said or assumed that what I *really* mean is that to *explain why* people were like what they were like, and to *explain why*, being what they were like, they did what they did, is in the last analysis what is important or basic in history.

At the personal level the only answer to such an assumption is that I *really* did not say that, and that I *really* am pretty good at saying what I mean and at not saying what I do not mean, that these are matters about which I habitually take considerable care, and that like Horton the Elephant, I meant what I said and I said what I meant. At a different level it may be worth pointing out that in history, as practiced by professional historians, the practical incentive to achieve explanation "why" is considerably less intense than it is for natural and social scientists. Certainly from the time of Bacon at least, one of those incentives in the natural sciences has been the hope, since partially fulfilled in rather a terrifying way, that explaining the natural environment would be a giant step toward controlling it. Certainly, too, it was the success of the natural scientists in this matter that moved social scientists to seek to emulate them and achieve control over the human environment. They sought it on the same conditions, or what could at least be disguised as the same conditions, as the scientists enjoyed—that the necessary knowledge did not demand self-knowledge, the achievement of control did not require self-control.

Humane learning and understanding operate on a wholly opposite set of assumptions. They assume that knowledge of other men and

[17] Is it, however, the dominant trait of *all* discourse? I think not. It is not so, for example, in the case of logic, dominated by rigor of demonstration, nor much lyric poetry, usually dominated by intensification of immediate sensibility.

self-knowledge are mutually interdependent. For them growing from infancy to maturity means precisely the synchronous growth from knowing nearly nothing of what it is like either to be another or to be one's self, to knowing a good deal about both. What we commonly refer to as immaturity or childishness is precisely a kind of simultaneous ignorance of what others are like and what one's self is like. So far is this kind of knowing of the human environment from being independent of self-knowledge that it grows symbiotically with it. An effect as well as a condition of this kind of knowing is not control of others but self-control, the ability to restrain one's self from interposing oneself between the Other and the light in which he sees himself and in which he reveals what it is like to be him.

As we have seen, the direct control of the environment which natural scientists achieve and social scientists hope to achieve through the power conferred by explanation scarcely rank high among either the hopes or the achievements of historians; most of the environments they try to explain have already passed irrevocably beyond their control; they have passed because they are past. On the other hand, history—but not history alone—can offer men a measure of that ability to know and understand what it is like to be another which is a prerequisite of a life of humane self-control. In the immediate circle of his vocation and family life, the historian Everyman regularly uses his historical knowledge of what it is like to be another. If he fails to do so, he is sharply penalized. The cab driver who cannot understand what it is like to wait half an hour for transportation to meet a pressing appointment loses his tip; the shopper who does not know what it is like to be a salesgirl before Christmas, the salesgirl who forgets what it is like to be a shopper, both lose their tempers. The husband whose expectations in dress and demeanor from his wife do not change with the lapse of half a dozen years and the birth of three offspring had better learn what it is like to be cooped up for ten hours doing household chores with three small children underfoot; otherwise his marriage bed is likely to become a bed of thorns. And every parent of an adolescent has heard the reproach—or seen it in a gesture or a glance—"You have forgotten what it is like to be young." As indeed, in part, all parents of adolescents have. It is only because most of them remember in part what it was like that family life may be a little less disastrous than any currently visible alternative.

Understanding what it is like to be another, always essential for men in the intimate communities of their day-to-day life and work, has become increasingly essential in the larger context of a society that more and more throws them into contact with people far different from themselves. Fortunately, many such contacts with others are rendered tolerable and orderly by the interposition of impersonal rules or laws.

At best, however, such rules are never quite enough and never quite good enough. Whether the rules ease contact with others or make it abrasive, whether the contact engenders conflict or mutual confidence, will depend on the quality of knowing what it is like to be another that goes into the structuring of the rules and that enters their interstices to lubricate their administration and operation. Knowing what it is like to be another, therefore, is what restrains civil intercourse from always escalating to confrontation. Unlike explanation "why," it aims at self-control rather than control of others. For this reason its results are themselves more controllable, more readily modifiable and corrigible and less permanently damaging than unsuccessful efforts to control others.

History is one of the disciplines most effectively organized for imparting knowledge of what it is like to be another. A historian is bound to try to grasp what it is like to be *all* of the major participants in a process in the past that seriously concerns him—Luther, Calvin, and Loyola; Henry III, Henry of Guise, and Henry of Navarre; Danton, Robespierre, and Hébert; Lenin, Trotsky, and Stalin; or, closer to date, Hubert Humphrey, Richard Nixon, and George Wallace. The very names on the list should make it clear that to know what it is like to be another does not require a historian to like that other, or to like what he is like. Of historians who encounter men in the record of the past their discipline does not demand universal mercy or love. Those are the prerogatives of God, not the obligations of historians. But to strive to do justice to those he encounters in the past, a fuller and more precisely measured justice than practical and procedural exigencies allow the law to attempt is the obligation of every historian. One of the wisest historians of my generation went right to the heart of the matter. The subject of his remarks was the Duke of Medina Sidonia, the Admiral of the Spanish Armada, which he had led to disaster in 1588 in its battle with the English fleet.

> There is a tendency of late to speak more kindly of Medina Sidonia . . . to recognize his courage and his administrative ability, but no one has yet said that he could not have done better. It is at least arguable, however, that no one could . . . Not that such a judgment would have been much comfort to Medina Sidonia. Whatever he did, it was not enough. Nor does it matter at all to the dead whether they receive justice at the hands of succeeding generations. But to the living, to do justice, however belatedly, should matter.[18]

Why was it important to Garrett Mattingly in 1959 to do justice to the Duke of Medina Sidonia, dead then for more than three centuries?

[18] Garrett Mattingly, *The Armada* (Boston, 1959), p. 375.

And why was it important to those who read his book to see and to understand justice to be done? To love all men or many is a gift of grace not given to all. But to do justice is a gift of reason, with which Everyman is in some measure endowed. To love is divine; to do justice is human; it is a large part of what humanity is; and wholly to turn one's reason from the quest for justice is to repudiate one's own humanity. To learn to do justice to others above and beyond what the law demands, Everyman needs to learn what it is like to be other than he himself. None of this learning is effortless; and although much of it is unsystematically acquired, some is attainable by systematic effort, if one looks in the right places. There are as we have said many disciplines, especially the natural sciences, to which the task of understanding and communicating what other persons or groups of persons are like is irrelevant, so it is useless to look for such learning there. There are others—painting, sculpture, music, lyric poetry, even some of the fictive arts—in which a practitioner can invest a fruitful lifetime without having to engage in the hard effort of seeking to understand what it is to be anyone other than himself.[19]

In historical inquiry, too, questions of what it was like to be another, can be avoided, but more evidently than in any other discipline the avoidance would be counterproductive of knowledge, understanding, and truth. It would require extraordinary restrictions, a series of arbitrary and stultifying measures to block and control the process of inquiry, serving no evident purpose but to render the flow of historical discourse sterile, narrow, and shallow. And while this futile diminution of history went on, the dammed-up answerable but unanswered questions about what people were like, what their vision of life was, on which depended explanations of why things happened the way they did, would pile up behind the dams, always threatening to engulf the few historical enterprises that alone were possible without them.

In the work of communicating what it is like to be another, history's most evident limitation—its commitment to operate within the bound of legitimate credible inference from the record of the past—is paradoxically its greatest asset. With his customary precision A. J. Liebling has put his finger on the limitation:

> The so-called creative artist . . . if he finds a character in his story awkward can simply change its characteristics. (Even to sex, *vide* Proust and Albertine. Let him try it with General de Gaulle.)

[19] The statement about the fictive arts may at first seem odd. It will seem less so if one keeps in mind a considerable number of genres from the romances of chivalry to expressionist dramas and beyond in which the "characters" were such beings as "never were on sea or land."

Or, the medievalist might add, Charlemagne. The fictive artist can at will add traits to the characters he has invented or subtract traits from them; he can invent without limit circumstances in which the traits he has chosen to assign to his *dramatis personnae* will most effectively manifest themselves. The historian has no such freedom. He cannot invent a character, he cannot ascribe to the characters he encounters in the records of the past any trait for which those records do not afford evidence; he cannot invent incidents to reinforce the reader's awareness of traits that the records show forth dimly.[20] Worst of all he cannot even disregard evidence that a character he has encountered had traits so incompatible as to render many things about him unintelligible, nor can he smooth such traits away. Or rather he ought and had better not. For if he does, he risks the penalty that historians corporately reserve for their fellows who err in this way individually—the Acid-Dipped Pen Torture. The purpose of the torture is to enforce a prime rule of the craft; to confess ignorance is forgivable, to ignore is not. For historians, it is the binding, overriding character of the commandment, "Thou shalt not ignore the record of the past," that constrains them to attain a view of what others are like and what it is like to be another that is more catholic than that required of the adepts of any other discipline.[21]

The historian has no place to hide from swarms of others, because once he embarks on a historical inquiry, he ordinarily encounters those swarms—other persons, other groups—in the records of the past. His encounters are not all in the nature of surprises. It would be more surprising indeed if a historian picking his way through a particular stretch of the record of the past did not expect in advance some of the encounters that take place. Only a most eccentric historian would expect to move around very widely in the early German Reformation without bumping into Erasmus, Luther, Charles V, Frederick of Saxony and Zwingli, the Münster Anabaptists and the Strasbourg Reformers.

---

[20] The most extreme experiment in such invention that I have come across in a historical work by a professional historian is in a chapter of Walter Webb's *The Great Frontier* (Cambridge, Mass., 1952), pp. 36–48.

The purpose of the chapter is to show the gradual reversal of leadership roles that took place between men moulded by the culture of the Atlantic Seaboard and those moulded by the frontier as Americans moved west. The device Webb employed was a journey west by an imaginary party made up of a military man, a businessman, a scholar, a man of the cloth, and a frontiersman. Granting what was deplorably evident, that Professor Webb was not a born master of the fictive arts, it still seems to me that what renders the chapter a historical disaster is its incongruity with the rest of the book in which it was encysted. The fictive rhetoric of the imaginary journey is not compatible with the rhetoric of history in the chapters that surround it.

[21] Anthropology, law, and psychotherapy are similar to history in this matter but for reasons too tedious to consider here the range of their view is more limited or the constraint to take a catholic view less exigent than that imposed on historians by the record of the past.

Moreover, when a historian does encounter such men and groups as these he rarely does so without any preconceptions at all about what they were like. It is almost certain that he will have heard a good deal about them from other historians; and he is both foolish and absurdly vain if he refuses to pay any attention to what such knowledgeable experts have said. But—and this is the crucial test—whatever the experts tell him, he must be ready to watch closely what the people he encounters do and listen closely to what they say when he encounters them in the record of the past. If what he finds them doing and saying there does not square with what he has heard about them from the experts, he must be prepared to revise his prejudgment about what they are like in the interest of doing them justice, for as a historian judges so should he be judged, and so ultimately will he be judged.

What is true of the historian's obligation and opportunity [22] with respect to persons encountered in the past applies equally to past human communities and collectivities. Indeed if history is not to forsake its singular humanity, it is especially important that historians take even greater care than they do with individuals to understand what the groups they encounter are like. We are somehow less prone to stereotype persons than we are to stereotype groups—less inclined to close our minds to what Oliver Cromwell was like than to what the Puritans were like, to what Robespierre was like than to what the Jacobins were like, to what George Meany is like than to what trade unionists are like. Why this should be so is not clear; perhaps it is because by casting persons into groups we have already partly dehumanized them, deprived them of their individual personalities. The results are clearer: stereotyping further dehumanizes our perception of others; it facilitates dividing the world into the Good Guys and the Bad Guys; and it ministers to the infantile need so to divide it when considering both the past and the present. It absolves us of all obligation to know what it is like to be one of those we have stereotyped as bad—a Puritan, a bourgeois, a courtier, a Negro, a cop, a Wasp, an Arab, an Israeli. In a world in which confrontation with rather than understanding of others looks like a suitable preface to probable annihilation, such absolutism is a luxury we might want to learn to forego, and history might do something to help us forego it.

The notion that at this late date history is likely to rescue mankind from the impending ultimate consummation of its propensity for self-destruction is one not likely to commend itself to a moderately skeptical

---

[22] With a nominalism perhaps excessively self-conscious I have throughout this primer preferred "historians," "a historian," and "some historians" to the implicit realism of "the historian." I deviate from my consistent usage here because I believe what I am saying applies universally to all historians and under all circumstances.

mind. It is indeed grasping at a straw; but then in the past by grasping at enough straws and somehow patching them together, groups of men have managed to keep themselves afloat, and it is just barely possible that we (all mankind this time) can do it again. If keeping mankind afloat seems at all worthwhile doing, any straw that helps in the least to prevent the enterprise from sinking is worth adding to the too scant mass.

The intention of the foregoing discussion is not to assert for the history that answers the question "What was it like to be that man or that community of men?" some sort of primacy over history that answers the question, "How did that event come about?" As we have seen, in the processive discourse characteristic of history these two questions are inseparably intermeshed aspects of a single activity or practice of inquiry and discourse. History is Janus-faced, looking in its own peculiar way toward explanation, a preoccupation it shares with the sciences, looking also toward knowing what it is like to be another, a preoccupation it shares with the humanities. Its two faces, however, share a common brain. In the practice of history writing, to separate one aspect of it from the other is to cleave through the crisscrossed network of connections necessary to intelligent historical discourse; if taken seriously it renders historical inquiry mindless. Without ever forgetting the other face or the common mind of history, it is possible, however, to contemplate one face at a time. We began this primer by a reasonably intensive scrutiny of the explanatory aspect of history, but almost from the outset to understand the expressions, so to speak, on that face of history we were forced to consider the common mind and intermittently but inescapably the other face. And for the last few pages we have reversed positions. Having inquired how the explanatory power of history augments knowledge, understanding, and truth, we have been trying to get some insight into the like powers of its humane aspects. The study of history, as we have seen, gives men the knowledge of what it was like to have been a *particular* person or a member of a *particular* human group in the past. In giving them that, however, it often gives them something beyond that. It gives them a certain habit of mind, a set of intellectual reflexes, that enhance their readiness to consider and try to understand now in the present what it is like to be another. If it could do this for Everyman in the range of relations that lie beyond his home, his friends, and his work associates, it might equip him, who is all of us, a little better for meeting the complexities and perplexities of living from day to day; it might make us a little less childish, a little more mature; a little less provincial and naive, a little more ecumenical; a little less mean, a little more generous. And in the Western world at a time when the practical application of the explanatory powers of the natural sciences has greatly enhanced the quantity and availability of things without bringing about an equivalent enhancement of the quality of life or the joy of living, any possible source of improvement in that quality merits some attention in its own right.

To claim that a discipline advances positive explanatory knowledge and truth and yet is not, cannot be, and perhaps should not be dissociated from the moral and civil education of society, raises questions about that discipline and about the very processes of knowing, understanding, and attaining truth that are most perplexing. Up to now we have but occasionally glanced at these large and difficult questions. We shall perhaps be prepared to scrutinize them more steadily and closely in the concluding chapter of this primer after we have dealt with some of the peculiarities of the microrhetoric of history.

APPENDIX[23]

The term "behavioral sciences" came into currency, one might even say into being, in the United States in the early 1950s. A decade and a half later, it appears to be well established in American universities and disciplines and is well on its way to acceptance abroad. Before 1950 the term was virtually nonexistent; since then it has come into such general use that it appears in the titles of books and journals, of conference sessions, programmatic reports, university departments, professorships, and courses, as well as in the names of a book club, a book prize, several publishers' series, and in the mass media of communication.

What happened to give rise to the term? The key event was the development of a Ford Foundation program in this field. The program was initially designated "individual behavior and human relations" but it soon became known as the behavioral sciences program and, indeed, was officially called that within the foundation. It was the foundation's administrative action, then, that led directly to the term and to the concept of this particular field of study.

The story begins with a committee that undertook a study for the Ford Foundation in the late 1940s, when the foundation was about to enter on the enlarged program that made it, overnight, the largest private foundation in the world. This study committee, given the task of suggesting how "the Ford Foundation can most effectively and intelligently put its resources to work for human welfare," concluded that

[23] Bernard Berelson, "Behavioral Sciences," *International Encyclopedia of the Social Sciences* (New York: Macmillan, 1968) 2: 42–43. See p. 154, note 5.

"the most important problems of human welfare now lie in the realm of democratic society, in man's relation to man, in human relations and social organizations"; and it recommended that the over-all objective be pursued in five "program areas—the establishment of peace, the strengthening of democracy, the strengthening of the economy, education in a democratic society, and individual behavior and human relations." Among the social science disciplines, political science became involved in the first and second programs, economics in the third, and, in a more or less residual way, anthropology, psychology, and sociology in the fifth. In the study committee's report appeared the term that soon became current, "the behavioral sciences," and the beginnings of a definition to distinguish them from the social sciences: "We have in the social sciences scientifically-minded research workers who are both interested in, and equipped for, the use of such techniques. Among these are the psychologists, sociologists, and anthropologists. In addition, there are psychiatrists and psychoanalysts, as well as natural scientists, including geneticists and other biologists" (Ford Foundation 1949, p. 92).

The conception was developed further in a staff paper, approved by the foundation's trustees in early 1952, that put forward the first plan for the foundation's program in this field. In that paper, hitherto unpublished, the notion of the behavioral sciences was characterized as follows:

1. It refers primarily to a program of *research*. A major part of Program Five is conceived as a program for research on human behavior, not as an "action program." Furthermore, it is not expected that the staff of Program Five will itself conduct behavioral research; rather, it will help to initiate and to support such activities.

2. It refers to the *scientific approach*. It encourages the acquisition of behavioral knowledge under conditions which, so far as possible, ensure objectivity, verifiability, and generality. It calls for conformity to high standards of scientific inquiry.

3. It refers to the acquisition of basic knowledge of human behavior and thus it is considered as a comparatively *long-range* venture. Basic study of the tremendously complicated problems of man cannot be expected to yield significant results in a short period of time.

4. It refers to the interest of the Foundation not in knowledge of human behavior as such but rather in knowledge which promises at some point to serve *human needs*. The program is thus oriented to social problems and needs.

5. It refers to an *interdisciplinary approach* and not to any single conventional field of knowledge or a single combination of them; traditional academic disciplines as such are not included or excluded. The program's goal is to acquire scientific knowledge of human behavior from whatever sources can make appropriate contributions. Social scientists, medical scientists,

and humanists, singly and in combination, can be engaged on the program. The intention is to use all relevant knowledge, skills, concepts and insights.

6. It refers to a broad and complex *subject matter*, since the program aims at a scientific understanding of why people behave as they do. "Behavior" includes not only overt acts but also such subjective behavior as attitudes, beliefs, expectations, motivations and aspirations. The program seeks knowledge which is useful in attacking problems of an economic, political, religious, educational or personal nature by studying the behavior of human beings as individuals or as members of primary groups, formal organizations, social strata, or social institutions. The program is vitally concerned with the cultural heritage by which men live, the social structures they have devised to organize their societies, the goals they pursue, and the means with which they pursue them.

7. Finally, it is definitely not considered as a cure-all for human problems but rather as a *contributor* to their solution, along with other sources of knowledge and judgment. The goal of the program is to provide scientific aids which can be used in the conduct of human affairs; it seeks only to increase useful knowledge and skills and to apply them wherever appropriate.

In short, then, Program Five is conceived as an effort to increase knowledge of human behavior through basic scientific research oriented to major problem areas covering a wide range of subjects, and to make such knowledge available for utilization in the conduct of human affairs (Ford Foundation 1953, pp. 3–5).

The report went on to identify the topics that constituted the subject matter of the behavioral sciences, at least insofar as the foundation's interests were then concerned: political behavior, domestic and international; communication; values and beliefs; individual growth development, and adjustment; behavior in primary groups and formal organizations; behavioral aspects of the economic system; social classes and minority groups; social restraints on behavior; and social and cultural change.

It was in this way that an administrative decision having to do with the programming and organization of a large foundation influenced at least the nomenclature, and probably even the conception, of an intellectual field of inquiry. The history of science contains several instances of intellectual concepts becoming administratively institutionalized, for example, psychoanalysis and gross national product (GNP). The concept "behavioral sciences" represents the reverse: an administrative arrangement that became intellectually institutionalized.

In the 1940s there were some similar stirrings within the universities themselves. In 1946 Harvard University organized a department of "social relations," which was, in fact, though not in name, a behavioral sciences department, even, to the exclusion of economics, political science, parts of anthropology and psychology, and, after a brief experimental period, history. And about 1950 a group of social and biological scientists at the University of Chicago began to seek a general theory of behavior under the term "behavioral sciences"—"first, because its neutral character made it acceptable to both social and biological scientists and, second, because we foresaw a possibility of someday seeking to obtain financial support from persons who might confound social science with socialism" (Miller 1955, p. 513). Earlier still, a somewhat similar effort was launched at the Institute of Human Relations at Yale University, although the line-up of specialties was different from what is now known as the behavioral sciences.

It is perhaps obvious that the Ford Foundation's commitment of several million dollars to this program had something to do with the term's acceptance and spread. In fact, one observer, upon learning that John Dewey and Arthur Bentley had in 1949 come close to using the term by distinguishing the *physical, physiological,* and *behavioral* regions of science (Dewey & Bentley 1949, p. 65), remarked that "the term may have been coined by John Dewey but it was minted by the Ford Foundation!" It would be a mistake, however, to conclude that the availability of funds was the only factor at work. Indeed, the term became so firmly established that it survived the termination of the foundation's program in the behavioral sciences in 1957. While money helped to establish it, the term did not die the day the money stopped; there seems to have been a genuine need for a collective term in addition to the traditional "social sciences."

CHAPTER IX:
Footnotes, Quotations, Name Lists, and Hypothetical Subjunctives, *or the Microrhetoric of History*

So far in this primer our attention has mainly fixed on large structures of historical discourse. Consequently, in the investigation of the forms taken by such discourses our concern has been with macrorhetoric, the principles, counsels, or maxims that govern the ordering of these structures. We have seen that the macrorhetoric of history is different from that of the natural sciences, not in a casual but in a systematic way, and that the differences are symptomatic of divergences in what scientists mean by knowing about nature and what historians mean by knowing about the past. Finally, it has appeared that efforts to reconcile or paper over these divergences in the interest of a uniformitarian dogma about knowledge and truth are a waste of time, since within their respective spheres neither scientists nor historians have serious difficulties with such problems in practice, and indeed the difficulties emerge only when an attempt is made to impose a uniformitarian dogma whether from the scientific or the historical side.

What happens if we transfer our inquiry from the macrorhetoric, the overall structure of historical discourse, to its microrhetoric, the small details of the language and syntax by means of which historians seek to communicate what they believe they know? If the situation is as described above, it is not unlikely that it will manifest itself in the microrhetoric as well as in the macrorhetoric of history. This chapter, then, will concern itself with a few items of that microrhetoric to see if the observable divergences between it and the microrhetoric of the natural sciences and (with less detail, because the problem is simpler) of the fictive arts are also systematic rather than casual.[1]

On the face of it, the outcome in detail of writing history, the microrhetoric of history, is unmistakably different from that of physics or poetry. Whatever a historian may profess that he is up to when he writes history, the result of his activity, an article, say, in the *American Historical Review*, sentence by sentence, does not look much like an article in the *Physical Review* or an epic poem or a sonnet. Indeed if it does look like either a physicist's paper or a poet's sonnet, its chance of publication in the *American Historical Review* is slim. And since—it is worth saying again—the serious commitment of craftsmen is better revealed by their common activity than by their often idiosyncratic individual professions of intent, by the look of what they write it appears that historians are committed to a different microrhetoric from that which science as exemplified by the physicists, or *belles lettres* as exemplified by the poets, or even the novelists, are committed to. By carefully examining and analyzing the differences, what can we discover about the infrastructure, the bone and gristle of the trade historians pursue? What do the manifest gross differences between the microrhetoric of history and that of the natural sciences on the one hand, of *belles lettres* on the other, tell us about the historians' often inarticulate conception of their vocation? Are the differences casual and trivial, or do the peculiarities of its microrhetoric mark history as a unique and separate domain of human knowing, in important respects incommensurate with the other two? One difference becomes manifest in the divergent attitude of historians on the one hand, of physicists and novelists on the other, to such lowly items as footnotes, quotations, name lists, and verbs in the hypothetical-subjunctive mood. These items are so lowly, indeed, that they may seem unworthy of notice. Yet the lowly and humble things of the earth are often more instructive than the high and mighty; after all, geneticists learned a good deal more

[1] The editors of the *International Encyclopedia of the Social Sciences* (New York, 1968) were generous enough to permit me to publish there under the title of "The Rhetoric of History" s.v. HISTORIOGRAPHY an exploratory essay on many of the matters that I have dealt with more fully and systematically in this primer. Neither the editors nor I were entirely happy with the way I divided the rhetoric of history in that article. I have adopted a different taxonomy here with no stronger sense of its merit. Refinement of categories which one dreams up ad hoc is generally desirable, but usually best done in the light of an adverse critical judgment for which there has not been time.

about genetics by considering the fruit fly than they could have learned in an equal span of time from a contemplation of the somewhat more impressive elephant.

First, footnotes. Fictive artists have used them on very rare occasions. When they look like footnotes in history books, they usually function as fictive devices, means by which those who employ them pretend to write history without intending to write it. If a fictive artist were consistently to employ footnotes as historians do and with the same intent, he would simply cease to be a fictive artist and become a historian. This is not at all to say that fictive writers never seek to grasp and communicate to their readers the truth about the past. Occasionally they seem to have both grasped and communicated it more successfully than historians have. I doubt if any historian with or without footnotes has ever conveyed to his readers what a shaky Latin American republic in the early twentieth century was like as effectively or economically as Joseph Conrad did in *Nostromo*. Yet to compare Conrad as a historian with other historians is absurd. Even when they share a common aim (to communicate in words what a Latin American republic was like), they play their game according to rules so different that it is unenlightening to think of it as "the same game." [2]

Suppose a critic had demanded that Conrad produce evidence that the outcome of the uprising in Costaguana was as he described it. Conrad would rightly have regarded the demand as absurd. Since Costaguana was a creation of Conrad's imagination, he was free to make the revolt come out as he chose. There is no record of the Costaguanan past against which to check Conrad's statements. He operates within a fictive framework. Given that his intent was to make it clear what a Latin American republic was like, there may be rules to judge his success in achieving his intent. Moreover, that judgment may be an ingredient in one's ultimate estimate of him as a fictive artist. The rules will not, however, include several that are binding on historians, so fully binding as to be an indispensable condition of their claim to be historians at all.[3] Thus the difference between the fictive arts and history in their use of that bit of microrhetoric, the footnote, are not casual and trivial; they are symptomatic and systematic—the consequence of fundamental divergences between two significant forms of human

[2] On this point see below, pp. 257–258, and note 7.
[3] Earlier from the historian's side we noted a grey area between history and the fictive arts exemplified by the imaginary westward journey described by Walter Webb in *The Great Frontier* (Cambridge, Mass., 1952). On the fictive artist's side a larger grey area is created by novels more strictly historical than *Nostromo*. These novels incorporate many details about specific events in the past in a more than casual way, as Tolstoy does in *War and Peace* and Stendhal in *La Chartreuse de Parme*. How far a fictive artist is bound to inform himself when his work actually includes specific *res gesta* and characterizes actual persons from the past is a difficult question.

activity. Both forms of activity are concerned with knowing, under-standing, and truth, but the rules under which they hunt for these, their Game Laws, so to speak, are incommensurate, so that the bags of knowing, understanding, and truth they can lawfully bring in are bound to differ in many respects.

Footnotes are part of the microrhetorical apparatus of physics as well as of history, and one of their uses is common to historians and physi-cists. Both use footnotes to cite to what is called "the literature." In an article in either *The Physical Review* or *The American Historical Review* "the literature" provides a relevant context of the subject under discussion. It consists of the work done by other experts who have previously dealt with the subject. Both historians and physicists cite the literature for several identical purposes—to support the assertions they are about to make, to provide a benchmark of the previous progress of inquiry, to specify the views they intend to challenge, refute, or con-firm.

Suppose both physicists and historians were prohibited from using footnotes for any purpose except citation to the literature of their sub-jects. The physicists, I suspect, would regard such a prohibition as a minor nuisance. But because it would bar them from citation to the records of the past, most historians would regard it as a major calamity. Those records are the data from which all history is generated. Citation to them makes an historian's professional commitment clear, just as the report of his experiment does for the physicist. In both instances it is a commitment to maximum verisimilitude (which does not mean exact replication of every detail). For the physicist it is a maximum verisimil-itude to the operations of nature as glimpsed through consideration of the experimental cluster; for the historian, verisimilitude to the happen-ings of the past and the relations among them as glimpsed through consideration of the surviving record. Experiment and citation to the record, then, are activities which more significantly than any theoretical pronouncements indicate the actual common commitment of physicists and historians to exploration, understanding, and rendering the best possible account of realities: for the physicist, the realities of the operations of nature; for the historian, the realities of what happened in the past.

As noted earlier, men's actual commitments are much more ac-curately revealed by what they do in the practice of their calling than by their quasiphilosophical excursions into methodology. The use of footnotes to the records by historians indicates that no matter what form of intricate epistemological fancy work they fiddle around with in their spare time, when they actually get down to writing history they all still commit themselves to trying to write about the past, as Ranke put it so very long ago, *"wie es eigentlich gewesen,"* as it really happened.

Today we might put that old and much derided aphorism in a somewhat more sophisticated language. We might say that historians are
committed to render the best and most likely account of the human
past that can be sustained by the relevant evidence. Still, we would
only be saying what Ranke intended. Let us call this statement about
the historians' commitment the "Reality" rule. And let us also add,
prescriptively for all historians, descriptively for the competent ones,
that this is their overarching commitment, their top priority. Insouciance in this makes vices of all virtues in a historian, as Lucifer's pride
did of his virtues. A historian may occasionally suggest a truth beyond
or above the record of the past. There can be no historical truth against
it.

Historians employ the footnote for a host of residual matters other
than citations to the record and to the literature—lists of names, minor
qualifications of assertions made in the text, polemical criticisms of
other historians, short statistical tables, suggestions for future historical
investigation. And these are but a beginning of the tasks to which historians have turned that versatile tool of their trade. If one allowed
them the footnote for citation to the records, they still would be loath to
forego its use for these many other jobs. And this confronts us with two
questions: (1) Amid the apparent chaos of "residual" footnotes can we
find any rule at all regulating their use? (2) What is the relation of any
rule we find to the first rule that emerged from our examination of the
peculiarities of the footnote as a device of historiographic rhetoric—the
"Reality" Rule?

As to the first question, the application of any rule about footnotes
requires an act of judgment in each case, and among historians
judgment about the uses of residual footnotes differs. It might seem
that in matters of judgment, as in those of taste, there is no disputing.
But is this so? Let us consider an example:

> At Shilbottle, in the case of three separate parcels of meadow, 31, 20 and
> 14 acres respectively, the first rendered 42s. in 1415–16 and 30s. in 1435–6,
> the second 28s. in 1420–1 and 23s. in 1435–6, and the third 24s. in 1422–3
> and 14s. in 1435–6. At Guyzance 6½ husbandlands each rendered 13s.
> 4d. in 1406–7, but 10s. in 1435–6. At Chatton and Rennington, on the
> other hand, the situation was more stable. At Rennington the clear reve-
> nues were £17.8s.3d. in 1435–6 and £17 in 1471–2 and at Chatton
> £40.18s.7d. in 1434–5 and £36.18s.7d. in 1472–3. At Chatton the de-
> cline was due to a fall in the value of the farm of the park, from £6.13s.4d.
> to £2.13s.4d . . .

This dashing passage is imbedded in the text of a study of the wealth
of a magnate family in the fifteenth and early sixteenth centuries and of
the effect on it of concurrent changes in the economy, the military

apparatus, and the political situation in England. Can it be suggested that the young man who inserted it in the text instead of quarantining it in a footnote did *not* commit an error of judgment? But to say he did commit one is to imply a *rule* from which his erroneous judgment made him deviate. Can such a rule—a "law" of historical rhetoric, of historiography, if you will—to cover this case be stated? I think so. As a rough approximation, the rule might go: "Place in footnotes evidence and information which, if inserted in the text, diminishes the impact on the reader of what you, as an historian, aim to convey to him."

So although in the matter of the use of residual footnotes judgment is inescapable, we are not at all confronted with chaos or anarchy or mere arbitrariness, but with a reasonably precise rule or law. We may name it the Maximum Impact Rule. Inevitably, there are marginal situations where there will be divergent views among competent historians as to how to achieve maximum impact or whether a particular rhetorical presentation has in fact achieved it. The existence of such marginal situations, however, does not mean that all situations are marginal, and that therefore there is no rule, or that any rule is as good as any other. Lawyers have a saying that hard cases make bad law, but they do not feel impelled thereupon to take a deep dive into a non sequitur and argue that there are no easy cases and no good law. Because there are some matters both substantive and procedural concerning which they are very uncertain, historians somehow have permitted themselves to be nudged into accepting the notion that everything about the past, including writing about it, is infected with a total uncertainty. This is not so. Specifically, as we have just seen, it is not so in the case of the residual footnote. Without difficulty we found a rule controlling its use not heavily infected with uncertainty.

But this turns our attention to the second question we foresaw earlier, that of the relation of the two rules—the Reality Rule and the Maximum Impact Rule—to each other. Note, first, that in our example the data that ought to be withdrawn from the text and consigned to a residual footnote, are informative and relevant with respect to the substantive historical argument the historian in the case is presenting, and that they are as complete, as accurate, and as exact as possible. Note, second, that what the historian, applying the second rule, is committed to seek to convey to the reader with maximum impact is his conception and understanding of the past as it actually happened, the "Reality" of the first rule. The clear implication of the two points we have just made is that *in the interest of conveying historical reality to the reader with maximum impact, the rules of historiography may sometimes require an historian to subordinate completeness and exactness to other considerations.* A look at our next rhetorical device of historiography may help us understand this peculiarity of history. The device is the quotation in the text. Let us again note a difference between the historians and the physicists. Suppose the editor were to issue an edict that in the text of the *Physical Review* neither quotation marks nor their equivalents would henceforth be permitted. Contributors would probably be annoyed, but with respect to the advancement of knowledge of the natural world they would not feel that much was at stake. Suppose the editor of the *American Historical Review* were to issue such an edict. At the very least he would promptly be fired. A convenience for physicists, quotation is a necessity for historians, indispensable to writing history well.

The kind of quotation that historians deem indispensable is quotation from the record. And again we may ask two questions: (1) Is there any rule governing quotation from the record? (2) How does the rule relate to the Reality Rule?

Let us start with a purely imaginary case of inept quotation. Suppose in writing the history of the Civil Rights Act of 1964, a historian were to quote verbatim from the *Congressional Record* the entire debate on the act in both the House and the Senate. The result would be undeniably relevant, accurate, and exact—and not only the judgment of the historian who perpetrated it but his very sanity would fall under grave suspicion. Again maximum completeness and exactness are not always essential, and they are not even always desirable in the historian's work of trying to tell the reader what really happened. In history what functions do quotation from the record of the past perform? An adept quotation from the record may help answer this question. It comes from the late Professor Harbison's *The Christian Scholar in the Age of the Reformation.* He says:

> Erasmus had absorbed Lorenzo Valla's historical perspective, his sense of the historical discontinuity between pagan antiquity and the Christian era . . . a sensitivity to anachronism. On one occasion he ridiculed the absurdity of the practice . . . of using Ciceronian words to describe an utterly different, modern world: "Wherever I turn my eyes I see all things changed, I stand before another stage and I behold a different play, nay, even a different world." The world of Cicero (or of Paul) can be understood and even in a sense relived—but only if we recognize that it has its unique existence, once, in a past now dead.[4]

What is the function in the text above of Harbison's brief quotation from Erasmus? Not mere validation or proof of his assertion that Erasmus was sensitive to anachronism; he could as well have proved that by putting a citation or a quotation in a footnote. By using Erasmus' own words in the text itself, he seeks a response not merely

[4] E. H. Harbison, *The Christian Scholar in the Age of the Reformation* (New York, 1956), p. 93.

of assent but of *conviction,* not just a "yes," but "yes, indeed!" Nothing
Harbison could have said about Erasmus' sense of history could produce
the conviction about it that the quotation in the text of Erasmus' own
assertion about his intense feeling of distance from antiquity produces.

The quotation aims at something in addition to conviction, however.
The quotation communicates the historian's own view of what happened in the past by the particular means of confrontation. It says in
effect, "In my judgment the most economical way at this point to tell
you what I believe Erasmus meant and to convince you that he meant
it is to confront you directly with what Erasmus said. Thus you will
learn from his words, not mine, what it was like to be Erasmus." This
provides us with a third general rule of historiography—an Economy-
of-Quotation Rule: "Quote from the record of the past only when and to
the extent that confrontation with that record is the best way to help
the reader to an understanding of the past *wie es eigentlich gewesen.*"

We saw, however, in the instance of our hypothetical case of the
Congressional Record that mere confrontation with the record of the
past is not necessarily the best way to achieve this understanding or
even to achieve confrontation. Indeed, far from being a clear glass
window through which the reader may capture an image of the past,
quotations from the record injudiciously used can be a thick, opaque
wall that cuts him off from it. Let us examine a converse instance, a
rejection of quotation from the record in the interest of confrontation.
In *Domesday Book and Beyond,* F. W. Maitland deals with the law of
status in Anglo-Saxon England in conjunction with *wer,* the legal
system of graded payments due a man's heirs if he is killed by another.
He consigns the relevant part of the record of the past to footnotes.
Here are a few bits of detail of two long notes:

> Leg (es) Henr (ici Primi) 70.1: In Wessex which is head of the realm and
> the law the villein's *wer* is £4 . . .
> (Law of) Aethelstan VI: a horse 120 pence, an ox 30 pence, a cow 20
> pence, a sheep 1 shilling (=5 pence).

Along with other supporting data this is tucked into the footnotes. In
the text Maitland remarks:

> Each *ceorl* or *villanus* has a *wer* of two hundred shillings . . . no trifling
> sum. At this rate the *ceorl's* death must be paid for by the price of some
> twenty four or thirty oxen. The sons of *villanus* who had but two oxen must
> have been under some temptation to wish that their father would get
> himself killed by a solvent *thegn.*[5]

[5] F. W. Maitland, *Domesday Book and Beyond* (Cambridge, Eng., 1897), p. 44.

Thus a great historian confronts his reader with a sense of what it was like to be a poor peasant in a somewhat primitive society which lumped crime and tort into a scaled table of damage payments. He does it not by quoting the record in the text but by construing it there in an act of historical imagination. Or as we prefer to say, by quick resort to one of the most richly stocked second records that any historian ever possessed. To insert into the text the flat dull fragments of the record of the past that Maitland relied on would not have increased but diminished the reader's sense of confrontation with the reality of the past. It would have been a witless violation of the Maximum Impact Rule.

Here perhaps we have escaped the perplexity occasioned by what may have seemed like a conflict between the Reality Rule with its roots in the record of the past and Maximum Impact Rule with its root in the second record. For what our examples suggest is that the microrhetorical means of historiography have to be adapted to its macrorhetorical ends, and that it is part of the task of the writer of history to mediate understanding and confrontation by devices of the rhetoric of history less direct but more subtle, more compelling, and more to the purpose than simple maximizing of completeness and exactness.

Awareness of this relation of the microrhetoric of history to its macrorhetoric enables us to cope with a problem that we have previously brushed past.[6] Consider the following statement. (1) "On January 19, 1943 (old style, January 29, 1644, new style) a body of arms-bearing men from Scotland, about 21,500 in number, moving south, crossed a body of running water named the Tweed River at north latitude 55° 47′, west longitude 2° 0′ approximately, and entered England." S. R. Gardiner describes this event in the italicized words of the following passage.

(2) All the current of events was setting against peace. *On January 19 the first regiments of the Scottish army crossed the Tweed,* and the Royalists of Northumberland after a short hesitation withdrew to Newcastle, where the Marquis of Newcastle soon arrived to put himself at their head. In Cheshire, in the last weeks of 1643, Byron had made considerable progress against Brereton with the help of the English soldiers newly landed from Ireland. One act of his indeed had roused that exasperation which is usually so dangerous to the offender. On December 26 he butchered to a man a detachment of Brereton's men who had taken refuge in the steeple of Barthomley Church, and who refused to surrender at the first summons.[7]

[6] See Chapter 6, p. 172.
[7] S. R. Gardiner, *History of the Great Civil War, 1642–1649,* 4 vols. (London, 1901), I: 294. (My italics).

To the foregoing sentences, one mine, one Gardiner's, we may add a couple more. (3) "Far to the north across the Tweed and toward the Tyne the Army of the Covenant of the Scots with their God and their English brethren were marching to the support and succor of the latter." (4) "In January the rebel Scots had marched to aid the rebel English against their lawful King and Lord." The four statements all refer to an identical event sequence in the past, E. In the mathematical rhetoric of the hard sciences, if A = B and B = C and C = D, then D = A. This transitive property of number permits free substitution of one form of mathematical statement for another if their referents are identical. Since $x = \sqrt{x^2} = \dfrac{x^2}{x} = \dfrac{2x}{2}$, in any mathematical statement any form of the number x can replace any of the alternative forms without affecting the other values in the whole mathematical expression in which x appears. By contrast consider the substitution of statements 1, 3, and 4 for Gardiner's statement 2, the referent of which is the identical event-sequence in the past. Clearly *none* of them will do; somehow they do not fit. The rhetoric of history, therefore, is not amenable to one of the most elementary rules of the language of science, mathematics. The transitive property of number does not apply to the language of history. Why does it not? Is it that it would allow substitutions of a less precise for a more precise reference? This may be true of statement 3 and 4 perhaps, but surely not of statement 1, the most precise and detailed of all. Actually, of course, there is no mystery about the matter. The first sentence in the quotation from Gardiner makes the rhetorical requirement clear.

"All the current of events was setting against peace." What the sentence requires is that the statement on the entry of the Scots into England appear as merely one element in the "current of events" setting against peace. But the statement in Case 1 slows the current into a mass of side eddies and irrelevancies; in Cases 3 and 4 it distracts attention from the current by an inappropriate display of verbal fireworks. In all three cases it impedes a processive historical discourse from getting on with what it has committed itself to getting on with. So while all four statements are true referents to the identical event-sequence, in the given context of Case 2 only Gardiner's statement is adequate, satisfactory and correct; the other three are inappropriate, unsatisfactory, and incorrect. It is easy enough to provide settings in which sentences 3 and 4 would be appropriate and satisfactory. Thus for sentence 4: "Whatever his subjects in London and Edinburgh might allege they were up to, Charles I had his own unclouded perception of what was going on. In January the rebel Scots . . . " And for sentence 3: "The despair of the partisans of Parliament who thought of themselves as the godly party was alleviated. Far to the north . . ."

To find an appropriate and satisfactory context for sentence 1, however, exceeds the capacity of my historical imagination. It is therefore a statement about the past, true in every respect, which I cannot conceive a competent historian making, because I cannot conceive any structure of processive historical discourse into which it could be satisfactorily integrated. And obviously the interchange of sentences 3 and 4 would be a historiographic catastrophe. It appears then that our four statements, all referring to the identical set of events in the past, are not interchangeable, equal or synonymous, that their full truth does not depend merely and wholly on the "facts" they put in order or on their right causal relations to antecedents and succeedants. As microrhetorical fragments their full truth value can only be assessed on the basis of the macrorhetorical pattern into which the historian fits them.

Or to repeat for emphasis the point with which we began: "the microrhetorical means of historiography have to be adapted to its macrorhetorical ends, and it is part of the task of the writer of history to mediate understanding and confrontation by devices of the rhetoric of history less direct but more subtle, more compelling, and more to the purpose than simple maximizing of completeness and exactness."

The point can be further pressed home by taking a look at another microrhetorical device of history, but not of history alone—the name list.

An inert element will not react or enter into chemical combination with any other element. In order of increasing atomic weight the inert elements are helium (4), neon (20), argon (39), krypton (84), xenon (131), and radon (222).

The average incomes of only three of the learned professions fell into the first quartile of all average incomes. In descending order of quartile and rank, the average incomes of members of the learned professions were as follows: surgeons (1,2), physicians (1,4), dentists (1,7), college professors (2,23), high school teachers (3,41), clergymen (3,47), grade school teachers (3,52).

The first list is scientific, it refers to nature; the second historiographic, it refers to the past. The lists are in many respects similar. In intent the words composing them are wholly denotative. They are not supposed to cast any shadow, to connote or evoke anything. Their arrangement (ascending order, descending order) is dictated entirely by considerations of rational utility. They both implicitly relate to an informational framework equally denotative in intention—the periodic table of all chemical elements, the table of average incomes of the total population classified by profession and trade. Both listings aim to achieve a purpose universal in the rhetoric of the sciences, common but not universal in the rhetoric of history. The scientist always wants the state, process, and set of entities he is dealing with so labeled that the labels unambiguously and unequivocally point to that state, process, and set only. For the scientist's purpose when he is formally communicating what he knows, words need to be free of contamination, of connotation, evocation, and emotive force, as sterile as the apparatus in an operating room. Otherwise he may find the means of communication fouled and, as a consequence, have to clean up an avoidable mess. In this matter the historian's purpose often coincides exactly with that of the scientist. It is only under the conditions and with a vocabulary of the kind above specified that he can to his own satisfaction transmit some of the kinds of information and understanding that he intends to communicate. Yet even the very close approximation to scientific rhetoric exemplified by the foregoing historiographic word list deviates from the scientific standard in ways that help to differentiate both the problems and the purposes of history from those of the sciences. Consider the question "Is not zinc (65) also an inert element?" To answer this question one can pour hydrochloric acid over zinc. Since one of the yields of this operation is zinc chloride ($ZnCl$), a chemical combination or compound, zinc is not an inert element.

The taxonomic system of chemical elements—the periodic table—is thus free of ambiguity. Suppose, on the other hand, the question were raised whether clergymen and elementary and high school teachers should be included as members of the learned professions when the executives of large corporations are excluded. The question points to doubts about a system of classification that might include store-front preachers and graduates of retrograde teacher-training colleges among members of the learned professions while excluding the products of the better graduate schools of business administration. These doubts thus revolve about the identifying traits of the learned professions and the expediencies involved in the selection of any one set as against alternative sets of traits for classificatory purposes. And the identification of a profession as "learned" itself still carries an honorific aura, derived from the past, which is difficult, perhaps impossible, to suppress.

In any developed natural science, traits are chosen as the basis of a taxonomic system because of their "importance" within the bounds of that science—e.g., in chemistry, valence and atomic weight as against color and taste. And importance is graded by applicability within the framework of generalizations or "scientific laws" that articulate the structure of the science in question and form the basis of its dominant mode of explanation. The dominant mode of historical explanation, narrative, emits no such clear, uniform signal for determining importance, and therefore in historiography the expediencies of alternative taxonomic systems often remain debatable. It is this situation which generates the interminable discussions among historians about whether sixteenth-century monarchies were *really* absolute, whether the Indians in the *encomiendas* in the Spanish colonies were *really* in servitude, whether the owner-operator of a small newsstand is *really* a capitalist. Such discussions seem futile because they purport to deal directly with the actual character of the past, a historical problem, when in fact they are concerned with the relative expediencies of alternative taxonomic devices for communicating knowledge of the past, a historiographic problem. The problem of taxonomy so considered, however, is anything but trivial, (1) because classification systems both condition effectiveness of communication and channel the course of historical thinking, and (2) because in the very nature of the rhetoric of history, terms like "capitalist," "absolute," and "learned profession" cannot be rendered wholly denotative to the consumer of history writing. Given the nonscientific values pursued in the writing of history, a historian using such terms will have to decide, for the purposes of the story or narrative explanation engaging him at the moment, how much time and effort he should expend in separating the connotative values from those terms and how important those connotative values are for advancing the historical understanding of the matter at hand. It is evident, in any case, that the microanalysis of historical rhetoric involves a study of problems of taxonomy in history closer than any undertaken up to now.[8]

One further trait of the above historiographic word list needs to be noted: it is either elliptical or meaningless. It acquires meaning only if time and place are specified, whereas no such specification is necessary in the above scientific list. A statement whose formal structure and manifest purpose seem very close to those that characterize the natural sciences illustrates the time-place specificity of the rhetoric of history as against the dominant time-space generality of the rhetoric of the hard sciences. Thus the analysis of a historical word list reinforces the conclusion that has emerged time and again in the course of this primer: despite occasional likenesses, history is not assimilable to the rhetoric of the natural sciences.

Here are two more historiographic lists; this time, however, they are rhetorically structured on principles quite different from that of the preceding scientific list of inert gases. I have imbedded both in contexts which, I hope, will be adequate to indicate their microrhetorical function.

---

[8] This is not to suggest that in the sciences taxonomic problems are all easily solved. Such problems seem to be acute today in the classification of mental illness. For decades a taxonomic failure prevented the consistent effective treatment of malaria with quinine. (Philip D. Curtin, *The Image of Africa, British Ideas and Action, 1780–1850*. (Madison, 1964), pp. 355–359.) In both these instances, however, the difficulty is a consequence of a defect of information, not a dilemma of rhetoric.

Trevor-Roper's protagonists and antagonists do not seem quite of a stature to bear the historical burden he imposes upon them. Perhaps that is why he pares down the burden, reducing that fairly magnificent upheaval, the Puritan Revolution, to the dimensions of a foolish farce that could conceivably have been brought off by the lowgrade louts and sharpers who people his stage. In the squalid setting of this farce there is not enough room for *William Chillingworth or Richard Baxter, for Edward Coke or Francis Bacon, for Thomas Wentworth or Oliver Cromwell, for John Selden, or John Lilburne, or John Hampden, or John Pym, or John Milton.* In such a setting men of such stature and others like them would poke their heads right up through the ceiling; for with all their limitations they stood high enough to see a little beyond the deedbox and the dinner table.[9]

The term Christian Revival describes a particular constellation of religious happenings to parts of which historians have given several names. The part which preceded 1517 has been called the Prereformation and the Religious Revival. Part of what followed 1517 has been called the Protestant Reformation or simply the Reformation, the Protestant Revolt, and the Protestant Revolution; the other part the Catholic Reformation, the Catholic Counter-Reformation or the Catholic Counter-Revolution. . . . Historians, however, have no covering phrase to describe the intensification of religious sentiment and concern that began long before 1517 and extended long beyond, that in its full span had room for *Cardinal Ximenes and Girolamo Savonarola, Martin Luther and Ignatius Loyola, the Reformed Churches and the Jesuits, John of Leiden and Paul IV, Thomas Cranmer and Edmund Campion and Michael Servetus.*[10]

The names in the passages above constitute historiographic lists, intended to serve the particular purposes of the rhetoric of history. Each emits a signal, and what the signal says to all who hear it is: "Draw on the reservoir of your knowledge of the times in which the men named lived to give meaning to this list." If that reservoir is altogether empty, then inevitably the list will itself be historiographically empty, meaningless, a mere collection of sounds, just as the sentences about the inert gases must have been empty of meaning to anyone who had no notion of what a chemical element, a chemical reaction, and atomic weight were. The reason for this similarity is that in the present case both the historiographic rhetoric and the scientific rhetoric presuppose that the reader already possesses a body of precise and exact knowledge of the particular universes to which they refer. The scientific and the historiographical statements conform to the Reality Rule; they are meaningless unless there are such elements as helium and neon, and unless there

[9] Hexter, *Reappraisals in History* (London, 1961), p. 142. (italics added).
[10] Thomas More, "Utopia," *The complete works of Thomas More*, ed. Edward Surtz and J. H. Hexter, (New Haven, 1965), 4: xcii–xciii (slightly emended and italics added.)

were such men as Chillingworth, Wentworth and Selden, as Loyola, Cranmer, and Paul IV.

The first of these two lists assists us to differentiate historiographic rhetoric from literary rhetoric with which it is sometimes confused, or of which genus it is sometimes deemed a species. We have just seen that although *sui generis,* historiographic rhetoric shares a common trait with scientific rhetoric: their overarching law, their Great Commandment, is the Reality Rule. The list of eminent participants in the conflicts of early Stuart England is good enough literary rhetoric; because of the demands of the Reality Rule, however, it is bad historical rhetoric. Moreover, it is improved as literary rhetoric by the very device that renders it bad historical rhetoric.[11] From a literary point of view the sentence has a certain rhythmic lilt that commands the reader's attention. It does so (1) by the three pairings "William Chillingworth or Richard Baxter, Francis Bacon or Edward Coke, Thomas Wentworth or Oliver Cromwell," (2) by the "or"-linked sublist of five names, none more than bisyllabic, (3) by the fact that all five surnames in the sublist are preceded by the same given name, John. Note that all the rhetorical devices that give the name-list literary force are relevant historiographically because they help maximize its impact. Note also that from the literary point of view "Edward Dering or Edward Coke" might be a rhetorically more effective pairing than "Francis Bacon or Edward Coke," and conversely that from a strictly literary point of view, if the names achieve impact through euphony and contrast, it does not matter particularly to whom they once belonged. Or to put it another way, from that point of view, the Reality Rule is irrelevant. But it remains the Great Commandment of the rhetoric of history. Therefore historiographically to substitute Edward Dering for Francis Bacon would be a serious error. Francis Bacon and Edward Coke balance off, not euphonically but historically. Both start under Elizabeth as champions of the queen *and* the law, but after her death Bacon and Coke are pulled in opposite directions, the former toward championship of the king beyond the law, the latter toward championship of the law above the king. Eventually they become the most effective and articulate exponents of their divergent views. Historiographically, they are good company. But in the rhetoric of history what would that third-level figure, Sir Edward Dering, M. P., moderate Royalist, moderate supporter of Episcopacy, a local and private man, not a central and public one, be doing in the company of a giant like Edward Coke?

The other pairings also have their rationale not in literary euphony but in the record of the past. But what of the five-name sublist? The very

[11] On the matter of literary rhetoric I accept the judgment of an expert, my neighbor at Trumbull College, Yale University, Michael O'Loughlin.

trait that makes it right as literary rhetoric makes it wrong as historical rhetoric. Historically they are five men, eminent on the Parliamentary side in the Great Rebellion, who—who what? Who happened to have the same Christian name, John. So what of it? Historically, nothing of it. Historically, the coincidence is at once a dead end and a distraction, what in baseball would correctly be described as a grandstand play by a "cute" player. Whatever additional literary impact the roll call of Johns may achieve is negated in the rhetoric of history by the fact that it leads the reader into an empty bag. It jumps the Reality Rule. That rule requires that the rhetoric of history always aim at enhancing understanding of the past as it really was. But the series of five Johns does not do this. It rather distracts the reader with a tricky but historically meaningless bit of word-music. It thus enables us to see very precisely the distinction between literary rhetoric and the rhetoric of history. It also enables us to understand a puzzling phenomenon. Nonhistorians will sometimes speak admiringly of the style of historians who are regarded by their peers as bad history writers. The divergence results from the historians' overriding commitment to the Reality Rule. A historian who seeks literary gains at the cost of diminishing his reader's understanding of the past is writing rhetorically inferior history. He is like the pacer who breaks stride in a race. An ill-informed crowd may think he has won because he crossed the finish line first. The judges, who know he has done so by breaking the overriding rule that makes a pacing race a pacing race, simply disqualify him. The restrictions the historians lay on their rhetoric, which render it subdued compared to the brighter palette and broader spectrum of the fictive arts, derive from their primary commitment to the Reality Rule.

Now let us compare the scientific name list with the second historiographic name-list. First consider the ordering of names on that second list compared with the list of inert gases. Given their common trait of inertness, the gases on the scientific list are arrayed in a way that indicates the scientists' normal preoccupation with establishing measurable differences of homogeneous traits—in this case, weight. In the historiographical list, on the other hand, no such preoccupation is discernible, yet the arrangement of the names lies at the very heart of the matter.

Note that there are three alternative ways of writing the second historiographical list, all of which maintain the structural elements of the arrangement.

1. Cardinal Ximenes and Girolamo Savonarola, Martin Luther and Ignatius Loyola, the Reformed churches and the Jesuits, John of Leiden and Paul IV, Thomas Cranmer and Edmund Campion and Michael Servetus.

2. The pre-Reformation cardinal who reformed the church in Spain,

and the pre-Reformation monk who was burned at the stake for his re-forming efforts in Florence; the first great figure of the Reformation and the first great figure of the Counter Reformation; the cutting edge of the Protestant attack and the cutting edge of the Catholic counterattack; the most fanatical prophet of the radical Reformation and the most fanatical pope of the era of religious strife; the Protestant martyred by the Catholics, the Catholic martyred by the Protestants, and the martyr who escaped death at the hands of the Catholics only to receive it at the hands of the Protestants.

3. Cardinal Ximenes, the pre-Reformation cardinal who reformed the church in Spain, and Girolamo Savonarola, the pre-Reformation monk who was burned at the stake for his reforming efforts in Florence; Luther, the first great figure of the Reformation, and Loyola, the first great figure of the Counter Reformation; the Reformed churches, the cutting edge of the Protestant attack, and the Jesuits, the cutting edge of the Catholic counterattack. . . .

The persons balanced in tension with one another are the same for each version, and the arrayal is identical in all three. On mathematical principles a member of any of the lists should be freely substitutable for the corresponding member of either of the other two, but in writing history *this is not so*. Each list must retain its integrity. On what grounds can an historian choose among the three? One might argue that the second list is preferable to the first since it explicates the rationale upon which the persons in the first list were arrayed; and that, in point of information about the past, the third is best of all, since it both names the persons and explicates the rationale of their array. Then why in the world would a historian committed to communicate what he understands about the past choose the *first* option—the bare list of names with no indication as to his grounds for choosing them, or for ordering them as he did? Remember what we said earlier about the signal emitted by the list: "Draw on the reservoir of your knowledge of the times in which these men lived to give meaning to the list." The writer assumed that most of his readers could and would in fact draw from their particular reservoirs the items of general information in the second and the third list. The effect of giving that information in greater detail, however, is to send another kind of rhetorical signal, a stop signal: "Stop drawing on the reservoir of your knowledge. I have already told you how I want you to think about these men." And this stop signal is just what the writer did *not* want the list to emit. The third version of the list is more exact, more overtly informative, than the bare names in the first list and just for that reason it is more empty, less ample. It dams up the informed reader's imagination instead of letting it flow freely, bringing with it the mass of connotation and association that those names have for him. Therefore to prevent such a blockage the writer chose the first list. In doing so, he made a judgment. He judged—or gambled—that the connotative evocative list would communicate a fuller meaning than the exact one, that it would more effectively confront the reader with the reality of the Christian Revival, and that therefore it was the more appropriate device for advancing the reader's understanding of it. Whether he was correct in his judgment is immaterial. In setting forth his findings, a scientist never needs to make such a judgment at all. Scientific rhetoric is purposefully constructed to free him of that need by barring connotative terms and evocative devices. To a scientist the idea that he had to choose between a rhetoric of clarity and precision on the one hand and one of evocative force on the other would be shocking. The idea that the writer of history has to select between *mutually exclusive ways of setting forth the same data* and that the knowledge of history which he conveys in some measure depends on his judgment in selecting among them is perhaps as disturbing and perplexing. But to the latter conclusion our investigation of footnotes, quotations, and word lists has driven us.

Further close scrutiny of competent historical discourse would bring to light other microrhetorical structures unique to it. The purpose served by this sort of scrutiny is not simply to provide a catalogue of the historiographic uses of particular rhetorical structures or to gauge their intrinsic importance. It is to discern through the functioning of those structures—perhaps themselves trivial, as is the name-list—in historical writing, the similarities of history to other forms of discourse, and its differences from them as instruments for the advancement of knowledge, the improvement of the understanding, and the perception of truth. It is not my purpose here to produce a compendious list of microrhetorical structures, but I would like to take a hard look at just one more of them—the hypothetical subjunctives "must" and "may." [12]

As near as I can make out, neither of these hypothetical subjunctives are part of the rhetoric of the natural sciences. This does not imply that they are no part of the psychology of natural scientists in pursuit of scientific discovery. Indeed I rather suspect that they are. In the present context, however, it may prevent confusion to draw a rather sharp line, as we have done earlier, between the psychology of discovery and the structure of discourse. If we draw such a line, we will observe that for communicating the results of inquiry in the natural sciences the appropriate verb forms are present indicative for the statement of the laws of a science and past indicative for the recording of experimental results or "boundary conditions." Although a covering law is a statement of maximum strength while hypothesis and statistical law are in different ways weaker, the rhetoric of natural science does not take

---

[12] I owe the grammatical labels to Professor Alice Miskimin of the Yale University English Department.

account of this difference by resorting to the strong hypothetical "must" for covering laws and the weaker "may" for hypotheses and statistical laws. Instead it states laws and hypotheses in unqualified present indicatives and finds mathematical means for incorporating qualification into a statistical law in a way that permits the law itself to be stated indicatively. And as for boundary conditions, to state them in any form less assertive than the past indicative is to deny them the replicability which alone renders them available for purposes of testing. If the account by philosophers of science of the ends of scientific discourse are correct, then there is no place at all for hypothetical subjunctives in its rhetoric.

In their discourse historians occasionally employ "must" and "may," the hypothetical subjunctive in both strong and weak form. What do they use them for? What are their functions in the rhetoric of history? We have already seen a use of the strong form by a master historian, F. W. Maitland, in his remarks on the Anglo-Saxon system of blood payments.

> The sons of a *villanus* who had but two oxen must have been under some temptation to wish that their father would get himself killed by a solvent thegn.

Granted that few historians, if any, have been Maitland's peer at bending the rhetoric of history to his ends, and that his ultimate end was always the illumination of the past as it actually was, why did he throw this sentence into the strong form of the hypothetical subjunctive?

The answer is necessarily conjectural since Maitland does not give a reason. I would guess that he avoided the past indicative "were" because it was much too strong for his purposes. It would imply the existence of evidence in the record of the past that sons of Anglo-Saxon *villani* entertained those thoughts. Maitland well knew that the records of Anglo-Saxon England would not yield such evidence. In any case it was not Maitland's purpose here to make a "factual" statement about the psychology of a particular social group. His is a general point which in fact cannot be driven home by reference to any small cluster of items from the record of the past. The "must" is not aimed at that record at all; it is aimed at the second records of the readers of Maitland's book, and at the "waste" of those records where the reader's unkempt life experiences lie. It serves as a reminder that although the book is taking its readers to the strange and dimly lit world of a thousand years ago, still even in those days long gone poor men might contemplate with a measure of equanimity the demise of their papa under circumstances that would bring them unimaginable riches—*and you had better believe it*. That is what the "must" is about. It emphasizes the credibility of some very general notions about men and human conduct which as a result of common experience flourish in our second records. That other things being equal or even a little unequal, men in general prefer moderate wealth to grinding poverty is one of these notions. Such notions, not universal, but very widespread, are links that bind us to men of different times and places, different nurture and status. Maitland keeps the human lines open between the sort of intellectual of recent times who might be a reader of *Domesday Book and Beyond* and the illiterate peasants who tilled the soil in England over a millennium ago. He does so by properly using "must" to imply that the burden of proving a fundamental difference among men in this particular matter lies on those who would allege that it exists.

Coincidentally, Maitland uses "must" for quite the opposite purpose when he discusses the burden of proof in early English law—proof by ordeal, by battle, and by oath and oath-helpers. In this matter Maitland himself alleges a decisive difference between our vision of life and that of the Anglo-Saxons. To understand the Anglo-Saxon notion of the way to arrive at a lawful and right judgment, he says:

> . . . we *must* transfer ourselves into a wholly different intellectual atmosphere from that in which we live. We *must* once and for all discard from our thoughts that familiar picture of a trial in which judge and jurymen listen to the evidence that is produced on both sides, weigh testimony against testimony, and by degrees make up their minds about the truth (my italics).[13]

In the Anglo-Saxon view the determination of truth could not safely be left to man's weak reason; it had to be referred to God's judgment. As Maitland proceeds to show, the ordeal, battle, and proof by oath were the means of effecting such a referral. If he is to understand what the "intellectual atmosphere," the vision of life, in Anglo-Saxon England was like, the reader needs to do the opposite of what he did in the matter of the sons of the *villanus*; in respect to early English ways of ascertaining innocence and guilt he had better extend his consciousness beyond its accustomed venue—*and this is an order*. The "musts" of the second quotation are not hypothetical subjunctives at all; they are imperatives.

The illustration of the second weak form of the hypothetical subjunctive, "may," comes from a little book of mine that I drew on earlier, *More's Utopia: The Biography of an Idea*. The third part of the book examines More's views as expressed in *Utopia* on the obligation of an intellectual with serious moral concerns, such as More himself was, to

[13] F. Pollock and F. W. Maitland, *The History of English Law* (Cambridge, Eng., 1895), 2: 596.

serve as an adviser to a ruler. At the very time he was writing about it, the problem had special poignancy for him, since he was under pressure from Henry VIII to become a royal councilor. Although More was ambivalent on the issues, after canvassing them carefully in *Utopia* he appeared to judge that in the long run such service would do no good, since it would implicate the intellectual in supporting or silently condoning policies that were wicked and merely self-aggrandizing for the ruler—especially policies of useless war. Yet a little while after he had had *Utopia* published, More himself became a royal councilor.

The brief epilogue of my book, called "The Bitter Fruit," dealt with the sequel to More's decision. Some years later, More found himself in the dilemma that he had grasped imaginatively in *Utopia*. Henry VIII got involved in a costly war. He needed money, and so he summoned Parliament. He required his councilor Thomas More to serve as speaker of the House of Commons and to encourage the members to lay a heavy tax on his subjects to meet the costs of his senseless military venture. More complied. As a reward he received £200, a very considerable sum in those days. In his letter to the king, recommending the grant of the gift to More, Cardinal Wolsey, Henry VIII's chief adviser and alter ego, remarked:

> I am rather moved to put your Highness in remembrance thereof, because he is not the most ready to speak and solicit in his own cause.[14]

My comment on Wolsey's letter was:

> More was never a ready solicitor in his own cause, but in this particular instance his tongue may have been especially tardy. The future martyr, the saint to be, the author of *Utopia*, the Christian humanist inextricably, wretchedly, unhappily involved in the betrayal and crucifixion of his own most cherished ideals may well have been diffident about asking for those two hundred pounds. *To him they may have seemed rather like thirty pieces of silver.*[15] [Italics added]

With that sentence my book ended.

What was the function of such a last sentence with its weak hypothetical subjunctive "may"? Supposing that I am not much less committed to advancing knowledge and improving understanding of the human past than other historians are, supposing therefore that every sentence that I write as a historian is immediately or proximately directed toward that end, just how does such a last sentence serve my purpose? Of course, it is possible that to Thomas More those £200 did

[14] Hexter, *More's Utopia*, p. 157.
[15] *Ibid.*

seem like the payment Judas received for betraying Jesus. But is there any evidence in the record of the past that they did so? Not a scintilla. Is there even, as in the case of Maitland's *villani*, a cumulation of experience in every man's second record to suggest that it is highly credible that they did so? There is not. Were there such a cumulation, I would have used—and have been right to use—the strong hypothetical subjunctive "must." What then does that "may" do historically? What is its place in the rhetoric of history? Perhaps we can approach the problem tangentially. Let us ask how we would translate that last sentence from a hypothetical subjunctive into an indicative to give it the maximum direct assertive force that I believe the record of the past warrants. The translation would go something like this: "It is not incredible that to More the King's £200 gift seemed like the reward Judas received." At first that seems to be saying very little, very softly indeed. But is it that little? Of how many men in the king's service would such a statement have been true? Of how many men in England? Of how many in Christendom? A thousand? A hundred? A score? Not many, God knows!

So that weak hypothetical subjunctive is fairly assertive after all. It asserts that More was a kind of man of whom there were very few in Europe: it asserts that he was a rare man and it tersely describes one of the characteristics which made him rare. It says he was a man who might suffer deep scruples at rendering a kind of service to his ruler, and receiving a reward for it which would not have given most of his contemporaries the slightest qualm. Once a historian makes an indicative assertion he is hooked on the Reality Rule that requires him to be able to document it from the record of the past. But in the book there is no visible documentation for that last sentence, no footnote with a serried array of references to the record. How then can it be squared with the Reality Rule? Easily enough. From one angle of vision my whole book was about what Thomas More was like, and what it was like to be Thomas More. So in one of its dimensions the whole book, the quotations in the text, and the citations in the footnotes were cumulatively a massive footnote to that last sentence. Or conversely the last sentence was an attempt to stamp on the reader's mind with maximum impact what the book was about. *Ecce homo!*

So we come to the end of our examination of four items in the microrhetoric of history—the footnote, the quotation, the name list, the hypothetical subjunctive. The inquiry has confirmed three conclusions that emerged from our study of historical macrorhetoric.

First, that history is a rule-bound discipline by means of which historians seek to communicate their knowledge of the past.

Second, that the relation of the rhetoric of history to history itself is quite other than it has traditionally been conceived. That rhetoric is ordinarily deemed icing on the cake of history; but our investigations indicate that it is mixed right into the batter. It affects not merely the outward appearance of history, its delight and seemliness, but its inward character, its essential function—its capacity to convey knowledge, understanding, and truth about the past as it actually was. And if this is indeed the case, historians need to subject historiography, the way they write history, to an inquiry far broader and far more intense than any that they have hitherto conducted.

Third, that there is an irreducible divergence between the rhetoric of history and the rhetoric of the natural sciences, that the vocabulary and syntax that constitute the appropriate response of the historian to his data are neither identical with nor identifiable with the vocabulary and syntax that constitute the appropriate response of the natural scientist to his. But the historian's goal is to render the best account he can of the past as it really was. Therefore, by his resort to the rhetoric of history, regardless of its divergence from that of the natural sciences, the historian affirms in practice and action his belief that it is more adequate than the latter as a vehicle to convey the kind of knowledge, understanding, truth, and meaning that history can achieve. Indeed, we discovered instances in which, in order to transmit an increment of knowledge and meaning, the very rules of historiography demanded of the historian a rhetoric which sacrificed generality, precision, control, and exactness to impact on the imagination, evocative force, and scope. The natural scientists never have to consider or make such a choice. They have constructed, and for their purposes I am sure constructed wisely, a rhetoric the rules of which eliminate the second alternative. The survival of this alternative in the rhetoric of history despite recurrent systematic efforts to eliminate it implies that in that rhetoric itself there are imbedded assumptions about the nature of knowing, understanding, meaning, and truth and about the means of augmenting them that are not completely congruent with the corresponding assumptions in the sciences, at least insofar as the philosophy of science has succeeded in identifying them. Concerning this peculiar and perplexing situation I shall try to say something in the next and final chapter of this primer.

CHAPTER X: The Dumblians and Another Ball Game, or An Extended Conclusion

WHAT has troubled me from before the beginnings of this primer has been the irrelevance or mistakenness of much that has been written in a prescriptive way about history by philosophers and historians. As concerns the historians I have not bothered about the prescriptions of the witch-doctor set, who will long be with us. In every generation they either profess to find in history the means of ultimate secular salvation for a soul-sick humanity, or they allege that history is bound to provide such salvation and is a swindle unless it can do so. Since, the human condition being what it is, humanity is going to keep on being soul-sick till Judgment Day, and since such sickness creates its own market for the nostrums of self-deluded witch doctors and mere quacks, historians in either of these lines of business have a permanent good thing going for them. Indeed if they move fast enough with the fashion and survive long enough, such historians may live through a whole cycle of nostrums and find themselves in their dotage peddling with renewed faith elixirs for what ails Man that they hawked and then abandoned in their youth.[1]

Life is too short—at least by now my own prospects for long survival are too dim—for me to find attractive the task of attempting to eradicate one of mankind's perdurable hallucinations and those who nurture it. In any case in recent years historians have shown less

[1] Nowadays if one dug around one might be able to come up with a few historians who peddled Marxism in the 1930's, abandoned it when the sales slackened, and are now hawking it again in a bright new package to a new generation of the soul-sick.

inclination toward such nurturing than succeeding generations of impenitent sociologues and psychiatrists. In any case, my concern has been with mistakes made by men of more sturdy intellectual purpose and more rational intent. Their aim has been not to win a saviorship award, collective or individual, and accompanying emolument, but to understand history as a significant form of knowledge, understanding, and quest for truth. Because the legitimate aim of getting things right has seriously concerned these men, I have tried to find out where they went wrong and to understand why they came up with prescriptions that no historian could actually follow.[2]

In most of the preceding chapters of this primer I have pivoted my arguments either around some particular course of events in the past or around everyday events—things the like of which have happened to or are part of the common knowledge of almost everyone. In this final chapter I will adopt a different strategy. Instead of taking past events or everyday events as a focal center, this chapter will pivot on a fiction in the nature of a parable. Here it is.

Imagine that the inhabitants of a most isolated village called Dumble have played and know of only one ball game—American football. Since they have never played or even heard of other ball games, Dumblians would then think of American football as The Ball Game. Suppose that they were then taken to see a game of Canadian football. After watching a while they might say, "Ah, that is The Ball Game with a few variations." Suppose further that then the best Dumblian players challenged the Canadian football team to play the Canadian variant of The Ball Game the following week. During that week the Dumblian team continued to practice and train as they always had for The Ball Game. They threw The Ball; they kicked it; they charged and blocked and tackled and ran; they went through their regular repertory of plays. If they were quite competent at The Ball Game, it is not unlikely that when they played the challenge match the Dumblian team would give a good account of themselves. If they were just a little better at American football than their opponents were at Canadian football, they might even win under Canadian rules.

We may conceive that their victory would entrench the Dumblians in their belief that all ball games were variations of The Ball Game. If the next ball game they saw was tennis, however, their illusion would almost surely be shaken. The number of players, the playing area, the equipment, the ball itself and what the players did with it—all these would be wildly at variance with what they were in The Ball Game. It

---

[2] The occasional disavowals of prescriptive intent by philosophers do not survive examination. Historians have been less shy or less disingenuous. They have known that when they describe a particular method or procedure as important, applicable, and nontrivial they are implicitly prescribing it for their fellow historians.

is hard to conceive that there would be Dumblians with minds so opaque and so resistant to what they perceived that they would not be driven to reconsider their belief that fundamentally there was only one Ball Game. Two readjustments of their notions would then be available to the Dumblians. If they were men of very flexible mind they might conclude that the ball game they were watching, tennis, was radically different from The Ball Game, and that therefore there were at least two quite disparate kinds of ball games. Their commitment to the Unity of The One True Ball Game having been shattered by experiencing tennis, they might even be able to conceive that there were more kinds of ball games still.

To Dumblians of minds at once more rigid and more nimble, however, an alternative would be open. They might simply deny that the object that tennis players batted about was a ball. After all it was a small object, about the size of a peach and even more fuzzy on the outside, and it was perfectly round. But a Real Ball, the ball used in The Ball Game, was covered with thick leather, it was fuzzless, it was about the size of a large honeydew melon, and it was oval. So they might conclude that while tennis was probably a Game, it was not a *Ball* Game. Notice that either response—that there was more than one kind of ball game or that tennis was not a ball game at all—would save the Dumblians a catastrophic mistake. They would not challenge the tennis players to a match the following week, train for it as they trained for The Ball Game, and then try to play tennis as if it were American football.

But the Dumblians might suffer just such a disaster if, immediately after they had successfully assimilated Canadian football to The Ball Game, they attended a soccer match. They would note a number of similarities of soccer to The Ball Game. There are eleven men on a soccer team; the playing field is not very different in size from an American football field; there is something more or less like a football goal at each end of the field; the team in possession of the ball aims to get it down the field and into the goal area; in the course of a soccer match, as in a football game, there is some catching of the ball, and throwing it, and kicking it, and a great deal of running up and down the field by members of both teams. Suppose that, rendered over-confident by their previous success with Canadian football, the Dumblians challenged a soccer team to a match the following week. Suppose, too, that drawing on their experience, they trained for the match as they always had trained previously for The Ball Game, that is, for American football. If they carried through and played the match as soccer under soccer rules, the Dumblians would suffer a thundering and unmistakable, but on their premises a quite unintelligible, defeat. Or instead, they might resort to football tactics—blocking, tackling, running the ball downfield, throwing forward passes—only to be told that they had broken the rules. Or after the first period, they might suggest that the rest of the game should be played with their kind of oval ball instead of a round soccer ball. This would get them into a raging argument with their opponents, who would have to reject a proposal, ostensibly so reasonable and moderate, but actually so preposterous, since given the rules of soccer on kicking, the game is a shambles unless played with a round ball.

Although under the circumstances the details of the course of events are unpredictable, a couple of results are easy to foresee. Inevitably, one outcome would be a perfectly terrible game, whatever game it turned out to be. Second, in the end the Dumblians would almost certainly come to one or the other of the same conclusions about soccer that they came to about tennis. They would be forced to conclude either that soccer is a different kind of ball game from The Ball Game, and that therefore there is more than one ball game, or that the round object soccer players kick about is not really a ball, and therefore soccer is not a real ball game. In the case of soccer, they might feel a good bit less comfortable about the second alternative than they were in the case of tennis. In the strategies, skills, and training that the game requires, soccer is similar enough to The Ball Game to make sensitive Dumblians uneasy about denying that soccer is a ball game. Yet a like result would follow either conclusion; once they stopped thinking of soccer as merely a variation of The Ball Game, Dumblians who wanted to understand soccer would no longer focus on its ostensible likeness to The Ball Game. They could then concentrate some attention on the differences. This would soon free them of the hopelessly erroneous illusion that because bits of soccer were in some sense similar to bits of The Ball Game, participants could make the appropriate responses in soccer if they knew how to play The Ball Game well. Having got over this mental block, they could begin to learn what soccer was like, and to grasp its patterns of play. Ultimately, they might understand and with practice even achieve the appropriate responses of a soccer player. But the prerequisite would be a qualitative discrimination, an awareness that soccer and American football were games different in kind.

And now to interpret the parable of the Dumblians as an image of what we have tried to get at in this history primer. Many inquirers— philosophers of science, scientists, and oddly enough even some historians—trying to account for the activities of historians as seekers, discoverers, and communicators of knowledge, understanding, and truth are like the Dumblians watching a soccer match for the first time. The model for such activity—the equivalent of The Ball Game—is and has long been the "hard" natural sciences. Consciously or subconsciously those inquirers have been on the lookout for things that historians do

which appear to be like things that natural scientists do. And thus they
have discovered that sometimes historians appear to be doing things
that seem comparable. Among other things historians accumulate
records; they commit themselves to the Reality Rule; they concern
themselves with proving that their assertions are properly supported by
evidence from the record and by coherent and convincing reasoning;
they offer explanations "why"; they seek to reduce the emotional over-
load born by some elements of their vocabulary.

At this point many inquiries into history as a discipline fall into what
in our parable may be called "the Dumblian soccer fallacy" or, more
generally, the morphological-physiological fallacy. In the Dumblians it
manifests itself for example in equating a soccer kick to an American
football kick, a soccer throw to an American football throw. We can
express this fallacy in something that approximates the rhetoric of the
philosophy of science. It would go like this: given that $s =$ soccer, $a =$
American football, $T =$ throw, $K =$ kick;

$$K_s = K_a, \text{ and}$$
$$T_s = T_a$$

But this is, of course, an error: kicking and throwing in soccer are
functionally different from kicking and throwing in American football.
Moreover, since actually $s \neq a$ the error is systematic, not incidental, and
it vitiates the Dumblians' whole perception of what goes on in a soccer
game. Indeed in respect to the *function* (f) of many of the throws and
kicks in soccer and American football, it is preposterous in the literal
sense of that term: it has got the matter arse-end-forward. Given $T_1 =$
throws by the soccer goalie and $K_1 =$ American football kicks, subclass
punt, and $K =$ all soccer kicks, then the functionally correct formulation
is:

$$\begin{array}{ccc} \text{Soccer} & & \text{American football} \\ (f)T_1 & \neq & (f)T \end{array}$$

(The soccer goalie's throw gets the ball as far down the field as his
strength allows at a high risk that his team will *lose control* of the ball;
all American football throws aim to *maintain control* of the ball.)

$$(f)T_1 = (f)K_1$$

(The American football kick called the punt has a function identical to
that of the soccer goalie's throw.)

And finally

$$.95 \, (f)K = .95 \, (f)T$$

(95 percent of all soccer kicks function like 95 percent of American

football throws: their purpose is to advance the ball *and* to retain control of it.[3])

Now, as we have said, it is evident that if the Dumblians actually took part in a soccer match their experience would soon persuade them of their initial error. If nothing else, the final score of the game would force them to the conclusion that their responses were somehow inappropriate and required reassessment. They might then become aware that they had fallen prey to the morphological-physiological fallacy; they mistook superficial and casual *structural* similarities between American football and soccer for a *functional* identity. At the same time they treated divergencies of large functional import as trivial and insignificant because all that they heeded and ascribed importance to was structural similarity.

The preceding exposition may help explain the sort of error that many philosophers of science and scientists are prone to when they try to understand history as a discipline. It may also account for the durability of their error. They reduce discussion of history to discussion of causal explanation in history, because it is at this point, they think, that the structure of history most nearly converges on that of the natural sciences. Having singled out this casual structural similarity, they imply or even state that whatever else historians do is not relevant for whatever truth value history may have. Therefore, by assuming that it has none, they absolve themselves from even asking what truth value a large part of the activity of historians has. It is a little like putting on blinders and insisting that what the blinders prevent one from seeing is scarcely worth looking at and perhaps not there at all. Yet to limit the scope of inquiry to the structure of a subactivity of a larger activity without investigating its function in that larger activity is likely to be an exercise in stultification. This is true, we have seen, whether the subactivities are kicking and throwing or causal explanation, whether the larger activity is soccer or history.

While it is easy enough to see how philosophers of science got themselves involved in this odd exercise, it is harder to understand why historians, who, after all, are professionally committed to writing history, should subscribe to views so contrary to their interest and opposed to their experience. It is rather as if a professional soccer player were to endorse Dumblian views on The One True Ball Game. There are perhaps two predisposing forces at work on a few historians here. The first is a fully justified respect for the great intellectual achievements of the "hard" natural sciences. For more than a century this led some historians to seek to identify their discipline as nearly as possible with

---

[3] The (roughly estimated) exceptional 5 percent on both sides are the soccer goalie's kicks and the American football quarterback's throws to "stop the clock."

those sciences. The easy way to achieve or at least create the illusion of identity is to pay heed only to casual morphological similarities and to disregard major functional differences. The other force on historians is a chronic crisis of confidence among some of them. Confronted with high and ghostly arguments in the celestial realms of epistemology and ontology, they tend unwarrantedly to lose faith in the common experience, common sense, and common language that has served and serves them quite well in their natural earthly habitat.

It seems to me that by taking a little thought, historians could spare themselves a good bit of the discomfort that their occasional forays into the celestial realms cause them. For example, in pursuit of their no doubt proper business philosophers have made pretty heavy going of what the past is and how it can be known—the ontological and epistemological status of pastness. Because of certain peculiarities of pastness (it never seems to be present) and because of even more marked peculiarities in their notion of what it is to know, some philosophers have verged on a position that implies that the past cannot be known.[4] Since this view suggests that what they believe to be the whole object of their inquiry is entirely inaccessible, at first sight one would not imagine that historians would find such a notion congenial. But because it has been sponsored by philosophers with an active interest in history (Croce, Collingwood), it has convinced or confused a good many historians, whose common sense might have told them better. In the interest of such sense consider the following brief dialogue. It exemplifies what is implicit in much human dialogue and discourse.

> PHILOSOPHER (loud and clear): Men cannot really know the past.
> HISTORIAN (stupidly): What did you say?
> PHILOSOPHER (irritably): I said, "Men cannot really know the past," and you know damn well that's what I said.

Note that in his reply the philosopher, irked by the historian's obliquity, assumes (1) that he himself knows what he said in the past and (2) that the historian also knows what he said. Whether or not this qualifies as "really knowing" under philosophical ground rules does not matter. It should be good enough for the historian since it assumes the existence of a kind of knowing about the past—knowing what someone said—that makes communication about it possible. It thus implies enough knowing about the past to enable historians to get on with their business. In this matter and a good many like it historians could save themselves trouble if they would mind their own business and not worry

---

[4] Jack Meiland has drawn this implication, with some justification, I believe—from the writings of Collingwood, Croce, and Oakshott. Jack Meiland, *Skepticism and Historical Knowledge* (New York: Random House, 1965).

about the ontological and epistemological problems of philosophers.

For almost two millennia philosophers and mathematicians wrestled with Zeno's paradox of the race between Achilles and the tortoise: given that the tortoise started a little ahead of Achilles, the latter could never catch up because in order to do so he would first have to traverse half the distance between them, and then half the remainder, and so on ad infinitum. From what I have been told I gather that in the end the philosophers and mathematicians found their long encounter with the paradox profitable, and that is all to the good. In the meantime the encounter need have been of no more concern to professional historians than it was to Everyman, safe in his knowledge that regardless of the mathematico-philosophical paradox the bookmakers paid off on Achilles.

Throughout this primer the differences between history and the natural sciences have been heavily emphasized. It is thus especially liable to be misconstrued by those who have encountered a similar emphasis in the pronouncements of writers with purposes altogether at variance with mine. To avoid misunderstanding let me stress this divergence of purpose. The purpose of the writers in question has fairly often been disingenuous; its unavowed aim has been to offer cover for a bootleg operation. It conceals an attempt to assert the superiority of history, its practices, and its practitioners to natural sciences, its practices, and its practitioners (or sometimes, of course, vice versa). The imputation of superiority to historical knowledge over all other kinds is one assignable meaning of "historicism." Unfortunately, that term has developed a prematurely middle-aged spread of meaning. To avoid confusion it has become necessary to specify with some precision how one intends to use it.

Historicism in the above sense implies that all human knowledge is "historical," that of such knowledge historicity is the only universal predicable, and that therefore history, the discipline which concerns itself with this unique universal, is the highest form of knowing, the Mother Superior, so to speak, in the house of the sciences. This is partly true; and like a good many part truths it has become the occasion for general error. All present human knowledge was indeed acquired in the past, and insofar as records of its acquisition survive, it is an appropriate subject for historical inquiry. But when this modest and reasonable claim is in the least extended it ceases to be valid. The claim asserts only that history is the appropriate instrument for rendering an account of the acquisition of scientific knowledge in the past. It does not assert that history has means of evaluating the methods and procedures for the acquisition and extension of knowledge of nature currently in use by scientists. In these matters merely being a historian affords no one any special insight. And, of course, professional historians as such have no claim whatever to knowledge of the present content or substance of the natural sciences, and nothing at all to contribute to it. To knowledge of the social sciences historians probably have something substantive to offer, since social scientists and historians have an overlapping interest in the nonbiological aspect of human activities. And the converse is, of course, also true. Valid discoveries by social scientists about the way societies work can be, have been, and will continue to be useful to and used by historians. To sensible historians with proper humility, megalomaniac claims by historicists therefore are both an embarrassment and a nuisance. With historicists as friends, history needs no enemies.

Imputation of guilt by association is an odious business, whether it is permitted to operate in the arena of politics or that of the pursuit of knowledge. Nevertheless it is unreasonable to expect particular associations to be viewed wholly without suspicion, unless one is clearly ready to disavow the general views of those with whom one associates and whose particular opinions one shares on matters of some importance. I hope that I have here made it evident once and for all that I do not in the slightest share the general views of historicists on the superiority or the special excellence of history and historical knowledge. Yet I believe, as they do, that the processes by which historians know and communicate what they know so diverge from the corresponding processes in the natural sciences that to avoid stultification and wasted effort history must be thought of as "another ball game." [5]

In the course of the preceding chapters we have discursively followed out the clues which suggested that history was another ball game, and we have tried to show that the differences they reveal are not mere matters of minor structural detail (like differences between American and Canadian football) but matters of major functional pattern (like those between American football and soccer). Now it is time to free the most important of these differences from the argumentative matrix in which they have been imbedded so that the contrasting patterns themselves will stand clear of the verbiage amid which they earlier appeared.

First, then, nature and the human past, the objects of investigation of

[5] This implies that cross comparisons between historians and natural scientists are misleading. Since history does not lend itself to revolutionary breakthroughs as the natural sciences do, there have not been and probably will not be revolutions in history comparable to those in the sciences. Therefore, there are no historians comparable to Copernicus, Galileo, Newton, Darwin, and Einstein. On this point see observations in my *Reappraisals in History* (London, 1961), p. 202. This is true even in the most general area historians are likely to work in, the area that concerns itself with the general way that history and historians work. Since that is the area in which this book is located, and since it is always gratifying to think of oneself as a possible Newton of history, I wish this were not so.

the natural sciences and of history respectively are fundamentally different. Nature as natural scientists perceive it in their work is not the same as the human past; the human past as historians perceive it in their work is not the same as nature. "Perceive it in their work," not "conceive it." It is doubtful whether either historians or scientists conceive the general objects of their investigations at all; it may be impossible to conceive them precisely; it may not be necessary to conceive them precisely in order to investigate them profitably. If natural scientists and historians did ordinarily perceive nature and the human past as the same it would be possible on grounds of synonymy ordinarily to substitute "the human past" or "history," "historical," and "historically," for "nature," "natural," and "naturally"—and of course vice versa—without significantly altering the meaning of the sentences in which natural scientists and historians imbed those terms. But this is not possible as one immediately discovers if one attempts such substitution, starting for example with such familiar titles as *Principia Mathematica Philosophiae Naturalis, Man's Place in Nature, On the Origin of Species by Means of Natural Selection,* The Museum of Natural History. Substitutions would radically change the meaning of each title or make nonsense of it.

Indeed we seem to conceive of the past as the human past and to conceive of man as man only at that point in time when an idiosyncratic primate began to behave unnaturally, that is, in a way in which nothing in nature ever behaved before. Historians of preliterate men begin to write boldly of *Homo*, rather than *Homo*(?) or *Pithecanthropus*, only when they find this primate in association with fires of his own making and of *coups de poing*, that is, only when he has embarked on the dangerous and unnatural business of messing around with nature in an unnatural and a systematic way. *Homo* thus defines himself to us against nature as *homo faber*.

Since they perceive the objects of their investigation as different, the records on which natural scientists and historians build natural science and history are and have to be different, because they are and have to be perceived differently. Those records are respectively the record of experiment and the record of the human past.[6] In his work a natural scientist does not perceive the record of an experiment as a record of the past. A historian of natural science, however, would perceive that "same" record as "not the same"; he would perceive it as a record of the

_____

[6] For reasons mentioned earlier I draw the contrast here between history and the "model" natural sciences and disregard paleontology or "natural history." Until very recently in the geological time-scale, the paleontological record has in any case been free of what appears soon after evidence of man appears in abundance—traces of the intentions of the creatures of which that evidence is a record.

past.[7] A natural scientist has no concern with the temporal (or spatial) locus of the experiment recorded, unless, of course, he can show that particular circumstances at that time and place broke through the "container" that the experimenter built around the experiment to shield it from accident and particularity. He is interested in a particular "then" and "there" only if they throw doubt on the "whenever" inference that he intends to draw, or when they involve a computable difference in the probability statement he intends to make. Historians face up to the fact that for them everything that the record records is at once open and closed. It is open because they cannot close out anything that happened to be there when the record was made; it is closed because they cannot alter the record itself without cheating. Historians have to be ready to take into consideration any evidence of anything whatever that at the time happened to be then and there which might affect their historical account. From the point of view of natural science as a way of knowing, whole masses of inaccurate experimental data which provided support for hypotheses subsequently falsified effectively cease to be part of the relevant experimental record of science; the same data do not cease to be part of the relevant record for historians of science, indeed they constitute the greater part of that record.

The second major divergence of history from natural science, which renders them inherently incommensurable, we found in the language of history, in its acceptable lexicon. We discovered this difference early when we recognized that Everyman was a historian, and that the common language of Everyman was the common though not the sole current coin of historical discourse. As we proceeded, our awareness of the divergence of the rhetoric of history from the rhetoric of the natural sciences widened and deepened.

It is now evident that while we may correctly speak of common language as the ordinary language of history, the total lexicon of history is universal; when we have sorted out the words of art of each science and discipline and skill we have to tumble them back together again to make up the vocabulary that historians claim as theirs and refuse to deny themselves access to.

Of this monstrous conglomerate the vocabulary of the natural

[7] Other notions propounded in this book I cannot confidently ascribe either to my own meditations or to the suggestion of others because I cannot remember or trace their genesis. This one I can pin down. The problem of sameness first occurred to me in the first draft of Chapter 5, when I noticed that "what happened" at Tacoma on November 7, 1940, was not the same for a historian and for an engineer both concerned to "explain" what happened there, and also that their "explaining" was not the same. I carried this notion further in dealing with dead Mr. Sweet when I inserted him into my revision of Chapter 1. It was only when at the suggestion of Quentin Skinner I got around to reading Peter Winch's *Idea of a Social Science* (New York, 1958) that I caught on to the strength of the idea of divergent identities of "the same thing." I have leaned heavily on it in this chapter.

sciences is one tiny, highly specialized segment, properly, meticulously, and painfully refined by the natural scientists. The special rule for entry into that vocabulary has been rigorously applied only in the past several centuries. The rule is that no term in the language of the natural sciences shall be ambiguous or value-loaded. The removal of ambiguity still requires some care, but the habit of scrubbing out value has become so automatic that mere entry into the vocabulary of the natural sciences cleans words like "cell," "mass," "positive," and "negative" of any taint of value they might carry in from common language. This process is indispensable to effective discourse in the natural sciences, and it has been almost entirely successful.

The same process is not possible in history, and were it possible it would not be desirable. Something odd often happens to the immaculately scrubbed terms once they move out of the carefully sterilized ambience of the laboratory and into the marketplace of common discourse. Like all pieces of common currency they show the soil and wear and tear of handling. What could be less value-stained than the billets of heavy paper used in computers or a whole number series like 863415? Yet the "IBM card" became the object of (probably quite undeserved) opprobrium, when in the faintly paranoid style recently deemed appropriate in adolescent behavior, students came to feel that they were being processed by means of computer cards (as they were) and generally treated like them (as they were not). Prisoners occasionally describe the sense of loss of human dimension and identity that they suffer in jail when they become "just a number" like 863415 instead of a person.

The use of the word "paranoid" above is another instance of the same point. In psychiatric medicine paranoid is as value-free as "rheumatoid" in orthopedic medicine. Both of these terms are used in medical science and their referants studied in the value-free manner appropriate to the natural sciences.[8] But back in the world of people, while rheumatoid stays as value-free as, say "deltoid," paranoid quickly gets value-stained.

This happens because men have to make choices and make those choices intelligible in the communities to which they belong. They can dispense, that is, neither with the choices nor with the language that enables them to vindicate, however crudely, the value-patterns which give a modicum of order and credibility to those choices. Consequently, common language is littered with terms and turns of phrase ineffaceably stained with value and judgment. Moreover, they will remain so, as long as their context is discourse in common language.

If by some linguistic catastrophe a whole set of indispensable value-

[8] Since its object is the alleviation of conditions almost universally deemed undesirable, and long held to be the consequence of divine disesteem, medical science, especially in the region of psychic ills, is the area in which the natural science scrubbing of vocabulary is most difficult.

terms lose currency in common language, at some cost in convenience people create new currency-equivalents for them. "Courage" and "prudence," for example, have ceased to circulate as freely as they once did, so previously neutral terms like "guts" and "cool" (as in "cool cat") help take up the slack. In certain kinds of common enterprise the traits once designated by courage and prudence are necessary. Since the existence of such traits is a matter of common observation and since the understanding of human doings requires a vocabulary approximately capable of describing intelligibly what exists and has existed, those terms or some equivalent for them and for what they communicate cannot be scrubbed out of common discourse. Before they recruit other men for shared enterprises in which those traits are required, people need to make a judgment about whether those men possess courage and prudence, and they will need terms to label the traits. *Common language has to adjust itself to common needs.*

Merely changing the tense of verbs does not alter such needs. In fact the tensing of verbs in the present is nothing but a specious cover for projecting experience in the past to make a rough prediction of the future. When I say that Jones *is* courageous or prudent, that he has plenty of guts or is a cool cat, my effective allegation is that Jones has so adequately displayed courage and prudence in the past that he is a good bet to display them when they are needed hereafter. The notion that statements of this sort can be made in value-free language is absurd, and indeed a contradiction in terms. What possible sense can one make of the notion of a value-free answer to a question that in its very formulation demands a value judgment? Such demands are not, however, confined to situations involving a present past and a present future. For a professional historian who takes his stand in a past moment they require judgments based on a *past* past which will render intelligible events in a *past* future. Suppose such a historian wants to make it clear what in the early 1640's was about to move John Pym, the political leader of the Long Parliament, not to trust a particular avowal of Charles I. From the record of the past it is easy enough to elicit overwhelming evidence (1) that in political matters Pym was no fool, and (2) that Charles I's readiness to deceive anyone who opposed him was exceeded only by his capacity to deceive himself. Can one possibly argue that these two statements are value-free? Of course they are not, and if they were, they would be historically worthless. They simply would fail to provide the reader with some of the information he needs if he is to understand why Pym distrusted Charles. A brief explanation would go like this: "In the circumstances Pym could not afford to credit Charles I's avowals. As Pym perceived the situation, a great deal was at stake. In matters political, he was anything but a fool, and he had learned from experience and report that in matters far less important the king had not scrupled to deceive those whom he conceived of as enemies—or for that matter even as friends." Yet although the necessary statements in this answer are value-packed judgments, they are easy to document, while "facts" about John Pym's sex life and eating habits, for example, are impossible to document, since concerning them the record of the past affords us no information whatever. More important, such judgments are part of the appropriate response of a historian to the question asked.

The point here made about the necessary difference between the rhetoric of history and that of the natural sciences reinforces the one previously made about the difference between the human past and nature. Intuitively, historians have continued to use a rhetoric not scrubbed of value coloration. Language must either adjust itself to need or block up and destroy communication to the extent that it fails so to adjust. The persistence of valuation in the rhetoric of history is a symptom of the difference between the human past and the "nature" of natural scientists, a difference which created and has perpetuated that rhetorical divergence.

The distinction made so emphatically here has been present in this primer, although latent, since the first chapter. When I began to write, I was not sharply aware of the point. Only during and through the process of writing, have the distinction and its implication become increasingly clear to me.

Yet both were present in the very first focal point of the primer, the Case of the Muddy Pants. Willie's third answer—the O.K. one from the point of view of a historian—is partly explanation and partly justification. Yet it is good history exactly as it stands. In context of the question to which his answer is addressed, "justification" cannot and should not be separated from historical explanation. To separate it or omit it does not increase but rather diminishes the truth value of the explanation. What Willie rightly seeks to establish and succeeds in establishing is that the mud on his pants cannot be imputed to acts of carelessness, stupidity, or cowardice on his part, that such a historical judgment on his actions would be unjust. He achieves this legitimate purpose of historical explanation with a minimum of fuss, with commendable and exemplary economy. Anyone who has ever been a little boy, reasonably anxious to get home on time and reasonably desirous of avoiding a fight over nothing against bigger battalions and long odds, will understand what Willie was like and what under the circumstances, it was like to be Willie. To that extent he will understand better what Willie is explaining about the past. And so Willie's third answer is a better historical explanation for including "justification" than it would have been had he left it out.

The recognition that historians' language is value-colored does not, of course, "solve the problem" of historical discourse. It merely spares historians from looking for a kind of solution, a value-free vocabulary, that is impossible, and that they would have to reject even if it were possible. Historians still face the difficult, because ever-recurrent, task of using the whole human lexicon to make the best sense they can of the past. What readers have the right to demand of historians is not lack of judgment (a most odd thing to demand, when one comes to think of it) but responsible judgment which sometimes may mean suspension of judgment or withholding of judgment when judgment is inappropriately demanded. For example, who was to blame for the movement of prices in England in the early modern era, that appears to have inflicted considerable suffering on the poor? Answer: if, as seems to be the case, at the time there was a considerable increase of population without an equivalent increase in productivity, and if, as also seems to be the case, the technological limitations of farm production made for a chronic, major, and irremediable underemployment of labor, then no one was to blame. Therefore: judgment withheld.

Part of the difficulty here has undoubtedly been generated by sects of historians (and others) who always want to have it both ways at the same time, *always* to have their cake and eat it too. They want to believe in a Law of History, that is, in a rule that determines the course of events in the past, does so now, and will do so in the future. They also want to be able always to hang on someone, or several someones, the rap for everything they do not like that has ever happened, is happening, and will happen. Therefore they find unbearable the notion that sometimes somebody is responsible for an event, and that then a judgment is not only possible but necessary, while sometimes no one is responsible and then a judgment is at once unnecessary and impossible.

The best effort of a historian to do justice to the past stumbles over another obstacle that natural scientists do not have to bother about— imperfect synonymy. Its consequence is that apparent synonyms can sometimes be freely interchanged and sometimes cannot.

Historians have to learn to live in a lexical atmosphere where an elementary postulate of mathematics does not always work. In mathematics if $A = B$, then *always* $B = A$. In the language historians use, however, sometimes in some contexts $A = B$, yet sometimes $B \neq A$. Consider two terms, "calling" and "occupational choice." In many contexts the two terms will be as readily interchangeable as two pennies dated respectively 1962 and 1963, and no confusion at all will result from interchanging them. But suppose a historian is confronted by evidence of a supply of Christian ministers in early seventeenth-century England in excess of the demand, and that he wants to account for this phenomenon. Soon he may come to the point where he needs to talk about the perception of many men that God picked them for the Christian ministry. At that point the synonymy of "occupational choice" and "calling" breaks down. These men truly believed God called them. For them there was no "occupational choice," or any choice at all but to obey God. Occupational choice was not what a calling meant to them. The historian then must make it clear that to some seventeenth-century Englishmen a calling was not a synonym but an antonym of an occupational choice. It is at this interface between what it was like for someone in the past and what happened in the past that historians are caught in a language crunch. Natural scientists never need bother about such a crunch, but no one has a recipe or a mission to save historians from it. For they can be saved from the crunch only at the cost of destroying history itself. Historians need to learn to work right at that interface, knowing full well that their undertaking will always be beyond their capacities and that their best effort will always fall short of their aspirations.

A third distinctive double trait of historical discourse or rather two complementary traits are the dependence of historians on large contexts to give firmness to their vocabulary and the processive character of their macrorhetoric. Historians need to pull up sharp when they find themselves worrying about the reality of ideas, realism versus nominalism, idealism against materialism or empiricism, nomothetic against ideographic thought. All those "-ics" and "-isms" should be warning lights for a historian. They should caution him to ask if there is actually anything in any of these boxes that as a historian he needs give much heed to. What they all ask in their various ways is how it is possible to come to terms with the simultaneous generality and individuality of things, with their generic and specific natures, and whether indeed it is possible to do so at all.

When a historian sees a question that starts "How is it possible—?" he should know that he has wandered on to the turf of the philosophers, and that he had better take heed where he is and where he is headed. The danger for a historian in this case is that if philosophers cannot show each other and him how something is possible, they and especially he may fall victim to the illusion that they have shown that something *is not* possible, although actually all they have done is show that they *cannot prove* that it is possible. This sort of illusion is especially to be avoided when the feasibility of what cannot be proved possible is manifested by its being done with reasonable effectiveness all the time.

Of course, communicating about both generals and particulars at a level of intelligibility adequate to the task is just what everyone does not only every day but very nearly every time he says anything at all. Except for those unable to keep two things in the front of their minds at once, it is not hard to do. Since almost all communication is actually about both generals and particulars, to believe that it is impossible to communicate about both is to believe that practically no communication at all ever takes place between or among men. And of course no one believes this, or acts as if he believes it, which for the purpose of historians is much the same thing. For professional historians, however, the problem is a bit more delicate and complicated than for the historian who is Everyman. They need to learn to write history that steers a firm line between the metaphysical sermons of *begriffstricken* Germans, who preach from one until four,[9] and Aunt Tillie's description of her appendicitis operation.

In this matter of the general and the particular, however, we can at least identify what makes it fairly easy for historians (and everybody else) to do what philosophers have trouble proving possible. Historians (and everybody else) can do it because they rely on common language, because their discourse has an extended context, because it is processive in character, and because its criterion is "enough to be going on with." In one sense the whole of common language *is* the extended context of whatever a historian writes. Ordinarily he uses words in their rough common sense without feeling constrained to whittle them finer, unless in the narrower context of the piece of history he is writing his language requires a sharper edge than that which rough common sense provides. Within this narrower context, if he avoids the initial mistake of excessively constricting himself by a rigorous denotative definition at the outset, each time he uses a particular word a historian has a fresh opportunity to refine its meaning. A number of analogies to this procedure suggest themselves; for example, the way scientists choose or design instruments accurate up to but not beyond the limits that the reliability of their data require—.9 or .99, or .99999. A better example, perhaps, is the bracketing fire of the field artillery. Their ordinary targets being (1) numerous and (2) people or things fairly responsive to the guidance of people, their need is less frequently for fixed precision firing (exact fixed denotative definition) than for quick appropriate response to targets of opportunity as they emerge—targets that might vary from a single mortar emplacement to a mile-long convoy. The ordinary way for coping with this variety of targets is "sensing" and "bracketing." [10] The artillery observer takes the whole ordinary landscape as his context. Then using his common sense of vision he "senses" whether the shells are "over" the target or "short." He does not expect to hit the target with the first shot fired. If he senses the first shot over, that

[9] The terminology here is a conflation of Wallace Ferguson's in *The Renaissance in Historical Thought* (Boston, 1948), p. 277, and W. S. Gilbert's in *The Mikado* (London, 1885).

[10] Since I wrote the above, it has been called to my attention that the German phenomenologist Heidegger makes use of a concept of bracketing. Since I do not know what a phenomenologist is, have not read Word One by Heidegger, and therefore have not the slightest notion how he uses the term, likeness, if any, between his use of "bracketing" and mine is wholly coincidental.

is, beyond the target, he drops the range of the guns so that the next shot is pretty sure to be "short." Having thus bracketed the target he continues to adjust fire until he senses that he has the range close enough for the purpose of the particular fire mission, whether it be disrupting a convoy or pinning down a machine gun crew in a foxhole. From there on, with the target in range he has the guns fire at will, but he never ceases to keep his target under observation. Especially if it is a moving target, he must always be ready to readjust the range of his guns to the changes in his target's position.

A historian needs to go through the same process in his use of words. He may have to make preliminary adjustments of a term to bring it to bear on what is in the record, and he may or may not choose to make the process of adjustment explicit and visible in the history he ends up writing. Still he is almost always dealing with people or groups of people in the past who are on the move, people whose movement has left traces in the record. He must always, therefore, keep his targets under close observation and adjust his language to their shifts. The term "Parliament," for example, has been used to designate an institution that has had a continuous history in England from the thirteenth century to the present. No exercise could be more futile than to try on first encounter with the term "Parliament" to fix permanently a definition of this moving body and then on subsequent encounters to argue about whether the somewhat changed body (by 1740 it had changed almost beyond recognition) was "really" Parliament. The first job a historian of Parliament has to do is to keep his observation close in on what in the record of the past is called Parliament in England. He must also keep under observation whatever trait of Parliament he happens to want to investigate—for example, the presence of representatives chosen by communities. Of course if he does this, he discovers that in the thirteenth century men did not think that Parliament always had to have present at its sessions representatives of communities, and that at the king's command representatives of communities assembled in gatherings that were not called Parliaments. Just by keeping this situation under continuous scrutiny he will be able to bracket the time span in which Parliament came to require the presence of representatives of the communities for some and finally for all of its official transactions. This simple-minded procedure will spare him the frustration of a quest for a *dingam sich* that is not there. He will not waste time arguing about whether without representation Parliament was *really* Parliament. He will have gently removed himself from the ontological and essentialist hook, a trap in which historians have wasted an appalling amount of time and energy. He will have identified an institution and bracketed it closely enough to call it "Parliament." And he will have bracketed a practice closely enough to call it "representation of communities." And finally he will have discerned a time span during which such representation became a required practice for what was called Parliament. And yet he will never have frozen himself into an eternal commitment on the "true" nature of Parliament or the "true" nature of representation. In so doing he will have been "true" to the one thing that all historians are always committed to be true to—the record of the past.

Historians, however, have a second task. They are obliged to take care not only that justice is done in their use of words, but that it is seen to be done. This means that they must use language in a way that gives them access both to the record of the past and to the second records of as many of their readers as they can reach. When he uses a word much trafficked in, it is very hard for a historian to be sure that his readers will actually have in mind at the start what they need to have in mind to follow his pursuit of those moving targets with which history must so often concern itself. This is why some of the best history ever written by some of the greatest historians, Maitland and Marc Bloch, for example, takes the reader through the process by which they initially have bracketed their targets. That is, they take their readers with them in their effort to discover what the people of the times they are writing about had in mind when they talked of a fief, or seisin, or a free man, or a villein, or a serf. When in full view of the public great historians work on these "semantic" problems, they do not lose their readers; rather they gain them. In addition, they also provide their readers with the two interrelated indispensables of history: some feeling for what it was like in the times and places that they write about, and the means for following the changes that took place over time in the subjects the historians are dealing with.

This brings us to a further trait that we have noted as distinctive of history—its processive character. Hitherto we have used the term "processive" with what we hope was a tolerable ambiguity. At times we have used it to describe what historians sense as needful in their discourse—not certainty, or perfect logical rigor, but enough to be going on with, enough, that is, to enable their readers (or in the case of Everyman, his listeners) to follow them in their effort to render the most likely account they can of the fragment of the past that they seek to elucidate. In a second sense, we have used the term "processive" to describe an overall trait of the macrorhetoric of history, the conformation of that rhetoric to its function of rendering intelligible changes in men and groups of men over time spans in the past. The two senses of the term are interrelated. The unit of written history—the essay, the article, or the book—is what gives the historian the *lebensraum* he requires, the writing space for bracketing his verbal targets with the degree of accuracy and the connotative force he needs to communicate effectively. It spares him the necessity of defining words with such rigidity that no collocation of them can render intelligible the processive changes that are the common experience of all of us. It spares him the obverse philosophical problems of the total Parmenidean immobility of being and the total Heraclitean flux of becoming. It further spares him the reductionist or assimilationist necessity of stripping actual historical discourse down to the bare bones of the logic of causal ascription imbedded in it, and then implausibly alleging that these bones are the sole repository of all the truth values that history offers. This skeletal metaphor seems to be curiously attractive to some analytical philosophers.[11] It may be somewhat less attractive to producers and consumers of history.

Equipped with the versatile and well-tuned instrument of common language and access if necessary to the universal lexicon, given contexts that extend even beyond what he actually writes to the common language of his day, and thus provided with means for discourse processive in both senses of the term, a historian can comfortably reject the claim that adequate historical explanation requires him to adduce necessary and sufficient causes. He can learn to live comfortably with the idea that the appropriate response to the quest and request for historical explanation is not all the relevant general laws and boundary conditions of an event. The appropriate response is simply the most credible story or account that he is capable of offering concerning the matter about which explanation is sought. He need not believe, indeed he had better not believe, that in rendering such an account he has arrived at the ultimate or final explanation.

The adoption, often tacit, of the standard of credibility instead of a number of possible alternatives is the final trait of history we wish to underline in our attempt to indicate why as a significant form of human inquiry, history is a different Ball Game from other forms of inquiry no less significant.

Credibility is perhaps the most elusive term used in this book. We have had the least success moving in on it with the bracketing fire in which we have caught other key terms in this primer. We seized on it, almost *faute de mieux*, because it seemed especially important to emancipate historians from one of the most frustrating and stultifying language traps into which some of them all of the time and all of them (including myself) some of the time fall by pursuing the quest of "real" causes which turns out on investigation to be a quest for necessary and sufficient causes. A great deal more needs to be said about the credibility standard than I have time or capacity to say here. In the end the term "credibility" may turn out to have been so soiled and debased by common use that it cannot be employed without creating more confusion

[11] Morton G. White, *Foundations of Historical Knowledge* (New York, 1965), pp. 220–221; Arthur G. Danto, *Analytical Philosophy of History* (Cambridge, Eng., 1965), p. 255.

than communication in the context in which I am trying to place it. In this region, however, the random noise level is so high and the communication level is so low, that throwing another term into the arena is not likely to make matters much more confusing than they now are, and it just might make them a little less confusing.

At any rate when people describe an account as "incredible," they have something more or less determinable and specific in mind. If we press them they may be able considerably to clarify for us (and themselves) what they have in mind. Let us return once more to the beginning and our first focal point—Willie's muddy pants. Suppose in answer to his father's question, Willie had replied, "You know Elizabeth Hawkins. Well, she is a witch, and she hates me. On my way home today I was crossing that intersection at Fifth and Main. Well right then and there Elizabeth changed herself into a mud puddle just where I was crossing, and I slipped in her or it, and got my pants all muddy. And right away she dried up and disappeared. O.K.?" Now if we compare this explanation with the one we earlier found both satisfactory and appropriate we note that they are alike in some ways. They focus on history, not on nature. They are in common historical language, not in a specialized natural science rhetoric. In context they address themselves to providing a historical answer to Willie's father's demand for an explanation. They are processive in both senses: that of giving his father enough of an answer to be going on with and that of dealing with change over a time span reasonably adequate to the requirements of the question. So far then both answers are good historical answers; so far in both instances Willie has played the right ball game. Still he goes wrong in his historical explanation about Elizabeth Hawkins. Not that Willie is lying; he may without reservation believe his witch story. If so, too bad for Willie; he is hallucinating; his story is incredible. Nowadays no one in his right mind will believe that what Willie said happened actually did happen or could happen. Conversely, anyone in his right senses will find Willie's account of his misadventure in Plumber's Field quite credible whether it turns out to be true or not. At least this brackets the term "credibility." It puts it somewhere in the neighborhood of common sense.

And this does indeed bring us pretty nearly full circle to a clear recognition of what this primer is about. If it has a pattern and a design, if there is a gestalt into which its parts make a fair fit, it is the protean notion that the interlocked entities, common sense, common language and credibility lie at the very heart of history as a significant form of inquiry. The existence of a community is marked by the ability of its members to communicate with one another in a common language; the viability of this common language creates the presumption of the existence among those who share it of a shared view of what is credible. It is the existence of this interwoven pattern of common language, common sense, and credibility that makes Everyman a historian and a quite competent one as long as he stays within the bounds of that part of the record of the past with which he is familiar.

The main argument of this primer, then, is conservative, old, and orthodox, so conservative, so old, and so orthodox that to a generation which has heard a great deal of fancy, futile novelty and heresy it paradoxically stands a chance of seeming new.

Since as concerns history it is all too easy to make ridiculous the claims for the common sense, the common language, and the feel for credibility of Everyman, since indeed the attack on these legitimate claims usually takes the form of exaggerating them and then caricaturing the exaggerations, we need to take care to mark out roughly the bounds and limits of the claims.

1. It is not claimed that the common sense of Everyman is a perfect and universal guide to historical certainty. Quite to the contrary, I do not for a moment believe that there is any such guide. It will not do, therefore, to point out that in historical matters the exercise of common sense has led men astray. Of course it has, and so has every other prescription for arriving at truth,—tradition, authority, mathematical reasoning, experiment. In one aspect, the whole record of man's quest for truth is a shambles of bloody error achieved by misapplications, myopia, and mistakes.[12] Of the ways for attaining truth preferred to common sense by clever men it is at least worth pointing out that they may sustain and indeed have sustained noxious illusions far longer and with more devastating effect than common sense was likely to have done. Among such delusional systems in the past, for example, were the Inquisition and the witch craze, kept to proper fever-pitch by some of the most powerful intellects in Europe, such as the members of the Dominican Order and Jean Bodin. Such yesterday was Leninism-Stalinism. Such today is the expert-fed insanity that writes off tens of millions of men as "an acceptable loss" by a thermonuclear explosion, without wondering whether the loss is all that acceptable to those consigned to destruction.

What is claimed is simply that common sense and the common language through which it is exchanged serve and always have served men fairly adequately for getting along with the necessary transactions of living from day to day, and that this creates a strong presumption for the use of both in history. The burden of proof therefore always rests on historians or any others who insist that in a particular case, one, the other, or both have to be jettisoned. This is not at all to assert that in history a case for jettisoning them cannot sometimes be made, but only

[12] In another aspect, of course, it has been that of a hard heroic climb toward truth despite error.

that in all instances a historian needs to make the case, even though tacitly, to his own satisfaction. He must never merely assume it.

2. It is not claimed that common sense is never contradictory, but only that contradictions are at times more apparent than real. It is a favorite ploy of writers with animus (or a vested interest) against reliance on common sense to point out that the old saws and sayings that are supposed to and do embody it frequently point in opposite directions. A favorite example offered is "He who hesitates is lost," and, "Look before you leap." They seem to be saying opposite things. But then what about: $2H_2O + O_2 \rightarrow 2H_2O_2$ and $2H_2O_2 \rightarrow 2H_2O + O_2$. They seem to be saying opposite things too. But that does not prevent both from being true. The question is which is appropriate at a particular point, and that question is unanswerable out of context. In context it is often easy to choose between apparently contradictory formulations of the conventional wisdom. By and large in the context of choosing a career common sense rooted in common experience seems to indicate that it is a good idea to look before one leaps. On the other hand he who hesitates very long about throwing a hand grenade on which he has released the triggering device is rather likely to be lost. There remains a considerable difference between a prescription to abandon common sense in history and a prescription to use it with common sense.

3. Finally the common sense of Everyman in the 1970 American model of course is not an entirely sound instrument for judging what it was like to have been Luther at the Diet of Worms or Paul on the Damascus Road, nor can common sense alone render credible here and now what those men experienced there and then. The humanizing function of history is precisely to liberate Everyman from the constricting limits of the common sense of here and now. This is a part of the vocation of professional historians and the relevance of history's irrelevance. It will not do, however, for historians to misconstrue either their problem or their task here. It is not to abandon the 1970 American model of common sense or to transcend it so far that it wholly disappears from view. To abandon common sense is to abandon one's readers except with respect to a few cramped corners of the past that can be made partly intelligible without common sense. To transcend it is to ascend into the empyrean of metahistory where ideologies war, and "isms" clash, and trends trend, but no man acts or suffers or even lives. Historians have another option in writing; they can take their readers with them, over the path they went, to where they got to. After all, they started their own journey, long ago perhaps, with only the equipment of here-and-now common sense. And if they were worth their salt, without ever wholly abandoning that common sense they extended it and intensified it, till they did begin to attain some intima-

tion of what it was like to have been Luther at Worms or Paul on the
Damascus Road. The certification that they had attained such an
intimation was the credibility of what they said and wrote not only to
those who followed after them along the path of understanding they
discovered but also to those who had hewn out not quite identical paths
themselves. By remaining in close contact with his own second record
as he writes, a historian stands a chance of carrying his readers, their
common sense transformed but not excised, with him to where he has
been in the past, and of enlarging their understanding so that they can
grasp what he has understood.

One of the few things in this primer that may be intellectually radical
or even revolutionary is its persistence in asserting a central role for
common sense in history. It is necessary to emphasize the point of
centrality. Otherwise notions about common sense in history lose out by
winning casual assent ("Of course, common sense has a place,
but———"), and end at the periphery rather than in the center of
attention to how history achieves explanation, understanding, and
truth.

To insist that common sense is and should be the prime mover toward
the advancement of learning in an intellectual discipline invites a fresh
evaluation of one of the most powerful and consistent developments in
the thought of Western men during the past four centuries. The beginnings of that development—the reorientation of science from Copernicus to Galileo—itself entailed one of the most abrupt intellectual turn-
abouts in chronicles of the human spirit. It was the beginning of the
greatest series of successes ever achieved by men in the intellectual exploration of the natural world around them, the series which we today
bunch under the general rubric, modern natural science.

Since the century of Copernicus and Galileo, there has never been a
time when all men have been free of misgivings about modern natural
science, and with more or less vehemence in every age some men have
expressed those misgivings. None of this opposition has enjoyed more
than passing favor, and that only from the ill-educated and the few.
Often it has been merely and demonstrably obscurantist, not to say de-
ranged. Often it took its stand on grounds that the advance of modern
science itself promptly and cleanly undercut. Modern natural science
showed extraordinary power to come through on its commitment to advance men's knowledge, and later their control, of nature, thus providing
a most effective and crushing rejoinder to the few who entertained
doubts about its efficacy. Today that power is greater than it has ever
been, and increases day by day.

The conditions surrounding the initial success of modern science and
the long continuation of that success impressed a number of distinctive

traits on the intellectual topography of modern man. Two traits need to
be singled out in the present context. First the major scientfiic successes
of the century and a half after Copernicus were scored in the regions of
what today we would call terrestrial and astrophysics, and they were
accompanied by a quantification and mathematization of proof in those
disciplines on a scale hitherto unprecedented. Ever since, physics has
been the exemplary natural science, the standard and model of what
such a science should be, or at least should aspire to. The strongly
quantitative character of its rhetoric has also been taken as normative
for scientific discourse. The impetus to quantify has received enforce-
ment from the considerable (though by no means perfect) correlation
between the rapid progress of other natural sciences and their mathematization. Recently Ralph Bradley put the point quite neatly:

> Scientific progress is made through the development of more and more
> precise and realistic representations of natural phenomena. Thus science
> . . . uses mathematics and mathematical models for improved under-
> standing . . .[13]

This brings us to and is indirect evidence of the second distinctive
trait of the modern intellectual topography which modern science has
moulded. That trait lies in the realm of folk psychology or at any rate of
the psychology of intellectual folk. The dazzling sequences of successes
of modern natural science habituated such folk to think of science as,
par excellence, the depository of truth, knowledge, and understanding,
if not indeed as their sole authentic and legitimate depository. In four
centuries from a view which was ecumenical, if slightly incoherent, a
view which depending on the circumstances found truth, knowledge,
and understanding in revelation, reason, experience, common sense,
tradition, custom, inspiration, intuition, and conventional wisdom,
many men came to equate the true, the known, and the understood
with what is scientifically true or scientifically verified or scientifically
verifiable.[14] A claim to being true, which was not also a claim to being
scientific was, therefore, dubious, or inadequately sustained, or in some
other way somehow second rate. This notion was not itself demonstrated or even, so far as I can judge, demonstrable. It was far more
pervasive and far more tenacious than any demonstrable conclusion. It
was a scarcely discerned and rarely examined assumption, a postulate,
a way of perceiving and organizing a range of experience, a focus of

[13] R. A. Bradley, "Multivariate Analysis Overview," *International Encyclopedia of
the Social Sciences* (New York, 1968), 10: 527–537.
[14] This sense of the matter is capable of surviving and indeed has survived quite
considerable divergences of opinion as to what constitutes scientific verification. It
is evidently independent of such opinion and such divergences.

men's visions of life. It became so pervasive that large areas of human experience which ill-fitted the notion remained unorganized and lacking focus. After each large stride of the natural sciences, men concerned with society and history tried to assimilate the substance of their disciplines to the latest great find in the natural sciences—Gallilean mechanics, Newtonian astrophysics, Darwinian natural selection, Einsteinean relativity theory. The abandoned, rusting, rotting remains of these endeavors attest to their failure. They also attest to the power of the preconception that the one right model for organizing knowledge, understanding, and truth stands in the region of the natural sciences.

One of the most remarkable capacities of science since Copernicus has been that of taking the grit of objections which detractors occasionally dump into the works and grinding them so finely that instead of creating friction, like graphite they lubricate the movement of the machinery they were expected to slow up or stop. Perhaps because most of the grit got so thoroughly and effectively pulverized, for a long while one fragment received only intermittent attention. The beginnings of "modern" history are harder to identify than the beginnings of "modern" natural science. The practice of history writing undeniably underwent considerable changes from sometime in the fifteenth century on, but there is no historical equivalent of Copernicus or of the Copernican revolution in history. By the time the writing of history became a professional academic activity the prestige of the natural sciences was such that almost every more or less systematic procedure purporting to advance knowledge—like history, philology, and phrenology—was sure to describe itself as a science. Adventitiously, history's claim to be a science found a readier welcome at the time it was pressed than it was likely to have had a century before or after. It happened to be put forward about the time that the natural sciences were undergoing the Darwinian revolution, the only one in their history that did not immediately and manifestly raise the level of and the demand for a corresponding intensification or extension of mathematical and quantifying skills. Moreover, the net for sifting claims to be a science was very loose-meshed during much of the nineteenth century and let pass foreign bodies a good deal grosser than history. Actually natural scientists were too intent on their ordinary business to pay much attention to history. After all, unlike phrenology, it evidently did yield steady increments of knowledge reasonably acceptable to sensible men, so why waste time arguing?

As one would expect, awareness that history presented some sort of special problem in the area of knowing came initially from philosophers concerned with the problem of knowledge. The story of what followed on this awareness is quite complex, and has been told elsewhere far better than I can tell it.[15] The upshot of the matter appears to be, that while keeping their grip on the claim that history is a science, a cluster of German philosophers much interested in history argued that it was a different kind of science from the natural sciences, and they tried to specify the differences. Their arguments resulted in a series of controversies of inordinate complexity and considerable opacity about the nature and conditions of knowing, the net result of which was to impress on philosophers mainly interested in the natural sciences the desirability of making it clear what science really was, what scientific truth, explanation, knowledge, and understanding were, and what henceforth should count as a science. This actually turned out to be quite a task, and the attempt to unify the sciences that it entails encountered and continues to encounter serious difficulties. One of the difficulties it encountered was history, for which some philosophers had already claimed a privileged sanctuary. Such a sanctuary is, however, incompatible with the conception of a unified science. Yet it is evident that readers of a competent work of history know more about the past and why things in the past happened after reading it than they did before. If history was not the only errant planet in the orderly cosmos of the philosophers of the natural sciences, it was among the most conspicuously errant. To authenticate the claim that all truth values and adequate explanations conform to models similar to those of physics, the model science, history therefore has to be dealt with. One can deal with it by minor tinkering with the model. Or one can deny the truth value and explanatory force of anything in historical discourse which fails to fit the model and assimilate the rest. Or one can do both.

Sporadically and unsystematically in this primer we have collided with parts of the enterprise that philosophers of natural science undertook in a heroic effort to fit history into their cosmos. In less than three decades this enterprise has traversed the route from the classic simplicities of Hempel's earliest essay on history in 1941 to a dense and almost impenetrable proliferation of complications, alterations, amendments, and modifications—the logical positivist's equivalents of the epicycles, eccentrics, and equants of Greek cosmology and astronomy. What orginally bore the innocent appearance of a quick and easy solution to a small but annoying problem in the philosophy of science gradually grew to the point where it absorbed the intellectual energies of considerable numbers of intelligent and technically proficient men and where men over spans of several years.

it commanded most of the professional attention of a number of such

The outcome has not been happy. The assimilation of history to the mode of discourse or rhetoric of the natural sciences simply did not hap-

[15] See Raymond Aron, *Introduction to the Philosophy of History: La philosophie critique de l'historie* (Paris, 1938; Boston, 1961).

pen. Instead of achieving assimilation, the intense scrutiny to which the planetary movement of history was subjected has merely made its eccentricity with respect to the system of the natural sciences more obvious. Only by fiat and by distortion of the structure of historical discourse was it possible to bring it within the bounds of rules both appropriate and necessary in the discourse of the natural sciences. Yet in their own erratic and (from the perspective of the rhetoric of natural sciences) errant way historians kept on improving and adding to available truth about the past and to the knowledge and understanding of it.

This primer is radical, then, only in that it proposes that historians and philosophers both give up on trying to shape history to a model of the natural sciences and in that it offers reasons for their giving up. It insists that if historians confine themselves to the simple and difficult rhetorics of those sciences and to the postulates of natural science knowledge, they will never understand more than a fragment of what they can readily know about the human past. There are postulates on which to erect an investigation into history more consequential than the hapless one of the past few decades:

1. That the object of investigation of historians, the human past, is incommensurably different from nature, the object of investigation of natural scientists;

2. That the special language of historical discourse is common language, not one of the uncommon languages characteristic of the natural sciences;

3. That the thrust of their special language requires historians to rely on common-sense judgments far more frequently than they do on strict logical entailments;

4. That the reliance of historical discourse on common language and common sense renders it inherently and inerradicably valuative rather than value-free;

5. That in history credibility rather than necessary and sufficient causes provides the standard of adequacy of explanation;

6. That the exploration of truth values in historical discourse requires the examination of large historical texts and contexts and not just of minute fragments wrenched out of context;

7. That historical discourse is functionally processive rather than formally logical in two respects: (a) of affording readers enough to be going on with and (b) of dealing competently with evidence of change, becoming, or process in the human past.

All these postulates are such that their support derives and must derive from history as actually written or spoken, not from an exploration of the psyches of historians. Throughout this primer we have kept the rhetoric of history rather than methods of historical investigation and the psychology of historical discovery at the center of attention. Our concern has been with what history does rather than with what historians do. The proper translation of the title of this book, *The History Primer*, is not *Elementary Manual for Historians* but (*Some*) *First Principles of Historical Discourse*. No one could possibly learn how to *do* history by reading this primer. This does not matter much because, as was evident almost from the outset, everyone who conceivably might read the primer already will have done history by the spoken word for a good many years.

The treatment of history in this book therefore does not render it vulnerable to the criticism that some philosophers have leveled at a number of attempts to write about historical knowledge—that those attempts center on the methods of historical investigation and the psychology of historical inquiry rather than on the visible yields of such investigation and inquiry—historical discourse, or history as a significant form of knowledge, understanding, and truth. Studies both of historical method and of the psychology of historical discovery are valuable in many respects. Nevertheless such studies usually do not join issue on shared ground with the philosophers in question. They address themselves only casually to the completed visible (or audible) historical work or statement. One of the very best studies of this kind unintentionally renders the distinction evident. In *De la connaissance historique*, Henri Marrou says,

> a completely elaborated history already exists in the mind of the historian before he has begun writing a word of it; whatever the reciprocal influences of these two types of activity may be, they are logically distinct and separate.[16]

Whatever the unspecified grounds for a logical distinction and separation between "these two types of activity" may be, I am perplexed at an account of historical knowledge that takes little or no cognizance of its embodiment in spoken or written utterance. Taken literally it seems to imply that before he starts to give utterance at all a historian already is in such full command of what he intends to set down that thereafter like a copyist he merely engages in a mechanical process of transcription. For a historian who gradually zeroes in on precisely what he means and in a sense discovers it sentence by sentence, word by word, as he sets it down, the severance of historical discovery from historical discourse seems highly artificial. What a professional historian has actually discovered as against how he has gone

---

[16] Henri Marrou, *De la connaissance historique*, tr. R. J. Olson as *The Meaning of History* (Baltimore, 1966), p. 33.

about discovering it is accessible for examination and evaluation only if he writes it down, only in the words written on the page. An inquiry into *connaissance historique* which pays little heed to historical discourse and concerns itself mainly with the psychological processes of historical discovery has a most elusive object. Unlike historical discourse psychological process is very difficult, indeed impossible, to submit to direct public examination and scrutiny as an intellectual artifact. As a historian I prefer not to be judged on my allegations about my psychological processes. I want to be judged by what I write, by the words I put on paper and into print after careful consideration, the words for which, therefore, as a historian I assume serious responsibility.

One of the novelties of this primer, then, is that by and large it meets the philosophers of science on their own ground. It starts off not from the psyches of historians or their intentions but from what they actually do or have done to render the past intelligible, whether in the spoken history of Everyman or in the written history of professionals. That is what most of the focal points are about. They exemplify historical discourse. Discussion of these focal points has pretty largely concerned itself with how they work (or fail to work) in the speaking and writing of history.

The units of historical discourse that are adequate to reveal its ways of eliciting increments of knowledge, understanding, and truth about the past are considerably larger than the minute fragments which philosophers of science have dissected. For this reason we first gave attention to macroscopic units of historical discourse. Only later did we turn to microscopic examination. The crucial judgment we came to was that the rhetoric, that is, the vocabulary and structure of discourse to which a historian often has to resort in order to achieve increments of knowledge, understanding, and truth is incommensurate with the rhetoric of the natural sciences and incompatible with the requirements and restrictions that the exigencies of those sciences impose on that rhetoric. The implications of this conclusion are in a minor way revolutionary. If the conclusion is correct, it means that in history, a region where quite evidently men can and do augment human knowledge, improve human understanding, and add to the store of truth, the natural sciences model, rendered sacrosanct by four centuries of success, breaks down. If this is indeed the case, then the natural science model that has done remarkable and durable service for a long time is in some matters inadequate. Consequently, notions about truth, understanding, and knowledge which imply the unique viability of the natural sciences in those domains need to be subjected to a difficult and far-reaching critique. I cannot guess how extensive that reexamination will need to be; I cannot do more than suggest a few points that might bear looking into.

One concerns triviality. Stringing together true answers to solicitations for information or explanation is by and large no more difficult for professional historians than for Willie back in Chapter 1. The trouble is that unlike Willie's answer to his father, which in the given context had enough existential pressure behind it to be of some importance to both Willie and his father, many true historical answers are trivial and banal. In effect nobody actually gives a damn, not even the professional historian who writes those answers down. The discipline is swamped in a deluge of midgetry. Nor, as I understand it, is this a peculiarity of history. Scientists, too, are being submerged in a tidal wave of true but trivial busy work, so enormous that with rare exceptions, they are reduced to the self-defeating process of counting pages to measure the competence of their colleagues. This process has the hideous effect of reinforcing the propensity to triviality which engendered it. Processes of orderly and consecutive thinking sometimes sink in a quagmire of error; but they may also get hopelessly lost in a dense undergrowth of trivial truth.

Still, no total catastrophe of the sort has yet taken place. This indicates that although they have not been subjected to systematic scrutiny, strategies to deal with the catastrophe exist. The common fact of common language is that unlike some adjectives such as "perfect" and "total," "true" has both a comparative form, "truer," and a superlative, "truest." This seems to correspond to a common sense that all true statements are not of equal truth value, and that it is not beyond human capacity to discriminate between statements and discourse of lesser and greater truth value even when none of the statements are false. In Chapter 5 we offered a suggestion as to how within a reasonably limited context historians adjust their accounts to do justice to new evidence and to maintain the fullest credibility, to tell the likeliest story of which they are capable. This process itself implicitly conceives of truth not as a packet of equal atoms, but as a structure or an organized set of structures, lesser and greater, better and worse. The organization of such structures may well turn out to differ among the sciences and between the sciences and history. In the natural sciences the most comprehensive general laws appear to be most potent in truth value. In history, after an indeterminate point as it broadens in scope generalization appears to increase in triteness, triviality, and vacuity.

A further matter that requires investigation is the relation of accessibility to truth. "Accessibility" as used here does not refer to the problem of avoiding the accidental seclusion of a major intellectual achievement, like Gregor Mendel's work on genetics, in a publication so obscure that decades elapse before it is discovered. In fact this sort of thing seems to happen rarely. Accessibility refers rather to a problem with which Charles Darwin had to wrestle more than a century ago. As he writes in *The Origin of Species*, "Nothing is easier to admit in words than the truths of the universal struggle for life, or more difficult—at least I have found it so—than *constantly to bear this conclusion in mind* [my italics]." With fine precision in a single sentence, Darwin has aligned the two dimensions of the problem. They both have to do with what we earlier called the second record.

The first dimension of the problem concerns those with whom one seeks to communicate. To deny any relation between knowledge, truth, and understanding and their communication does not seem particularly sensible. If a man claims to be in possession of truth, knowledge, or understanding that he cannot communicate at all to anyone, we may acknowledge that this is possible; but since we have no way of knowing or understanding *what* it is he claims to know or understand, we will have no way of dealing with his claim. For all practical purposes such a claim has to be treated as meaningless. It makes poor sense, then, to put truth in one hermetically sealed compartment and communication of truth in another. If this is the case, we cannot wholly reject the responsibility to render the truth or understanding or knowledge we possess intelligible to others. Nor can we wholly deny that maximizing their accessibility or their accurate transmission has truth value.

Of course, we cannot assume total responsibility for all failures either. At some time or other almost every one who has written with the intention of communicating must have had the deflating experience of seeing in print what purported to be a statement of his views and noted with horror that the purported statement was a misstatement of them so gross that, as he read, he could scarcely believe his eyes. While very few people are totally idea-deaf, all of us have a lot of wax in our ears. Some of it is extruded by ignorance, and in the case of difficult truths the ignorance of many of us is invincible. Such truths are and for all our lives will remain out of our range of perception. This common human defect natural scientists have learned to accept and expect. The artificial languages of mathematizing scientists are more difficult to master than the natural languages of other communities of men. Inevitably, most of what is communication among members of scientific communities is mere confused and confusing whispering to those ignorant of their languages. All our hearing blockages, however, do not result from invincible ignorance. Some are a consequence of prejudice, of misconceptions and preconceptions, and of sheer mental laziness. These impediments to understanding are in principle removable. They do not concern historians only, but they concern them in a special way. Given their commitment to common language, historians cannot entirely shift to the consumer of history the blame for their failures to penetrate his second record. Common language, which daily must find its way through the prejudices, misconceptions, preconceptions, and sheer

mental laziness of those with whom we need to communicate, has resources for this purpose unknown to the more sparse and rigorous
rhetoric of the natural sciences. Yet in both cases the attainment of
access to the second records of those toward whom discourse is directed
is one of the functions and values of all utterances that aim at truth. In
this matter we acknowledge the indissoluble liaison of truth and
rhetoric.

   Darwin's observation, however, points to a further and more interesting problem. The second record to which initially Darwin had trouble
maintaining access was his own. For him the struggle for existence was
the very ground of his theory of evolution, yet he had trouble "keeping
it in mind," before and while he wrote, *The Origin of Species*. The
difficulty Darwin felt in maintaining constant access to his own central
conception is of particular interest   to historians. In the past four
hundred years, the natural sciences have undergone several upheavals
of such magnitude that experts on the history of science are willing to
defend the practice of calling them revolutions. Of these revolutions
only one, the Darwinian Revolution, had at the eye of the storm an
intellectual operation that bore a considerable likeness to history.
Darwin was a naturalist, and *The Origin of Species* is a masterpiece of
natural history. It deals with living creatures in the past. Unlike the
scientific revolutions in classical mechanics, astrophysics, chemistry,
relativity theory, quantum mechanics, genetics, and most recently
molecular biology, it did not rely for credence on a crucial experiment,
a small cluster of such experiments, or a small cluster of crucial observations. Instead it relied on investigations of the record of the past of
life on earth by Darwin himself and by other naturalists. It relied, that
is to say, on natural history. In Darwin's day, such investigations were
abundant, many of them were accurate, and most of what they reported was well verified. One of Darwin's most difficult problems therefore
was that of a plethora of true accounts along with lacunae, traceable
not to the inadequacy of other natural historians but to vast lacunae in
the then available surviving record of the "natural" past. The trouble
with the accounts was that they were at once too numerous and not
quite true enough. Darwin's problem was to order the abundance of
knowledge and truth in them into a history of the natural past that
focussed the attention of his readers on the struggle for existence of
living things in their earthly environment and its consequence, natural
selection. He had to make those readers aware and keep them aware
that the excess capacities of living things for reproduction tended constantly to overcrowd their environment so that only well-adapted creatures survived. He believed that a history so written and abundantly
documented would tell a more likely story of the past of life on earth,
and order the "natural" record of the past into an account of the variety

of animal and plant species extant and extinct, more persuasive than any hitherto offered.

Darwin's effort was successful. Within two decades and with some modifications it displaced all alternative accounts for men whose minds did not permanently reside in the outback of the human intellect. His general views were not absolutely original. Evolutionary views of the origin and variety of species of plant and animal life had in fact been propounded before. Darwin vanquished resistance to a view that hitherto had gained few adherents by painstakingly searching his own second record and dealing with those obstacles in it that prevented him from constantly bearing in mind the point of the story he aimed to tell. Men speak of Darwinism; they never speak of Wallaceism, yet the theory of evolution by natural selection occurred independently to Darwin and Alfred Russell Wallace. The bare bones of the conception came to Wallace in one day. In one week he had set them down in a memorandum of 4,000 words which he sent on to Darwin in 1858. If one strips off the elaboration of detail, "explanation" and "truth" about evolution are nearly the same in Wallace's communication of 1858 and in Darwin's *Origin of Species*; "essentially" one is about as true as the other. In fact Darwin had arrived at his hypothesis on evolution more than two decades before he published *The Origin of Species*. In the years between he gave his energy to rendering what he already "knew" more fully accessible first to himself and then to his readers. From all sides he laid siege to resistance in his own mind to his conception of the origin of species. The result was more than the bare bones of the argument which his book had in common with Wallace's communication. He piled up applications so massive and so irrestible that his hypothesis remained far forward in his own mind and ultimately in *The Origin of Species*. That work is a masterpiece less of the logic of scientific discourse than of the macrorhetoric of natural history.

What Darwin's experience exemplifies occurs frequently in histories. Bad historians so successfully bury under avalanches of true statements the consequential truths they have found that they obscure the lines of access to them from the sight of their readers and sometimes they themselves wholly lose track of them. At this point the very notion of "knowing" becomes slippery and elusive. Suppose a man utters a truth that he believes to be true as he utters or writes it. Does he know it, if an hour later when he needs it he has so completely lost access to it that he never finds it again? Something similar can happen even to excellent historians. One of the very best writes as follows about a longish review of his book, "Thanks to this . . . article, *I can now see things that I never saw before.*" [17] Yet the article referred to added scarcely a jot of

---

[17] *Journal of British Studies* 8 (1968): 82.

evidence to what was already present in the book. All it did was juxtapose and thus render more accessible to the author of the book evidence that he himself provided. Once the juxtaposition had been made, the appropriate inferences from it were easy enough. The author had not made them simply because he had chosen a macrorhetorical structure which scattered the evidence that when juxtaposed enabled him to see things that he "never saw before." Consequently, he did not bear that evidence in mind, did not have ready access to it, and therefore did not recognize how it could have helped him to write a more persuasive history.

The preceding scattered investigations are only that. It will be necessary to carry such investigations further to arrive at the reordering of our conceptions of knowing, understanding, and truth that the partial collapse of the natural science paradigms require.[18] One aid to rethinking such problems might be a careful search for the inexplicit metaphors that constitute or control the beliefs of scientists and philosophers of science about the increase of knowledge, understanding, and truth. There is no intention here to suggest that such metaphors are universally misleading. A few now in use may always be misleading. In the natural sciences a few may always be suitable. Many, however, are of a utility limited by circumstances, particularly by the circumstance of the character of the particular intellectual art to which they are applied and by the condition of the art at that particular moment. And some metaphors generally applicable in the natural sciences are almost irrelevant to history. What follows is only a couple of brief examples of the problems of the metaphorical foundations of natural sciences. One is an example of the time-bound character of a natural science metaphor, the other an example of the irrelevance of a natural science metaphor to the advancement of knowledge, understanding, and truth in history.

The first metaphor is that of the sand heap. This metaphor suggests that by an ant-like activity science advances as scientists add one grain of knowledge or truth to another in an ever-increasing pile. The previous description of the Darwinian Revolution illustrates the limitation of the sand-heap metaphor. For a long time before Darwin, the advancement of the knowledge of living things proceeded and needed to proceed pretty much on the sand-heap principle. After wallowing in something close to pure fantasy for centuries the study of living nature required a large reliable data base, and in the seventeenth century it began to get one. From the 1650s to the 1850s, hordes of worthy and

---

[18] As I indicated before the beginning in the Nonchapter in the past few years I have gotten dim intimations that such investigations are in fact already taking place. I have not followed up these intimations partly because of a firm conviction that scholars usually do best when they write with care on matters they know a good deal about rather than amateurishly on matters about which they know little or nothing. What I know most about is history.

industrious workers dropped grain after grain on top of the pile. As the data base spread, it became painfully evident, however, that the level of truth was rising at a rate exponentially lower than the quantity of knowledge-and-truth input. In a very large area of inquiry the mere cumulation of discreet bits of knowledge, once indispensable, was no longer enough. An analogous phenomenon is quite familiar to every child who has played in a sand pile. Without any effective agent of coherence, increments of sand, dumped on top of a pile, roll down the sides broadening the base of the pile without correspondingly increasing its height. *The Origin of Species* drastically altered this situation. The theory it set forth served as a general agent of coherence. It enabled natural scientists to build available knowledge into a higher structure of truth and to continue to raise the level of that structure as further knowledge now coated, so to speak, with a cohesive agent was added to it.[19]

A second metaphorical model for the advancement of knowledge, understanding, and truth has been up to now implicit in the natural science perception of these matters. It is the simple two-dimensional planar graph. Here is what it is like. Assume a zero-point of total ignorance at the intersection of line X and line Y. Assume further a truth line T, T^n as here illustrated.

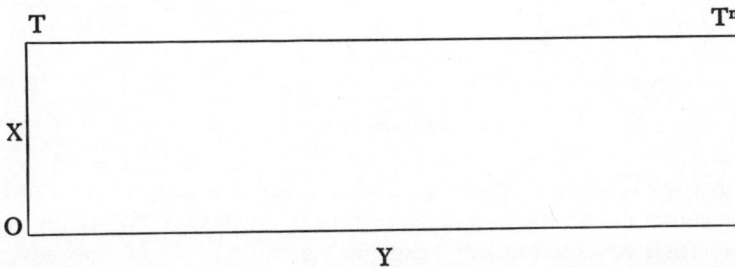

Figure 7

Question: Starting at O, what is the shortest route from line Y to line T, T^n? Obviously on a planar graph the route is OT. The logical-scientific surrogate for the planar graph is Ockam's razor: do not multiply entities beyond what are necessary. Or, in effect, introduce no more assumptions

[19] I do not believe that any hypothesis about the human past will serve for human history a function similar to that served by Darwin's theory for natural history. The empirical evidence for this view is quite considerable. Since the eighteenth century many such theories—laws of history, so called—have been propounded. Under scrutiny and criticism their survival value has proved negligible and their life span short. The only exceptions to this rule are those hypotheses whose lives have been unnaturally prolonged by the support of men holding a monopoly of the instruments of violence. Any attempt to deal in general with such putative laws of history in this primer has been rendered otiose by a skillful and destructive discussion of their untenable character by Danto, *The Analytical Philosophy of History* in Chapter 1, "Substantive and Analytical Philosophy of History," pp. 1–16. Here

into your postulates and no more logical steps into your argument than you need to reach your conclusion. Or, the correct explanation of an event is the statement of the minimum number of boundary conditions and the minimum number of general laws strictly to entail the statement that the event happened. The shortest way is somehow also the best, truest, and most scientific way.

Once that from the metaphor which treats the movement from ignorance to knowledge and truth as rectilinear motion over a flat surface we have shifted to one which treats it as ascent over tilted irregular terrain, a view of the process more complex than that just offered suggests itself. Consider the following diagram:

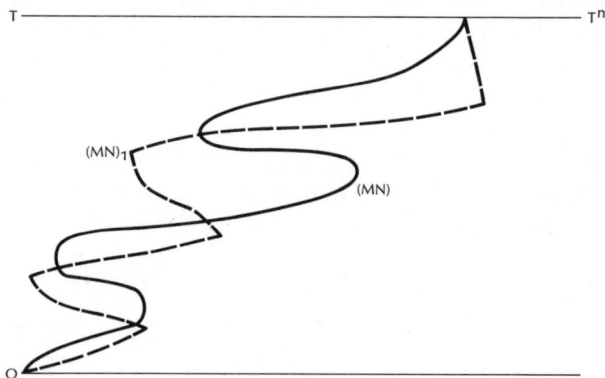

Figure 8

To proceed from O to T along axis X on a planar graph is one of the serious concerns of mathematizing natural scientists. Whether they describe such proceedings as "elegance" or avoidance of unnecessary hypotheses, they devote much time to achieving it. They might find odd the view that the shortest ways to T, T^n could be graphed as follows and that MN could be that way.

The figure is intended to suggest that the best path of ascent to the same or like truths may not be unique, that paradoxically $(MN)_1$ and $(MN)_2$ may be at once incommensurable and equal. In any ascent there are two components—the ascended and the ascender. In any single case

perhaps is a good place to rectify an injustice I once did to a most thoughtful book. In reviewing Danto's work some years ago in *The New York Review of Books* I concentrated my attention on his treatment of historical explanation, which seemed and still seems to me to be dogged by the same difficulties as Morton White's book earlier referred to, difficulties that I have tried to give full attention to in this primer. In so concentrating I failed to give due praise to other parts of *The Analytical Philosophy of History*, which were both illuminating and perceptive. For that injustice I wish, as far as possible, to make amends here, fully recognizing that belated admission of an injustice are meager amends indeed.

the best route to the top is the one that maximizes the fit between the traits of the one and those of the other. Sometimes a question put to the record of the past is such that, because of its character and that of the record, there is only one way to the answer. But such questions are special cases, and frequently alternate routes to the answers through the record are possible, and are adaptable to varied gifts of different seekers.[20]

The metaphor of the slopes and the climbers suggests a more ecumenical conception of explanation, knowing, and truth than has prevailed in philosophical analysis and the philosophy of science. It is, I am sure, overloaded with pitfalls and booby traps. So be it! Nothing ventured, nothing gained; and as Spinoza said, all excellent things are as difficult as they are rare. Yet if we think of the movement toward truth as the climbing of a slope, Fig. 8 makes sense as a possible planar projection of the movement actually going in three-dimensional space. Then we might think of OT in Fig. 7 as a special case of MN in Fig. 8, the scientific case. It represents the instances in which because of special traits of the subject matter and the discipline 1) explanation in general is equal (or nearly so) to explanation "why," and 2) the rhetoric of the discipline is wholly (or nearly) logical-mathematical in structure.

These two limitations do not hold for much explanation "why," less for explanation in general, and less still for all truth-communicating and knowledge-advancing discourse. The most inexperienced hill-climbers, explainers, and discoursers know that the least linear distance up a hill is not always the best way to the top. Even very inexperienced climbers are aware that looping up steep slopes does not diminish but increases rate of ascent, that beating around the bush is often a faster way to the other side than plunging into the thicket, that the assessment of the shortest way up a broken rough slope is better left to an experienced climber than to a geometer. The sort of discourse that historians often find they need to engage in—processive discourse, that shapes itself to the peculiarly casual character of the record of the past—better fits the metaphor of irregular mountainous terrain than that of a smooth planar surface.

The planar metaphor, useful in discourse in the natural sciences,[21] is useless in history except for the fragments on which most analytical

[20] For example, Professor Lawrence Stone, Professor H. R. Trevor-Roper and I ultimately arrived at markedly similar conclusions about a number of issues in seventeenth-century English history. Yet the macrorhetorical and microrhetorical courses we took to our common destination varied considerably and were adjusted to our particular skills. Apparent continuing divergences among us are largely illusory and are probably to be ascribed to one of our few shared traits—a voracious appetite for controversy.

[21] The planar metaphor evidently does not work well at all in some natural scientific discourse either, as the discussion of *The Origin of Species*, above, indicates.

philosophers have done most of their whittling. For the larger structures of historical discourse it will not serve. On the other hand, for historians the metaphor of mountain climbing may be helpful. It will permit them to consider their discourse not only in its logical but in its rhetorical dimension. Considering it in the latter dimension, they may be able to introduce a whole range of considerations related to the rhetoric of history, such as accessibility, impact, and intensity, into their conception of how their professional activity increases the knowledge, understanding, and truth available to men who seek for them in the study of the human past. That the rhetoric of history does actually effect an increase has been a recurrent theme of this primer.

The argument that minimizes the claims of history to achieve increments of knowing, understanding, and truth usually focuses at first on the truth claim. With ostensible reasonableness it is put that, after all, there are many human activities excellent and generally accepted as desirable, such as eating, drinking, and rolling in the hay, for which no incremental truth value is claimed. They are fine things to do, ends-in-themselves, as Kant might say, and if they have nothing to do with adding to truth, they are not the worse for that. Nor is history. Truth is a rather gray and often tiresome affair. History can be and sometimes is charming, exciting, lively, and entertaining. What need then to clutter so attractive an activity with the claim that achieving increments of truth is one of its prime and constant objectives? The argument here is seductive; pleasurably it suggests there are ways that historians can avoid much tedious work; and remembering the fate of those who listened to another siren's song, historians would do well to close their ears to this one. For historians cannot detach their claims to increase knowledge or enhance understanding from their claim to achieve increments of truth. To forego the latter claim is to forego the former. If historians do not increase knowledge and enhance understanding of truth about the human past, just what is it that they claim to increase knowledge and enhance understanding of? Or do they not claim to increase knowledge and understanding at all? What do they think they are up to? What are they trying to wrestle out of the record of the past? What is their painstaking search of that record in aid of? What is the scrupulous examination and construal of that record for? If truth is not the aim of the game, what is its aim?

No, it simply will not do. On examination the whole argument appears to be a slightly disingenuous maneuver directed toward a seizure of lexical bastions that historians surrender at their peril. We have already seen that in discourse about men, terms neutralized in the vocabulary of the natural sciences take on value-tonality. Even in their own discourse, however, natural scientists do not imagine that they can render terms like "know," "understand," and "true" value-free. For one natural scientist to say of another that his reports on research do not achieve any increment of knowledge, understanding, and truth is to say that the latter has wasted his time and the time of all his readers. To say that, and then to allege that such a statement is value-free would be either nonsense or hypocrisy; but I know no natural scientists who would make such an allegation. No sane natural scientist would be so stupid as tamely to surrender the lexical bastions on which his own credibility and that of his science depend. With respect to that science he will regard any attempt to substitute the terms "ignorance" or "fun" for "knowledge," "error" or "play" for "understanding" and "false" or "nonsensical" for "true" as an outrage and a betrayal of his discipline. Every pseudoscience and science from astrology to zoology explicitly or implicitly makes claims that it advances knowledge and understanding of truth, knowing well that if it does not do so, it will go out of business. And unless he has lost his mind, a historian will make, and seek to make good, like claims for his own discipline. It has been one of the key arguments of this primer that historians do make such claims and do make them good. Historians can thankfully accept the added concession that history may be and sometimes is lively, exciting, entertaining, a pleasure and a delight; but they must not and need not for a moment concede that they are without concern for or that they fail to achieve increments of knowledge, understanding, and truth about the human past.

Then there is the opposite alternative. If we accept, as I think we must, the view that historians are in the increment-of-truth game, why not go into it all the way? Why not claim that, although a different kind of science from the natural sciences, history is nevertheless a science? There are serious inducements to historians to press such a claim. Especially in the past quarter century, the higher learning has received large subventions from government and from the private sector of the economy. Of these, historians have received a most meager share. Overwhelmingly, rather, such subventions have gone to disciplines that call themselves sciences—physical sciences, life sciences, earth sciences, social sciences, behavioral sciences, administrative sciences. Many of the crumbs that came to history from this lordly banquet landed on the plates of historians who most loudly proclaimed themselves social scientists. When historians refuse to count their discipline as science, they impose relative poverty upon themselves. They do so, because as Mr. William Sutton once so sagely remarked of banks, science "is where the money is." It may help historians to continue to resist the temptation to make so remunerative a claim if they will recall (1) that Willie was a safe cracker, (2) that his observation was his response to the question, "Why do you rob banks, Willie?", (3) that in the end Willie was caught up with and sent to jail.

Motives, less dubious, may also suggest the arrogation to history of the name of science. The most persuasive, perhaps, is that such an arrogation already has the sanction of general usage in most European languages. The French have their *sciences historiques,* the Germans their *Geschichtswissenschaft,* and so on. The argument from such usage, however, is not wholly persuasive. The structure of discourse is not something one usually wishes to subject to democratic process on the principle of "one language, one vote." A particular language may preserve a most useful distinction that other languages have lost or never clearly made. In such circumstances imitative desolation by equalization seems to have little in it to commend it to sensible men. French *science,* German *Wissenschaft,* and their cognates in other languages are words of wider spectrum than "science" is in English; they tend to embrace all scholarship, all learning, nearly all highly organized knowledge. On the other hand French *bon sens* and German *gesunder Menschenverstand* are not as rangy as "common sense." Indeed when Germans and Frenchmen come upon the phrase "common sense" in English, or when they aim to expound the traits it connotes, they rarely translate it. In this there is something slightly wistful, as if they wish both that their language had a truly equivalent phrase and that their compatriots were slightly better endowed with the trait it designates.

This situation speaks directly to our preference that historians be bold in their claims to an ability to advance knowledge, understanding, and truth while refusing to describe their orderly inquiry into the human past as a science. So to describe it is to blur beyond any need and in a way that creates useless confusion the boundaries between science and common sense. Such blurring ill serves the purpose of intelligible discourse. No one who asserts the worth of common sense wants to claim that all of science, or indeed very much natural science or even social science, lies readily within its reach. Nor conversely, one imagines, would scientists, natural or social, care to claim that all common sense is science. This is the case whether one conceives of science in the somewhat stricter English sense or in the broader sense of *science* and *Wissenschaft.* One may well hesitate to ascribe a scientific outlook to anyone earlier than Plato and Aristotle, and to them only with reservations. On the other hand, it is reasonable to infer that men have had a modicum of common sense for several hundreds of thousands of years, ever since they made the transit, whenever that was, between mere animal and human. *Sapientia,* which may be as close as one can get except in English to "common sense" is probably antecedent to the species *homo sapiens* and coeval with the genus *homo.* To describe as science all that men learned and came to know about organizing and ordering their remembered experience of living with other men would be stretching the term "science" a bit further than most scientists are likely to want to stretch it. Indeed to describe it as History is going further than men who think of themselves as Historians may want to go.

I am not a Historian, however, just a historian, but so I am ready to go all the way with describing men's ordinary understanding of their own past and the place of other men in it as history. It is indeed the reason for my repeated insistence on the competence of Everyman and Everyboy as a historian, for my emphasis on the importance of common sense and common language in history. Within the limited horizons of man's immediate milieu, history is not what he understands and has understood least and worst, but what he has understood most and best. It is there that we started this primer, with Willie's third explanation of his muddy pants, a story that we immediately recognized as good common sense, but not as science. In subsequent chapters we have tried to bracket the notion of history in a series of successively more accurate approximations. Now we can reassess that third account of Willie's in the light of our later effort. We therefore note:

1. That it was skillfully adapted to its context;
2. That its macrorhetorical and its microrhetorical structure throughout rendered it maximally accessible to the second record of its presumptive consumer (Willie's father) and maximized its impact on that record;
3. That it was economical, with scarcely a word wasted;
4. That its explanatory effectiveness depended on and successfully projected what it was like in a particular set of circumstances to be Willie;
5. That it was processive in both of the senses in which we have used that term, that is, (a) it was quite enough to proceed with, (b) it rendered an account of the relevant process of change through time that could scarcely be faulted;
6. That in context it was wholly credible;
7. That there was not a word in it that lay outside the common language of its producer or its consumer.

Note that every major element that we have identified as prerequisite to a good true historical account is present here. But I had concocted the account before I worked out explicitly what the prerequisites for such accounts are. In some respects all that followed in this primer has turned out to be a clarification of what I already knew with my finger tips, so to speak, from the very beginning.

Again here we have an instance of the problem of accessibility, of the difficulty of keeping constantly in mind what one assents to. What we need to keep in mind is that a twelve-year-old can produce *an account of the past that is at once good common sense and well-nigh perfect history and that it is the latter because it is the former.* Again this is not to argue that historians can rely altogether on common sense and common language alone. It is most emphatically to argue that history which wholly abandons either is likely to be bad history. Professional historians then may do well to abandon a claim to being scientists, if and to the extent that such a claim requires them also to abandon free recourse to common sense, or to deny its worth for them. For all historians, Everyman and the professional, common sense is, and is likely long and perhaps always to remain, their greatest resource for gaining increments of knowledge, understanding, and truth about the past—a vast and inexhaustible sea of resources, antedating and surrounding those tiny islets of highly organized knowledge called the sciences.

The reliance of history on common sense presages and brings us to the final concern of this primer, which is the obverse—the possible role of history in the regeneration of common sense. We have tried to drive home the point that discourse about the human past in the common language of common sense can never be wholly cleared of value-loading. The only way to write history free of such loading is to dehumanize it, that is, to inquire into human conduct only to the extent that it conforms the behavior of men in the past to the behavior of nonhuman living creatures. This is the strategy of behavioral psychologists. It is applicable only to the range of activities of *homo sapiens* which are similar to those of *troglodytes gorilla, canis familiaris,* or *mus decumanus.* For the purpose of rendering an account of such human activities this sort of inquiry is useful. The trouble is that the relevant activities are few and not distinctively human. In the daily conduct of men, even of the behaviorists themselves, the range of activity relevant to such inquiry is miniscule compared with the range of human behavior concerning which effective discourse is possible only with a rhetoric that bears ineffaceable value-marking. In this wider range what is required of writers and especially of historians, is care and responsibility in the use of language on which the traces of judgment are bound to be present, and especially a sensitivity to value shifts that occur in the course of one's lifetime in words one has become habituated to using as if their values were fixed.

This last monition on the shift in the value tone is especially relevant in the present context, since it bears heavily on the term "science" and its cognates, which we have used frequently in this primer. For about two hundred years science has ordinarily evoked at least three widespread responses. (1) Science seems most generally to have been sensed as having to do with controlled experiment and mathematization; that is, the term "science" has tended to bring to men's minds an image of the "hard" or physical sciences, not by and large of geology or botany. (2) Science has been and still is associated in men's minds with the notion of control over nature. (3) Overwhelmingly, science and its cognates carried a positive or honorific value-loading, until, as pointed out earlier, it came to encompass almost all knowing and truth that men deemed worthy of the name.

Each of these three traits requires attention in the present context. With respect to the first, it has always engendered a scattered and fragmentary hostility to science. The "hard" sciences are hard in two ways. For one thing, especially as a consequence of their mathematization, the difficulties of understanding them in a more than trivial way are considerable. That is, putting the matter loosely, they are hard to master and in the process of time have become harder and harder to master. Unlike the "creative arts," they are also hard in the sense that they are resistant to the more egregious foibles of fashion. Phony claims to large achievement are quickly and accurately assessed and rejected, incompetence is detected readily and soon. These traits have rendered the hard sciences repulsive to men who seek readier and easier ways to recognition and repute. Such men imagine that they add to their own stature by seeking to diminish the stature of men of science, their keen minds and hard work.

For many tens of thousands of years the victims of the disasters and horrors of human life—starvation, plague, drought, flood, and fire—sought alternately to appease and control what they conceived as the source of their miseries, the rivers, the winds, the gods, the demons. Most of their efforts, those that lay in the realm of magic, seem not to have been notably successful. Others, based on technological improvement, like agriculture, irrigation, flood control, and metallurgy were of greater efficacy. Up to the time when the findings of modern science began to be systematically applied to the control of nature, however, the acceleration of that control was irregular, sporadic, and uncertain. With the application of modern science men's mastery of nature moved along at a scarcely credible clip until it became the wonder and then quite recently the terror of the world.

Although it had earlier penetrated the periphery of some men's attention that improvements in human control over nature uncomfortably seemed to be accompanied by an equivalent increase in human aptitude for mass mayhem and homicide and by no perceptible abatement of the propensity to perpetrate them, this phenomenon did not gain widespread attention until rather recently. Then suddenly a remarkable forward leap in the hard sciences had as one of its consequences, an ultimate forward leap in the human capacity for homicide. It was ultimate in the simple sense that for the first time it rendered feasible the total and rapid destruction of human life on earth by human agents. The instruments of that destruction were nuclear fission and fusion. This spectacular achievement was not accompanied by the slightest indication of any decline in men's appetite for mutual slaughter. Quite to the contrary, in this matter neither the men with authority nor those over whom they govern inspire a bit more trust than the statesmen and rulers who boldly marched or stupidly stumbled into wars in times past or than the people who blindly followed their leaders into orgies of blood-letting. The dream of science remaking the world has been transformed into the nightmare of science destroying it.

The events so sketchily outlined above produced a value-upheaval generative of mass psychoisis in large sectors of the intellectual elite. Actually it generated two or three forms of psychosis. The older genera-tion and most markedly scientists themselves developed toward science itself an ambivalence varying from schizoid to schizophrenic in inten-sity. Having exalted science to a most lofty eminence among the means of attaining knowledge, understanding, and truth, partly because of the power of control it gave men over nature, they found themselves in a paradoxical situation, caught on the horns of a most uncomfortable dilemma. The control over nature, which was rightly one of their chief sources of self-esteem, continued to grow at an unprecedented rate. Yet this very control had released from the bottle not just one but several genii that threatened to destroy not only those who released them but everyone else—the genie called "the population explosion," and the one called "environmental pollution," as well as the one most immediately threatening, "thermonuclear catastrophe." The older generation also discovered that about such matters, except with respect to technical detail, the community of natural scientists had nothing more sensible or fruitful to say than ordinary men with no scientific claim to expertise. Indeed they found something even more horrifying. While the natural scientists were wondering what to do, others had seized their creden-tials, and, flourishing them about, were gaining credence from ordinary puzzled and frightened people for claims to possession of scientific knowledge that any competent natural scientist could recognize as pre-posterous. There were phony gurus, self-deluded "saviors," oppor-tunists, and quacks that called themselves psychiatrists, sociologists, behavioral scientists, and what-not. Because these men claimed to be scientists, because like natural scientists they spoke in a special lan-guage with a special vocabulary, ordinary people accepted their cre-dentials. They accepted them because they accepted science as the only broad highway to knowledge, understanding, and truth, because they did not expect science to make sense to their ordinary untrained minds, and because whatever their other errors the gurus and quacks did not make the mistake of merely making common sense.[22]

[22] These remarks are not directed at the hardworking, skillful, modest, social scientists whose serious and valuable investigations are proof of their detestation of fraudulence.

The Dumblians and Another Ball Game

The young are not ambivalent about science, and their delusional system is not schizoid but paranoid. The children perceive one hard fact about the scientific image of truth, a fact that a child in an old fable perceived: in the relevant matters the emperor has no clothes. That he imagines he has clothes is simply evidence that he is crazy. Yet he still, albeit, somewhat shakily claims not only to be sane but to have privileged access to sanity. If that is all that sanity has to show for itself, it is scarcely surprising that in partly justified distrust of their elders a great many young people not only reject the value of science but literally seek lunacy whether in political madness, or in drugs, or in apocalyptic millennialism, or in the revival of ancient gnostic heresies and of superstitions, Kabalism, and astrology. The young surely have misperceived some of the claims of some scientists and philosophers. Dimly, however, they have perceived that for reasons unintelligible to them many of their elders have entrapped themselves in an idolatrous worship of their image of science.

The lunacy of such idolatry—and all idolatry is lunatic—becomes evident only when the idol manifestly fails to fulfill the expectation of its worshippers. The worshippers are the last to recognize and admit the defect of their idol; they have staked too much on its own power. Instead of acknowledging the limitations of the thing they have made of sticks and stones, they ascribe its failure to the inadequacies of their sacrifices and pour out yet greater largesse on the cult's increasingly skeptical priesthood. The very naïveté of the young spares them this foolishness. Offered no reasonable alternative to a cult whose excessive pretension they have penetrated, what more human (and young) than that they fall into an anarchy of weirder cults or into mere desperate nihilistic iconoclasm.

Roughly this seems to be where we are now in this year of grace, 1970. The evidence piles up that the control over nature which natural science promises fails disastrously with respect to human nature. Some people are still unwarily committed to the faith that the sciences confer control over man and that such control, attainable through the social sciences, will "solve our problems." The young denounce the aims of much investigation in the social sciences as "manipulative," which insofar as it is concerned with control over men it in fact and avowedly is. Then they demonstrate the false pretension of such investigation by themselves successfully rejecting and defying all efforts to control them. They demonstrate, that is, the powerlessness of the power that the idolaters of science once believed science would confer on men. Against such power claims the young have frequently and sometimes astonishingly shown the power of powerlessness. Unfortunately, though not surprisingly, some of them have become obsessive captives of the very demon they began by denying. Rejecting manipulation they become

manipulators; repudiating the power of others over them, they ruthlessly exercise naked power over others; having at the outset rejected
force and violence even as the ultimate recourse, some of them come to
resort to force and violence immediately, denying the existence of any
alternative to such resort in any case whatsoever.

Amid the infernal din created by the *Götterdammerung* of the idols
of science and the inhuman *Walpurgisnacht* of self-indulgent youthful
desperation, historians may wish to raise a still small voice in behalf of
what they know—the value of common sense. Paradoxically in all the
racket it stands a chance of being heard only if it is a still small voice. It
also needs to be a humble voice, since it will be telling people only
what they themselves know already, but what they have lost track of
amid all the screaming. Surely its message is a part of the message of a
very great teacher, a Man who was more than a man, when He said,
"My Kingdom—that is my power—is not of this world." Again, alone in
the desert with Satan He refused to turn stones to bread, that is to show
His power as control of nature. And yet again He refused all the king-
doms of the world and all the glory of them. That is, He refused to
show His power as control of men. He thus showed the powerlessness
of the great power of darkness over Him. And in the face of temptation,
He also showed the power of His powerlessness, the power to control
Himself. What Christ showed in an ultimate way is a gift that all sane
men have in lesser measure—common self-control that has its source in
their common humanity and their common sense.

That historians owe to common sense most of what they can rightly
claim to know and understand about the human past, most of the truth
that is theirs, has been the main theme of this primer. It has been its
theme more than at the outset I ever dreamed it would be. For me
writing this primer has been an unanticipated voyage of discovery, not
the discovery of strange new truths but of old long-known ones. I have
long known that common sense above all else vindicates the truths of
history, and that history beyond all other disciplines, scientific or
humanist, vindicates the claims of common sense. Knowing this, as I
have for a long, long time, my difficulty has been precisely that of
Charles Darwin: "I have found nothing more difficult than constantly
to bear it in mind." As I wrote this primer my wandering attention
again and again was drawn back to the indissoluble links that bind
history to common sense. I realized those links are so strong that historians cannot and should not give up on the claim that in common
language by the disciplined exercise of common sense Everyman in his
daily affairs is a good historian. If they do, they also give up their
proper claim that in the practice of their profession they achieve increments of knowledge, truth, and understanding. Much of this primer has
been devoted to examining the implications and shadings of the rela-

tion between professional history and common sense and in working
out a rhetorical strategy that may secure firm lodgment and a conspicuous place for this obvious notion in the second record of my readers.
Now I no longer have any difficulty in bearing the notion constantly in
mind, in having it constantly accessible. I hope by now I have rendered
it almost as accessible to readers of this primer as it is to me.

Since historians do owe so much to common sense, it may not be
presumptuous of me to suggest that now might be a good time to pay
back a few installments on their debt. Rarely has common sense had so
few articulate champions, and rarely has the world stood in deeper
need of heavy drafts of the common sense of common men. And never
have professional historians been in better shape to make a repayment.
For my whole lifetime as a historian in America, in the greater society
of learned men historians have been perhaps the largest corporate
group to resist solicitation to become loud-mouth peddlers and shills of
phony panaceas for the ailments of humanity. On the whole they have
refused to claim a monopoly of the instruments of secular salvation and
have shown an encouraging tendency to doubt that such instruments
exist. The leaven of fanatics, lunatics, and ideologues who are always
with the professional historians, as with all intellectuals, have received
little encouragement from them in recent decades.

This modesty and humility is not at all the consequence or mark of
any innate superiority in historians. If they have been moderately
modest and humble, it is because they know they have a lot to be
modest and humble about. At the end of the last century and the
beginning of this one, some of their predecessors had their try at setting
up History as an idol for worship and the Historians as its priesthood
and the trustees and depositories of its mysteries. In the decades from
1914 to 1944, the absurdity of their claims to power based on a special
kind of knowledge became painfully evident, and all who made such
claims, except those artificially propped up by Marxist proprietors of
the instruments of violence, slid into the muck of abandoned nonsense,
a place that their intellectual pride had well earned them.

I would like to believe, and do in part believe, that there is something
here still more creditable to professional historians. Perhaps the ties
that bind them to the historian Everyman render them a little more
respectful of the capacity of the common sense and common language
of common humanity to achieve a modicum of understanding and
arrive at a modicum of truth than are those students of society whose
pretensions commit them to seeking ways to control other men. Historians may be, therefore, a little less prone to see human situations as
just a series of problems to be solved or their fellow men as eggs that
may have to be broken to make an omelette. The link with common
sense that is built into their profession forces them to recognize that

besides presenting men with problems, the experience of living confronts men with comedy and with tragedy. But while we may solve problems or fail to solve them, we do not solve comedy or tragedy. The appropriate human response to comedy and to tragedy is not a solution; to comedy it is laughter, to tragedy pity. Laughter and pity do not solve problems, they humanize life, and make it a little less terrible. When he recognizes comedy and tragedy, Everyman is capable of and often makes the human and humane response of laughter and pity. But as a historian Everyman lives within the narrow perimeter of his daily life. Professional historians can perhaps do a little to extend that perimeter and to extend the common sense and the common humanity of their readers. Such readers might thus acquire some sense, beyond the boundaries of their daily lives and daily experience, of what it is like to be other than they are. In order to do this professional historians must believe that it is worth doing. For to doubt that they can do it and that it is worth doing is to doubt that the vocation to which they are giving their lives is worth much. And although surely they will often fail, they must not despair of doing it in some measure, for if they give up hope, they will cease to try, and then surely they will live their lives in the desperation of failure.

Above all historians must not be careless of common sense. Carelessness is not taking care, not caring. Not taking care with common sense, not caring about it is not caring about the most important means they have for knowing and understanding the truth about the human past. But to be careless about understanding the human past is to be careless of most of what we can know about men. It is to fail to cherish one of God's greatest gifts to humanity—the capacity in many things, if we exercise it with care, to judge men justly and rightly, and to understand men humanly and humanely. Not to cherish those gifts is to deny to other men their humanity and thereby to abase and destroy our own.

To cherish these gifts, to care for them, is to hold them dear or *carus*, and the gift of holding them dear is *caritas* or love. To love such gifts to us is, with however little perception that this is so, to love both God their giver, and men for whom they were given to us; not to love them at all is to reject the Great Commandment. It may seem odd that what began as a vindication of the common sense of common men should end as a plea for faith and hope in it and for love of it as a gift of God. It may seem even more odd that the author of a history primer, a man not generally given to the wilder flights of fancy, should be drawn to end that primer with words Paul wrote the Christian congregation in Corinth almost two thousand years ago. I can only hope that to my readers it will seem neither odd nor fanciful for me so to end, but a piece considered, thoughtful, careful, and therefore loving common sense.

Though I speak with the tongues of men and of angels, and have not charity, I become as sounding brass, or a tinkling cymbal.

And though I have the gift of prophecy, and understand all mysteries, and all knowledge; and though I have all faith, so that I could remove mountains, and have not charity, I am nothing.

And though I bestow all my goods to feed the poor, and though I give my body to be burned, and have not charity, it profiteth me nothing.

Charity suffereth long, and is kind; charity envieth not; charity vaunteth not itself, is not puffed up

Doth not behave itself unseemly, seeketh not her own, is not easily provoked, thinketh no evil;

Rejoiceth not in iniquity, but rejoiceth in the truth;

Beareth all things, believeth all things, hopeth all things, endureth all things.

Charity never faileth: but whether there be prophecies, they shall fail; whether there be tongues, they shall cease; whether there be knowledge, it shall vanish away.

For we know in part, and we prophesy in part.

But when that which is perfect is come, then that which is in part shall be done away.

When I was child, I spake as a child, I understood as a child, I thought as a child: but when I became a man, I put away childish things.

For now we see through a glass, darkly; but then face to face: now I know in part; but then shall I know even as also I am known.

And now abideth faith, hope, charity, these three; but the greatest of these is charity.

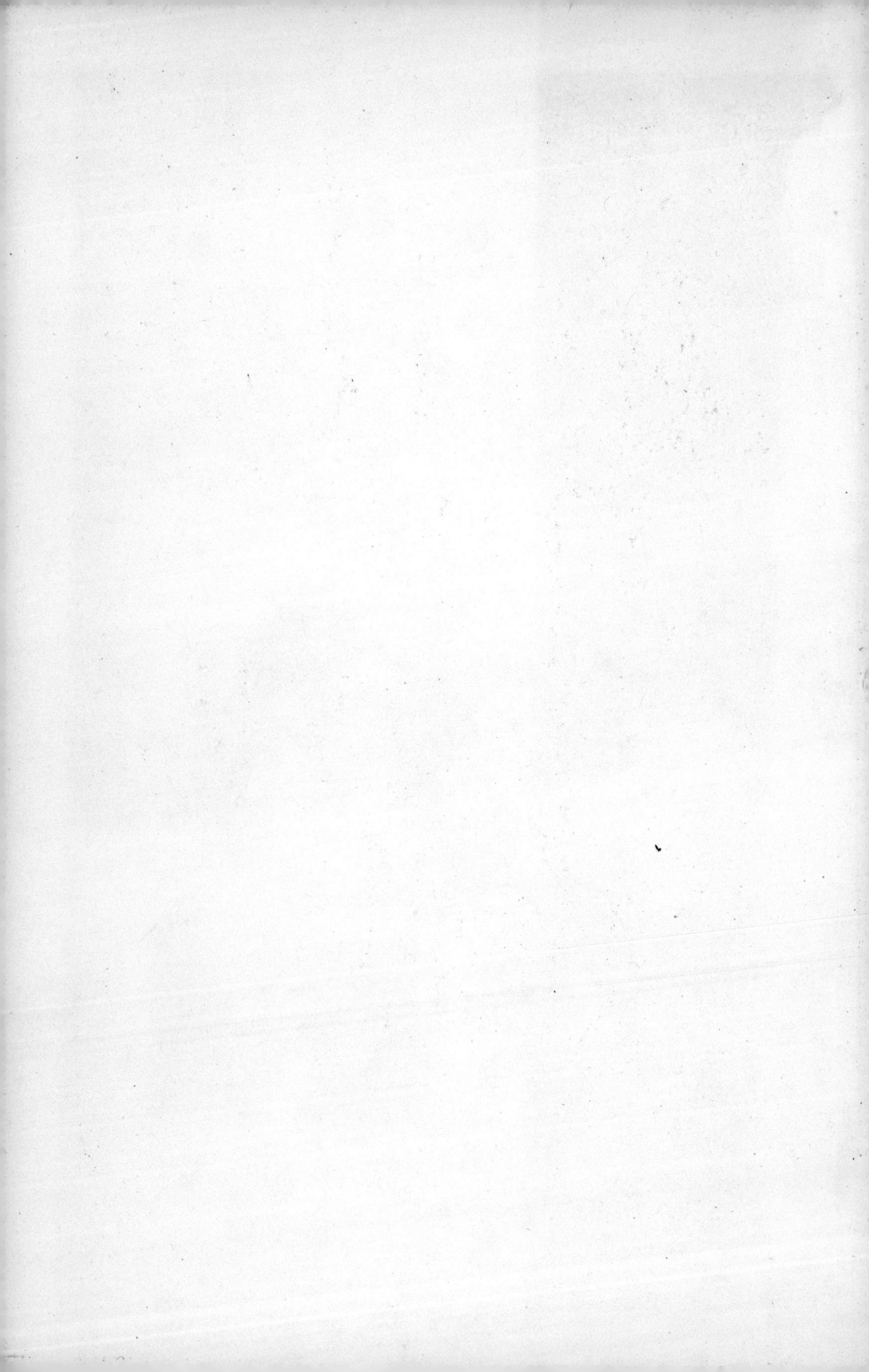